The Force-Free Dilemma

"Dogs in Our World" Series

Canine Agility and the Meaning of Excellence: Formulating an Ethical Approach (Beth A. Dixon, 2024)

Canine Crania: Your Dog's Head and Why It Looks That Way (Bryan D. Cummins with Kaelyn Racine, 2024)

Dogs of the Railways: Canine Guardians, Companions and Mascots Since the 19th Century (Jill Lenk Schilp, 2024)

The Force-Free Dilemma: Truth and Myths in Modern Dog Training (Nicola Ferguson, 2024)

I Know Your Dog Is a Good Dog: A Trainer's Insights on Reactive, Aggressive or Anxious Behavior (Linda Scroggins, 2024)

My Broken Dog: Living with a Handicapped Pet (Sandy Kubillus, 2024)

The Peace Puppy: A Memoir of Caregiving and Canine Solace (Susan Hartzler, 2024)

Police Dogs of Trinidad and Tobago: A 70-Year History (Debbie Jacob, 2024)

We Saved Each Other: How Rescue Dogs Help Us Through Hardship (Christopher Dale, 2024)

Horror Dogs: Man's Best Friend as Movie Monster (Brian Patrick Duggan, 2023)

The Most Painful Choice: A Dog Owner's Story of Behavioral Euthanasia (Beth Miller, 2023)

Your Service Dog and You: A Practical Guide (Nicola Ferguson, 2023)

Dog of the Decade: Breed Trends and What They Mean in America (Deborah Thompson, 2022)

Laboratory Dogs Rescued: From Test Subjects to Beloved Companions (Ellie Hansen, 2022)

Beware of Dog: How Media Portrays the Aggressive Canine (Melissa Crawley, 2021)

I'm Not Single, I Have a Dog: Dating Tales from the Bark Side (Susan Hartzler, 2021)

Dogs in Health Care: Pioneering Animal-Human Partnerships (Jill Lenk Schilp, 2019)

General Custer, Libbie Custer and Their Dogs: A Passion for Hounds, from the Civil War to Little Bighorn (Brian Patrick Duggan, 2019)

Dog's Best Friend: Will Judy, Founder of National Dog Week and Dog World *Publisher* (Lisa Begin-Kruysman, 2014)

Man Writes Dog: Canine Themes in Literature, Law and Folklore (William Farina, 2014)

Saluki: The Desert Hound and the English Travelers Who Brought It to the West (Brian Patrick Duggan, 2009)

The Force-Free Dilemma
Truth and Myths in Modern Dog Training

Nicola Ferguson

Dogs in Our World
Series Editor Brian Patrick Duggan

McFarland & Company, Inc., Publishers
Jefferson, North Carolina

LIBRARY OF CONGRESS CATALOGUING-IN-PUBLICATION DATA

Names: Ferguson, Nicola, 1971– author.
Title: The force-free dilemma : truth and myths in modern dog training / Nicola Ferguson.
Description: Jefferson, North Carolina : McFarland & Company, Inc., Publishers, 2024 | Series: Dogs in our world | Includes bibliographical references and index.
Identifiers: LCCN 2023059532 | ISBN 9781476692579 (print) ∞
  ISBN 9781476650715 (ebook)
Subjects: LCSH: Dogs—Training. | Dogs—Behavior. | Dogs—Training—Moral and ethical aspects. | BISAC: PETS / Dogs / Training & Showing
Classification: LCC SF431 .F47 2024 | DDC 636.7/0887—dc23/eng/20240130
LC record available at https://lccn.loc.gov/2023059532

BRITISH LIBRARY CATALOGUING DATA ARE AVAILABLE

ISBN (print) 978-1-4766-9257-9
ISBN (ebook) 978-1-4766-5071-5

© 2024 Nicola Ferguson. All rights reserved

No part of this book may be reproduced or transmitted in any form or by any means, electronic or mechanical, including photocopying or recording, or by any information storage and retrieval system, without permission in writing from the publisher.

Front cover image: © Nikiforova Viktoria/Shutterstock

Printed in the United States of America

McFarland & Company, Inc., Publishers
  Box 611, Jefferson, North Carolina 28640
    www.mcfarlandpub.com

For Anna Wilson Ferguson

Table of Contents

Introduction   1

Chapter One. Definitions, and Dog Training Through the Ages   11
Chapter Two. An Introduction to the Science of Dog Training   25
Chapter Three. Myth Busting   48
Chapter Four. Corrections and Management   88
Chapter Five. More on Training Tools and Equipment   102
Chapter Six. The Science   117
Chapter Seven. The Innate Drives of Dogs: Brain Structure and Physiology   140
Chapter Eight. Balanced Training versus Force-Free Training   157
Chapter Nine. Legal Beagles   174
Chapter Ten. Cults   193

Conclusion   212
Glossary   229
Chapter Notes   237
Bibliography   255
Index   257

Introduction

In the last few decades there has been a massive shift in the way we keep dogs and in our relationship to them. This is to be expected, as with each generation the values of society change, sometimes for the better, sometimes not. However, the growth of social media in the last ten to fifteen years has been particularly detrimental to the welfare of dogs, as it has been used to push an agenda of **force-free/purely positive dog training** (hereafter force-free dog training) and the humanizing of dogs, changing the fundamental way in which we view dogs and consequently how we train them. (Terms that can be found in the glossary are set in bold type on their first appearance.)

No longer are dogs primarily seen as working animals or valued pets; rather, many people now see their dogs as "fur babies," small, vulnerable child substitutes that are to be treated in the manner of the most entitled of toddlers and must be kowtowed to at all times. Indeed, the *Cambridge Dictionary* now defines "parent" as "a mother or father of a person or an animal,"[1] and the *Collins Dictionary* goes further, with the inclusion of the more specific "pet parent" and a note stating that the term "is considered by some people concerned with the rights of animals to be more acceptable than *owner*."[2]

As a pet owner myself, I personally find this a tad insulting, given that I have devoted much of my life to serving the best interests of animals, having worked as a dog trainer and a welfare officer for a major animal charity, not to mention running my own small rescue operation with my summer practice supervisor while I was studying veterinary medicine. Not that I ever qualified as a veterinarian: those tuition fees are as vicious as an angry honey badger.[3] Nevertheless, I wasn't sitting safely behind a computer screen during those years, acting superior; often I was out alone at midnight in a rough part of the big city where I lived, in order to investigate a report of an animal in distress, which at times turned out to be a hoax. So yes, I am *very* concerned with the rights of animals.

To be fair, though, what you call your dog or yourself does not really matter much to me. After all, I once trained a beautiful German Shepherd Dog whose owners had named him "Adolf." Not terribly politically correct, but Adolf he was, and Adolf I very reluctantly called him. In fact, maybe people *should* both name and treat their dogs more like their kids. The vast majority of people would never let their kids behave as badly as their dogs do: mouthing off, acting violently, urinating wherever they choose, and issuing all sorts of threats—in short, behaving like a drunken teenager. In the bar or in the park, one day the aggressor will encounter someone bigger and tougher than he is and trouble will ensue.

There is nothing wrong with worshiping and adoring your dog. I'm autistic, and my dogs and cats provide me with unconditional love and a sense of belonging. They are my family, pure and simple, and there is rarely a cross word between the five of us. However, I respect my dogs for who and what they are, a very different species than me, one with strong predatory instincts and drives, not to mention acute senses, which as a human I can never fully understand.

Most dogs have forty-two sharp teeth which are designed for bringing down, killing and consuming other animals. My dogs would not hesitate to eat me if I passed away at home, nor would your dogs. If a dog is hungry, he will eat, and, unpleasant as it is to think about, he will start to chow down on you in a far shorter timeframe than you may imagine.[4] Although dogs may be intelligent and adorable, they are *not* small, hirsute child substitutes, no matter how much we may wish that were so.

In common with many other mammals, a dog's brain has the same basic structure as that of a human. However, dogs do not understand language, ethics and moral concepts as a human does, their prefrontal cortex being particularly small and undeveloped compared to ours. To treat dogs as anything other than the wonderful creatures that they are disrespects their unique talents, including their olfactory superpowers. Putting it simply, no matter how he is "brought up," a dog cannot comprehend why you might expect him to share his raw, meaty bone with grandma's dog who is visiting for the day. His mind and language capabilities are not up to that.

The babying of dogs has not been beneficial to them or to society at large, which has to live with these sad parodies of the superb hunters they were designed to be. More than ever, veterinarians, dog trainers and behaviorists are confronted with spoiled, genetically nervous, overweight, understimulated dogs who are living unhealthy, miserable lives with little exercise, training or appropriate enrichment activities. Anyone who has visited a public park has at some point had a rude, out-of-control dog come up and harass them, and as dogs are given fewer and fewer boundaries, this is becoming more and more of a problem.

Introduction

We all want to do the best for our dogs. We love them and want them to live happy, fulfilled lives. I can see why modern dog owners and younger dog trainers, veterinarians, and the like have bought into the fantasy that dog training *must* be *entirely* force-free and purely positive. Didn't you know dogs never, ever deliberately put a foot wrong? All **corrections** are unnecessary and cruel, they say, and will result in a shut-down, suppressed, miserable dog who is constantly quaking in terror. If you try to get a word in edgewise with staunch force-free advocates, the words "science says…" will be parroted out. I guarantee it.

But the passionately force-free trainer is only just hitting her stride, and why would you not listen? We all want well-behaved dogs who are enthusiastic and happy when being trained. She may mumble a bit about the UK **e-collar** studies if questioned about the "science," and, not having read the studies herself, she is quite unaware that those she is referencing and relying on have been largely debunked regarding their scientific merit and integrity.[5] I suppose what you don't know doesn't hurt you. It is hurting our dogs, though.

If you're unlucky, you will now start to be criticized for the **martingale collar** you have on your dog. You know, the one that sits loose on his neck but which, if needed, stops him slipping his leash and legging it after rabbits. You will be told to immediately remove it. "Martingales, **slip leads**, **choke chains**, e-collars and **pinch collars** must all be banned as they *always* cause fear, pain and suffering!!!"

No matter how loudly it is squawked, that does not change the fact that the statement above is fundamentally false. "Always" is a definitive word. Rarely in life is anything all good or all bad. A tool is only as harsh as the human hand that wields it. Indeed, a hand in and of itself can be used to caress a dog or to punch him. Berating a dog by shouting loudly at him is extremely personal and can be emotionally abusive. Or you can use your voice to whisper sweet nothings into your dog's ear, setting his tail helicoptering, ready for takeoff. Never forget that science is not necessarily objective, particularly when studying animal behavior. Researchers are human and are not above reaching the conclusion they want to believe, whether the data supports it or not.[6]

When used correctly, tools such as martingales, slip leads, pinch collars and e-collars are humane, fair ways to communicate with many dogs. If used wrongly, like the hand or voice of an abuser, they are unfair and can mete out pain. If these tools are not for you, then don't use them. What I would say, however, is to keep an open mind, but do not petition to have them taken away from other people who *do* require them in order for their dogs to live a happy, fulfilling life.

If you have never tried any of these tools yourself, why would you blindly take the word of someone else? A person who, similar to yourself, has never tried training a dog with the tools in question, who has never looked into their history, nor read the research studies which confirm their efficacy and fairness to the dog when used correctly and appropriately. That makes no logical sense. As my mother used to say, "Would you jump off a cliff just because someone told you to?"

We already have laws to prevent animal cruelty, laws which are not adequately upheld as it is. We do not need more laws demonizing tools and training techniques which may be the best way to communicate with certain dogs, particularly when the argument for banning such tools is made by a small but vocal minority of extremists. These proposed bans are not drawn up in consultation with a wider group of veterinarians, dog trainers, behaviorists, or even just the general public, but only with a very small number of people who may have a vested interest, financial or otherwise, in the banning of certain tools. Nor do the advisory papers put forward by government-sponsored researchers include any legitimately conducted science on the *correct* use of these tools.[7] All they contain is opinion. Opinion with a biased slant.

The tool should always be appropriate for the dog in question. I'm not saying to automatically put a pinch collar on your elderly, arthritic Labrador should he dare to pull on the lead with the strength of a cup of weak tea. However, if your adolescent Cane Corso is yanking you into the road, right in front of cars, whenever he sees another dog in the distance, then what? Perhaps, after consultation with an experienced trainer, a pinch collar or an e-collar may turn out to be an appropriate tool. It may not, but do not take away the rights of the Cane Corso owner if this is indeed the right tool for her dog.

Always bear in mind, all of our dogs should be able to enjoy a good quality of life *as a dog*. When certain tools and training techniques are banned, the ability of *all* dogs to live a happy, species-appropriate life is removed. Either that, or loving owners are turned into criminals, dodging the long arm of the law, all because they continue to use the tools which keep their dogs safe and give them a high quality of life. This is currently the situation in many Western European countries, where many kinds of training collars have been banned. Recently, in Switzerland, someone was fined $1000 for animal cruelty, as the dog she was walking was wearing a pinch collar.[8]

The reality is that many successful, self-professed force-free dog trainers use a whole host of harsh corrections, and even **aversives**. Common tools and techniques include food deprivation, ignoring dogs to the point of severe frustration and distress, **head collars**, and front-pull harnesses, not to mention castration and spaying. Most recently, sedatives and other "calming" drugs have become popular. Balanced trainers—those who rely on both **rewards** and aversives—may use the self-same things, and why not? What matters is that the tool is used judiciously, with correct training, and that it works for the dog in question. However, most balanced trainers will try several different tools and training techniques before scheduling a visit to their veterinarian. More often than not, this is the best approach for the dog and owner's bank account alike.

Even though the same tools and training techniques are being utilized by both force-free and balanced trainers, most force-free trainers claim the moral high ground, and a great many are quite salty about balanced trainers. Why so insecure? A lion doesn't have to roar for everyone to know he's King of the Jungle. No need to put others down. I'm not a fan of head collars, for example, but they work great on some dogs, so I'm not going to call for them to be banned. Why, then, should a force-free trainer tell me that *my* tools must be banned? I'm very much against hypocrisy and the abuse of animals. The terms *force-free* and *purely positive* are simply marketing tools to play on dog owners' emotions, force-free dog training being a practical impossibility.

I'll say it once in this introduction, and many more times throughout this book: *Force-free dog trainers use corrections, and many go further than this and use aversives—yes, they use extreme, at times very harmful, force.* However you define it, collars, harnesses and leads are restrictive devices. Making a dog uncomfortable with even the mildest of corrections is "force," and there is absolutely nothing wrong with this. Ignoring a dog until he eventually works out what he is doing wrong and complies or starving him into ignoring distractions are not positive experiences for a great many dogs. Often these techniques are more frustrating and unpleasant for dogs than a simple "no," yet they are increasingly being promoted as good practice.

Some force-free trainers will admit to enforcing boundaries and having rules their dogs must follow, though others will insist that everything in life must be the dog's own choice, and he must have bodily autonomy, meaning you must ask a dog's permission before you even touch him to administer medical care. This is where we stray into exceptionally dangerous territory for our dogs, and I hope that force-free trainers who are not extremists would agree with me on this point at least.

Now, many force-free trainers will say, "Everyone knows we use force; using no force at all is impossible." I agree, it is impossible, but it is *not* true that everyone knows this, which is my issue with the promotion of force-free dog training as the cure-all for any and every training or behavioral issue that a dog may have. Many members of the general public now believe they must give their dog no boundaries or rules whatsoever, and that the word *no*, when used with a sharp tone, will cause their dog to either have a mental breakdown or to go nuclear.

I see so many dog owners who have in the past trained and loved dog after dog, often of challenging breeds, and who are now stuck with reactive, rude, undisciplined dogs that they are faintly afraid of. The fair, consistent training they used in the past, they have now been told, was not ethical, and was scaring, indeed *hurting*, their dogs. Such owners invariably end up wishing they had never gotten another dog and are unhappy that standards have changed so much. Was their previous dog really so unhappy? He never seemed miserable, being a coffee shop dog who went everywhere with them, in comparison to the reactive monster they now have lording it over them as King of the Living Room and who can only be walked late at night or early in the morning, lest he terrify small children and send pensioners to an early grave.

Force-free trainers who say in their promotional materials that all the training they conduct is based on positive reinforcement only, while at the same time advertising head collars and front-pull harnesses for sale on their websites, are displaying hypocrisy at its finest. Some trainers (including famous ones), when put on the spot, will admit, "Oh yes, of course I use force in my training. I don't need to spell it out on the website or to my clients, as it would upset my sponsors and decimate my client base!" Is that what matters? Making millions of dollars for yourself, at the expense of the lives of thousands, if not millions, of dogs?

This sort of behavior is unacceptable, particularly from dog training celebrities with their own TV series and training schools. It's bad enough when local trainers tell lies, taking business away from more honest trainers, but when a well-known dog trainer puts out a misleading message, it affects far more people overall.

The fact is that a great many force-free trainers are now not only admitting but *emphasizing* that they do indeed set boundaries and have rules their dogs must obey, stopping short of using the words *correction* and *force*. This tells you that they, too, are seeing dogs being let down, falling prey to the extremists within their own movement. At one time, no force-free dog trainer would admit their dogs were trained with consequences for bad behavior (i.e., corrections, using the **Koehler method**) in addition to rewards for good behavior. But admitting that you train your dogs with corrections is an oxymoron when you are also saying you are "purely positive" in your training techniques.

The truth is, in the real world, *good* dog trainers use *exactly* the same basic techniques, whatever they call themselves. It doesn't matter if you say you're a **balanced dog trainer**, a force-free dog trainer, a purely **positive dog trainer**, an **emotional dog trainer**, a reward-based dog trainer, a

play-based dog trainer, or a dog trainer with pink and purple spots. In the vast majority of cases, given the same small- to medium-sized dog to train, there would be absolutely no difference at all in how the opposing camps would approach training that dog. None. None at all. Each and every one of those trainers would start with teaching correct behaviors using positive reinforcement and go from there when any problems arose.

The tools used on the dog may differ slightly, as may the types of rewards and corrections, but that is due to personal preference on the part of the trainer and also what suits the individual dog. Trainers have varying levels of experience and skill, and different owners want very different things from their dogs. A pet dog takes less time to train than a working dog. A seeing-eye guide dog needs a different trainer than a police dog. As we will see in this book, the real difference between trainers who admit they use corrections (and this includes reward-based trainers) and those who insist they are force-free or purely positive is in the marketing. The bad force-free dog trainers, those extremists who are letting down dogs, are masters of marketing and manipulation; it's their bread and butter. They do not get clients through skill but through deception.

This book is not a dog training manual. I will not tell you to turn to page 69, for instance, to teach your dog how to be his most sexy self, detailing the techniques to train him to use a hump pillow. Yes, this is a thing with some extreme force-free dog trainers who believe a dog needs to be free to openly express his sexuality at all times. In my view we should *not* be encouraging and normalizing such behaviors from our dogs.

Carrying swiftly on, this book is a look at how we came to live in a world where using the word *no* is considered tantamount to abusing dogs. I'll look at the misconceptions that have become so common in dog training, examining the corrections and aversives that force-free and balanced trainers alike actually use. I'll debunk the myths and bad science that have been unfairly wielded to demonize certain training tools and techniques, and I'll finish by explaining why all of this matters, including examining the soaring rates of dog bites and dog-bite fatalities for humans.

I will make as much reference as I can to scientific materials, articles, and the writings of well-known dog trainers, in addition to visual aids, which can be of great benefit when discussing a practical skill such as training dogs. Whether the trainer uses purely positive methods to train agility dogs or is a balanced trainer who produces personal protection dogs, every school of thought has something to contribute.

I want to give you different points of view and direct you toward the information you need in order to do more research and ultimately make informed choices on behalf of your own dogs. I don't expect or want you to just take my word on trust. Your conclusions may not be the same as mine, and that's fine. We are all entitled to our own opinions, and we live with and love very different dogs.

If you have a well-behaved dog, why bother reading this book? Who cares if pinch collars and e-collars are banned? Well, you may care when your family silver is stolen but the police can't pursue the thief as there are no operational police dogs available.[9] You may care when your new terrier won't recall and is miserable being permanently on-lead on his walks.[10] You may care when crates are banned[11] and your adult dog redesigns your kitchen cabinets, while your Goldendoodle puppy swallows a tea towel and later dies in surgery. You may care when your favorite breed is banned, the Labrador Retriever being one of more than 80 breeds banned in Lviv (Ukraine) as recently as 2016.[12] You may not be affected now, but one day you invariably will be. Consider the dog laws from around the world.[13] Ask yourself, "Where are the force-free extremists taking us next?"

For me, it's a matter of animal rights as well as human rights. We need to have a discussion within society about what we feel is and is not permissible, for *all* members of that society, not just a chosen few. I'm writing this book because we are letting dogs down, each and every one of us: balanced trainers, force-free trainers, veterinarians, dog walkers, and dog owners. Increasingly, dogs are being managed, medicated, sent to shelters, recommended for euthanasia, and passed from pillar to post by the more extreme factions within the dog training industry.

The general public does not know where to go for advice anymore, and people are getting berated for setting any boundaries for their dog. Others think they're doing their best by their pets by giving them no discipline, rules, **leadership** or structure in their lives. This is a recipe for disaster with a great many dogs, both large and small.

For too long, those of us in the balanced training community who are peaceable, nonconfrontational folks have had a "live and let live" attitude. That has been our mistake and our undoing, letting down dogs and owners alike and leading to the banning of useful tools such as crates, e-collars and pinch collars. Good, decent force-free trainers are also guilty: for not standing up to the extremists within their own community, one that has somehow assumed all the power just so they can have a marketing advantage over other trainers in a competitive world.

Plus, there are more sinister intentions afoot, which I suspect include doing away with working dogs entirely and banning all large, high-drive dogs.[14] Oh, and brachycephalic dogs. *Any* pedigree dog eventually, given that the mantra "adopt, don't shop" is very popular with activists,[15] whose views are gaining more and more traction with the general public. Have you ever seen a Landrace dog?[16] Landrace dogs are bred and trained to perform specific functions needed by their people—herding, guarding, hunting. Depending upon their purpose, they will have a typical look but no kennel club pedigree. They are a far cry from the small handbag dogs many people prefer these days, but we had all better get used to them, as my guess is that within thirty years Landrace dogs of indeterminate parentage may be all that's left, the breeding of pedigree dogs being banned entirely until shelter populations are at zero. Finally, I think no dogs will be permitted to be kept as pets, since this will be morally questionable,[17] in the way the use of training tools and even corrections are increasingly being seen today.

I hope this book will make you stop and think about the issues we are facing as dog owners. Some of you may even consider learning how to use tools which you have bought into believing are cruel when you have never even touched them, never mind seen them correctly used. You may be pleasantly surprised, or you may decide such tools are not for you and you'd prefer to soldier on by "managing" your wayward dog. That is absolutely your prerogative, but nevertheless please accept that there *is* a place for such tools, and you do not have the right to tell other people how to live their lives with their dogs.

If those of you in the U.S. and other countries that value personal freedom remain complacent, it will be at your peril. If you do not start to actively campaign for the rights of dog owners, all sorts of bans will be introduced by stealth, and when you finally wake up, it will be too late. This has happened to many of us in Western Europe, to our deep regret, not to mention that the U.S. already has laws which limit personal freedoms, such as bans on certain dog breeds in many cities and states.[18]

Pit-bull breeds are the main ones banned in the U.S., but there are also bans that apply to other large, powerful breeds, including Rottweilers, wolfdogs, Chow Chows and Cane Corsos, to name just a few. The breeds most commonly favored by the police and military, including German Shepherd Dogs and Belgian Malinois, seem to have escaped unscathed.[19] How very odd; it seems to be one rule for them and another for us. Who would have guessed such a thing would ever happen? It's not just breeds that are being banned; the U.S. is following the lead of Europe in terms of bans on tools and training equipment.

Unless we pull together as a united body, worldwide, the extremists *will* triumph, and in twenty or thirty years' time we will look back and say, "I wish...." Just as we currently devour sci-fi movies about dinosaurs, if we do nothing we will end up watching movies about the magnificent species we currently call "the dog" that soon will no longer exist in the many wonderful forms we now know and love: large and small, fat and thin, dogs built for comfort, others for speed. Maybe that's fine if you're rich, with your own secret Jurassic Park to play in. But if not…

Welcome to the world of force-free dog training.

One final word of advice: training benefits from keeping things in perspective, and you will see traces of my ~~suppressed rage~~ lighthearted humor throughout this book.

CHAPTER ONE

Definitions, and Dog Training Through the Ages

Let's start at the very beginning, a very good ... well, you know how it goes. I don't want to infringe copyright and all that. (If you do want a thrilling, feel-good tale of nuns, Nazis and strict parenting, watch *The Sound of Music*.) In this chapter, I'm going to go over some technical terms which are used throughout the book, but don't worry if you're a bit uncertain around scientific dog training terminology; all will become clear. Pinky promise. There's a glossary at the end, and I'll try to make my explanations as clear as possible, using normal language such as "reward," which we all understand.

Even if the next pages on terminology and old dudes in white lab coats seem like tough going, keep reading. By Chapter Two, I aim to give you the scientific tools and language to thrill and impress everyone you may meet at a party, or at the very least have a meaningful conversation about your dog's martingale collar if, for example, it is being called "cruel." You'll even be able to effortlessly counter any arguments you may have hurled at you by the force-free mafia. No need for your dog to bite them. We've all been there, being told "I don't use force" by a person whose dog mopes along in a head collar put there by force. Nothing wrong with this necessarily, but there is also nothing wrong with your own well-behaved dog in a martingale collar.

Before we get into it, it's essential we are all on the same page regarding definitions, so I will take some pains to state *exactly* what I mean by some words and phrases you will see over and over again in this book. If I say "sugar" and you think it means "salt," we are hardly ever going to ever agree, are we? Sugar and salt can look alike, and indeed can both be used in the same dish, depending on taste, as is the case in the use of tools in dog training. Where I come from in Scotland, porridge (one of our national dishes) is traditionally eaten with salt, whereas I much prefer it with sugar myself.

If you're already vehemently disagreeing, having misunderstood me in the introduction, now is the time to get a nice cuppa and a few choice chocolate biscuits. I am *not* advocating for the abuse of dogs, and as you read on, even if you're a committed force-free dog trainer, you may realize we are actually on the same side. Mostly.

The word reward comes up a lot in this book. As it should, being the most important term, and far and away the most frequently used tool we have at our disposal when training dogs. It is also a tool which is greatly misunderstood and not utilized as correctly as it could be. For example, used on their own, or overused, the effectiveness of rewards diminishes rapidly, particularly when a dog is established in a certain behavior, so care must be taken! But alas, this is not a technical dog training book.

Also, some dog trainers differentiate between a reward and the feeling of relief, while others do not and consider relief to be a reward in itself, given that it has a strong link to positive emotions. Relief does not have to be artificial; it can be a natural consequence. For example, the dog may gain relief from the discomfort of his legs and shoulders disappearing once he stops yanking and lunging when wearing his front-pull harness. I would tend to say that in many instances when training, relief in and of itself is insufficient to most effectively promote good behavior, so whenever a dog performs correctly, even if that has been instigated via discomfort from a tool, for maximum benefit the dog *must* also be rewarded for doing as he is asked.

The *Cambridge Dictionary* definition of *reward* is "something given in exchange for good behavior or good work."[1] I think we can all relate to this. The definition of *relief* is "a feeling of happiness that something unpleasant has not happened or has ended."[2] So the real divide between the two words is that it's possible for a reward to have nothing bad associated with it, whereas relief will always involve something unpleasant, whether real or simply anticipated or imagined.

If a dog is hungry during training, giving him a reward for good behavior will have the effect of relief, as his hunger is satisfied (if only partially). Hence dog trainers who say they are force-free yet ask you to not feed your dog breakfast before the training session are using discomfort in the form of hunger, providing relief from that hunger when giving rewards. This can be great, and a very sensible move provided the dog does not skip too many meals.

Going back to *reward*, the main thing to remember is a reward is something the dog likes and which makes him happy, such as playing, food or affection. What a reward is will entirely depend on the dog, and the amount or value of the reward will depend on the circumstances. When teaching a dog a new skill and he gets it right, give him a fantastic reward. Act as excited as a tween with her first TikTok account. If you're asking for something simple which the dog knows very well and has performed many thousands of times, he may just get a brief "Good boy," if anything at all.

Most dogs like food as a reward, and the vast majority of trainers will use food as a reward at some point. Many trainers will use both high- and low-value food rewards, depending on the circumstance, examples of this being chicken and **kibble**, respectively. Other trainers use one type of food only, which may be part (or all) of the dog's daily food ration. When the dog is only fed during training, this is called the **ditch the bowl** training method.[3] I am not a fan of this technique for a reliable dog that works in the real world, but many people swear by it.

Often food is used to lower the dog's energy and as a reward for calm behavior, though much depends on the dog, his preferences, and what we are training for. There are also ways of using food to create excitement and **engagement** in a dog during training, mainly by using a bit of movement when dispensing the **cookies**.

Play is also an excellent reward, either instead of food, where we want to up the energy of the dog and activity, or where a dog is too excited to eat but will most certainly engage in a game. As with food, what is a good game is up to the dog to determine. Some dogs love fetching a ball or jumping up to catch a Frisbee. Others prefer playing more directly with their owner, such as enjoying a game of tug together.

In addition to food and games, most dogs greatly enjoy being praised by their owner, since this is very personal to them. I use a lot of verbal praise with my dogs, as well as food and games. After all, my voice is something I cannot mislay or forget when going on a walk. Many of us live in the same home with our dog, and therefore we are (or should be) our dog's leader, and some of you may also see yourselves as your dog's parent or guardian. Food or play coming to the dog as a reward can be impersonal, but praise from you will raise the dog's level of oxytocin, the feel-good love hormone.[4] I would not rely on verbal praise alone when training; rather I use it in addition to food and play.

There are a great many dogs who are not very active, or who are old, or who simply are a bit too anxious to eat and enjoy food rewards when out and about. For many of these dogs, a soft stroke under the chin and kind words are very meaningful, and act as a good reward. All dogs are different, and their own individual preferences should be respected to get the most out of what we offer them as a reward during training.

Let's move on to the next important term, which is *correction*, another word I will use often in this book. A correction is simply a stimulus the dog does not like, which you as a trainer use in order to show him he has done the wrong thing. A correction can also be *removing* a stimulus he *does* like. So the dog performs an unwanted behavior, you use the correction and he decides not to repeat the behavior he was engaged in. Ideally, an alternative preferred behavior should be asked for after using a correction, so the dog can be rewarded for making a good choice. In the future, this gives him more reason to not repeat the undesired behavior and instead choose the one we are trying to encourage. Let me emphasize straight away that a correction is *not* a punishment. Neither does a correction cause fear, pain or anxiety.

Just as with rewards, some dogs will regard a stimulus as a correction, while other dogs will be totally unaware that the stimulus in question is supposed to be something they dislike. Many anxious dogs will find hard, sustained eye contact from a trainer to be a very frightening experience, whereas very confident dogs will see the trainer staring at them as an invitation to approach them for affection. What sorts of stimulus can act as corrections, then? Any that engage the dog's senses. Most commonly a trainer will use body language, voice, or physical touch in some manner, more often than not using a tool to convey that physical touch, such as pressure from a collar and lead.

So a correction can be as simple as hard eye contact or body language. It can be the trainer using her voice to deliver a hard, firm "No!" the tone alone letting some dogs instinctively know you are not pleased whereas other dogs require the word "no" to be paired with a negative stimulus to undertsand it is a correction. With my own dogs I often say "no" in a soft, kind tone, using it as guidance to my dogs, meaning they are doing great and I am very pleased with them but the response they are giving me is not right, so they should try the task once again. This "no" is encouraging and sets tails wagging despite being a correction, since we are working together and doing something fun in our training session. This is very distinct from my hard "No!" which means they should immediately stop whatever they are doing. I also use a hard "Ah, ah!" to mean "Do not do what you were thinking of or are about to do."

Physical corrections via a tool could be lead pressure, in combination with whatever type of collar the dog is wearing, or stimulation from an e-collar. Some trainers will use light pressure directly on a dog's body in order to manipulate the dog physically. This could be pushing lightly on a dog's bottom until he sits down on the ground to get away from that pressure. This is a more traditional way to teach "sit" (I prefer to lure with food), and I find it causes many dogs to push back, but some dogs find the pressure helpful. They are all different.

Chapter One. Definitions, and Dog Training Through the Ages 15

Another correction that can be very useful is removing a pleasurable stimulus, usually via stopping play when the dog does not want to abide by the rules of the game. All games have rules, after all; yes, even Monopoly. An example of this type of correction would be not throwing the dog's ball if he does not bring it *right* back to his owner's feet so she can easily bend to pick it up. We've all had dogs dropping a ball several yards away, making us walk over to get it. It's annoying. If the game temporarily stops as we refuse to walk over to get the ball, only restarting when the dog drops the ball a bit closer to our feet, over time we can use this type of correction to ensure the dog always drops the ball right at our feet.

Please note that in this book, unless it is explained otherwise, a correction is simply something that is unpleasant enough that it cannot be ignored by the dog, and therefore the dog is motivated to take action to stop the correction. Some corrections we want the dog to remember very well, aiming to make sure he never wants it applied to him again, such as discouraging a dog from raiding trash bins, and yes, those corrections will be a little more unpleasant. Raiding bins can kill dogs. It is not an acceptable behavior.

In other situations, often when teaching behaviors during a training session, it's essential we maintain the dog's enthusiasm and energy for what we are doing. In such a case, the corrections are usually very mild, and more in the form of helpful guidance. The dog is working as a team partner with the trainer, and the trainer is explaining what she wants, all the while trying to give the dog better options than the incorrect behavior he is performing, which may be the easiest option for him. The dog responds to the correction, temporarily stopping the behavior, but the trainer knows the dog may need many, repeated small corrections.

An example of this is competition heelwork, where the dog should be moving with a lot of energy at his trainer's side, all the while looking up at the trainer, trying to make eye contact with her. This is a somewhat artificial position, and it takes time for the dog's muscles to get used to walking or running like that. Often the dog wants to look at where he thinks his reward will come from, for example, the trainer's hands (if that's where his ball is) but not at her actual face. We want the energy and passion of the dog maintained, but also to give corrections, so the dog understands he cannot look at the incorrect part of the trainer. It is not easy!

Ninety-nine percent of the time, a correction is not something that strikes fear into the heart of the dog, as changing your internet router password no doubt would do to your kids. Nor is a correction the same as a punishment. However, if your fourteen-year-old kid, who should know better, "borrowed" your credit card and bought thousands of dollars' worth of toys and clothes online, then perhaps taking away her internet privileges would be justified. It's the same with dogs.

Very occasionally it *is* necessary to give a dog a short, sharp shock to convince him he *never, ever* wants to repeat that behavior again. It does not have to cause pain, but it does need to be effective. Similarly, a correction should not be a nag, nag, nag. Corrections delivered in this way will cause the dog to become habituated to the stimulus and quickly ignore it.

Therefore a correction must be unpleasant enough so the dog pays attention immediately, and ideally strong enough to have a long-term, lasting effect, bringing about meaningful change, though, as with the heelwork example, how much pressure is optimal will depend on what we are doing. A correction should not cause a strong, negative emotional reaction, but where it is necessary, it should act as an aversive.

A correction, then, needs to be well thought out and suit the individual dog in question. A correction *does not* and indeed should not be painful, deeply unpleasant or scary in any way, unless it is an emergency situation where the dog could suffer serious harm from repeating the behavior and it's essential we stop it immediately. In such cases, the correction should be as hard as is necessary, and yes, more often than not it will act as an aversive, and if it causes fear or pain, so be it. Perhaps this was what was required. Such corrections are administered to the dog in order to preserve life and limb without a visit to the ER or veterinarian.

Many force-free dog trainers will insist that the only permissible correction is ignoring a bad behavior and offering an alternative good behavior, continuing with this until the dog makes the right choice. This is similar to putting down rules via play. However, though this works well in many circumstances, it is not the best method for every dog. After all, if aliens visited the Earth and the correct way to greet them was to lie flat on your back and make snow angels, how long would it take for you to work that out on your own, with no direction or help? Dogs benefit from direction in the form of fair, kind corrections, not from being left to wing it alone.

As an example, many dogs get extremely excited when visitors come to the house, jumping up on the stranger and, when it is a big dog, clawing at her, trying to lick her face. Force-free trainers often advise the guest to ignore the dog and turn her back on him, only petting him when he calms down, while the owner offers the dog cookies to encourage a basic alternative behavior, such as not flattening the person. For a dog that is not terribly excited, this can work well, as can management strategies such as putting a dog in his crate for the length of the visitor's stay. However, some dogs will sit in their crate and scream the house down for hours on end, and others who are unconfined will not stop jumping up, scratching the visitor's back and legs as she and the dog twirl round and round, as if performing a canine *Danse Macabre*.

Chapter One. Definitions, and Dog Training Through the Ages

When a dog is extremely excited and aroused, he cannot effectively use his brain to work out that if he stops jumping up, the visitor will stop moving away and may eventually give him some attention. Similarly, his excitement means he will not accept cookies, nor find plonking his bottom on the ground to be a better, alternative behavior. Many dogs enjoy having someone turn their back on them and then twirl away, as it's a fantastic game to them, and they get more and more excited and rambunctious. This is not a good state for your dog to be in, and can result in a dog taking a nip at the visitor out of pure excitement, not aggression. This is particularly the case with working breeds that have been bred to bite when aroused, such as the Belgian Malinois. What do you think will happen then?

I once knew a Labrador who developed this very problem. There was not an aggressive bone in his body, but he got very excited at playing the "ignoring, twirling game," and one day he nipped a guest, which elicited loud yelling, which was a double bonus. A force-free trainer told the owners that their dog was nipping out of fear and he must be **counter-conditioned** with lots and lots of cookies. Being a typical Labrador—in other words, a canine waste disposal unit—the dog found visitors to be even more exciting, as cookies were everywhere, and eventually he bit a guest using a full grip with his mouth, not letting go until he was offered sufficient cookies to make it worth his while.

This was not puppy mouthing. But, being a good boy, he always used bite inhibition, as his intention was never to hurt anyone, just to have fun and get fed. After a while this lovely dog started biting any strangers he encountered while out on walks and off-lead, as he found yet again that when he bit someone, there was excitement and lots and lots of cookies. His owners were actually told to yell at any people he approached and to tell them to start giving him cookies, to prevent him biting. Keeping him on a lead or muzzled was seen as an infringement of his canine rights, but, as you can imagine, had he bitten the wrong person, he would have been seized and euthanized. This is *not* what you want to teach your dog, and force-free training can be incredibly harmful when used incorrectly.

These sorts of dogs, who get excited on receiving guests, do not benefit from being ignored, left to work it out themselves, or offered cookies; rather they do best when given clear directions and leadership from their owner, regarding the behavior required of them. This could be as simple as the dog being put on a lead and being firmly but calmly told "no" by his owner, with a lead correction, when he tries to jump up to say "hello" to a visitor, who, ideally, ignores him and who does not turn away or start to spin. When the dog starts to listen to his owner, he can be asked to obey the very basic commands he knows well, obedience to which are generously rewarded. It is the dog's owner who needs to be calling the shots, though. It is not right for your visitor to be left to train your rude, bad-mannered dog.

Don't get me wrong, an excited dog who is over threshold, in a state too excited to learn, will not suddenly calm down as if by magic just by being told "no" once or twice. The owner must restrain the dog until he is on or under threshold, where he is capable of taking instructions and receiving both corrections and rewards. Unless the dog has serious issues with **barrier frustration** or redirecting onto his handler, both of which require expert intervention, his arousal will gradually wane, and he can then learn the acceptable way to greet guests. The most important thing, however, is that the dog is not getting more and more excited, and that he is kept safe and will not be taken away by the police for biting someone.

Dogs which are under threshold when visitors arrive can effectively be trained using appropriate corrections and rewards, and will learn very quickly the behavior expected of them. They are not given the chance to get more and more excited, soaring over threshold and becoming incapable of learning; rather they are immediately given direction and rewarded for good behavior, in addition to being corrected for bad behavior. This, in and of itself, is of great benefit to them. A more excitable dog will need some additional time, and to be restrained until he is less excited and is on threshold and ready to learn. If that is the dog you have, that is the dog you must work with. It is part and parcel of dog ownership.

Please note, adult dogs are *very* different from puppies. (Unless I state otherwise when I am discussing a behavior, I am talking about an adult dog, *not* a puppy.) Any dog under a year is considered a puppy, though how long a dog takes to mature, both mentally and physically, will very much depend on the breed and the individual. Larger dogs mature later, with some breeds being two or even three years old before full maturity. Dogs of six months of age or under, of whatever breed, are very much puppies. Like human toddlers, puppies have less control of their emotions and require you to be much more forgiving and patient, jollying them along, setting them up for success, instilling confidence, and managing behaviors which would be totally unacceptable in an adult dog.

We now must define aversive. The *Cambridge Dictionary* defines *aversive* as "making someone feel a strong dislike for something, or making them not want to do it."[5] Many people use the word in relation to dog training, and there is nothing inherently wrong with this, as corrections may or may not be aversives. I will not often use the word *aversive* in this book when describing a correction, as, unless stated otherwise, I will not be talking about a correction that results in a strong dislike or emotional reaction. All corrections should correspond as much as possible with the

Chapter One. Definitions, and Dog Training Through the Ages 19

LIMA (least intrusive, minimally aversive) approach. Force-free extremists claim that each and every correction causes pain and fear, which is untrue, but which is another reason for me to differentiate between a correction, an aversive, and a punishment.

Similarly, I do not like the term *punishment*. The *Cambridge Dictionary* definition of *punishment* is "rough treatment,"[6] which is certainly not what we want for our dogs. B.F. Skinner—basically a science dude whom we'll discuss in Chapter Two—used the word *punishment* when coming up with his theory of operant conditioning,[7] but I'm not going to use it even in that context, as the word has no connection with learning and therefore no place in dog training. Instead, I have replaced *punishment* with *correction*. If that is arrogant of me, so be it.

In general, *punishment* is used to describe actions performed out of spite or anger. Dog training should always be about teaching a dog, *never* about getting angry and emotional ourselves, inflicting pain via a punishment, just so we feel better. When I think of punishment, I also think of the type of force used to make a dog do something which is an unreasonable thing to ask of him, either due to the ask itself, his level of training and understanding, or whatever else. That is not good dog training.

A correction should not cause pain, only a degree of discomfort, but this in itself is pretty subjective, and is one of the reasons why dog training has undergone such a large split between its various factions. Force-free trainers condemn tools such as pinch collars, claiming they cannot be used in an ethical way as they *always* cause pain. Always. On every dog in existence. But balanced trainers know that different dogs react to pinch collars in totally different ways, many not experiencing any observable pain whatsoever, some hardly acknowledging any discomfort unless given a hard leash "pop." Other dogs will yelp with only a tiny amount of pressure, often out of surprise when the collar is first used.

Every person has a different pain threshold and perception of pain, and this is also true of dogs. A recent survey of dog owners and veterinarians regarding which breeds have higher or lower pain thresholds was extremely interesting.[8] It shows that the general public—that is, dog owners—believe smaller, lighter dogs experience pain more intensely than larger, heavier dogs, particularly breeds that are commonly banned under breed-specific legislation, their perception of such breeds having been colored to quite a large extent. So, giant breeds such as Great Danes are perceived to experience more pain than American Pit Bull Terriers, even though the Pit Bull is not a very tall dog. Yes, we were discussing definitions, but to keep you from becoming comatose, we are going on a slight detour into the world of pain.

The views of veterinarians in this study were more diverse, with less prejudice toward certain breeds, except perhaps the poor old Pit Bull, which everyone agrees does not feel as much pain as other breeds. We also have to take into account the dog's genetics and what he was bred to do, in addition to his temperament and level of stoicism, which veterinarians consider much more carefully than the general public, given that they may lose an arm if they make a misjudgment with a Mastiff. Hence the difference in the study's overall results.

Veterinarians do acknowledge that both the German Shepherd Dog and the Siberian Husky have low pain thresholds in comparison with what would commonly be expected, given their size and weight. From my own experience, I would agree with this when such dogs are being given veterinary treatment, though it has to be said that both these breeds are very vocal, and is that more what we are judging rather than pain? Also, if we look at the working lines of the German Shepherd and Husky, they can in no way, shape or form be said to be weak dogs and not able to endure a high degree of pain. A Siberian Husky team can pull a sledge 120 miles per day.[9] Yes, you read that right: that's some distance, in the harshest of conditions. This is not a dog that gives up the ghost and calls for an Uber when feeling a bit of cold, discomfort and misery.

Now, the smarty-pants out there will be thinking that perhaps skin thickness correlates with pain, and that many of the veterinarians thought about which dogs tried to nail them when being vaccinated and which dogs didn't. It seems the skin of a Saint Bernard is the same thickness as that of a Yorkshire Terrier, something I was not aware of, and yes, I would perceive a Yorkie to be more pain-sensitive than a Saint Bernard. The study also considered genetics and whether we sympathize more with small dogs, as many look like human infants, with large, wide-set eyes—a bit like Puss in Boots from *Shrek*—which is known to bring about an instinct to mother and protect.[10]

The real point in bringing up this study is that different breeds of dogs experience different levels of discomfort, and indeed pain, from the exact same stimulus, be it a shot, an e-collar correction, or a lead correction. It would not, then, be fair or scientifically logical to ban pinch collars, martingales, slip leads and e-collars on the basis of their causing pain and suffering to all dogs, as we know they simply don't. That is what science says, not those e-collar and pinch-collar studies that call themselves "science" but which always have an agenda, as we shall see in Chapter Six.

Which dog feels the least pain? The Mastiff. Is he to have no life outdoors if we ban pinch collars, **choke chains**, martingales and slip leads? A hard-pulling Mastiff would tend to find an appropriate pinch-collar correction useful, but not painful or unacceptably uncomfortable, so why should *he* never get to be walked in public or have a tool used on him

Chapter One. Definitions, and Dog Training Through the Ages 21

which gives him precise, fair guidance? He's not a Pomeranian, a breed that would find a pinch collar to be too much, but he deserves the same rights and respect as a Pom. Why can't all dogs enjoy a nice lifestyle, subject to an appropriate tool as and when required, which they understand and which suits the specific breed, instead of blanket bans being imposed? Force-free campaigners should love all dogs, not just small, cute ones. In ignoring the needs of large dogs, they do these dogs a disservice and can hardly be said to be dog lovers.

Types of Trainers

So what do I really mean by force-free or purely positive dog trainers? It should be obvious from the introduction, but it may not be, so let me be clear: When I am discussing force-free and purely positive trainers, I mean those trainers who tell people they do not use *any* corrections whatsoever in their dog training, and that all of their techniques are based *only* on reward-based, positive methods. The dog will not be forced to do anything he does not want to do, and bad behaviors will never be corrected, they will simply fade away like a bad dream. The trainers who actually abide by this are extremists, and tend to have very little knowledge of dog behavior and training, either practical or theoretical.

Such trainers tend to be extremely arrogant, believing their way is the only way and that dissenters must be destroyed or, at the very minimum, assimilated. They will seek to "educate" every person they meet, no matter her level of expertise. So often I see a self-proclaimed twenty-something "expert" force-free dog trainer being brought into a police department as part of a woke agenda. This trainer may have previously held the lead of a show line German Shepherd, but has never worked a dog in protection, *ever*, yet is telling police dog trainers of thirty years' experience to offer their doggies some kibble to get them to "out" on command instead of using a break stick.

The officers smile politely, try to see the mandatory training as a day off work, and laugh about the trainer's naiveté for the next few months. Some wonder if she has been on the wacky baccy, given that their drug detection dogs were keen to indicate anywhere other than her kibble pouch. The boys (and girls) in blue are not swooning in admiration as this trainer imagines, boasting as she does on Instagram of how she educated the police. Hiring her is a box-ticking exercise regarding dog welfare, no more, no less, and has nothing to do with actually improving the training of the department's general purpose police dogs. If anyone has asked for her phone number, it's because she is blonde and into Pilates, not because she is a good dog trainer.

There are many trainers who used to market themselves as purely positive or force-free trainers but now call themselves reward-based trainers. I have no issue with this, as it's honest and a great many of these trainers are ethical, fair, and produce beautifully trained dogs. They now admit that they use appropriate corrections, as they want to differentiate themselves from the force-free extremists, who tend not to be good trainers at all. Many of the most famous **clicker trainers** would now say they are reward-based trainers. I would describe myself as a reward-based trainer, in addition to a play-based trainer and a balanced trainer. The dogs I train get lots and lots of rewards; however, there are also boundaries and rules. If you are looking for a trainer, a reward-based trainer is not a bad place to start.

Compulsion trainers are at the opposite end of the spectrum from force-free trainers. As with the genuinely extreme force-free trainers, the words "wouldn't touch them with a bargepole" come instantly to mind. Compulsion trainers damage plenty of dogs, as do extreme force-free trainers, just in different ways. These trainers may get results quickly, but they produce, at best, shut-down, depressed, sad dogs, and at worst, dogs who are suppressed in their behaviors but who one day will explode and perhaps redirect on their owner. Don't go near a compulsion trainer.

A quick internet search will show you what are considered the main schools of dog training, which change all the time. I am not going to cover them all, but it's worth noting that a few are really not what it says on the tin. Science-based dog training, which tends to be very aligned with force-free dog training, picks the aspects of science it likes, and rejects the science it disapproves of. Yes, I agree that positive reinforcement, using lots of rewards, is best for teaching a new behavior we want to instill, but it will not hold up around competing reinforcers that look better than the rewards offered. To deal with that, we need corrections.

Model-rival training utilizes another dog as a role model.[11] Therefore it only works if you already have one well trained dog, or one that already understands the exercise you want the other dog to copy; it is best used while training new behaviors in a quiet setting. Relationship training is a method I don't consider to be a separate training methodology, and is rather what all good trainers should be doing as a matter of course: looking at each dog as an individual and building up a relationship with that dog based on trust and respect. We have already seen the acronym LIMA, for least intrusive, minimally aversive, and again, this is what all good trainers do. LIMA does *not* mean using no corrections or only negative corrections, but using appropriate corrections for the dog in question.

When I speak about balanced trainers, I am speaking about trainers who admit they use corrections as well as rewards and who generally

Chapter One. Definitions, and Dog Training Through the Ages 23

utilize all four of Skinner's operant conditioning quadrants, to a greater or lesser degree. Many balanced trainers use the exact same techniques as reward-based trainers, though some may use additional tools, including pinch collars and e-collars. Some balanced trainers specialize in one area of training, in much the same way clicker trainers do, using e-collars and "pressure and release" in extremely sophisticated ways, not zapping the dog into oblivion like a displeased Greek god, but rather using the e-collar as a line of communication that the dog really responds to and understands well.

Before I bore you to death with definitions, one final comment: I have mostly used the male gender for dogs in this book, and the female gender for humans. Not for any particular reason other than I didn't want to use "he/him" for every creature in existence, as is the case in many books. Hopefully "he/him" for dogs and "she/her" for people is easily understandable.

Having gotten all of the most important definitions out of the way, let's now take a brief trip through the different scientific experiments relevant to dogs. Or just the ones which interest me. This could take all day, or rather all year, but I will try to be brief, and to this end I have created a little table for you, mainly concentrating on scientists, though I've added a few schools of thought too. I have also put in the endnotes links to some cool YouTube videos which show the dudes and dogs concerned. Finally, I thought it would be fun to give the guys some "fighter" names. Enjoy.

1890–1930. Ivan "Ding That Bell" Pavlov: classical conditioning.[12] There is even a really groovy game on the Nobel Prize website where you can try to condition Pavlov's dog.[13]

1898. Edward "The Puzzle Box" Thorndike: the Law of Effect.[14]

1913–1948. Burrhus Frederic "Don't Turn Me into a Hat" Skinner: operant conditioning.[15]

1920. Watson and Rayner: Little Albert Experiment,[16] aka "Let's Torture a Small Child."

1959. David "I Prefer This over That" Premack: **Premack principle** of responses as reinforcers.[17]

1960s. Keller Breland, Marion Breland Bailey and Bob Bailey, the "Party of Three," followed by Karen "I'm a Good Type of Karen" Pryor: clicker training.[18]

1968. David "The Wolfman" Mech: pack and dominance theory.[19]

Now, there have been loads of different dog training methodologies since then, plus many really famous dog trainers who have large social media followings, which does not necessarily equate with competence. There are also loads of scientists I have left out, but let's give a final special mention to Nikolaas Tinbergen[20] for his awesome name (so like my own) in addition to his scientific work, and also Konrad Lorenz,[21] who made many contributions to science.

I have lots more definitions in the glossary, but I thought it best to get the main ones understood at the start. Now that we are on the same page regarding corrections and rewards, plus the different types of trainers, let us move on to more exciting stuff.

Chapter Two

An Introduction to the Science of Dog Training

This will be a more technical chapter, but basically, all of the experiments on dogs discussed here have concluded that (a) dogs do more of the things they enjoy and (b) dogs do less of the things they do not like. I also want to include (c): most (though not all) dogs seek to obtain a better deal in life for themselves, even just in very small ways. One day it's their dog bed, the next your super comfy king-size bed, plus all of the duvet, while you lie shivering, not wanting to disturb their sleep.

I'm going to be contrary and start with Skinner and the operant conditioning quadrants.[1] We should start with Pavlov, the father of classical conditioning,[2] but as there are some fundamental definitions and concepts which we need to understand first, we are starting with Skinner. Yes, Skinner, a name if there ever was one that you don't want to hear if you're a laboratory animal. "What are you doing with that scalpel, Dr. ... gulp ... Skinner?" I can hear those poor animals think, as echoes from the past. You may be tempted to skip over this bit of the chapter, but please do persevere as best you can.

Skinner came up with four operant conditioning quadrants which explain how animals, including dogs, learn. They are (1) positive reinforcement; (2) negative reinforcement; (3) positive correction (punishment); and (4) negative correction (punishment). Please note, I have changed two of the terms Skinner used, from *positive punishment* and *negative punishment* to *positive correction* and *negative correction*.

Positive means adding something; it does not necessarily mean adding something "good," though usually it does. So adding something could be adding food to the situation or it could be adding discomfort to the situation. Conversely, *negative* means removing something—it could be removing discomfort and providing relief, or it could be removing play. Reinforcement is encouraging a behavior to happen more often, whereas correction (punishment) is concerned with stopping a behavior.

Positive reinforcement means rewarding a dog so he will do something more often, and positive correction (punishment) means doing something unpleasant to a dog so he stops doing something he should not be doing. Remember, both include the word *positive*, because we as trainers are adding something to the mix—an action the dog likes or one he doesn't like—with one of these quadrants encouraging a behavior (via reinforcement) and the other one stopping a behavior (via correction). They are polar opposites.

We also have negative reinforcement and negative correction (punishment). These are discussed less in training, though in practice they are used a lot, particularly negative reinforcement, which is simply pressure and release. Also note, these quadrants can be used pretty much simultaneously, as at times we want to stop one behavior while encouraging a different one (e.g., stop pulling and start loose lead walking). So if you just don't "get" them or can't decide which is which in a given situation, don't worry about it. It may be that both are in play. The main quadrants to know are positive reinforcement and positive punishment.

Positive Reinforcement

In relation to dog training, positive reinforcement is just a fancy name for encouraging the dog to increase a behavior in order to get a reward from the trainer. Positive = adding something. Reinforcement = encouraging a behavior so it will happen more often. If the dog gains something he likes as a result of his behavior, then that behavior will increase. Positive reinforcement is simply giving the dog a reward when he does the right thing.

Example: The trainer gives the dog a piece of food whenever he does not pull and instead walks on a loose lead at the trainer's side. The result is that the dog walks on a loose lead more often and does not pull on it, in order to ensure that the trainer will keep giving him pieces of food.

Negative Reinforcement

Negative reinforcement is also called avoidance training. In relation to dog training, negative reinforcement generally means encouraging the dog to increase a behavior to stop the trainer from continuing to put pressure on him. Negative = removing something. Reinforcement = encouraging a behavior so it will happen more often. If the dog learns how to remove something he does not like, then the behavior which gains relief will increase. The words *negative reinforcement* sound contradictory. How can something the dog feels is negative increase the likelihood of his performing a behavior more often? When we look at this in the context of pressure and release, then it starts to make sense.

Example: If we put gentle, continuous pressure on the lead, the dog will walk closer to our side in order to release the pressure, making the lead loose. The loosening of the lead is a relief to the dog, so the behavior of walking closer to our leg increases, as the dog does not want to experience pressure on the lead again. The dog walks on a loose lead more often and does not pull on it, in order to ensure that the trainer will not put continuous pressure on the lead again.

Positive Correction

In relation to dog training, positive correction generally means getting the dog to stop a behavior so that the trainer does not give him another correction. Positive = adding something. Correction = discouraging a behavior so it will happen less often. (Skinner called this positive punishment.)

This is confusing, as when we hear the word *positive*, we automatically think it must mean something good—not so! Positive means adding something, and here it is adding a correction—so, adding something the dog does not like. Understandably, it can be a bit confusing.

Positive corrections have nuances in that they can be used in three main ways: (a) to give a correction when the dog is doing something wrong, so he does not want the correction to be given again; (b) to give a correction which is fully intended to be an aversive that will stop the behavior immediately and, ideally, permanently (this can either be recognized by the dog as coming from the trainer or simply be something that "just is" and comes from nowhere, the trainer not saying anything, making eye contact with the dog or reacting to his bad behavior, and perhaps not even being present when the aversive occurs, leaving the aversive to do the work for her); and finally (c) to give a correction to tell the dog to both stop the bad behavior *and* to perform the behavior he should be doing.

When the aversive is not seen as coming from the trainer, it is generally being used to stop behaviors such as counter surfing, chasing cars, raiding bins, etc., which are dangerous and often take place when no people are present. Not linking the aversive with the trainer means the dog does not try the behavior when the trainer is out of sight, as he believes the aversive came from the behavior he was performing. Or the correction can be a "hand of God" aversive with the trainer present and needing to exert absolute control, as when the dog is chasing a sheep with a view to killing it, in which case it's essential the dog stops dead in its tracks.

Example: The dog is pulling on the lead, so the trainer gives a pop on the lead, a pop being a short jerk, to act as a correction and to cause the dog momentary discomfort. The pop is most commonly used in (a) or (c) two paragraphs above, ideally (c), as the dog should first be made to understand he should walk to heel by **luring** him with rewards. The result is that the dog pulls on the lead less often, and walks on a loose lead in order to ensure the trainer will not pop on the lead again.

Negative Correction

In relation to dog training, negative correction (also called negative punishment) generally means getting the dog to stop a behavior as the dog does not want the trainer to withhold an expected reward. Negative = removing something. Correction = discouraging a behavior so it will happen less often. Again, this is counterintuitive, as the word *negative* combined with *correction* instinctively makes most people think of a trainer using a correction such as a lead pop, whereas the trainer is actually removing a reward.

Example: The dog is pulling on the lead, so the trainer stands still, preventing the dog from walking forward toward the park. Walking is rewarding for the dog, as he enjoys going to the park. The trainer (and hence also the dog) standing still acts as a correction. The dog learns that if he wants to walk toward the park, this only happens when the lead is loose and he is not pulling. The result is that he pulls on the lead less often and walks on a loose lead in order to ensure that the trainer will keep walking.

Summary to beat all summaries:

POSITIVE REINFORCEMENT. The dog walks on a loose lead more often, and does not pull on the lead in order to ensure the trainer will keep giving him pieces of food.

NEGATIVE REINFORCEMENT. The dog walks on a loose lead more often, and does not pull on the lead in order to ensure the trainer will not put a continuous pressure on the lead again.

POSITIVE CORRECTION. The dog pulls on the lead less often, and walks on a loose lead in order to ensure the trainer will not pop the lead again.

NEGATIVE CORRECTION. The dog pulls on the lead less often, and walks on a loose lead in order to ensure the trainer will keep walking.

Force-free trainers say they *only* use positive reinforcement, giving the dog rewards for walking on a loose lead beside them and never using corrections. The extremists even recommend running after a pulling dog, so he never gets any pressure on his neck when he pulls on the lead. However, being able to do this is not realistic, as most force-free trainers are aware of.

It's also worth bearing in mind that some trainers who call themselves force-free will admit they use boundaries—mainly those trainers now marketing themselves as reward-based. They may say that they use the "stop walking when the dog pulls" technique and insist it is force-free but will refuse to use the words *correction* or *punishment*, even though they are technically using negative correction (punishment) plus negative reinforcement via pressure and release on the lead. Stopping walking until a dog "gives in" and stops pulling potentially involves three different quadrants if rewards are also used, though mainly this is a negative correction method: I take away something you want so that you will stop doing something I dislike. Yet other reward-based trainers admit they will actively initiate pressure and release or even a small lead pop.

How exactly can you trust an extreme force-free trainer who uses a method formally called negative punishment but will not tell this to clients, maintaining a "holier than thou" attitude and insisting that just stopping walking will not cause the dog any significant lead pressure, discomfort or negative emotions at all, and so it's a purely positive training method. This is simply not true. Of course it causes discomfort, and some dogs simply *cannot* work out why the reward of walking to the park has been taken away. Such dogs get increasingly frustrated, excited and upset, start to refuse food rewards to come to heel, and end up very confused. This is unfair to the dog.

Such a dog often benefits far more from being given very clear instructions. He is taught loose lead walking via a combination of reward for keeping the lead loose (positive reinforcement), pressure and release (negative reinforcement), and later, if required, a lead pop (positive correction). Initially this is done in order to teach the dog about pressure and release, the trainer deliberately putting very light but constant pressure on the lead (negative reinforcement). As the lead loosens when the dog moves toward the trainer (usually when encouraged to come to her), the dog gets relief from the pressure. A good trainer also immediately rewards the dog when the lead is loose and he comes toward her (positive reinforcement). We therefore see a constant pressure on the lead, then the relief of a loose lead being backed up by a reward, which can be praise, food or play.

So with this technique there are massive rewards for the dog, but also corrections via negative reinforcement and positive correction. In combination, the positive reinforcement, negative reinforcement, and positive correction are used to teach the dog the concept that keeping a loose lead is the most beneficial way for him to walk with his trainer. This method can be much clearer than using other quadrants in a confusing manner, as a way of trying to "be kind."

Once the dog fully understands that walking on a loose lead is how he should behave, being given a lead pop (a positive correction) when he pulls reinforces to him that putting pressure on the lead is uncomfortable and is a choice he should not make. This is generally used when the dog moves away from a quiet environment, becomes a bit more excited, and starts to pull; even though he knows full well he should walk on a loose lead, he forgets himself a little. A lead pop is hard enough to act as a deterrent to pulling in a way that constant pressure isn't, as, after all, it takes two to pull. Once again, the dog is rewarded by the trainer when the lead is loose, having been asked to come to heel.

You can see that for this dog, using *three* quadrants instead of two (or, at worst, only one) still involves lots of rewards. Where required, adding fair corrections to the training mix can be the clearest way possible to teach and enforce loose lead walking. This is the best technique for the vast majority of dogs. There are lots and lots of rewards used in this technique, often many more than if the dog cannot work out the negative correction method of stopping walking and subsequently gets too upset to accept any food rewards at all.

Not every dog requires many corrections in training; some dogs will stay calm and use their brain, working out that they only get to walk forward when the lead is loose. If using fewer corrections suits you and your dog, then there is nothing wrong with it. Every dog is different. I'm not going to tell owners and trainers their business when I don't have their dog in front of me to assess him. However, you may find that this method can take a very long time, even with a calm dog who is trying to think things through. On the other hand, when he finally "gets" it, the results can be effective and long-lasting.

There are good ways to use negative reinforcement as a training technique, in my opinion, and I do not rule any training technique out. We always have to do what is right for the individual dog we are training. This is where many adamant force-free trainers fall down. They have a very limited range of techniques and tools which work on only an extremely small range of dogs. They are not prepared to expand their training repertoire, keep an open mind, and to train the dog in front of them. It's good to recognize your limitations, and if such a trainer is doing badly with a dog but refers the dog to a balanced trainer, or just a more experienced reward-based trainer, then all is well and good. I *do* object, however, when a client is told her dog cannot be helped when the dog absolutely *can* be helped and trained in a fair, ethical way—just not by that trainer.

For those of you who want to plow on and take a deeper look at the four operant conditioning quadrants, you will probably have noticed that there is a lot of crossover between the quadrants, as, after all, we can be discouraging one behavior and encouraging another all at the same time, which does of course cause confusion. It's a "which came first, the chicken or the egg?" type scenario, and personally I would rather not get caught up in it, though I am sure I will get criticism from other trainers saying I have gotten things wrong. Positive reinforcement and positive correction tend to be super clear, the other two quadrants not so much, and there is great disagreement about them, even among the top trainers of today. If you want an example of this, watch Ivan Balabanov's Training Without Conflict video on negative reinforcement.[3]

Bart and Michael Bellon are masters of the quadrants, and if this is an area that interests you, please look at their NePoPo system,[4] which works a lot with negative (and positive) reinforcement, utilizing e-collars and food restriction. Ivan Balabanov is also an expert dog trainer and a master of the quadrants, and his Training Without Conflict system[5] should not be missed, particularly if you are interested in play-based training. However, it is very, very expensive and beyond the purse of most mortals. These trainers work very differently but get very good results with similar high-drive, high-energy dogs, and also with pet dogs, often those with severe and challenging behavioral problems.

A quick note on differences: With positive correction, the dog must make a mistake by pulling on the lead in order to elicit an uncomfortable leash pop by the trainer. With negative reinforcement, *the handler* initiates the pressure and the dog responds by making the lead loose; he may never actually initiate the undesired behavior of pulling on the lead himself, as the handler is the one who starts the pulling. It is used as a tool to teach the dog not to pull, but if he does end up pulling—and they all do—it is used to teach the dog how to switch off the pressure he then feels on his neck and body.

Some trainers say the difference between the quadrants has to do with the dog's *knowledge*. With positive correction, the dog makes a mistake, pulls, and the trainer pops his lead. With negative reinforcement, this is not necessarily the case. In both cases the trainer initially uses rewards to teach the dog, via a lure, to walk by her side. Then, when the time is right, she introduces continuous pressure (negative reinforcement) in order to teach the dog that a tight lead is uncomfortable, so he should strive to keep the lead loose. Other trainers say the real difference is in the intensity of the correction. With positive correction, the correction generally is more intense and uncomfortable than with negative reinforcement. In many respects, this will depend on the trainer.

When negative reinforcement is used, the trainer is in control and initiates the pressure, and therefore she can start low, increasing the pressure by degrees until she gets the reaction she wants from the dog. With positive correction, the trainer responds to the dog pulling, so if the dog is pulling hard on the lead, the trainer in turn will need to give him a harder lead correction than she would if the dog had only pulled lightly. Or, in response to a first light pull, the trainer could give quite a hard pop, to really surprise the dog so he thinks, "Wow, I won't do that again!" He may of course be used to pulling on the lead, but not with the trainer. He may be used to there being no consequences, and sometimes a short, sharp shock can be useful with such a dog to quickly change his mindset.

Again, this would be down to what the trainer thinks is right for the dog. A small Poodle is unlikely to ever pull hard on the lead, and may happily work on a flat collar. A Rhodesian Ridgeback who is physically dragging his owner around as a nine-month-old puppy will almost certainly pull worse as an adolescent unless he is trained not to. In such a case the trainer may introduce a pinch collar so she can give a tiny pop to the dog, which is subtle but which gets the message home. The client can then be taught to work with her dog on the pinch, the dog now understanding that his owner can command the same measure of respect as the trainer. Please note that I do not advocate pinch collars on puppies.

A commonly given example of negative reinforcement is the "ding ding ding" noise to remind you to fasten the seat belt in your car.[6] You don't like the seat belt, but you like the noise even less, so the nagging of the noise can be enough to act as a negative reinforcer, in that it encourages an action—i.e., fastening the seat belt. This makes most (but not all) people buckle up before they even hear the noise. If it was a positive correction, some trainers will argue, it would be a loud siren and you would jump out of the car and not get back in, as the noise hurt your ears so much you want to avoid it again at all costs.[7] But some people are not noise-sensitive, so they just turn the radio up louder and start to sing along, not putting the seat belt on; therefore the "ding ding ding" noise has not acted as a negative reinforcer or as a positive correction. So it is with the dog, as we discussed in Chapter One regarding sensitivity to pain.

We cannot treat all dogs the same, and this is what the force-free movement refuses to recognize. Gentle lead pressure on a harness, the equivalent of the "ding ding ding" of the car seat belt alarm, may work well with a French Bulldog. It is ideal to enforce loose lead walking with this small, low-drive dog that often struggles to breathe. Frenchies are delightful dogs who want to please, and have little inclination to pull hard on the lead.

But the harness so beloved by owners of brachycephalic dogs will not work well with a large, heavy Cane Corso who barely feels even a front-pull harness in his excitement. He needs the equivalent of a smoke alarm, perhaps a pinch collar working on him as a positive correction, in order to make him walk on a loose lead, particularly when under **distractions**. Offering food or stopping walking (negative correction) are not going to prevent him from pulling.

Hence we have to wonder, is there a secret agenda? That of getting rid of high-drive, "tougher" dogs? We are being told that in order to be ethical and kind trainers, *all* our dogs must be trained to respond well to rewards and rewards *only*. Pressure on a flat collar or harness should be used only at a push. If rewards alone don't work, and the method of negative correction and stopping walking does not work either, then as a very last resort a tool such as a front-pull harness can be used to cause discomfort, but the smoke alarm, the pinch collar, must be banned. This will be the death knell for larger, higher-drive breeds.

I can see that sticking to one quadrant, positive reinforcement, is in line with some trainers' client bases, even though it is not a true reflection of how they actually train dogs. Now, the haters among you who claim to be force-free trainers may very well have skills far in excess of mine in some areas, such as agility or trick training. I will not refute this. I am in awe of many of you! I would love to study under you, as I never want to stop learning and would no doubt sharpen up a lot of my own skills, which is why I'm sad that often never the twain shall meet.

We all want different things with our dogs. Some of us are fascinated with the mind of the dog, and with teaching tricks in a very controlled environment. Others want a dog that is competitive in international-level dog sport competition, and yet others want a nice, well-behaved family pet that knows little more than sit, stay, loose lead walking and recall, all of which is done in public with lots of distractions around, which is no mean feat. I enjoy dog sport, and my own dogs live in a city, so they must be well mannered canine citizens first and foremost. However, I am fascinated by trick trainers who use a lot of positive reinforcement to produce great **free shaping** results (see below).

Let's talk about different kinds of rewards.

Direct rewards. The reward is given directly to the dog. The best example of this is luring. We hold the food reward in our hand, the dog puts his mouth next to the food and follows our hand as he learns to walk at our side, and the food is released when he is in the correct position. The food is all he cares about, not the fact that the hand is part of the trainer's body; the trainer simply uses her hand as a receptacle for the dog to follow.

Indirect rewards. The reward is given indirectly to the dog. There is a *bridge* between the dog and the food, the bridge being you, the trainer. The dog may look at you for guidance, and not solely be concentrating on the food and where it is located. The best example of this is shaping. The dog may have to perform several small steps in order to get to the final, desired behavior and the food reward. The steps are taught one by one, and the dog needs to eventually link these steps. This takes some brain work on the part of the dog, and he will often look to his trainer for help and guidance, which may be verbal and not part of the food reward, such as the trainer pointing to an object he must go toward.

With luring and direct rewards, the dog does not look to his trainer for help as he does with shaping; luring means the dog is following the food and the food alone. With luring, there can still be linked commands, but there is less trial and error on the part of the dog than there is with shaping. The dog is "fed" the answer rather than encouraged to work out what he needs to do himself as is the case with shaping, particularly free shaping. However, working together as a team can be extremely valuable for both dog and trainer.

This may not seem like a massive distinction, but shaping tends to encourage the dog to be creative and to dare to make mistakes. With luring, the dog knows he has to do the exercise in a very precise way, otherwise there is no reward. However, his absolute focus on the food may stop him from being creative and trying new behaviors, so it really depends on what we are trying to achieve at any given moment.

When we have a shut-down dog that has perhaps had some compulsion training, and we want the dog to benefit from increased confidence and to enjoy his training once more, we may use luring to initially build him up, so as to avoid a situation where if he gives the wrong answer, he simply gets confused, depressed and gives up. Later we may start to use shaping, where he can have fun, build a bond and work closely with his trainer, taking hints and direction from her rather than always just looking for the food. The trainer is linked to the reward, which we also want to encourage.

A dog whose mind wanders, is excitable, and can't keep concentrating very long or very well may also benefit from first doing luring work to learn some impulse control. The intense concentration on the reward which comes with luring may be exactly what he needs, teaching him that when he gets overexcited and can't self-regulate, it takes longer to get his reward. Later, as his thinking becomes more controlled, shaping can start to come into play.

Still unsure of the difference? Dolphins are commonly trained with rewards, primarily indirect rewards. The trainer can't swim through the water to lure the dolphin along and show him how to jump out of the water

Chapter Two. An Introduction to the Science of Dog Training   35

after her hand. So shaping and indirect rewards are used, particularly free shaping. For example, the dolphin may be rewarded every time he spontaneously does something the trainer wants him to repeat at a later date, such as jumping out of the water. The trainer can't lure for this, but she can shape and reward the behavior when she sees it, eventually turning it into a behavior she can ask for. Classical conditioning also comes into play here.

Many trainers of whatever persuasion, balanced or force-free, put little thought into how they use rewards or the basic fundamentals of training. They do not think through the quadrants, clarifying whether the reward is direct or indirect, or set a reward schedule, and they make other mistakes such as just whipping out cookies, not taking the time to use a clicker or a **marker word**. If they *do* decide to use a clicker or marker word, no time is spent in **charging** it. Yes, you can get by without using any clicker or marker word, but for many activities the clarity that such tools provide makes it much easier for the dog, particularly when you are shaping and can't physically get the reward to the dog quickly.

A clicker and marker word are simply signals that allow the trainer to tell the dog he is right. Some people call them a bridge. A clicker is a small device that makes a distinct "click" sound, and a marker word is a specific word said in a specific way, such as a very enthusiastic "yes!" This word, whatever it may be, is pronounced in a consistent, distinct way to make it different from any other word the dog may hear as part of the common speech patterns of the trainer.

Having no clicker or marker word in any of your dog's training makes you miss out on so much of the clarity and also subtlety which you can put into the work. If a dog is marked for a correct behavior, he knows he has given the right answer and that a reward is forthcoming. I like to use clickers and marker words when I am teaching new behaviors and using a continuous reward schedule, so the dog gets rewarded every time I click/mark. For **partial reward** schedules I also use clickers/marker words, but I never mark a correct behavior and then not reward the dog. Some people do, **marking** each correct try and rewarding only as per the schedule they are using, but I prefer to always back up a click/mark with a reward every time.

When you do want to use a clicker/marker word, it must be properly charged, which takes time and which many people just skip. "Charging" is simply making sure the dog realizes that the clicker/marker word *will* result in a reward. How do you know the dog understands this? Well, if the dog hears a clicker/marker word while just sitting and relaxing, and comes running to you full of enthusiasm (or even just looks round to you) as if he is expecting a reward, then he has made a link between the sound and the food. If he does nothing, more time needs to be spent clicking/marking and then immediately rewarding, even if this takes a few more sessions or even a week. It's a fundamental.

After a while you can extend the time between the clicker/marker word and the reward arriving, with the dog understanding it will come, as he knows he has performed the correct behavior and he just he needs to wait. There are more complexities regarding types of reward schedules, whether they are determined by time or the number of clicks, which I will go over below. I just want to emphasize that for me, a click/mark always has a reward. If you are not rewarding every try, just don't click for those tries you do not intend to reward, for example if you are only rewarding a *better* try.

Do the majority of force-free trainers use positive reinforcement and rewards to their fullest possible extent? Sadly, no. Such a trainer may argue that all her client wants is to get a dog that understands basic obedience, calmly walking to heel with no tension on the lead. The client doesn't want to learn a whole lot of nonsense about clickers/markers, direct and indirect rewards, or reinforcement schedules, so why bother learning it herself? My argument is that, along with such knowledge being essential, force-free trainers are supposed to be the absolute *experts* in positive reinforcement and reward, since it's all they use. Logically, then, each and every force-free trainer must know the theory of positive reinforcement inside and out? If not, why not?

I see many force-free trainers who only use food as a reward. They have no idea how to deal with a dog that has too much food drive, or dogs that have no food drive. They do not utilize play, which can be a massive mistake, as many dogs tend to learn best while in a higher state of arousal. A lot of research has been done on play in humans, particularly in relation to video games, and play does indeed enhance cognitive ability, including in older people.[8] Play is not just for puppies and teenagers.

Unless you are withholding food to some extent, keeping the dog in a state of constant hunger and making the food a very valuable resource, food will not generate as much arousal or, to my mind, as much enhanced learning, as play will. The dog should always be the one to lead us in recognizing what is truly rewarding for him, not what we *think* should be rewarding or what we prefer to use as a training tool or technique. Also, it depends on what we are trying to train. For some things, I find play works best as a reward, and for others, food.

In addition, and very importantly, play utilizes a great many boundaries. The dog will select the play he prefers, whether that is tug or throwing a ball or Frisbee. In some games there are food rewards as part of the game, and this has started to become a "thing" in dog training circles, though I myself do not consider this to be "play" as much as an

Chapter Two. An Introduction to the Science of Dog Training   37

inexperienced force-free trainer attempting to muscle into the games market. However, if the dog thinks his play should involve food, and indeed prefers it, who am I to argue? Mainly, though, I will use a ball on a rope, a tug toy, or something else I can throw and which can be tugged as well as retrieved.

We have already discussed in Chapter One how to use play to enforce rules, and this is a good use of negative correction, or "force," would you not agree? We are playing and having fun, yet we still have boundaries and rules, and you cannot dispute that it is *force* via negative corrections which is creating these good behaviors. Why, then, is all force defined as cruel, and always causing pain and suffering?

Getting a dog to focus absolutely on me when he is very excited, and using play in training, stands me in good stead in the real world when I ask for a behavior when there is a **competing reinforcer** present, i.e., something the dog would prefer to focus on rather than me. Walking nicely past a lunging, barking dog, remaining at my side on a loose lead when asked, and not barking back, becomes easier when the dog can control his emotions, concentrate on me, and think about what I am asking of him, even when very aroused, having developed these skills when we were playing tug.

In addition to bringing the energy and enthusiasm of a dog up by using rewards, I also want the skill to use rewards to take the high-energy dog down a notch or two. Often food is very good for this rather than play, so being able to utilize many types of rewards (and also corrections) is vitally important. Most force-free trainers are more familiar with the use of food in this way, to teach quiet compliance and obedience to commands in a training room. This is fine until the dog goes into the real world, and there is a competing reinforcer which is more exciting than food.

However, what do we do with the dog that has no interest in play or food? How do we train him if we cannot reward him? If this is a shut-down dog, this is not who he actually is. Generally this type of dog can be brought out of his shell if given enough time and we find out what he likes most, and then work sympathetically with that. Many abused dogs, including those terrorized with compulsion training, may be too scared and nervous to eat during training, as they know their trainer wants something from them, and past experience has shown them that getting their trainer's individual attention and being asked to learn things does not end well for them.

On the topic of food and abused dogs, many force-free and balanced trainers who use food as their main or indeed only tool in training a dog understand all too well how food drive, and hence handler engagement, can be dramatically increased. This is done in not such a nice way, mainly via starving the dog. I have no objection to a dog being trained before feeding him or after having him skip a meal, or being trained when slightly hungry. Hand feeding can wonderfully build up a dog who lacks trust and confidence. These are all good uses of a dog's biological need to eat.

What *is* a big bone of contention for me, however, is when a trainer calls herself force-free and yet is using excessive hunger, both as positive and negative reinforcement, the positive reinforcement being the reward, and the negative reinforcement being that the hunger pain goes away. Some dogs are starved for days. Not for hours, not overnight, but for days. Let that sink in. A dog does not eat for three, four, five days or longer, just so the trainer can boast she is force-free but still gets *results*. This is totally unethical.

Should not we as trainers be able to train *any* dog, to adapt ourselves to the dog, and not the other way around? If you hold yourself out as a force-free trainer, then I expect you to be able to use *every* type of reward, on every type of dog, especially the rewards the dog likes best. After all, is that not your selling point, that you work with the dog and let him lead you? That the dog gives permission to be trained? How is that so when he has not eaten for days and will do anything for food, even if he is still terrified, working for food being the lesser of two evils?

It may seem a bit pointless to go into all of these technical aspects of dog training in a book which purports to be about a broad debate over how we should approach dog training and indeed is not about the minutiae of dog training. I am in fact skipping over many concepts, and being a bit basic with the ones I have touched on. Truly, this is not a book for a deep dive into how to train a dog or use different techniques; it is meant, rather, to make you aware of the tools and techniques all trainers use, so you can understand what is being discussed in the force-free debate, and also to help you ask questions of any trainer you may be considering studying with, or using with your dog. A trainer should have a much, much deeper understanding than I present here of rewards and corrections, but not all do.

I see many force-free trainers these days who do not understand the science behind dog training and *constantly* use rewards, employing a continuous reinforcement schedule.[9] The dog is literally being rewarded for breathing. With every few steps, he is given food simply for staying beside his owner in the training room. He is not learning a new skill, and he does not really care about the food. No **jack-potting** is used, no partial reinforcement schedule with fixed or variable rewards, just constant luring and cookies. As the training session goes on, the dog gets fatter and fatter.

Why is this wrong? Why *not* reward the dog every time he does something right? What about corrections? Well, there's a big difference

Chapter Two. An Introduction to the Science of Dog Training 39

between the beginning stages of training a dog to understand a behavior, improving on a behavior, and maintaining good performance of a behavior he knows very well. When learning a new behavior, the dog needs to be having *the best time ever* in the training, with a reward every single time he gets it right (a continuous reinforcement schedule) and a correction every time he gets it wrong which may be simply witholding a reward. The corrections are there for communication purposes only, as kind and helpful guidance for the dog, not "Don't do that again, or else," but more like "Yay, good try, buddy, but not the right answer, so have another go."

As we move on in a dog's training and the dog fully understands what he is being asked to do, both rewards and corrections change. For a simple task he has done a thousand times, when the dog does as I ask, I may just give a brief "good boy" but not give food or play. I may not even do that. He does not need to be rewarded each and every time he does as I request. As we will discuss below, constant rewards for a well-known behavior during training impedes learning and good behaviors rather than promoting them. If we are making a fair request, but for whatever reason the dog does not want to do as we ask, we must figure out why. Was he is paying attention to us or was he daydreaming? Is he a bolshy adolescent?

We must *always* ensure that a refusal is not due to pain, and that we are asking the dog for a behavior he genuinely understands. For example, I might be out for a walk and ask my dog to "sit" at the traffic lights. He does not sit, yet stays standing and gazes off into the far yonder. He might or might not have flicked an ear back at me, indicating he heard me. Now, a refusal to sit could be because of a sore back or a pending tear in the CCL (cranial cruciate ligament, your dog's ACL equivalent), but if this refusal to sit is not a common thing, and the dog is looking lovingly across the road at another dog or a squirrel, the chances are it's not about pain.

I will ask my dog to sit again, and this time if he refuses I will not ignore the disobedience but give the dog a small correction, perhaps say his name and repeat my instruction to him, or give a small lead pop if I feel I really need to get his attention, and again repeat the command. I would not just ignore my dog and fail to correct him, letting him ignore me, particularly for several requests to do something reasonable. When I am *sure* he heard me the first time, having seen him flicking an ear or even looking at me but then disobeying me, I would correct that first disobedience.

I love my dog, so why not reward him for every single thing he does when asked, via a continuous reinforcement schedule? Scientifically there are very good reasons not to reward each and every time, and indeed the top force-free clicker trainers tend to not reward dogs constantly with food, depending on what they are teaching. Stuffing a dog full of food for very basic behaviors the dog knows well, particularly in real life and outside the training room, tends to be a habit of more inexperienced force-free trainers. Often this happens when they have little control, and worry (rightly) that the dog will head off and do his own thing if there is no food on offer. The food is acting more as a bribe than a reward, and there is no real working partnership between dog and trainer.

If such a trainer *does* reward her dog every single time he does something he knows well alongside the things he is learning, what happens when the food runs out during a long training session? Once the food is gone and there are no consequences for ignoring the trainer, the dog has zero incentive to continue and may start to misbehave and amuse himself. I keep my training sessions short, often only ten minutes each, but what if you are out for a long walk on a sunny day with a dog trained in this way? Does your dog behave, or does he become disobedient when no food is forthcoming for correctly performing a simple task such as walking beside you without pulling?

A partial reinforcement schedule[10] means we do not give the dog a reward every single time we ask him to do something, and it is used when a dog already understands a behavior and we want to maintain his correct performance of it. There are four different classifications of partial reinforcement schedule, and if you look at the link in the endnote above, there is a great article explaining them.

At its most basic, a partial reinforcement schedule can be variable ratio, fixed ratio, variable interval or, lastly, fixed interval. Back to a few brief definitions. *Fixed* = well, fixed. The reward *will* be given provided the dog meets the criteria that has been set. There is no guessing involved. *Variable* = there is *randomness* involved in the provision of the reward, keeping the dog guessing. *Interval* = a time period, mainly in seconds, as dogs forget pretty quickly. You don't want a reward to be given minutes later. *Ratio* = proportion in relation to the number of correct responses. It will all make sense when you look at the difference between fixed and variable ratios.

Variable Ratio

The dog receives a **random reward**[11] (or by using an average) when he gives us the behavior we are asking for. Let's say we are asking him to bark on command, the correct response being one bark and one bark only. With a variable ratio reinforcement schedule, we may ask for a bark seven times in a row, only rewarding him the second time he barks and the seventh time he barks. Variable ratios work well to reinforce an already learned behavior, but not to teach a new behavior, as the dog would become confused and lose interest. While using a variable ratio reinforcement schedule, the trainer can tailor the reward to how the dog is performing at the time, so she is flexible in her allocation of rewards.

In practice, most people do not work out averages but use random variable ratios while training. The randomness does not act as a deterrent, rather it's a bit like playing the lottery; it's exciting for the dog to not know whether he will win. Variable ratios elicit the most dopamine production, and maximum dopamine is released when the ratio is 50 percent reward,[12] but the dog must know the task well. Often trainers will recommend a higher ratio of up to 85 percent reward.[13] Much will depend on the dog's personality. An important point: It has been found that it is the anticipation of the reward that causes a big dopamine hit, *not* when the reward is actually received.[14] Bear that in mind!

Dopamine is a neurotransmitter, responsible for feelings of euphoria and happiness, but it has many more roles than that, also contributing to memory, learning, movement, behavior and motivation.[15] Some dopamine is made in the brain, but it is also produced in the adrenal glands along with adrenaline, as it is also a hormone. Dopamine is involved in eating, drinking and other activities we enjoy—in a dog's case, being trained.

A variable ratio reinforcement schedule is a useful technique when we only want one repetition of a behavior: to bark once, or to sit when asked. It's also fine for a small number of linked behaviors, though linked behaviors of any complexity generally benefit more from a continuous reinforcement schedule,[16] i.e., rewarding the dog for every correct repetition of the behaviors. If we want the dog to bark and keep barking until we ask him to stop, instead of one bark per "ask," these may all be barks but they are linked, making a variable ratio reinforcement schedule not the best choice. If the dog has been asked to bark and has barked twenty or thirty times, and your variable ratio is on "asks" four and five out of each group of seven, he may get frustrated with the training session, feeling he rarely gets rewarded, and give up. It is better in this scenario to use continuous reinforcement.

Fixed Ratio

Here the dog is rewarded after a *set number* of correct responses.[17] For instance, I ask the dog to bark, and my fixed ratio is to reward him every third time he barks. I ask him the first time, he barks, no reward. I ask the second time, he barks, no reward. I ask the third time, he barks, and he gets rewarded. We start again (or keep going, depending on how you view it) and on barks four and five he is not rewarded, only getting a reward on bark six. With fixed ratio schedules of reinforcement, if you make the reward too far off, the dog may just give up, though it's surprising how many repetitions you can get from a motivated dog who understands the task.

Variable Interval

With a variable interval, the reward comes at *different times* after the behavior has been correctly performed; these times vary, being random.[18] So, the dog may be asked to bark once. He barks once, but is not given the reward until five seconds have passed. We repeat the exercise, and this time he is given the reward after two seconds; we go again and he gets the reward ten seconds after he barks. The dog needs to fully understand the exercise and what the correct response is. A dog who barks once, is waiting, waiting, waiting for the reward and barks again has "got it wrong" and so will not get any reward.

With variable interval reinforcement schedules, it is not a case of the dog giving the correct response, the trainer immediately clicking/marking and then fumbling about in the treat bag and the dog having to wait and getting the reward fifteen seconds later. Rather there is no clicker or marker word, or if there is, it is only used after the time delay, which is random. This method may be appropriate when teaching a behavior such as a stay, where the behavior in and of itself has a timed aspect which you want to gradually extend, yet you want the dog focused on you while he is waiting, since he may be rewarded after ten seconds or thirty.

Fixed Interval

I don't like this kind of schedule in relation to dog training, as it means the reward only comes at a certain fixed time interval after the desired behavior.[19] This makes more sense in a laboratory experiment, not so much if we are training for a behavior. For example, if the behavior we want in the laboratory is a bark, with a fixed interval reinforcement schedule the dog barks and is rewarded after, say, ten seconds. If he barks again during the ten-second delay, he gets nothing. The dog learns that he has to *wait* until the ten seconds are up in order to be rewarded, and only then can he offer up another bark and thus set the ten-second reward timer ticking once more.

When training a dog, we are generally *asking* for a behavior: we can't ask again before the ten seconds are up and then deny the reward, as that's not very fair. Also, if we are using this method to teach a dog to stay, say, and we linger too long on the time interval, the dog will start to anticipate that ten-second mark. I would rather extremely gently correct a dog for

Chapter Two. An Introduction to the Science of Dog Training 43

anticipating than try to get him to work out that unasked-for barks during the interval will result in his waiting longer, which seems to be the point of the laboratory experiments.

So those are the four types of partial reinforcement schedules. Please bear in mind, there is a massive difference between teaching behaviors in a training room or for a competition of some sort, and living with your dog in real life. When training for competitions, we tend to be more methodical and carefully plan what type of reward schedule we want to use during a specific training session. Living with your dog is a very different matter.

In real life, I am not going to reward my dog for every little thing he does for me when asked. Some good behaviors are taught and then simply expected. I may reward my dog verbally or, very occasionally, with a treat, but on the whole when we are around the house I do not reward basic behaviors, which are merely good manners. These could be as simple as his sitting or standing still to have a collar put on, or going into his crate when asked at bedtime.

Many force-free trainers say *every* behavior should be rewarded on a continuous schedule to ensure the dog always does as he is asked, but for me this is just not realistic. A verbal "good boy" is fair enough, and I do talk to my dogs a lot of the time at home. It's a bit like being polite and saying "thank you," so in many ways this is the background chatter of daily life rather than a genuine reward.

When I give verbal praise *meant* as a reward, it tends to be very enthusiastic, except when a dog has been disobedient and then decided he had better comply. In such a case, I may say a terse "good boy" to let him know that yes, I am pleased he obeyed, but since he was disobedient to begin with, he's not going to get a gushing verbal reward from me, just an acknowledgment that he did finally do as he was asked.

Another example: I am not going to reward my dog for loose lead walking when going to the park, given that it's such a simple request he has known for years, plus I cannot reward him every few steps when it's a ten-minute walk. Yet some force-free trainers say you should do this! Reward the dog every few steps, every single day, for the rest of his life. How much food do these trainers go through? If they are using no overt corrections, just ramming treats into the dog, this is the only way they will be able to get to the park without the dog yanking them about. I go to the park two to three times a day, with two large dogs, and I am not carrying a rucksack of food with me. So, no treats for basic walking, but on the other hand, during a focused heelwork training session, there will *always* be lots of high-value rewards given, since this is physically hard for the dog and requires a great deal of concentration from him, so he needs frequent and lavish rewards.

Jack-potting[20] is another technique that is very useful in dog training, and it is simply, every now and again, giving the dog a *massive reward*, sort of like winning the lottery. It gives the dog a lot of incentive, as once he has won big the first time, he hopes it will happen again. This big win, and the subsequent hope that it will happen again, releases a lot of dopamine and makes for a very happy, motivated dog who enjoys his training sessions immensely.

Usually we give a jackpot for a behavior we rarely see but want to encourage, or for a breakthrough in training. Say a dog has been struggling to learn a command such as "down." The dog is a Dachshund, and with his short legs it's not that easy or necessarily comfortable to achieve an obedient down position. The owner has tried several things, but nothing has worked. In such circumstances, I may offer a food reward in my hand, luring the dog from underneath a low coffee table, say, so that in order to get to my hand and the food, he has to lie down. When he does this successfully for the first time, he does not get a piece of kibble, he gets a handful of cooked chicken. I may stop the training there, with the dog very eager to be asked to lie "down" again. He will remember the jackpot of the cooked chicken fed piece by piece (not in a lump) and be keen to get busy in his next training session.

We are having it shoved down our throats that force-free training produces the most happy, contented, ethically trained dogs. That we should always be rewarding everything the dog does, feeding him every few seconds and never saying "no" or denying him a reward. This is not how learning optimally happens, or what makes a dog the happiest and creates the most hope in life. Isn't that what you live for as a human, hope? Dogs do too.

I see many adult dogs trained by fanatics who are having food given to them to do something as simple as to sit when asked. That's all. To sit, while paying attention to the handler and looking about them only occasionally, as the handler is scared that if the dog looks elsewhere he will see something more interesting and break his sit. This does not happen just in the real world; I've also observed it in the training room, with older dogs who have been in training for months, if not years, and for whom sitting when asked is not a new skill.

This is not a complex behavior that is being asked for. What do I see in the dog constantly lured with food in this way during his training? At very best, a dog mildly interested in the training session. At worst, a dog deliberately ignoring the trainer, looking for amusement elsewhere and yanking the trainer about at the end of the lead. But usually I see an obese dog with his ears and tail down in a state of **active submission**, as he's bored, reluctantly coerced into obeying for hours on end while taking low-value pieces of kibble as a reward.

Chapter Two. An Introduction to the Science of Dog Training   45

A dog with this posture of active submission is not a dog having a great deal of fun, nor learning particularly quickly. He is not necessarily unhappy, but neither is he very engaged or interested, and hence he is not producing much dopamine. Now, the point of this training session may be to teach the dog to be quiet and calm. A **service dog** for a disabled person, for example, is a dog we want to be extremely quiet. For me, though, during training and learning I *do* expect some raising and wagging of the tail, for the dog to be producing dopamine, and hence the dog enjoying working with his handler.

Always, always bear in mind that outside a laboratory setting, we have the distractions of the real world, and consequently we have emotions at play ... both of the dog and the trainer. When a trainer is scared, a dog can smell this and will react to it. This is how many force-free trainers get in over their head and increase bad behaviors in dogs that are too much for them and that they refuse to correct.

As you can see, it can be hard to decide what is actually happening when discussing operant conditioning. Really, I could write a book about it, and indeed many people have, if you want to do further study on the matter; some of their books are listed in the bibliography. But it's now time to journey to simpler times, as far back as the 1890s, to Russia and the laboratory of Ivan Pavlov, the king of classical conditioning.[21]

Pavlov's most famous experiment involved bells, bowls and salivation.[22] When food came in for his study dogs to be fed (for a different experiment entirely), Pavlov saw that as the dogs anticipated eating, they salivated. He called the food an unconditioned stimulus, bringing about the salivation, which he called an unconditioned response—something that the dogs were not in control of and that was hardwired into them.

Pavlov realized that after a time, the dogs started to salivate at the appearance of his laboratory assistant, not just as the food was put in front of them. This was because they had learned that the laboratory assistant was the one who fed them, and they linked him with food. This sounds pretty basic, but Pavlov's subsequent experiment was groundbreaking at the time. One day when Pavlov was feeling crazy, he decided to introduce a bell and ring it just when the dogs were about to be fed. The bell rang and, seeing their dinner appear, the dogs salivated in anticipation of eating. Pavlov did this for a while, and then one day, even when there was no food, Pavlov rang the bell to see what would happen. The dogs still salivated on hearing the bell.

The bell was originally something the dogs were not interested in (a neutral stimulus). However, once it was paired with the food, the dogs learned over time (i.e., they were conditioned) that the bell meant they were going to be fed, and they started to salivate when it rang. Eventually they salivated even if no food was present. The bell was able to elicit a conditioned response, salivation. Once conditioning had taken place, the bell, at first a neutral stimulus, was now a conditioned stimulus.

What lesson can we learn here? The principles of classical conditioning are important, as, where we can, we use them a lot in dog training. Through repetition we teach behaviors (condition our dog) so that the dog no longer needs to *think* about what he will do, his response being one which *just happens*. This can be for good or for bad. When performing focused heel-work, my dogs know that when I come to a halt, they immediately sit beside me, maintaining eye contact with me. We have practiced this so often that I do not need to give the command to "sit," I just need to come to a stop. The sit is a conditioned response to my halting and standing beside the dog.

However, if I have a young puppy and I'm scared of other dogs, if I start jerking on the lead and making him yelp on seeing another dog, then I could create problems. My puppy, who has never had any bad encounter with another dog and never previously feared them, may end up with a conditioned response, yelping and being scared whenever he sees another dog, even if I have not yet seen the other dog myself and did not (yet) jerk on the lead.

It's very easy to inadvertently train our dogs in bad behaviors, as anytime we are with our dogs, they are learning. It also must be remembered that *dogs do not generalize well*, and what we train in one environment may not carry into another one. A dog that understands "go to your bed" in your living room would not understand the same command if you put her bed in a training room. The more the stimulus has become a truly conditioned response, the less a dog's inability to generalize will be an issue.

We've just been talking about generalization and conditioned responses (i.e., training/learning), but a big part of Pavlov's work was on unconditioned stimuli and unconditioned responses, such as salivation on seeing food: responses that are hardwired into dogs. This is important when training dogs, as they have many responses to certain stimuli which we as humans do not experience and so cannot understand.

Although dogs learn in the same general way, leading many force-free trainers to claim their methods will work on all dogs, this is not the complete truth. Some breeds are wired very differently than others, and hence a dog needs to be trained in a way that respects the drives and innate responses of that individual dog and its breed, in order to be fair to the dog and for him to get the most enjoyment and fun, plus clarity and ease of understanding, out of training.

Many dogs have a great deal of prey drive, and the best tug toy or largest handful of high-value food alone cannot and never will compete with that innate drive kicking in when they spot a squirrel (for example), no

Chapter Two. An Introduction to the Science of Dog Training   47

matter the quality and quantity of training you have put in. So what to do if, as a force-free trainer, you encounter such a dog and can get nowhere with his training, as this is a large dog who is terrorizing his owner, not a terrier that can be picked up? Do you start to petition to get rid of these breeds, as you have done with pinch collars and e-collars, getting them banned? Do you insist that breeders dumb these breeds down, so they no longer have so much drive and you can finally handle them? It seems many countries in Europe are going down these routes, and dogs and their owners are paying the price.

Or, do we agree we all have different skill sets and train each and every dog as an individual, using the tools and techniques which suit that particular dog, which may mean making a referral to another trainer? With a large, high-drive dog, the force-free trainer who refuses to set boundaries would be better off referring the client to a trainer who takes a balanced approach. Or, when the owner selects a trainer who turns out to be a big fellow in person, whether he is a balanced or reward-based, it can be too much for some dogs, who may have issues around large men. This trainer should also refer the dog, this time to a reward-based female trainer who specializes in nervous, sensitive dogs. It works both ways.

Chapter Three

Myth Busting

There are many myths surrounding the training of dogs, some old, some new. What they have in common is the way in which they have been commandeered and used by the force-free mafia in order to promote their extremist agenda, claiming their way is the only way, sounding a little like the bad guys in a dystopian sci-fi novel. A small proportion of these myths are harmful, but the majority are little more than old wives' tales. Some are funny; others are irritating and initiate an automatic eye roll, the like of which leaves even your average teenager behind.

Logically and practically, I will explain why these myths are incorrect or not, as the case may be, so you can amaze and amuse your crush with these factoids at the dog park. I'm going to start by debunking a myth that will be pretty cherished by a small number of readers, and not by the majority. Those of you who own a Border Collie can skip to Myth Two; everyone else can put the champagne on ice. It should be just ready to enjoy by the end of this chapter.

Myth One: Border Collies are the most intelligent breed of dog.

If you actually own a Border Collie, whenever this myth is mentioned, your feet will start to twitch uncontrollably, and in a heartbeat you'll be dancing around the room, punching the air and clicking your heels together in glee. For everyone else, this myth will make your teeth itch. I *know* Border Collies are *not* the most intelligent breed: believe me when I tell you that the best, most intelligent, most easily trainable, most affectionate, most loyal and loving breed in all of creation is in fact the Rottweiler.

There is an old saying in the dog showing world, which is "every person takes the best dog home," and this is the truth. We *all* own the best dog in the world, no matter if it's a pedigree or a mixed breed, expensive or cheap, from a world-class breeder or from death row at the local shelter, a working dog which saves lives day in, day out or a pet that simply saves yours by his presence.

There are many dog trainers who compete in various dog sports at an extremely high level. Examples of these sports typically include obedience, doggy dancing, trick training, flyball, dock diving, and agility competitions, where force-free and balanced trainers alike enjoy massive success, primarily with one breed in particular: the Border Collie. This is no accident. Border Collies excel in these activities, in part due to their athleticism and in part due to their intelligent, biddable, trainable temperament. They are undoubtedly the "go-to" breed for serious competitors in any of these areas of dog sport.

On the other hand, we rarely (read "never") see Border Collies successfully compete in sports such as IGP (Internationale Gebrauchshund Pruefung, or International Working/Practical Dog Test), where there is a component of bitework, and plenty of it. These sorts of activities generally require a dog with the right genetics. While any dog can be taught to take an item and hold it in his mouth, true bitework involves confronting and tackling big blokes and is another thing entirely. A dog either has the courage, nerve and passion to bite and "take on" a human aggressor with enjoyment and gusto, or he does not.

Many of you may have watched *America's Top Dog*,[1] where Border Collies can be seen performing very basic bitework, generally biting and holding a trainer in a bite suit for a few seconds. However, the dog in each case is hesitant and clearly not terribly willing to take the bite, grabbing hold of the bite suit with reluctance. If that guy wearing the bite suit were to put any pressure on the dog, even as mild as hard, sustained eye contact, the Border Collie would tuck his tail between his legs and run faster than Scooby-Doo and Shaggy from the big, bad villain dressed in a ghost costume.

This lack of courage and the willingness to bite a human with a sustained grip, instead of just rapidly darting in and out to give a nip, is why you will never see a Border Collie as a general purpose police dog. Never, not even for simply tracking criminals. There may exist a tiny minority that perform specialized explosives or drug detection, though Spaniels, Labradors and other breeds with less nervousness tend to be recruited into these police roles. You *will* see Border Collies excel in locating people who are lost or injured, mainly in rural environments, as part of a search-and-rescue team, though they are not the preferred choice for urban searches. Occasionally you may see a Border Collie as a service dog, but this is exceedingly rare, once more due to the breed's innate fearfulness and basic lack of nerve in busy places with a lot of noise.

I must emphasize, my noting the fearfulness and noise reactivity of Border Collies is *not* meant as a criticism of the breed, but if we are evaluating intelligence, then we have to take account of how a breed is used, and what the attributes and limitations of that breed are. Border Collies are truly remarkable dogs, and retain many of the characteristics which have made them outstanding sheepdogs and which now stand them in such good stead for rural search and rescue, as sports dogs, as pets, and for trick training. Sensitivity often goes hand in hand with nervousness, and when put to work in the right way, the flightiness of the Border Collie is not a big issue.

The majority of pet dogs do not have and *do not need* the courage and guts to bite people with a full-mouth grip and hang on under pressure, or to attack on command, as a police dog, personal protection dog, or IGP sports dog is taught to do. This type of work is extremely skilled, nuanced and specialized, and should be left to experts in this field. It's highly inadvisable to buy a bite sleeve from the internet and then try to go all John Wick with your pet dog. Can you imagine the awkwardness if you met someone with a broken arm and a plaster cast on it in the park? Training bitework without expert supervision and training generally ends in tears. Don't do it.

Due to the Border Collie's dominance in certain sports, an urban myth continues to state that it is the most intelligent dog breed on the planet, just as a similar urban myth used to state that IQ tests determine who are the most intelligent humans. In the past this latter myth was widely accepted, though these days we acknowledge that there are many different types of human intelligence, and that there may be better indicators of happiness and success than a standard IQ test, which concentrates on just one aspect of intelligence. Indeed, it is now thought there are between eight[2] and twelve[3] types of human intelligence, including visual-spatial, naturalistic, logical-mathematical, extra and interpersonal.

The same can be said for dogs. There are certainly many different types of intelligence in dogs, and intelligence does not necessarily equal easy to train. In fact, some of the most intelligent dogs I have trained have been the most challenging, and the, ahem, stupidest dogs the easiest. Although smart dogs cotton on quickly to what is being asked of them, they often are constantly anticipating what you might ask of them next, leading them to make mistakes. Other dogs are thinkers. They may take longer to understand what they are being taught, but once they do understand, they never forget. It all equals out in the end.

There is no doubt that Border Collies are highly intelligent, trainable dogs, and this is one reason they dominate certain dog sports but not others. As I have explained, they only excel in specific areas. However, do a

Chapter Three. Myth Busting

Google search and the Border Collie will rank as the most intelligent dog in pretty much every online article you find, as if they excel in everything. But do the same search on PubMed (a database of research literature in the field of life sciences), and Border Collies fall way down in the rankings of dog intelligence in the vast majority of research papers. How so? Why the discrepancy?

There has not really been that much scientific research into dog intelligence. Not as much as you might suspect, at any rate, probably because it's highly subjective, each of us believing our own pet's breed to be the most intelligent. And indeed our own pet's breed will tend to show the greatest intelligence in areas specific to the purpose they were originally bred for. A dog such as a Caucasian Shepherd Dog,[4] like the Border Collie,[5] works with livestock. However, the Caucasian Shepherd Dog is a guardian breed, extremely brave and bold and working independently from man on their own initiative, quite the opposite to the Border Collie in personality. Both breeds herd and work with sheep, and both are intelligent, but this intelligence is manifested in very different ways, and one breed could not do the job of the other.

Some of the scientific studies which have been done on dog intelligence correlate body weight, height and craniometry, as has also been done in humans. However, different researchers have come up with different conclusions when this methodology is applied to dogs. In a 2021 research paper using this method, the number one rank for intelligence goes to the Doberman Pinscher, followed by the German Shepherd Dog, Labrador Retriever and Golden Retriever.[6] The latter three breeds are extensively used as working dogs by the police and military and as service dogs for the disabled; the Doberman Pinscher unfortunately suffers these days from a lot of health issues and thus its popularity as a working dog has significantly declined. In this list, the Border Collie ranks below the Rottweiler at numbers seven and six, respectively. Obviously, the Rottweiler declined to excel and take the number one spot in this study in order to give other dog breeds a chance.

In terms of internal cranial capacity, the Rottweiler actually *is* ranked as the most intelligent dog breed[7] (told you so), along with the German Shepherd Dog. And if we look at the encephalization quotient—a numerical comparison of brain mass to body size using the von Bronin formula—the Rottweiler ranks as top dog in terms of intelligence (yes, the Rottweiler again). It is only when we use the Saganuwan formula that the Border Collie gets any sort of boost. However, even though the Saganuwan formula was used in this particular research paper, when other relevant parameters were added the Border Collie dropped down the rankings to number seven, behind the Rottweiler, who would probably have ranked first overall if the von Bronin formula had been used to determine each breed's encephalization quotient.

Measuring the physical characteristics of body and brain is just one method of determining intelligence, but it's interesting that the breeds which most commonly go out and do a decent day's work fared best in this particular study.[8] Of course, the use of certain breeds of dog in real-life working scenarios is not necessarily the be-all and end-all, since for some breeds the purpose they were designed for has all but dried up, or there may be other external factors that render a breed unsuitable for work in certain public-facing jobs in today's fast-moving, noisy world, a category which would include the Border Collie.

What does all of this tell us? Well, mainly that scientists don't all agree, and that slight differences in scientific formulas can make for vastly different results. What we can say is that certain breeds, namely the Border Collie, the Rottweiler and the German Shepherd Dog, repeatedly seem to rank in the top ten of most intelligent dog breeds, both across scientific research and also in articles based on common knowledge and the practical experience of dog trainers and dog owners.

Sometimes we will see Labrador Retrievers and Golden Retrievers listed in online surveys as intelligent dogs, and sometimes not. A breed that rarely seems to feature, which I consider a gross oversight, is the Belgian Malinois, perhaps because they are "too much dog" for the average pet owner and thus are mainly still used as true working dogs. They were not part of the test group in any of the dog intelligence studies I read, though they have been included in other studies on dog training and behavior, particularly where police and military dogs have been selected to take part in the trials.

Personally, I *would* rank the Border Collie, along with the Rottweiler and German Shepherd Dog, as being three of the most intelligent dog breeds, but the exclusion of the Belgian Malinois and many of the Spaniel breeds renders the typical online dog intelligence list more of a popularity contest than anything else. Labrador Retrievers and Golden Retrievers, I find, are not necessarily striking in terms of absolute intelligence. I never go "wow!" when I train one, as they can be a little slow on the uptake, but they do make up for this by virtue of their exceptionally high trainability, and also their reliability and kind, sweet, unflappable natures, making them, overall, fantastic dogs as pets and for certain types of work, particularly as service dogs and for many scent-work tasks.

I think, then, we have established that Border Collies, if not necessarily number one in intelligence, are certainly deserving of being repeatedly ranked in the top ten, both scientifically and in more subjective online articles. What about trainability, though? For an experienced trainer in

Chapter Three. Myth Busting

the right environment, Border Collies are extremely trainable, but take them out of that quiet, peaceful training room and into a world of noise and distractions, and the Border Collie starts to crumble. This leads neatly into the question of why Border Collies are the dog of choice for force-free dog trainers. It is not by accident.

We really can't get away from it, can we? Border Collies are *the* preferred choice for force-free dog trainers worldwide, with photos of the breed festooned all across their videos and social media. They are widely used as demo dogs for training tricks, as well as for competitive obedience, agility and flyball. It's hard not to be impressed. *I* certainly am! However, there are other highly intelligent breeds that do not get the same attention from force-free dog trainers, even though their intelligence and athleticism are on a par with that of Border Collies. What about the Belgian Malinois? Why are *they* not dominating the agility, trick and obedience rings with force-free trainers? Why not, indeed?

Leaving the Malinois aside for a moment, there is a case to be made for preferring Border Collies in certain dog sports such as agility and flyball, where heavier but equally intelligent dog breeds, including German Shepherds and Rottweilers, would not excel to such a great extent, lacking nimbleness. However, there are other sports, such as obedience, where frame, athleticism and weight have little bearing. So where are the breeds that in reality are as intelligent as Border Collies and that were actually the more traditional choices for obedience many moons ago, before the force-free revolution? These breeds include both the German Shepherd Dog and the Rottweiler. Now, despite the evidence I have presented, you may be thinking, "You mean the stumblebum and the dunderhead?" Careful! I may be just words on a page, but I can haunt you when I die. Don't think I do not have an ample amount of spite lodged in my black little heart for people who dislike Rottweilers and German Shepherds.

German Shepherds and Rottweilers are highly intelligent dogs, no less intelligent than the Border Collie and more so if you believe the studies I outlined above. This is particularly true of the working lines of these breeds, so let's put the show lines aside for a moment. Along with the equally brilliant Belgian Malinois, German Shepherds and Rottweilers are just as able as the Border Collie to excel in the obedience ring and in trick training. After all, we see their brilliance in obedience when watching the sport of IGP, whose obedience phase I would say is actually harder than the highest level of traditional obedience tests. Why, then, are these breeds not wildly popular with force-free trainers?

All of these breeds are highly intelligent, extremely energetic, sensitive and eager to please their trainers, and all were originally bred as herding dogs. They are all high-drive dogs that require a lot of exercise and mental stimulation to be happy, albeit they do display slightly different types of drive these days, the German Shepherd, Belgian Malinois and Rottweiler all possessing significant quantities of boldness, toughness, high defensive drive and guarding ability. For me, the most important distinctions between the Border Collie and these three other breeds are that the Border Collie lacks courage, has weak nerves, has high noise reactivity, and is very easily intimidated by his handler.

The main reason Border Collies are used so much for trick training and demo training in a controlled environment is that they are easily intimidated, and hence they are easy to tell what to do, using seemingly invisible commands. This plays right into the force-free trainers' hands, and is for them a distinct advantage. It is this factor more than any other which makes Border Collies so popular with purely positive activists and why Rottweilers, German Shepherd Dogs and Belgian Malinois are not.

Force-free trainers will wax lyrical about how they do not use force. They do—we know that. However, the force they use, their "go-to" corrections, if they are smart, are very subtle and almost undetectable unless you know what to look for. Such corrections are well suited for, and extremely effective with, the easily intimidated Border Collie. Balanced trainers use the self-same tools and techniques on their dogs, but primarily as mild corrections, employing somewhat stronger corrections to control their dogs when they are in high drive and extremely aroused.

I'm sure you're wondering exactly what I mean. Wonder no more. Let's directly compare the Border Collie with the Belgian Malinois and see why one breed is the force-free trainer's dog of choice and the other is avoided like a dodgy chicken curry. I have selected the Belgian Malinois[9] primarily because the breed has similar athleticism to the Border Collie,[10] more so than the heavier German Shepherd Dog[11] and Rottweiler.[12] Given this, in addition to obedience, which all four breeds excel in, why is the Belgian Malinois not the dog that force-free trainers flock to buy, since they are physically just as capable at obedience, flyball, doggy dancing, and agility as Border Collies, and have stronger nerves and more confidence? Would that not make them the better option? Yes, it does if you're a balanced trainer; no, it doesn't if you're a force-free trainer with an agenda to protect and defend.

The Border Collie was historically a sheepdog,[13] and not much has changed about the drive, intelligence and sensitivity of these amazing dogs. Border Collies originated in my home country of Scotland, along the border with England, hence the name. This is hill country and the dogs were worked far away from their handlers, so they needed to be quick and responsive to their handler's voice commands or whistle over very long distances. Border Collies are *extremely* reactive to sound, and therefore

Chapter Three. Myth Busting

super-responsive to even the softest of verbal commands. They have been bred to be this way for more than a hundred years. It is in their genes.

How easy it is, then, for a force-free trainer to influence a Border Collie via her voice, using it as a reward but also as a remarkably effective punishment. In order to successfully influence a Border Collie, there is pretty much no need for anything but the voice, plus some hard eye contact and/or body language if required as a backup. In order to correct the dog, the trainer can simply use a quiet but harsh tone. So sensitive are they to noise that a low murmur which observers will not even hear can act as a strong aversive to a Border Collie and quickly get him in line and acting obediently. An equally sensitive and intelligent breed such as a Belgian Malinois would barely register that anything had been said to them if the trainer's voice was used in a similar way, never mind seeing it as a punishment.

In addition to their noise sensitivity, Border Collies lack any real nerve or courage, being fearful dogs. They rely on their handlers to keep them safe and feeling secure, and therefore they are very reluctant to challenge their handler's authority or try to impose their own will. Well, unless you are a sheep. When a Border Collie would rather do something other than what you want him to, such as stop to sniff an interesting scent, a mild verbal reprimand is sufficient to bring him to heel and comply with his trainer's wishes, giving the impression the dog is super-obedient as opposed to super-anxious.

No wonder force-free agility competitors, trick trainers, and obedience competitors prefer the Border Collie to the equally intelligent and athletic Belgian Malinois, a breed that also has a herding background but does not have so much voice reactivity, coming as it does from the relatively flat Malines region of Belgium,[14] where the shepherd's voice does not need to carry over hill and dale. This breed now excels in the police and military and is exceptionally courageous, making it a very different dog from the Border Collie and thus a dog that requires different corrections in order to influence it to the same degree that a voice command and hard eye contact would for a Border Collie.

Now, of course there are force-free trainers who very successfully work breeds such as the Belgian Malinois in dog sports, including in IGP—a sport that comprises tracking, obedience and protection. Admittedly, they are far better trainers than I ever will be. I do not dispute that, though I have yet to see a force-free trainer win a title at the world championship level in IGP *at all*, never mind repeatedly. They also use corrections and, just as with everything else, the corrections they use are suited to how much force they believe is acceptable. It is not that they use no force at all—nowhere near.

Some "force-free" trainers competing in IGP use slip leads in the protection phase, as it conveys more clarity to the dog, keeping him under control and making the training easier for the dog to understand, though the trainers are loath to admit this. There's nothing wrong with using a slip lead; it is hardly a harsh tool if used correctly. But it's not considered a "positive" tool, and if word got out, such force-free trainers would be stripped of their halos and subjected to public stoning by their cohorts.

Will minimal corrections enable force-free trainers to win on the world stage year after year in IGP? I do not think so. IGP is a dog sport where, unlike competition obedience—another sport which has a subjective element and judges who give scores—dogs are heavily marked down for looking stressed, worried or anxious. When a dog shows a lot of stress-related behaviors, he can be eliminated. In regard to many animal sports, I would say that trainers will do what they have to do in order to win, regardless of animal welfare, but where winning and losing can come down to which dog looks happiest, well, the dogs have to be enjoying their work.

IGP therefore provides us with a proving ground where training techniques are always evolving and where competitors prefer to and indeed *must* use the minimal amount of corrections to enforce obedience. The dog has to be genuinely happy and having fun—all while maintaining an exceptionally high level of control in three different spheres, often when it is extremely aroused, such as in the protection phase. Something as simple as flat, pinned ears and a tucked tail can lose a world championship trophy, so you can bet the handlers will use the most effective, kind techniques available for training their dogs to keep them happy and enjoying the work. If typical force-free training techniques were the best way to get a happy, super-obedient dog that wins world championships, the top IGP competitors would be doing it. With Border Collies. They are not.

This is not to say you cannot keep control by using a flat collar or harness on a breed such as a Belgian Malinois, even when working these dogs in a high state of arousal, as the handlers of operational police dogs do. This is the case in countries where commonly used tools such as martingales and pinch collars have been banned. As always, it depends on the dog, its amount of drive, its training and aptitude, and also what the trainer herself can cope with. However, if training a high-drive, courageous, determined dog in a flat collar is so quick and easy, why did the Berlin police force ask for an exemption to the 2022 law which banned "pulling collars"? To prevent 49 out of 130 dogs being taken off active duty, that's why.[15]

In my view police dogs in countries where pinch collars and other tools the force-free brigade dislike and are consequently now banned are "dumbed down" versions of the breed, nowhere near as "hard" as the dogs in the police forces of old. It cannot be denied that for some dogs, in general nervous, sensitive dogs training with only a flat collar or harness is effective. But where it is *not* effective, it can produce a dog that is not safe in operational work, no matter the extra time taken to provide a better foundation of training. The dog simply may not have the level of respect he should for his handler, and a massive amount of brute force may be needed to drag him about. Where the dog will not "out" he will almost always tear the flesh of the criminal he is biting, so it is hardly safe or effective for anyone concerned.

Not every police dog handler is built like Arnold Schwarzenegger in his prime, and I would argue that it's more abusive to lift a dog up and hang him by his neck in his flat collar, legs dangling in the air, than to use a pinch collar judiciously, with a small degree of pressure. Or we can just get rid of police dogs altogether, which some campaigners are advocating for, both on welfare grounds and because many dogs are inadequately trained and loath to release their grip on a suspect.[16] If police forces are being bullied into using ineffective training techniques and equipment by the force-free mafia, who have never themselves trained a protection dog nor worked as a police officer, then what we can expect?

Is this what we want? No police dogs, no female handlers, or shall we only have "soft" dogs without the mental hardness to do the job and confront a violent criminal? Dogs that are lower in courage and determination, and have never received any sort of strike or pressure during training but are then supposed to stand up to criminals who will punch and kick them. In such a situation the dog may quite rightly be shocked and back off. Is this fair on the dog? On the handler? The "sovereign citizen" movement, among others, I am sure will approve.

It's not just police dogs, other working dogs are also under threat, including service dogs for disabled people. Some service dog organizations are insisting that dogs be trained only in a force-free manner. For owners to have control and enforce loose lead walking while around distractions, head collars are being recommended or even mandated for larger, higher-drive dogs, with no care for the fact that many dogs find them extremely aversive. So long as the PR machine whirs and the dollars and cents donated by the general public keep flooding in for "dogs trained with only positive methods," dog welfare be damned.

No person should be demonized for being disabled. Why should an individual with arthritic hands, who uses a loose martingale because her dog can slip it over his own head from a hook on the wall, be told she's evil and a dog abuser? She is told that if she wants to stay in her service dog organization, she must now use a head collar on her dog as a safety measure, regardless of the fact that such a potentially aversive tool is not required since her dog does not pull, and which she does not have the dexterity in her fingers to put on her dog, who hates the thing.

In conclusion, the real reason Border Collies are so popular with force-free trainers is the trainers' ability to correct their dogs using only their voice, some eye contact and body language, corrections that are often too subtle for anyone watching to pick up on. They hold these dogs up as shining examples of their training methodology, claiming that since they can train their oh-so-high-drive, energetic Border Collies in a flat collar using only treats and their soft, loving voice (plus a hard lead pop when no-one's looking), then everyone should be able to do the same with their own dog, of whatever breed, if only they followed their good force-free advice.

These trainers do not acknowledge that they cannot take their Border Collie into the park around other dogs, bikes, and screaming toddlers, at least not without reactivity issues. Nor could they work their dog in Walmart on Christmas Eve, amid grabbing hands all intent on nabbing the last viral video game. Their "obedient" Border Collie would have a complete mental breakdown. Which may be fair enough. I have run the gauntlet of Christmas Eve gift shopping and suspect I have been traumatized for life, my Rottweiler service dog not so much, since she thrives on attention.

Many balanced trainers have challenged force-free trainers to compete with them, to take their Border Collie out of the training room and into the real world, and they do the same with their Belgian Malinois, German Shepherd Dogs and Rottweilers, with a cash prize to go to the dog which performs the best. In one such challenge, UK dog trainer Jamie Penrith, backed by many U.S. trainers such as Larry Kohn, offered $55,000 to any force-free trainer who could cure a dog that was reactive to livestock using no corrections, only rewards.[17] None of these challenges were ever taken up by the force-free mafia, never mind publicly tried and then failed, which I think says it all regarding their confidence in their own training techniques. This is where I will finish, having discussed everything from beautiful Border Collies to hard-working police dogs.

Myth Two: Ignore all bad behavior and never correct a dog.

In general, I do not ignore bad behavior (being that which I do not like) on the part of an adult dog, or even a puppy. Many behaviors that we as humans categorize as "bad" occur because they are natural behaviors for the dog, in addition to which the dog does not know any different. For example, digging up your prized geraniums and burying a bone among

Chapter Three. Myth Busting

the scattered petals and torn roots is a fun activity for a great many dogs, since burying food to be enjoyed later is a natural behavior and one which is rewarding to the enthusiastic amateur gardener that your dog may be.

No matter how smart your dog is, he does not have a crystal ball lodged firmly inside his skull cavity. If he did, I would have requested the winning lotto numbers long ago and would currently be sunning myself on my very own private tropical island. Alas, I am in cold, bleak England, and the only way your dog is going to learn whether a behavior is "bad" or "good" is if we tell him which is which. We can do this by means of a redirection, usually followed by offering an alternative behavior, or we can do it with a correction, which may also be followed by offering an alternative behavior and/or rewarding the dog for obeying a simple command.

Ignoring bad behavior in a dog is a gamble which very rarely pays off, unless the behavior in question was not *that* rewarding to the dog to start with and so he may just pick up a better behavior by chance. Some dogs will deliberately perform a behavior they know displeases you simply to get attention, any attention, since they are so bored. Once the dog is given adequate exercise, enrichment activities, training, and mental stimulation, such behaviors often cease.

Sometimes ignoring bad behavior in a dog, although touted as force-free, is a correction in and of itself and can be an extremely harsh method of training. One example is letting a puppy "cry it out" alone in his crate. The puppy is ignored when he whimpers and whines and, it is true, eventually he will stop, but only when he is exhausted. Gradually the barking and whining get less and less, but he is not learning resilience; rather he is developing an ever-increasing separation anxiety coupled with **learned helplessness**. Not a good combination.

The vast majority of force-free trainers will accept that when ignoring a dog does not work, a redirection followed by offering an alternative behavior is an acceptable way to teach the dog that a certain behavior is wrong. The hope is that, if this approach is repeated often enough, the bad behavior will stop, the dog instead choosing to engage in the good behavior which you offered to him as an alternative and which he finds more rewarding, this last part being the clincher. He must find what you offer as an alternative to be better than what he has been doing.

For example, say your puppy is chewing on the table leg. You might give a sharp "ah ah" to get his attention and then, as he looks around in surprise, offer him a chew toy to play with instead. Provided the chew toy is more fun than the table leg, after a few repetitions the puppy should look for his chew toy when he has the urge to gnaw on something, rather than molesting the table. However, if he does not perceive the chew toy to be a better option, he will ignore it and do what gives him the most satisfaction, i.e., practicing his woodwork skills with his sharp puppy teeth. The efficacy of a redirection/offered alternative depends on being able to provide your dog with a better deal. Sometimes this is possible, but sometimes it is not.

Redirection/offered alternative is a relatively benign training method and is almost always a positive experience for the dog, and hence it is widely used by both balanced and force-free trainers alike. However, the more extreme force-free trainers will not even permit this, as the redirection in itself can cause discomfort and/or alarm, particularly if a dog is extremely engaged and intent on a certain behavior and it's hard for the trainer to get his attention via a redirection.

Say your new puppy is chasing your cat. No matter how much you call with a sweet, encouraging voice, he is lost in the moment, and unless you have him on a house line (not recommended for very young puppies), or grab and remove him, or use a redirection harsh enough to startle him and break his focus, he is not going to take his attention away from Mr. Fluffykins' tail to look at the pathetic pieces of kibble you have on offer.

Unfortunately many force-free trainers will leave a puppy to do his own thing if he will not respond to a kind, encouraging voice, believing it is for the puppy to decide when to stop a behavior and return his attention to his owner. They also have the notion that animals in a household will sort things out for themselves without human guidance. In the cat example, it would be deeply unfair to allow Mr. Fluffykins to be terrorized, and may not end well for the puppy either, one of the top causes of eye injuries in puppies under six months of age being cat scratches.[18] Even with more harmless activities such as chewing the table leg, it is not good to let the puppy decide. Puppies should not learn that it's acceptable to ignore their owner whenever she calls to him. This is setting him up for failure and a lifetime of being "managed" in the future, when as a grown dog he does whatever he likes unless his movements and environment are severely restricted.

In some circumstances we can relatively easily redirect a dog away from an unwanted or bad behavior, giving him a better alternative, and all is well with the world. This is my preferred method whenever possible, particularly with young puppies, where I always want to be Mr. Nice Guy and set them up for success. But what if we cannot do this? Life is neither fair nor kind, and there will be times when we cannot get an adult dog's attention or, even if we succeed momentarily, there is nothing we have to offer which can compete with the bad behavior he is engaged in, such as pouncing on and nipping Mr. Fluffykins' tail.

In such a scenario, a balanced trainer will use a correction to teach the dog that what he is doing is unacceptable, stopping him from deciding to engage in that behavior again. This correction does not have to scare or hurt the dog; it simply must be sufficiently clear to get the trainer's point across, i.e., that the behavior is *not* one which the dog should repeat, and if he does there *will* be consequences, though if he will listen and do as he is asked, life will be amazingly, stupendously fun.

The Mr. Fluffykins scenario is a complex example, and if you are in this position you really need a consult with a good trainer. A young puppy and an older dog alike needs to be made to see the cat as a positive thing in his life, and not to make an association between the arrival of the cat in the room, tail waving, with an angry owner telling him off. We want the puppy/dog and Mr. Fluffykins to end up best mates. This requires assessing your environment and the temperament of cat and puppy. With an adult dog it is important not to suppress his emotions (which can explode unexpectedly) but rather to change his reaction to the cat, away from one of excitement in the chase to one of neutrality and not finding the cat terribly interesting.

Dogs like to know where they stand, as it allows them to relax and get on with life. They do not enjoy being unsure and anxious about what to do, preferring to know what is what. Training should be consistent, not one rule on Monday when it's sunny and warm and another on Tuesday when it's raining and you just want to watch Netflix and chill. Corrections should be educational and a learning experience for the dog, enhancing his life, not making him shut down and fearful.

We have already looked at different types of corrections, including "wrong answer" and "no, don't *ever* do this again." However, it's worth repeating that the entire picture must always be looked at, including the long-term welfare of the dog, which at times must be prioritized over short-term discomfort. It's better for a dog to learn that chasing cars and biting tires will have painful, unpleasant consequences—either imposed by his trainer or, he thinks, by the tire—than that he is run over and killed.

Although force-free trainers tend to go down the management route with a car chaser rather than correct him, I dispute that extreme management techniques are in the dog's best interest. A high-energy working dog was made to run, to use his nose, to chase things (just not cars) and not to sit on the sofa all day, drugged to the eyeballs, allowed to stagger around a fenced-in paddock once a week off-lead, as he can't be walked outside the house without slipping his flat collar and dashing into the road after anything that moves.

Not everything can be managed, particularly for dogs that go out and about in the real world and do not live in the ivory tower of a training room or their owner's large garden. I prefer to teach my dogs right from wrong, and that when I ask them to do something it is not an optional request to be pondered and debated at their leisure; rather, they *have to* do as they are told, and do it *now*. This sentence will have force-free enthusiasts snorting their tea out of their noses. The outrage! How dare I demand my dogs obey me!

Well, as I said, I do live in the real world, and as a human it is my job to keep my dogs safe. I love my dogs deeply, so I take this responsibility very seriously. In order to achieve this, I train my dogs to be obedient. This is always done with 99 percent play, rewards, kindness and fun, plus 1 percent fair corrections as and when needed (which is very rarely with a trained dog), never asking more than the dog is able to give.

I do not issue corrections like the drill sergeant in *Full Metal Jacket*, rather I form a partnership with my dogs based on mutual love, trust and respect. However, my dogs *must* recall when I tell them to, leave or drop any items I tell them to, and act neutral around other dogs, even if they want to bounce around and try to instigate play. In this way, I believe my dogs are both safer and have much less "force" used on them than an unprepared force-free trainer would use in an emergency situation.

Far better to kindly but firmly put boundaries in place from the start, letting the dog know he *must* do as he is told. No confusion, no ifs and buts: when he is asked to do something, it is compulsory. Do not say to your dog, "Please do this for me, darling, but only if you really want to." It makes you sound creepy. Rather, tell your dog, "We are a team, but nevertheless you *will* do this for me when I ask you to," being much more like a parent, which is the type of relationship many people aspire to with their pets but who in reality treat them with a level of leniency they would never afford their human children.

In summary then, using a correction correctly—there's a tongue twister for you—is not traumatic or harmful for a dog, it is a learning experience, particularly when it provides the dog with some much-needed clarity. Corrections are the only way to stop a behavior that the dog truly values when the trainer has nothing better to offer as an alternative. It is a fact of life: Corrections in some form are necessary in order to produce a well-mannered, happy dog.

Myth Three: It's all in how you bring them up.

Yes and no. This is a phrase which has been taken up by some of the younger trainers of today, though "no bad dogs" was actually coined by the one and only Barbara Woodhouse many years ago.[19] Really, though, we need to distinguish between "bad" and "fault" and be extremely clear in how we define these terms. Barbara Woodhouse notwithstanding, there are a lot of bad dogs out there, ones I would not sleep near without one eye open, whether they are crated or not. Is it these dogs' *fault* they are bad? No. In many cases they have been designed this way, irresponsibly bred by **back yard breeders** for a quick buck, or abused by past owners who either didn't know better or didn't care about their dogs.

When I was younger I liked to think every dog could be helped, and that we should always try to rehabilitate every dog whose owner comes to the veterinarian or trainer for advice on dealing with aggression toward humans. I now have little patience with dogs who are aggressive and who will bite people—not just nipping, I mean really nailing them with the intent to do damage. I particularly do not like such dogs when they have the opportunity to back off but instead choose to move forward and attack. Again, it's not the dog's fault: he may have been beaten or abused, he may be genetically fearful or crazy, he may be a bully and simply used to getting his own way. But nevertheless this is a dog that will happily use his teeth, and use them hard. This is not a dog I want in my life, not as a client, and not to meet in the park when relaxing with my own dogs.

In a shelter situation, dogs with a repeated history of severe bites, even if just the one, do not have a promising future. Whether due to ill treatment or poor genetics, some dogs may never gain sufficient confidence to be trustworthy around anyone but their owner, and sometimes not even her. They often require a very experienced handler who understands their triggers and what may provoke an aggressive reaction. Yes, for sure, many of these dogs could be helped immensely by a good trainer, but most shelters simply do not have the resources to allocate hours and hours of a trainer's time to one dog.

All too often these dogs languish for years in kennels, the criteria for rehoming so strict that no prospective owners can meet them. Who never has visiting children under sixteen; does not have, or want, a partner (!); and does not work and so is home all day, not to mention is fit, healthy, sprightly and has no other pets? Experience as a dog owner, if not as an expert trainer, and familiarity with the breed in question may also be prerequisites, in addition to having a secure garden in the countryside, as the dog cannot be taken into public but still needs plenty of exercise as well as peace and quiet away from traffic and other noise pollution.

Very few people can offer this, and so these dogs live their lives in fear, in noisy, overcrowded kennels full of barking dogs, where, due to their bite history, they may not even have any daily human handling, very few staff being qualified to deal with them. They don't get exercised outside, in the fields shown on the charity's fundraising page. If they are lucky, they are put into a tiny concrete run, alone, while their kennel is cleaned. This "privilege" is granted for ten minutes, once a day. They are generally housed with no other canines for company, and receive no love or affection from any other living thing. This is no life for any dog. Better for such a dog to be quietly euthanized, and for the pain and fear to stop.

There are some dogs who are more in the middle of the spectrum. For example, a dog whose bite may be considered a one-off and was understandable, and which, realistically, will not bite again, as he is friendly and sociable, with no behavioral issues. Or a dog that is just bossy and, with a good trainer, quickly accepts that things have changed and that threatening humans is no longer an option. This could be a six-month-old puppy that was playing tug with an unsupervised child, grabbed at the toy and accidentally caught the child's hand. It could be a small, old dog that has never bitten in his life but nipped a person who picked him up, squeezing his arthritic leg. Doggy doo-doo happens. These are not bad dogs; they are often low-risk and absolutely deserve another chance should their owner not want to keep them.

Then there are dogs who lean a bit more toward the "bad" side. The best-case scenario for these dogs is where they are surrendered to rescues that understand the breed in question, including its genetics and inherent drives. This can work very well when the rescue has expert trainers and foster homes that are also familiar with the breed and that will put sufficient time and energy into making an informed assessment of the dog, what can realistically be done with him, and whether he indeed poses a danger to the public. In many cases, such dogs can be rehabilitated and go on to live long, happy lives.

There is also another side of the coin, where dogs with a serious human bite history are not taken seriously enough, the shelter staff believing, as I once did, that there is a home out there for every dog and that a dog that has bitten someone is not necessarily bad, he simply needs some love and proper training. In general, given the larger shelters' struggle to obtain affordable legal liability insurance for staff and visitors to interact with aggressive dogs, it is only the smaller, independent shelters and breed-specific rescues that will still take dogs that have bitten a human badly and/or repeatedly.

Often these rescues are run by very well-meaning individuals for all of the right reasons. But unfortunately at times they make bad decisions, trying to rehabilitate dogs that are very bad indeed and that are a legitimate danger to the shelter staff. No matter how experienced the handler, everyone makes mistakes and either lets their guard down or has something untoward happen, resulting in fatalities involving shelter staff as was the sad case in Scotland not that long ago, where a very good man lost his life. Rest in peace, Adam Watts.[20]

The very best of these shelters consider all life sacrosanct and have special facilities to safely manage high-risk dogs. The dogs are never rehomed, and may not be handled by humans at all anymore, but they are given a good quality of life, with access to large outside areas and, in some cases, company with other suitable dogs, living in this manner until they pass. Provided people are kept safe and the dog is content, that's a best-case scenario and I'm happy when a dog can be saved in this way. However, such shelters are very rare.

Unfortunately, there does exist a tiny minority of uninformed, unrealistic individuals who run rescues and who think every dog can be cured of severe aggression problems. This can be a bit of a mixed bag. There are shelters run by force-free trainers who believe love solves all, and then there are those who are run by compulsion trainers who have the arrogance to think all behavior problems can be solved with enough force, lighting a dog up constantly on an e-collar to simply suppress the bad behavior. This is more of a trend in the U.S. (no offense).

In one tragic case, an elderly lady was killed by a dog her daughter had recently adopted.[21] Rest in peace, Margaret Colvin. This should never have happened to you, and is an example of the very worst goings-on in the dog training industry. The dog, Blue, had a lengthy bite history, yet was advertised for adoption with no mention of his aggressive past. He had also been shipped between states to avoid euthanasia, which is a common tactic with these sorts of shelters, along with giving dogs a cute new name and identity. "Angel" or "Princess" sound more appealing than "Hannibal the Cannibal" or "Brutus the Destroyer," it has to be said. Well, unless you're a drug dealer or have alternative gastronomical tastes.

Trainers of every variety are increasingly being brought dogs that have serious aggression problems and are being expected to work miracles, putting their lives at risk in the process. Some trainers will no longer take on large, powerful dogs with a serious human bite history, having been bitten in the past and having been out of work for some time as a result. This is just common sense. Some dogs will choose to bite, and dogs that are fearful but at the same time have a high degree of defensive aggression, preferring to advance rather than to retreat when under pressure or scared, are very dangerous dogs indeed.

Many people will tell you that it's all in how these dogs were raised, not giving enough credit to genetics. I do believe that each and every dog should be judged as an individual, and that legislation which bans certain breeds is unwise and does nothing to prevent bites. There is always going to be another big, tough designer breed that is not on the "banned list" and that people will flock to buy from back yard breeders—dogs with unsteady nerves and bad genetics, often bred for color and appearance, with no thought to temperament—whereas lovely dogs of banned breeds are unable to have any freedom or real quality of life, permanently muzzled and on-lead when they have done nothing wrong.

My breed, my passion, is the Rottweiler, and although my dogs are good-natured and kind, I do not view them through rose-tinted glasses. They are large, powerful dogs that could do a lot of damage if they bit a person, another dog, or livestock, or even just ran into a person, knocking her down like a bowling pin. I am very careful to set them up for success, to spend time training them each and every day, to walk them and meet their exercise requirements, to play and have fun with them. But I do not forget what they are capable of. While they should not be stigmatized by their looks, each dog should be judged by its actions.

When buying a dog, many people do not take enough account of genetics and what the dog was originally bred to do. Just because you know a person with a lovely, dog-friendly Pit Bull (for example), it does not mean that all Pit Bulls are going to be wonderful around other dogs. If you want a Pit Bull, great care must be taken when selecting a breeder, and you must accept that the dog you end up with may *not* be good around other dogs and be prepared to put in the extra work required for training and caring for such a dog.

There are certain dog breeds that unfortunately have been bred for fighting, and also breeds whose purpose was to act as guardians, whether of livestock, people or property. These dogs retain within their genetics a degree of aggression, suspicion around strangers, and defensiveness concerning their owner and her property. Although each dog is an individual and yours may show none of these traits and be the sweetest dog ever, nevertheless these traits may appear at some point in his life, and it disrespects your dog and his unique heritage to forget what he was designed for.

No matter how well brought up a dog is, his genetics will determine much of his innate behavior. An Akita with a tendency toward aggression, for example, can be brought up by the most kind, loving, well-meaning owners, who expose him to extensive socialization, but that dog will still have a tendency to dislike other dogs. That is who he is. When he tells you, believe him! He can be managed, and he can be taught to be neutral around other dogs and not act in a reactive way, but he cannot be taught to actually *like* them—not by beating him, and not by shoveling treats down his throat. He will never like other dogs, just as you may never like sandals with socks on an otherwise smartly dressed man.

Similarly, a dog that is genetically fearful, of whatever breed, can be trained kindly and with compassion, the owner always looking to build up the dog's confidence, but the results will be mixed at best. Most fearful dogs will try to get themselves out of a situation which scares them, but, if on-lead and restrained, and therefore not free to run away, they may feel they have no choice but to defend themselves. Sometimes such dogs will act first, taking the part of an aggressor, as they have found in the past that barking and snarling will make other dogs and people back off. When the dog is a big, powerful breed, this presents a very real danger.

Abusing a dog, or raising him to have no boundaries or limitations, contributes to bad behavior and dangerous habits, even when the dog has good genetics. Inexperienced owners can inadvertently create such problems by encouraging resource guarding, thinking it's funny when their small dog growls when anyone tries to sit on "his chair," or by allowing their kids to pull a dog's ears or tail, or even to climb onto its back, when the dog is clearly showing via his body language—if not yet resorting to a growl—that he is deeply unhappy.

This is far from amusing, and invariably one day someone gets bitten. However, a dog with good genetics and a sound, friendly temperament without fearfulness has very little, if any, reason to bite a person unless he is abused or mistreated. More often than not, a well-balanced dog will find a way to leave or diffuse a situation which is annoying or scaring him, rather than to bite. Yes, accidents can happen, but they are few and far between with good dogs.

So, to my mind, there certainly are bad dogs out there. Sadly, given how many genuinely lovely dogs need a good home, and given the limited shelter places up for grabs, the worst of the bad ones should be euthanized for their own good. This is not a judgment on the dog. I have the utmost sympathy for all of these dogs, but due to the unlikelihood of such a dog having anything close to a good quality of life in the typical shelter, keeping him alive out of sentiment is unfair to the dog. He has already been let down by people. If he cannot live a happy, species-appropriate life in a specialist center, let's not keep punishing him. Euthanize him and put him out of his misery.

Myth Four: Balanced trainers never reward dogs.

This is not so. There is a big difference between compulsion-based trainers and balanced trainers, and balanced trainer, like force-free trainers, tend to either sit in the middle or toward one or the other extreme of the dog training spectrum. In reality, a great many *good* force-free dog trainers, the ones that turn out really nice, well-trained dogs, are in reality balanced trainers and use corrections in addition to rewards. They find value in marketing themselves as force-free trainers, and a minority now say they are reward-based trainers, which is much more honest, as it describes what most balanced trainers are but without ruling out the appropriate use of corrections.

Any corrections given to a dog by a balanced or reward-based trainer are, of course, in addition to a *massive* amount of rewards and positive reinforcement, as the dog must first of all, before we do anything else, learn to trust us and know he will have great fun being with us. Then he must understand that there are boundaries and rules he must adhere to, as we are his leader, but the upside of that is his guaranteed safety. When we are encouraging a behavior, positive reinforcement is a good trainer's default, as is having a dog that is engaged with the trainer and interested and enthusiastic about the training session.

For an owner or trainer, being friends with and having the trust of one's dogs is vitally important. This can't be achieved with force, and is best done with fun and the use of rewards, particularly play. Some play can be with toys, some with food, and yet other play can involve just the dog and owner. More and more trainers are catching onto using play, though I would say it is more prevalent with balanced trainers that train working dogs than with force-free trainers, who concentrate more on pets and tend to use food as a reward more than an element of play. Play benefits all dogs, though the type of play must be tailored to each dog.

A dog with a positive emotional connection with his owner will do far better than one without such a connection. There should be respect on both sides, and a dog will not respect an owner acting as a bully toward him. In an ideal world we reward a dog for good behavior choices, redirect away from making mistakes where appropriate, and, where we have to stop a behavior, we teach the dog with fair, consistent corrections that it is in his best interests to choose good behaviors over bad behaviors. Those good choices then become increasingly important to the dog, much more appealing to him than being corrected for choosing to perform an undesirable behavior.

Time and again it comes back to educating owners that every dog must be evaluated and trained as an individual. Balanced training does not equate to abuse and giving a dog no rewards—not when it is done correctly, which involves much, much more rewards than it ever does corrections. Force-free training may work for a minority of dogs that respond well to the corrections which *are* used, but a methodology labeled force-free does not necessarily work for every dog. This is particularly true when a dog has bad behaviors which desperately need addressing and the force-tree trainer either does not understand that she actually is using corrections (badly) or is using the wrong corrections and tools for that specific dog.

Myth Five: Never reprimand a dog that uses your home as a toilet.

Now, this is a popular one, and though it comes from good intentions, it often causes a great many problems for dogs as well as their owners. In particular, I have seen people inadvertently use grossly inappropriate, indirect corrections on dogs for indoor toileting say they train their dogs exclusively in a force-free, purely positive manner.

A small, nervous adult dog (not a young puppy) that urinates or defecates inside your house simply because he hates the torrential rain knows he's put you in a bad mood. As you curse and swear, all the while scrubbing urine off your prized antique rug, your dog is scared and his anxiety is soaring. There is a rule he does not understand, but he knows he has somehow upset you. I am saying small dog here, as it usually is the small, sensitive ones who are most affected by thunderstorms, though of course any breed can hate getting wet and be reactive to loud noises.

Shouting and showing aggressive, threatening body language is being abusive to your dog, even if it's indirect and you're trying your best not to ~~skin him and make him into a new rug~~ let him know you are angry. Swearing under your breath in frustration with your back turned to him, pushing him away as he comes to see what is wrong while you are scrubbing the ruined rug is being mean, pure and simple. Your dog is not a fool. He knows it's about him, he just doesn't know what he did to upset you. Fairer to let him know that indoor urination is off the table, even if Noah is packing the ark.

Is it understandable for you as a human to be annoyed about your expensive rug, now ruined by a turd or pool of urine, staining the white with a less than pleasing shade of yellow? Well, yes. I would be a bit annoyed too, but that's life with dogs. I just shrug my shoulders and get on with the cleanup. Many people do not. We are all different, and although I'm laid back by nature, I recognize that not everyone is and that some people get very angry with their dogs over things that should be non-issues, that would have never happened if the dog had received some appropriate corrections and direction in life instead of being expected to guess what is right and what is wrong.

For sure, you do not want to teach a dog to be scared to urinate or defecate in front of you. But at the same time, it's perfectly possible to teach an older puppy or adult dog, via rewards and fair corrections, that indoor toileting is *not* permitted. Remember, a puppy is any dog from birth up to twelve months of age; I will correct older puppies and adult dogs, but not very young puppies that physically and mentally are not able to be totally clean indoors.

Almost all of my initial work with a very young puppy is to build trust and love, to play and have fun together, instead of drilling him in obedience as most people like to do. However, I still want a clean home! I teach my puppies to go to the toilet on command (via rewards) from day one of coming to live with me from their breeders, at about eight to ten weeks old, and they usually learn this extremely quickly and with great enthusiasm. If an older puppy or adult dog starts toileting indoors, I am beginning from a good place, as he already trusts me and pees and poops in front of me with a level of gusto that would be alarming in anyone other than my dog.

Once my older puppy is physically able to have some effective control over his urination and defecation, I *will* give a light correction for toileting in the house in front of me. Large-breed puppies may not have complete control over their bodily functions until as late as six months old, particularly during vigorous play, when they may stop to urinate with no warning. Small-breed puppies usually can control themselves a lot earlier. Much will depend on your own individual puppy, and care must always be taken that there is no underlying cause for indoor urination, such as a urinary tract infection.

All of their lives, my dogs are rewarded for toileting in front of me, either on command or spontaneously on walks. These rewards are on a partial schedule, meaning they are not given every time, just occasionally. We have covered this, but to recap, a partial reinforcement schedule, particularly a random variable ratio schedule, builds hope and can increase the likelihood and speed of a behavior once the dog understands what is required. As in playing the lottery, when you only win occasionally and are looking forward to a pleasant surprise in the future, you are more keen to play than you would be if you won every single time and there was no mystery.

So all of my dogs, from puppies to geriatrics, trust me and happily toilet in front of me on our walks on a daily basis. Sometimes they are on-lead and sometimes off-lead. (They are never turned out into the garden for an hour or so and just left to their own devices. Much as I would love to do this, my garden is too small.) If my older puppy or adult dog does pee or poop *in front of me* inside the house, provided there is not a suspected health problem or a fault attributable to me such as my missing him asking to go out, I let him know it's not OK. Most dogs only need to be told once or twice not to toilet inside, and usually all that is required to do this is a very sharp "No!," followed by immediately taking him outside to toilet, where he is massively rewarded.

Now, I know 911 will be called and the copper chopper scrambled at the very thought of telling a dog he cannot use the house as a toilet, the poor little lamb's heart pounding from fear and the sheer injustice at being told "no" and put into the cold, wet garden. Force-free trainers will insist that if you ever use a correction for indoor toileting, your dog will forevermore hide from you behind the sofa to toilet and the problem will only get worse. Yes, this happens, but not because of fair corrections. It's due to owners refusing to correct their dog and then eventually exploding in frustration and rage, giving a massive overcorrection, having watched their dog make direct eye contact as he repeatedly does his business inside the house whenever it suits him.

Myth Six: Castration will solve all your dog's behavioral problems.

Sadly, this myth is pushed by veterinarians and dog trainers alike in relation to male dogs. This "solution" shows a real lack of understanding of the effects of testosterone as well as learned behaviors. Before I say anything else, I want to emphasize that removing a dog's hormones, whether by spaying a bitch or castrating a male dog, has a lot of negative health *and behavioral* implications and should be considered very carefully on a case-by-case basis.[22]

Very briefly, some of the health risks associated with early spaying and castration relate to longevity and increasing the risk of your dog becoming ill with certain serious cancers, including osteosarcoma, a bone cancer that is a prevalent killer in my own favorite breed, the Rottweiler, in addition to other breeds such as Golden Retrievers.[23] According to many vets, spaying and castration can encourage skin allergies and other joint issues,[24] particularly if carried out early, before the age of one, though much depends on the breed of dog and whether it is male or female.[25]

Often, sexual behaviors in adolescent dogs, if not discouraged, will become an ingrained habit. Even after castration, some dogs, particularly small ones with too much autonomy, will continue to hump pillows in the home, along with engaging in scent marking and attempts at roaming.[26] A lot depends on how long the behavior has been going on and how it is managed.

Testosterone is a hormone present in both males and females (as estrogen is) and does not in itself cause aggression. Rather, testosterone heightens the volume of emotions,[27] turning them up and reducing self-control. If a dog likes to fight, chances are he will still like to fight after castration. Maybe he will want to fight a bit less since he has reduced energy, but if his "go-to" behavior for any issues he has with other dogs is aggression, then his answer will still be aggression after castration, and he may actually be worse, particularly if he is a dog that lacked confidence.

Lowering testosterone decreases confidence, so in a nervous dog it can make some behavioral problems much, much worse.[28]

As with all science, there can be discussion and disagreement, particularly with behavioral issues, where results can be subjective. A recent study in Poland,[29] conducted via owner surveys, gave the main reasons for castration as being undesirable behaviors, but the conclusions, though expected, were slightly worrying. Although castration did reduce unwanted behaviors, including roaming, mounting and urine marking, it "did not reduce the presentation of anxious behavior in fearful dogs. Castration increased the number of dogs that were fearful of unfamiliar dogs/humans, as well as dogs with sound phobias...."[30] Clearly, this is not good.

Now, the vast majority of veterinarians energetically promote spaying and castration, citing health reasons and behavioral benefits. This is poppycock. Along with the vaccination of older animals (and kittens and puppies, which *must* be vaccinated), spaying and neutering is the primary source of income for many veterinary clinics. Veterinarians may study the effects of hormones in their college classes, but they do *not* study dog behavior to any great extent. It's not emphasized on the standard curriculum, though some universities offer electives on behavior. Several hours of study cannot compete with the years of practical knowledge that dog trainers have, not to mention that the science surrounding hormones and dog behavior backs up the observations of trainers.

Myth Seven: Dogs must always give us their consent to be trained.

A common narrative some extreme force-free trainers bandy about these days is that dogs are never deliberately disobedient or strong-willed and that, as sentient beings, they should not be *told* what to do. Dogs must give us their consent whenever we require something from them. Consent to being trained, consent to having their nails or coat trimmed and even consent to receive medical treatment. "Just offer him some kibble to encourage him," we are told, and "don't you dare jerk on that lead," all while a 130-pound Mastiff tries to swallow a Pug whole for lunch.

Again, I have to emphasize that it's bad trainers who are to blame, and within this group there are two polar opposites: force-free trainers and compulsion trainers. The terms *force-free* and *purely positive* are misleading, but nevertheless there are good force-free trainers who train many well-behaved, nicely rounded dogs with effective corrections, taking control of the dog and not pleading for consent. However, most force-free trainers will get hot under the collar when a balanced trainer says a dog *must* do as he is told and that corrections should be used as appropriate if the dog deliberately disobeys.

Dogs like what dogs like, and it may very well be different from what we humans like. Do you enjoy chasing and then killing others of your own kind? If your answer is "no," keep reading. If it is "yes," then I'm sure there must be a Psychopaths Anonymous site somewhere on the dark web you would like reading more than this book. Many dogs, it has to be said, do very much enjoy chasing and killing dogs smaller than themselves. Make no mistake, they are not stupid and they know it's a small dog and not a squirrel or rabbit. They need to have it explained in no uncertain terms that this behavior is totally unacceptable and they do not have a choice to say "no" when we point it out to them.

Dogs are like us in that most have a mind of their own, and their own likes and dislikes—and why shouldn't they? This is not "dominance," using the term in the way many trainers throw it around—just common sense. Who does not like getting their own way? Having a strong character and knowing what you want in life is not a bad thing! Dogs will absolutely do the wrong thing and not make the right choice when obeying us is optional and there is a behavior which is more rewarding to them. This is why corrections are successful in stopping bad behaviors and rewards are not, particularly when compared to the taste of fresh Pug.

Personally, I am always a bit suspicious of any dog that is too well-behaved, that shows no love of life nor any personality or happy interaction with his owner. I *want* my dogs to make mistakes when trying to give me the right answer to a new task, and also to make appropriate suggestions to me, as I like them to have some choice in their lives. "Let's take the path toward the sea today and not the one through the forest" = appropriate suggestion from my dogs. "Let me run off after this rabbit, ignoring all recall, and return to the car three hours later when I'm hungry" = totally inappropriate suggestion from my dogs. If I had a dog like this, that had a good understanding of recall but preferred rabbits to me and was not afraid of giving me the finger and disappearing, I would use an e-collar correction to let him know that being off-lead does not mean obedience is optional.

I am ignoring the abuse klaxon that force-free trainers are now sounding, screaming that e-collars are torture and that there are many other ways to stop a dog from chasing rabbits. I am not denying there can be, depending on the dog. However, most dogs are not stupid. They know when they are on a long line or Flexi lead, and when they are not. The *habit* of always recalling when on a long line may persist for some dogs when eventually the line is removed, as we are all creatures of habit, particularly if the dog has also been taught to be really engaged with his owner and is not that fussed about the rabbit. Don't count on a perfect recall with a smart dog that has a high prey drive, though: some will be gone like a Jack Russell down a rabbit hole. Which may be your exact problem.

For some, though not all dogs, chasing a rabbit is far more fun than the highest-value food, or playing with a ball, or whatever is the best reward the owner can think of to offer her dog in exchange for returning to her. These dogs, if never taught obedience and respect for their owner and what is being asked of them, will just disappear and choose to do what their instincts tell them, which is to give chase and not to obey us. This is *incredibly* dangerous and will invariably end their lives in one way or another.

A good recall is taught by positive reinforcement, by the dog *wanting* to be with his owner, wanting to come back to her to play and be given food rewards, and not by buzzing him with an e-collar. However, when a dog refuses to listen when his owner calls and runs off after something better, that is a bit different. An e-collar can essentially act as an invisible lead, and occasionally as a "hand of God" to stop a fixated dog dead in his tracks, and so prevent him from dashing onto the road while chasing a ball (for example) a ball being an item which you would not typically carry out predation e-collar training with.

A dog with high drive and no reliable recall—or at best a slow, reluctant recall, gazing back longingly into the distance (who would that be, my dear Rottweiler?)—can be "managed." The most frequently provided solution for such a dog is to live permanently on-lead. If you have a large garden or can afford regular trips to fenced-off secure areas, this may not be a concern for you, as your dog still has some off-lead time. If you have no such luxuries, you can simply train your dog with an e-collar so he *can* enjoy off-lead exercise with you when in the park, the beach or the forest.

A dog needs careful conditioning with an e-collar, so he learns how to turn the stimulus off. Just blasting an untrained dog is both unfair and dangerous, as it can make him run faster and harder away from you, not understanding what is happening to him or how to make the sensation go away. You need a good balanced trainer who is experienced in e-collar use to (a) teach your dog engagement with you and therefore a solid recall; (b) find the level of stimulation which does not cause your dog pain but is uncomfortable enough to persuade him to listen to you; and (c) teach your dog that ignoring his owner has negative consequences for him. *Do not* just sneak a cheap e-collar on him behind your trainer's back, hoping you can use it in an emergency.

Once trained using consequences for bad behavior and *loads* of rewards for being obedient, bad choices on the part of the dog become very rare indeed, meaning he can enjoy life, not needing to be exercised off-lead only in a fenced field and able to experience freedom and the joy of running and playing with his owner. Some dogs do better with an e-collar as a backup, no matter how well trained; others do not require this and just need some initial work to enforce the ground rules. As I say all through this book, it depends on the dog.

Veterinarians and groomers are seeing more and more dogs that are aggressive, prepared to bite in order to enforce their "back-off" signals. These dogs have been taught that they have bodily autonomy and that if they don't want to be touched in a certain place, they have the right to say "no." This is plain wrong and, again, puts your dog's life at risk. Many popular breeds, including any with "Doodle" or "Poo" in their name, need professional grooming, suffering from deeply uncomfortable mats in their hair if not attended to every four to six weeks. If your dog needs emergency veterinary treatment but cannot be touched, you may have to pay a whole lot more for sedation just so he can be examined, and you may eventually find yourself asked to leave the practice, as no one there wants to be bitten. You may even be banned from the majority of veterinary practices in the area. Do not let this be your dog.

Myth Eight: Never punish a growl.

One more myth whose debunking will end up with me getting bomb threats is the squawked "Never punish a growl, or you'll get bitten, girl! And next time he won't growl, he'll go straight for the jugular!" Now, *punishment* is a word I don't like when talking about dog training, as the dictionary definitions tend to mention penalties and retribution rather than learning. Therefore, punishment is quite rightly *not* what we should be doing to a growling dog. Or any dog.

However, this is not what is meant by "never punish a growl." What is really being said is, "Never correct a growl. Do not tell the dog this behavior is unacceptable." The vast majority of force-free trainers will insist that dogs should be allowed to articulate to you that they do not agree with you and what you are asking, and that it's OK for them to threaten people in order to maintain their seat on the sofa or get whatever else they want. These trainers strongly advocate that growling dogs should be left alone, respected, and permitted to remain undisturbed while you and your guests sit on the floor. I'll go along with that if the dog is paying my mortgage, but he's not. Neither are the cats.

This bit of the chapter is like a video with stunts where the presenter says in a gravelly voice, "Do not copy what you are about to see at home … these are paid professionals … blah blah blah." Same here.

If you have an aggression problem with your dog, go get professional help. Do not tackle it on your own.

I just want to clear up some of the hysteria over growling. Anti-stab vest on: check. Riot shield at hand: check. Hard hat: check. But bite suit? Not required. After all, aggressive, force-free humans are the problem, not dogs. Have you not been taking in a word I have been writing?

If a growling dog is not cornered, is not growling out of fear or restrained with nowhere to go in order to escape pressure he is uncomfortable with, and is not growling in play as part of a game, but instead is growling to threaten me or another dog, as he thinks he should be able to do whatever the hell he wants, you know what? I may use a correction on him. I just might. Not out of anger, and not to hurt him, but because a dog throwing his weight around and issuing threats is never a good thing. Cuddles growling at Auntie Marge for sitting on "his" seat is all fun and games until it ends in tears.

A dog threatening me, another person, or another dog or animal that is not doing him any harm is not acceptable. *Ever.* Yes, we must always be fair to the dog, both in our requests and regarding the circumstances at hand, and this includes leaving him in peace as appropriate (e.g., to eat) and dealing with any concerns regarding his health: dogs who are sick or in pain are often aggressive and grouchy. Scared dogs that cannot escape what is frightening them will growl, which is perfectly understandable. However, a healthy, confident dog that is free to move away at any time but instead wants to hold his ground, growl and issue threats, *has to* understand that this sort of behavior is not acceptable. EVER.

A correction may or may not be appropriate for the confident dog that wants to take you on. In some circumstances the situation should not be escalated, particularly where a dog is extremely aroused and will back up a growl with a serious bite if you correct him. However, unless it's essential for my safety or that of others, I certainly *will not* back down and take pressure off a dog who growls as a warning to me. If I do this and back away, I am rewarding that growl. I never want the dog to gain confidence that he can move me about and tell me what to do and where to go. The moment he stops growling, depending on the circumstances, I may back off as a reward for the growl ceasing, but not until then.

The more entitled a dog gets, and the more he expects people to give in and back away from him, the more likely he is to (a) bring that behavior into other scenarios where he wants his own way; (b) start to redirect on his handler when told "no" or corrected; or (c) escalate to a bite, especially when someone who usually scuttles away eventually stands up to him. When we let this continue, it is not going to end well for anyone. Management is not the answer, as the day always comes that someone makes a mistake, such as coming too close to the sofa where the dog has made it clear he does not want anyone disturbing his beauty sleep.

A dog trainer who is confident in handling such a dog, and who the dog suspects will cause him *much* more trouble than it's worth if challenged, will often be able to quickly change the dog's mind about issuing threats. If the dog is not entrenched in this behavior, his growl may be very tentative and just meant to test the water, with no real intention to follow it up with a bite; the dog just wants to see what is going to be permitted. One well-timed correction may be all it takes to convince this dog that a growl is *not* appropriate and that he has not been behaving as he should. Working with the trainer, he can learn to expand this to apply to the people he lives with, as it very much should.

Other dogs, usually those who have been allowed to growl and threaten people for a long time, will expect the trainer to back down just as everyone else does. Such a dog can be much harder to retrain, and if it's a confident dog, I will be honest: things may get ugly. Context must always be borne in mind. The trainer's first priority is always her own safety, and it is not always the case that you can spend time tiptoeing about a dog, afraid to administer even a mild correction, as the dog will redirect and let you know that *no one* gives him orders. Sometimes the dog must simply be told, and told extremely firmly, that the equivalent of Freddy Krueger will appear if he even dreams of growling again, never mind biting.

This type of work, with bold, confident, "hard" dogs, is best left to experts in the field who actively *want* to do it, as it's emotionally draining for both dog and trainer. No trainer enjoys being hard on a dog. It may be necessary at times to save a dog's life, but it takes a toll. It's hard to find a trainer who is proficient in this kind of work, as most older trainers who have dealt with a lot of such dogs feel that they have done their time. They don't enjoy dealing with truly aggressive dogs and no longer financially have the need to take on this type of client and risk their own mental and physical health. And younger trainers often don't have enough experience.

Corrections for growling are rarely harsh. When an entitled, spoiled dog growls at a balanced trainer and is corrected, the trainer is not shouting, hitting or using violence on that dog. This *never* happens, unless in a tiny number of circumstances such as I described in the paragraphs above, where the spoiled, entitled brat intends to put the trainer in hospital and is very much capable of doing so. In such a case all bets are off, and the trainer will do anything she needs to in order to defend herself. Human safety always, always, always comes first.

When acting in defense, I draw the line at executing a Mike Tyson maneuver and biting the dog's ear off. That would be too much, especially with a hairy dog, where I would be flossing forevermore. I am joking, by the way. But some people do think an appropriate correction for biting is to bite the dog back. Do not do this, it's plain stupid. Who do you think you are, Crocodile Dundee? You are not another dog with suitable canine teeth (Mike Tyson notwithstanding), and there are far better ways to correct a dog.

Not all growling dogs are scared, but some are, and it can take a lot of skill to decipher the emotions a dog is feeling. When correcting a growling dog, I do not want to merely *suppress* the behavior, and this is where the "do not ever punish a growl" myth comes about. A dog that is scared and is having a negative emotional reaction, but that is threatened by the trainer with harsh corrections for growling, may comply and keep quiet, suppressing his emotions. He only obeys because he does not want to feel even worse about his life; however, his emotions about the situation have not changed, and, if anything, he is even more scared than before. Such a dog is a ticking time bomb, as the underlying cause of the growling—fear—is still there, and often the fear will build and at some point the dog will explode.

Avoiding **suppression** is particularly important with fear-based aggression. Decision-making is affected by emotion, and the decision not to growl and issue threats should not be made out of fear of harsh repercussions but rather because the dog learns he can cope with the situation he is in. A feeling of safety does not come from a trainer issuing threats of violence. But, and this is a big but, not all growling dogs are scared. Force-free trainers will say there is no such thing as dominance in dogs, and that all dogs who growl are actually scared. This is not so. I do not buy the explanation "he is scared that he will have to sit on the cold floor instead of on the sofa." No. Just no. Not acceptable. He can move his "scared," hairy little butt elsewhere. If a dog dislikes sitting on the floor, he will just have to suppress his annoyance, as he will no longer have sofa-sitting privileges until he understands it is not his place to tell family members where they can and cannot sit.

There are lots of reasons for a growl. Dogs growl when they play, both with each other and with us, the growling issued with no genuine aggression or intention to bite. Many dogs are excitable, and (for example) want to play with other dogs they spot while on walks. When they are restricted on-lead they often find it hard to control their emotions and may start to vocalize, displaying barrier frustration. However, loudly barking and whining is not acceptable behavior and can be misinterpreted by other dogs and their owners, causing fear and alarm.

I never want my dogs to be an inconvenience to other people, not when they can be quiet, which, don't get me wrong, may take work. However, for most excitable dogs it is achievable, and is a matter of developing the dog's impulse control and working on his barrier frustration, which are very valuable life skills for any dog. Yet despite this, we are expected to adhere to the one-size-fits-all mantra of "never punish a growl."

It is not actually an easy life for a dog who is allowed to growl, vocalize uncontrollably, or otherwise issue threats, having to make all his own decisions and take total responsibility both for himself and his inept owner. With no direction, leadership or support, what is a dog to do? He is a dog, and as such he cannot fully understand the world in which he lives. Dogs like this are rarely, if ever, truly happy. Structure and boundaries are generally readily accepted and appreciated by almost every badly behaved dog, including those who are aggressive and feel they must be the ones in charge, making all life choices for themselves and the humans they live with.

A dog needs to learn to be neutral in his reactions, and his emotions toward a given *situation* must ideally be positive, even if they are not necessarily positive toward the particular thing or circumstance he has growled at in the past. I can't make a dog like other dogs if his genetics are screaming at him to hate them. However, he *can* learn to enjoy his walks when other dogs are close by, no longer having the need to growl or vocalize as his impulse control improves and he learns to become neutral in his reactions and to trust that I will never again put him in a position where his emotions feel unmanageable to him. He may see other dogs close to him, but never so close that they are a concern. This takes work.

The corrections used on such a dog will vary depending on many factors, including the reason for the growl and the emotions behind it. A correction can be as simple as keeping a constant pressure on the lead until the growl or vocalization stops, then releasing that pressure as a reward for the growl stopping. This may be followed by engaging with the dog, asking for a basic behavior that he knows well, such as "sit," which can then be rewarded, so the dog does not write the trainer off as the worst thing ever to happen in his life.

If a dog is on the sofa, for example, and threatening me for simply wanting to sit beside him, I will not back down at his growling for me to go away. I will not issue him with a direct challenge either, but will instead quietly maintain my distance from him until he stops growling. Then and only then will I back off. The lesson for him is that growling has not worked, but silence has. I would then encourage him to get down from the sofa and reward him for doing this for me. Thereafter, changes will be made within the home, and the privilege of sitting on the sofa will be revoked until the dog learns he does not have the absolute right to sit there, and if he is allowed back on the sofa at some future date, he will be sure he cannot *ever* threaten people again.

With many non-fear-related aggression problems, the source of the dog's issues is in the home. This is the type of house where the dog has no boundaries, where he can sit on the windowsill and bark at passersby (it's his hobby, don't you know), where he has *his* chair and people are scared to walk past it. Where if the owner asks the dog for simple obedience, he ignores her completely. This is where the real training begins: in the home, not around more complex distractions. It starts with simple obedience and the dog learning to be nice to live with. It is important for the owner to learn to engage with her dog and to start to enjoy training him, and for the pair to become a team as opposed to housemates who do not really like each other. There should ideally be no conflict, and yes, as force-free trainers insist is best, there may be a period of time with a lot of management, but unlike such trainers, we should not see this as the entire solution.

So the work starts in the home, with the emphasis on engagement so that the dog wants to be trained and have fun working obedience with his owner, but also with the owner *insisting* on that obedience. When eventually we progress to working around other dogs, leaving the training room, the problem may not be there anymore, the dog having learned enough about obedience, respecting and trusting his owner in a controlled environment, to take it into the outside world. Or the problem may persist, and we now must work on the dog becoming a nice, well-mannered dog when taking walks around distractions.

In behavioral modification, particularly involving reactivity to other dogs and matters of a similar nature, we work with thresholds, meaning there is a point—a threshold—we do not want to cross. If we go too much *over* threshold, we put undue stress on the dog, which we do not want to do. We never want to put the dog in a position where he has a strong emotional reaction he cannot cope with. The dog must always be able to think logically and to make decisions, whether good or bad. *Under* threshold is where the dog has little to no reaction. If you're confused, think about weddings, where there's always a drunk guy starting fights and who cannot be reasoned with. That is the same as a dog over threshold. He cannot understand what you are saying to him, as his emotions are in the way.

"On threshold" is a term I personally use for when a dog is reacting to a stimulus but can still think and make logical decisions, responding to commands I give him. He is not so triggered that he is struggling to learn or understand directions. Many trainers will say this is "over threshold," but my book, my rules. I use the term *on threshold* to make it clear that this is a place that is not abusive and is not pushing the dog so far that he cannot cope emotionally. Many trainers, particularly force-free ones, flood their dogs, thinking they are performing counter-conditioning and that if the dog is given enough cookies and allowed to pull the trainer about, all is good. This is not so. Working with reactive dogs takes a lot of skill.

On threshold is where the work really takes place, meaning we get enough of a reaction that while the dog may not be the paragon of relaxation around other dogs, say, he is also not too tense. It is here where learning and behavioral modification can take place. The dog is not so scared that he cannot think, but at the same time he is unhappy enough that he feels some stress and discomfort. Stress, discomfort—these are not dirty words! The dog reacts in a negative way, and I can kindly correct him and tell him that his behavior—barking and pulling on the lead, for example—is wrong asking for an alternative behavior which I have already taught. Over time, "on threshold" becomes "under threshold," and we can close the distance between him and other dogs. If we have a setback, or just a bad day, there's no shame in increasing the distance and the threshold once more.

Some dogs can just sit beside you, parked on a bench (you, not the dog), and watch the world go by, learning that the universe is boring and that reactivity gains them nothing. They are happier having a snooze than getting all worked up to no avail. This is often a good strategy with puppies, and can be a useful part of a young dog's education. Others are better kept moving, particularly when they have reactivity or fearfulness about other dogs approaching, as opposed to excitement, which wanes with exposure.

I like to keep reactive, fearful dogs on the move, particularly when approaching another dog. Asking them to maintain a nice, brisk pace on a loose lead when parallel to the other dog is a good strategy, as we can move in and out of threshold. With some dogs, where I have misunderstood what they can cope with, I may need to retreat, getting them out of the situation and well under threshold again before asking for any simple commands. If I have to drag a dog away barking, so be it—the fault is mine and I do not correct him for not walking to heel if he is so far above threshold that any instructions are incomprehensible to him, in addition to which he may redirect his fear or frustration onto me, which I do not want. Once within a situation he can cope with, when he has calmed down and is on threshold, I may ask for simple commands he understands well and correct (and very much reward) as necessary, always ending the session on a good note.

Now, many force-free trainers will say they can do threshold training and never use a correction, but the problem is (apart from the fact that they are lying, as they do use corrections) it can take so long in practice that a year later the client still has a dog she cannot walk on her own. Or she simply cannot reduce the thresholds to a place where she never has unwanted behaviors, and the trainer gives up and tells her to keep the dog at home. These trainers are playing guessing games with the dog, which is hit or miss at best, the dog never being informed that hauling his owner around like a semi-truck, complete with loud honking, is not conducive to healthy eardrums, though his owner invariably develops nice biceps and calves.

Unless we *tell* a dog that is lunging, pulling on the lead, and vocalizing that these behaviors are wrong offering an alterative behavior that is rewarded, how is he ever to know? We need to tell him he is wrong initially via corrections when he is under threshold, so that he fully understands how to walk on a loose lead (for example) or to be quiet, which may be achieved by teaching cues for barking and silence. Then we repeat the exercise when he is on threshold, where he is still capable of learning, with no high emotions. But we do not ignore bad behaviors; instead, we address them using the same corrections and rewards for alternative good behaviors he already understands, and this is how learning takes place.

We don't want to take the dog to a place where he is lunging—that would be over threshold. We just want to take him to where he is allowing the lead to tighten ever so slightly. Or he may simply stop paying attention to us, concentrating intently on someone or something that is not his owner. In this case, I would ask for a simple command. If I am ignored, then I would correct the dog. If he returns his attention to me and obeys, I would lavishly reward him. He can still look, but he can't touch, and I would expect him to listen to me and give me his entire attention when I ask him to.

Many dogs that seem a bit rude when seeing another dog are having no real negative emotions; rather it is a mixture of barrier frustration and excitement, as they are on-lead and are not being turned loose so they can run up to the other dog and play with him as they would like. As long as they are on threshold or not too much above threshold and their brain can understand corrections and rewards, they do not need to be backed off.

With a genuinely rude lout of a dog, I may use a firm correction for ignoring me, such as a hard lead pop, and then immediately ask him a question which I know is within his capability to answer and make the right choice, for which he is rewarded if he is a good boy and does as he is asked. Ideally I will not have to correct him again for ignoring me but can reward him and aim to get him really engaged with me, concentrating on having some fun working on obedience, not on what other dogs are up to.

With a confident dog like this, the rewards do not need to be gushing, overenthusiastic outpourings of admiration when he does what I ask after a correction. I may just say "good boy" or quietly mark the good behavior. Massive rewards are not necessarily appropriate when a dog has just received a correction for ignoring a request for something reasonable, which he thought about and *chose* to refuse to do. Force-free trainers will say all rewards should be massive, and provided for every good behavior asked for, but I disagree.

If you ask your teenager to keep her room clean, you expect it to be done. Finding you have no dishes for dinner one evening, you peer into her domain, bypassing the "keep out" signs, and see a month's worth of dirty plates. "Hey!" you say, pointing, expecting them to be taken straight to the kitchen and washed. After asking several times, you finally resort to threatening to change the internet password. She throws the plates in the dishwasher. Do you hug and kiss her when she sullenly does as you have asked? No. No, you do not. Probably you simply say a polite "thank you." Similarly, a rude dog that is being asked something reasonable, which he knows how to do but chooses to disobey, should not be rewarded with generous helpings of food and praise when he really does not deserve such treatment.

Depending on the dog, his emotions, and the situation, my response to a growl or vocalization from one dog may be a hard leash pop and a firm "no," and with another it may be simply maintaining pressure on the lead, indicating that growling at another dog is not the right answer. A correction should never make the dog concerned that I am angry with him, causing additional worry or anxiety. But, when he is confident in himself, knows well what I am asking, has the capacity to obey and chooses not to, it does not benefit him to be too nice. Subsequent corrections can be more of an encouraging "Not the right answer, try again to find what I am looking for" rather than "You did wrong; don't you dare do it again, you little brat." We are teaching the dog, not threatening him, and every dog needs a slightly different teaching style in order to thrive.

There are very few force-free trainers who will deal with aggression and reactivity, particularly where large dogs are involved. They may train some small and medium-sized dogs who are overexcited, shoving on a head collar and front-pull harness, but as they never use corrections (liars!) and only use food to try to distract the dog while he is being restrained, the dog never actually learns that vocalizing and lunging is wrong. He instead hovers under threshold for months, if not years, and the trainer eventually gives up, as whenever she does go to a place where the dog starts to react, the food she is offering is not as rewarding as the endorphin release that comes from barking and lunging.

Haven't we all seen small dogs that are scared of their own shadow, are very dog-reactive, and display fear-based aggression? Their owners only venture out at night to avoid meeting other dogs, and you can bet they pray to the God of peace and love every time they leave the house. They are terrified that they are going to meet a large dog with similar reactivity issues who is being walked late at night for the exact same reason—to avoid other dogs. The large dog's problem may be that he is overexcited and too friendly, or it may be that he has a gastronomical interest in smaller dogs. Life is full of surprises in such matters.

The small dog does not necessarily have to suffer like this. In many cases, his confidence *can* be increased and his fear lessened, but to do this someone has to step in and make decisions for the team, which include keeping him safe but also putting him in a place where he *does* experience discomfort in order for him to learn. At some stage he must go on threshold, meaning he still experiences fear but only a small amount, not so much that he cannot retain the power of logical thought.

Part of keeping him safe and building his confidence is letting him know what he can and cannot do in life. As he stops vocalizing, the approaching dog will tend to be more relaxed, and instead of a situation that escalates, with both dogs using threatening body language and the fear of one dog feeding the fear of the other, the aggressor gains confidence and becomes less fearful, and the approaching dog, seeing a relaxed, neutral animal, himself stays relaxed and neutral.

The trainer of this scared dog needs to be very skilled at reading dogs, putting aside her ego and backing off if the dog cannot be worked with on that day, or maybe even ever. The corrections and alternative good behaviors must be appropriate and well timed, practiced and understood under threshold as well as when working on threshold, in addition to the rewards being sufficiently high-value to make the training sessions enjoyable for the dog and a positive learning experience, not just something to be endured with gritted teeth.

The confident but excitable large dog also does not need to live like a vampire. However, the force-free trainer has the same problem with large dogs, but for different reasons. Once again she struggles to find a working threshold, one where the dog will pay attention to her and is not so excited that he will not accept food. All too easily, the dog goes from relaxed to overstimulated in an instant upon seeing another dog, and as the trainer uses no correction to insist he pay attention to her (and take rewards), once the dog's threshold is breached, she has no option but to back away and try to get him well under threshold again. That is, if she is not being dragged at Mach 5 toward the other dog.

This is a big dog. He cannot just be picked up and marched off with if things get to be too much. Very often the force-free trainer is scared to approach the dog's threshold and therefore it is impossible for any meaningful learning to occur, as she *knows* the head collar or front-pull harness she has on him will do diddly-squat to stop him from dragging her toward the approaching dog. Then a fight may ensue, something she knows nothing about stopping. Safety has to be a paramount concern, but at the same time, the dog needs to learn while under control. This is not achieved with ineffective tools.

As a balanced trainer, my use of appropriate corrections means that I can safely train a large dog and work on his threshold, and the dog can learn what is expected of him. I don't worry that I am going to be dragged along the ground face down if I get it wrong, as I will have done some loose lead walking work already, using tools such as a martingale, e-collar or pinch collar if need be, which the dog respects and which provide clear communication between me and the dog. What sort of restraint will work on the dog will vary massively according to the root of his problem, but I need to be able to use a clear, respected correction and to remove the dog safely from a dangerous situation if I have to.

Now, with a large, fearful dog I almost certainly will *not* use a pinch collar or an e-collar, as I do not want any extra discomfort added to the mix. When a dog is fearful and backs off, a slip lead is usually a better choice. What we consider aversive and what a dog considers aversive can be very different things, and we should be led by the dog in this regard. With a big thug of a dog that is just disrespectful, has no fear, is unfriendly and will not concentrate on me when asked, hell yes, I have no problem with a pinch collar or e-collar, letting such a dog know I am not to be messed with like a force-free Barbie girl.

If you have these sorts of problems and have been told that management is your only option, at least have a chat with a good balanced or reward-based trainer. A force-free trainer may have tried and failed, or told you that these things can't be ethically fixed. Often this is untrue. And you don't have to use tools you don't agree with if you don't want to. A balanced trainer will work with you and respect your wishes, but *only* if it is safe to do so, for you, your dog, the trainer, other dogs and other animals, including livestock. Sadly, there are some dogs with incredibly poor genetics where perhaps nothing can be done and they are happier left at home and managed. But at least you'll know you have tried.

Myth Nine: My dog is autistic.

This comes up a lot and it is nonsense. Your dog does not have autism, which is a developmental disorder in humans. And autism does not get better over time. It cannot be cured if you put the work in, trying to be someone you're not. It's genetic, not a choice to behave badly as it seems your dog is making, flipping you the bird when you ask for a recall.

Your dog very much understands the body language of other dogs and is capable of communicating with them instinctively. He understands your body language too, and is probably better at recognizing human faces and expressions than I am. Many of us who are autistic learn to mask it and pretend to be something we are not, which is incredibly damaging. I have autism and I am not a dog to be trained, thank you very much. I should not have to state "I am not a dog" in the way the lawyer said he was not a cat during his Zoom call filter mishap.[31] However, such is life.

I'm glad your force-free trainer helped your dog (to an extent), but if, as you say, your dog actually *is* "autistic," then all you and your trainer have done is suppressed his behavior around other dogs or people or whatever else he was struggling with, not "cured" him, and so you have a ticking time bomb on your hands. Or you have a perfectly ordinary dog who has been successfully taught to deal with his reactivity issues and now has an improved emotional response to the situation at hand. Which is it? You can't have both. Autism does not go away, including the extreme anxiety and constant feeling of being perplexed that surrounds pretty much every human interaction. It's a spectrum, of course, but that's where many of us are at.

Do you mean to be ablest and massively offensive when you say these sorts of things? You seem to be implying that like your formerly disobedient, reactive, badly behaved dog, with a little effort and training all of my own problems, of not being able to relate to other humans, could be cured, disappearing in a puff of fairy dust. At this point I want to use language that makes a sailor blush. Where did I put that axe again?

Stop taking dogs that have reactivity problems, or don't recall, or generally are disobedient and horrible-to-live-with miscreants that you don't like very much, and start bragging to people that you cured this "autistic dog" when you finally found a good trainer. No miracles have occurred. You did not cure your dog's "autism," as it never existed except in your own deluded head. Probably your dog was an easy case to work with. All you did was come across as a total nitwit to every parent, sibling, and family member of an autistic person, every healthcare professional who works with autistic people, and, most importantly, every autistic individual who is struggling to get through life as best they can. Am I being unfair? Possibly. Have I got my point across regarding "autistic" dogs? I hope so. Rant over.

So those are the top nine myths busted, nine being a particularly nice number given that three, six and nine are the keys to the universe.[32] You may agree with me, or you may not. About dogs, that is, not the universe. Some people may think I am simply making things up, as they have a fantastic veterinarian who gave their dog "the snip," or their dog's behavioral issues could not be helped, irrespective of whether the trainer was force-free or balanced. I am introducing you to ideas, some of which may be new, others not so much.

Whatever you do with your dogs, love them and have fun. Look up the endnotes, watch some of the YouTube videos and read the articles and books. Take a deep dive into more research. Relax and binge on *America's Top Dog* with some cheesecake. I hope I have effectively covered some of the misconceptions surrounding these myths and that there is a grain of truth in what I say, but don't take my word for it. Call your dog of whatever breed, grab some treats (ideally ones you can share), go train, and have fun!

Chapter Four

Corrections and Management

Corrections

Proponents of force-free dog training and errorless learning do use corrections, despite what they may say. Think about it. How is life possible without anything bad or unpleasant happening? Even if it *was* possible, it would not necessarily be beneficial. We need a certain amount of stress in our lives to make nice things meaningful. It's possible to have too much of a good thing, and this is pretty much a universally agreed-upon concept—except in relation to dog training, where we are told the dog must only be given pleasure and never be corrected for any bad behaviors.

Many force-free trainers primarily use negative corrections (withhold rewards) as their "go-to" correction, ignoring all bad behaviors rather than issuing a positive correction. They claim they are the most kind, humane trainers *ever*, as they only use rewards in training (untrue). They tell clients that even the word "no" is abusive to dogs and training should be totally led by the dog, that the dog will calm down and do the right thing on *his* time schedule.

"Just ignore the dog and his bad behavior until he takes the food you offer to him for good behavior," they preach. These dogs can be seen everywhere, yanking their owners down the street while the owners desperately try to keep up, pleading with them to take some kibble and not wanting to put the slightest resistance on the lead as it "might hurt his poor neck." I suppose at least the owners learn to run and get fit. Wax on, wax off and all that.

I know quite a few force-free trainers who laugh at criticism like this, saying, "This does not happen! No one recommends running after the dog to keep a slack lead!" Sadly, they are wrong. This is genuinely what is being taught by militant force-free trainers in the UK, including those in some service dog organizations, which is why decent trainers—whether we call ourselves balanced, reward-based, or whatever—need to stand together against this madness. If we don't, it will spread worldwide and soon there will be no well-behaved, high-drive large dogs anywhere, adding to the number of badly behaved handbag dogs that are simply picked up and carted off when they misbehave. Soon after that, no horses will be allowed to be ridden, because if you ban pinch collars you must also ban bits and bridles. Saddles too, perhaps.

If you don't believe me, as I write, Assemblywoman Linda Rosenthal is in the process of introducing legislation which will ban the sale of e-collars in the state of New York. Once the sale of such tools is banned, it is only a small step to ban their *use*, and indeed if you read the comments of Assemblywoman Rosenthal, this is exactly what she has in mind.[1]

Similar bans are being petitioned for in California, with campaigners in San Francisco seeking to ban both the sale and use of e-collars there. If a person is caught a third time using an e-collar, the draft ordinance wants her imprisoned and her dog taken away from her.[2] Who is behind all of this? Official supporters[3] include pet shops and dog businesses of various types (primarily force-free), including trainers such as Jean Donaldson and Michael Shikashio, who is described as "a world renowned aggressive dog trainer." In my experience, if it has to be spelled out that you are a world renowned expert, how true is it? Jean Donaldson did not need, nor get, such an introduction.

Campaigning against these unfair laws can work. In 2017, Toronto implemented a bylaw[4] banning pinch collars, slip leads, choke chains, and similar devices, after thirty-three councilors voted unanimously for the ban. (Martingale collars and police dogs were exempt.) Weeks later the ban was overturned after a public outcry,[5] including from the Canadian National Institute for the Blind, which was worried about the training of their dogs and the ability of blind people to control and rely on their dogs.

This method of ignoring bad behavior can be very dangerous for dogs that get confused, excited, frustrated or desperate for attention; a lot of issues can result. You may scoff, claiming that ignoring a dog for an unwanted behavior cannot be so bad. It can. As I explained in a previous chapter, some dogs will start nipping and redirecting when they are frustrated at being ignored, leading to their being euthanized. This happens more often than you think.

A slight deviation, but if you still believe dogs do not get frustrated and angry when the cookie supply stops unexpectedly, watch the documentary *Blackfish*,[6] in which Tilikum, an orca (killer whale), kills his trainer, Dawn Brancheau, due to frustration, which turns into anger, during a show at SeaWorld. Rest in peace, Dawn Brancheau, Keltie Byrne and Daniel P. Dukes, all of whom Tilikum killed.[7]

Tilikum took the lives of these people in part due to his miserable living conditions and lack of family, and in part due to his training. This included the techniques he was subjected to, the basic methodology being positive-reinforcement clicker training (or, in Tilikum's case, whistle training) using food deprivation. Over the years, I think we can correctly assume, Tilikum became traumatized by his living conditions and treatment, causing some sort of psychotic break. There is a short clip of *Blackfish*[8] on YouTube, but if you can watch the full documentary, you should. You can find it on the main streaming providers, but, as a trigger warning, you may well cry. I did.

Positive reinforcement using clicker training is used by a great many balanced trainers and force-free trainers, and, when done correctly, is an excellent training technique. Some force-free clicker trainers use food deprivation in order to avoid more overt corrections, though claiming that food deprivation does not cause discomfort is an oxymoron. Who has never been hangry? Hunger can create more engagement in the work, or it can be used to distract the dog from competing reinforcers (things the dog would prefer to do). The more enticing the competing reinforcer, the more hunger is required.

Ninety-nine percent of trainers who utilize hunger in training do not use starvation, nor do they use the abusive techniques Tilikum was subjected to. For example, no good trainer would condone marrying clicker training with the long-term withholding of food and keeping a dog extremely hungry in order to force compliance. Having a dog skip a meal or fast overnight is not a problem, but not feeding him for days on end is abuse.

Former SeaWorld trainers state in *Blackfish* that Tilikum missed a "bridge," a signal that he had successfully done what was asked and should come back to his trainer for a reward.[9] In Chapter Two we briefly discussed bridges and free shaping with the use of a clicker/marker word (here a whistle), the trainer being part of the reward process (as opposed to luring, where no bridge is used). Tilikum missed a bridge and a reward, so no big deal if he was used to a partial reward schedule, as is common with clicker training, right? Yes, but he was also corrected when he did the right behavior, which, it seems to Tilikum, *was* a big deal.

Tilikum had performed a perimeter pec wave, a circuit of the pool while waving his pectoral fin. His trainer blew her whistle (the bridge), indicating he was right in his behavior and should return to her for a reward of fish. It is thought that Tilikum did not hear the whistle, since he did not stop and come back for a reward—which, as he was hungry because food was withheld during training to force compliance, he most certainly would have done. Instead, he made another circuit of the pool in an effort to please. He then returned to the trainer, hoping for a reward. Instead, he was corrected.

In Tilikum's mind, he had performed perfect behaviors, circling the pool twice, and yet he was being corrected for being bad! As Tilikum had not done as his trainer had taught him and returned to her for a reward when she blew her whistle, she did not reward him when he did come back and instead gave him a "three-second neutral response" to let him know he had been disobedient and the show would continue without his getting a reward since he had performed incorrectly.

Tilikum was clearly frustrated by this. He had been a good whale but had not been rewarded for it as he had hoped. To add insult to injury, he had even been corrected. Plus, there was hardly any food left! This was an issue, since training and performing was his only access to food. It was the last show of the evening, and, as I understand it, there would be no more food until his training session the next day. Tilikum was asked for more behaviors and, as there was very little food left, he was not rewarded for performing them. Unfortunately, the sequence of events created a perfect storm and an angry orca that killed his trainer.

The force-free community likes to hold orcas up as the epitome of what force-free training can achieve. This is misleading. Yes, the free-shaping ability of orca trainers is out of this world, but—and for me this is a massive *but*—these orcas are kept and trained in an abusive manner, one that Attila the Hun would pale at. They lead miserable lives that are nothing short of torture, living away from their families in tanks that are much too small, tiny concrete pens with no environmental enrichment, not to mention the withholding of food to force good behavior. Yes, force. No getting around it—*force is used in abundance* in these shows, and by clicker trainers as a whole.

Food deprivation was also used by Tilikum's previous trainers,[10] to the extent that another orca was encouraged to bully him when he did not perform tricks in the desired manner, no doubt as part of a model-rival training approach.[11] Both whales were asked for a behavior simultaneously and if Tilikum messed up but the other orca performed correctly, neither got a reward. This led to the larger, stronger whale attacking Tilikum. The whales were kept hungry to ensure they worked hard for their food.

For orcas in captivity, food is both an essential resource and the only pleasurable thing in their lives. These whales were kept hungry in order to force compliance, in the same way clicker trainers, including the famous ones who tout themselves as force-free and purely positive, withhold food from their dogs. I can assure you, being bullied into working for food would not make me form a bond of friendship with my trainer/torturer, nor, it seems, was this the case with Tilikum.

Tilikum died in 2017 from a bacterial infection,[12] which is common for captive orcas.[13] Rest in peace, Tilikum. There was a lot of victim blaming of poor Dawn, his trainer, which was grossly unfair. Yes, it is true that she participated in unethical training practices, but Tilikum was not her whale, to love and train as she pleased. She did her best under the direction of her superiors, who just wanted a flashy show for tourists. A great many orca trainers stay in their jobs to make the best life possible for the whales they love, breaking their own hearts in the process.

As we have just seen, negative emotions in training can be fatal. We all make mistakes as trainers, and some of us work with genuinely dangerous dogs that could seriously mess us up. There is nothing inherently wrong with corrections, though I can understand the force-free enthusiasts grabbing hold of this poor, frustrated whale as a weapon for their cause, saying all corrections cause frustration and violence and that he should have been rewarded for performing every behavior—still clinging onto the notion that they use no corrections, or, at a push, yes, they do use *negative* corrections (e.g., ignoring a dog that wants attention).

What about the *positive* corrections many balanced trainers commonly use (e.g., the word *no*)? Surely they are not worse? Yes, they can be! Positive corrections can create a lot of negative emotions if used on the wrong dog, in the wrong circumstances, with the wrong amount of pressure, and with the wrong tools. The consequences of getting it wrong include causing a redirection, where the dog vents his frustrations on his handler, in some cases biting her. Absolutely, we need to be careful with positive corrections too, not to mention negative reinforcement (e.g., pressure and release), since this can also cause negativity if done wrong. As can too much positive reinforcement. Really, anything in life, if used in excess, can go wrong.

Some dogs with too much food drive have to be handled carefully when food is around, even in a training session, even when there is no food withholding and the dog gets two solid meals per day. It may be that another method of reward is less stressful and exciting for such a dog, perhaps low-value food that tastes like cardboard to him. We must always train the individual dog in front of us, taking into account his mental and physical state.

So, there *are* dogs that can be trained using minimal aversives and few overt corrections, whether positive or negative. Most bad behavior can be ignored and a simple "no" used for behaviors which it is not appropriate to ignore—in addition, of course, to rewarding good behaviors. However, some dogs *cannot* be trained without effective, well-timed corrections of a type that would devastate a weaker dog. A martingale on an elderly, 10-pound Yorkshire Terrier that just wants to stop and smell the flowers occasionally as he toddles slowly along? Not appropriate. How about on a young, 40-pound Springer Spaniel that pulls his owner off-course in order to smell that delicious rabbit scent on the ground? A martingale collar, along with correct training in engagement plus pressure and release on the lead, may be a very good choice indeed. The methodology in training should always suit the dog and his owner.

We know that force-free trainers will often use ignoring a dog as a correction. What else do they use? Well, some will admit to using positive corrections, such as the word *no*, though these more typically are reward-based trainers, who believe that *no* is OK. As discussed, a very soft "no" or "wrong answer, but you did good, try again to please me a slightly different way" can be encouragement for a dog to keep seeking a solution, so they may use it in this manner, or they may use it as a genuine correction, as in "no, you have done the wrong thing, do not do so again."

"No" in this context, being a hard "no," is clearly not purely positive, yet many trainers I would categorize as reward-based market themselves as force-free or purely positive, which is deception. To them it may be common sense, in order to satisfy the requirements of the market, since everyone knows there have to be *some* corrections, right? An itsy-bitsy "no" is so mild compared to a balanced trainer's techniques and corrections that it's just fine to claim the moral high ground, isn't it? No. Not to me.

Many members of the general public do not understand that trainers may advertise themselves as force-free or purely positive and yet absolutely do use force, even aversives. Some trainers will not deny it if asked, others will parrot the line that their corrections of choice are kind and ethical, yet effective in stopping bad behaviors. Which is it? It can't be both. So how are potential clients to distinguish between the hordes of force-free trainers out there, to sort the wheat from the chaff, when they're being sold an impossibility and don't know what questions to ask?

This is damaging for the really good force-free trainers (or, to call them what they are, reward-based trainers), who do a wonderful job. Putting your name beside those of the fanatics in the force-free dog training industry will ultimately bite you in the bum. (For the trainer's sake, I hope it's with the force of a French Bulldog, not a Tibetan Mastiff.) On balance, I would rather clients choose a good force-free trainer who may market herself deceptively but trains dogs well, with appropriate corrections, than a bad trainer of whatever variety, be it a compulsion trainer or a loony-tunes purely positive trainer.

The majority of force-free trainers use corrections *they* consider to be mild, perhaps in conjunction with tools that I personally believe can never be described as positive or kind, acting as an aversive to some (but not all) dogs. A common correction for such a trainer on a large, strong dog will not be a lead "pop" but constant lead pressure along with a tool such as a head collar, which puts a lot of pressure on a dog's head and neck and which many dogs spend more time trying to remove than concentrating on walking beside their handler. Some trainers may also pop a dog with a head collar, which risks whiplash if done with enough force on a small or medium-sized dog.

In general, though, when the dog starts to pull, as he invariably will, the trainer does not immediately try to follow him to release the lead pressure, but allows the dog to maintain the pressure until he feels uncomfortable enough in the head collar to stop pulling on his own initiative. He may or may not be asked to come to heel and be rewarded for doing so. There's nothing wrong with this technique if it works for the dog and owner. Nothing wrong at all.

Often with a new tool it can be good to let the dog make his own mistake and come to his own conclusions as to whether he will pull again. Despite my dislike of the tool, I would rather a trainer use a head collar than run after a dog to "save any pressure from his neck," though a dog pulling hard into a head collar and getting whiplash as his head is yanked around is obviously not recommended. Depending on the tool, making his own mistake can be good, particularly when he already understands what is required in loose lead walking. As in all cases of using negative reinforcement and pressure and release, the dog should be taught how to take the pressure off himself in his new gear.

As you can see, many balanced trainers and force-free trainers are using the exact same techniques, not to mention the same tools, depending on the dog. What a force-free trainer misses out on, however, is the ability to back up the milder tools and training with something more meaningful should they prove to be insufficient motivation for the dog to listen to his handler. Once the dog understands pressure and release in the new tool but decides he will pull anyway as pulling is not *that* uncomfortable for him, what then? Depending on the tool, a lead pop may be required to get the best results, more often than not backed up with a reward for walking nicely. I am not talking about yanking and cranking, just applying sufficient pressure in conjunction with a tool the dog respects; the more respect a tool inspires in a dog, the less of a "pop" required. I do not like lead pops with head collars and no-pull harnesses; I like them more with a well-fitted collar (of whatever variety).

We now come to the next correction used, which is the withholding of food. You may imagine this is mainly used when teaching flashy heelwork. Not so. Many force-free and balanced trainers alike use a little bit of hunger as a motivation for a dog during general training sessions, as well as in more specialized training such as obedience and scent work, and there is nothing wrong with this. It is not unkind, and it effectively creates motivation. The kind of food withholding I object to is far more sinister. In some cases it involves starving dogs for days on end, which is unethical, cruel and in no way force-free or positive.

When an extreme force-free trainer cannot, or rather will not correct a dog, and when the dog will not engage and pay attention to her since there is something he would prefer to do (a competing reinforcer), the trainer has few tools in her toolbox. Say the dog wants to pull toward a squirrel tree, for example. She will not use a lead correction or any tool other than a flat collar, which the dog disrespects. What to do? Withhold food glorious food, of course. Once he is finally hungry enough to obey, most of the dog's **gut villi** have died and he has lost half his body weight.

A piece of cheese will never be as rewarding as the squirrel tree, with delicious baby squirrels frolicking beneath it, when we are dealing with a high-prey-drive dog. However, if the dog has not eaten for four or five days, the squirrel tree loses its shine somewhat and the dog will work for food, desperately grabbing for the proffered cheese from his trainer's hand as they walk past the tree full of mooning, taunting squirrels.

When this type of food withholding is attempted for behavioral modification—for example, learning to just walk nicely past the squirrel tree— it fails completely as soon as the dog is given a bit more food. There are only so many days a dog can be starved before he loses so much weight that he becomes emaciated. And this type of training is supposed to be ethical, science-based, force-free and purely positive? Don't make me laugh.

Management

Balanced trainers use management. Force-free trainers use management. There is nothing wrong with management: it can be an essential part of training a dog. Once again, it comes back to finding the best way to deal with a particular dog's issues, over both the short and long term, and a dog's issues will simply never be dealt with by not considering all the training options. Management is another one of the "go-to" techniques many force-free trainers turn to when they refuse to use corrections and their other techniques have not been working on the dog in question.

If this is the case, if you are a force-free trainer who cannot find a solution for a client, then put away your ego and refer the client to another trainer who *can* help. It is that simple. Do not berate the client for asking if there is another way, and start lecturing her that force-free training is the only ethical, scientific manner in which to train dogs, while the dog is now miserable, permanently confined to a tiny garden. Or a crate. Or never let off-lead. Or put into a shelter. Or euthanized. No. Just no.

This does not just occur with behavior modification, but also with pretty basic training such as working with a large dog that pulls on a lead when on walks. Not lunging at or attacking other dogs, simply pulling. For the owner, this can be very serious. Even small dogs yanking suddenly on their lead can cause injury, spraining arm muscles or even pulling people right over and breaking their bones, particularly old or disabled people. With a large dog, the owner may be too scared to walk the dog anymore. Or a dog walker may be hired, but this negates a major part of the pleasure of owning a dog: going for walks! It's also hideously expensive, and invariably the dog is not walked several times a day but, if he is lucky, once or twice a week.

Not every dog that pulls on the lead can be cured by engagement and treats only, or by stopping and refusing to walk with them anymore. Neither do head collars and front-pull harnesses work with every dog, particularly bigger, high-drive, powerful dogs that have been bred to be very resistant to discomfort. A martingale collar or slip lead may be effective, but if not, a pinch collar or e-collar may work well with such a hard-pulling dog. The dog can then be taken on the kids' school runs, go for walks alone, and overall live a much happier life than if he can only be exercised by a dog walker, maybe once a day if lucky.

On a similar note, many force-free trainers—yes, *trainers*, not owners—will announce with great pride that their own Border Collie, Rottweiler or other high-energy breed is only allowed off-lead in an enclosed, well-fenced area, as he has *no recall*. They call themselves responsible dog owners and yet seem to think that their dog having no recall in public is … err … admirable, wearing it like a badge of honor. Management may be necessary for a fearful dog that may flee if off-lead and scared of something, but it should absolutely not be considered the norm for an ordinary adolescent dog that just finds other things more interesting than his owner, and possibly always will.

Being on a long line or Flexi lead is not the same as being off-lead, especially for a high-energy dog, and, if you don't have a massive garden, renting an off-lead fenced enclosure is prohibitive on a daily basis, never mind two or three times a day. So these dogs only get to be off-lead and enjoy the freedom to be a dog once a week or so. For what? As the owner has been taught, e-collars are torture devices. Again, it depends on the circumstances. An e-collar is not for every dog and owner, but, when used *correctly*, it will quickly and effectively ensure recall in your typical confident, adolescent dog, allowing him freedom and allowing you not to have to be hyper-vigilant for any distractions.

Chapter Four. Corrections and Management 97

Other management techniques typically relate to inside the home. Cats are confined upstairs or re-homed in favor of the new dog (I will see you in hell for this), or the dog is crated or kept in a utility room away from the family, particularly if he nips at the heels of kids or has other unacceptable behaviors such as counter surfing and raiding trash bins. Corrections would prevent this, but they will not be used by the force-free trainer, so the management technique of excluding the dog from daily life is used instead. Or, in some homes, the management is achieved by every inhabitant of the house tiptoeing around the dog.

Castration/spaying is another management technique, and we have already discussed in Chapter Three why this does not necessarily work. Sadly, a management technique that is increasingly popular with force-free trainers is the use of drugs to control a dog and calm him down, preventing him from having any personality or joy in life. All so he can conform to "normal" standards of behavior (for humans, not dogs) without the use of corrections. This is plain wrong. Such trainers can take a run and jump off a high cliff.

Now, I am not 100 percent against the use of medications when there are severe behavioral issues and a dog needs to have the edge taken off him while a good balanced or reward-based trainer kindly and sympathetically puts rules and boundaries in place. In addition, some dogs have canine compulsive disorder (CCD), which is an anxiety disorder involving behaviors that are natural but taken to the extreme. This can involve repetitive, obsessive behaviors such as fly catching, tail chasing, and excessive licking, causing sores.[14]

One of the worst cases of CCD I have seen involved a dog staring at her reflection in puddles, oven doors, mirrors, tablet screens—you name it, she stared at it—for 99 percent of the day, panting and distressed, watching for the slightest movement. Such extreme behaviors are mainly down to genetics, and if every attempt has already been made to meet the dog's legitimate needs, medication may give her relief from CCD and a better quality of life, even if it has to be permanent for the rest of her life.

In general, though, veterinarians and other balanced trainers, including myself, are seeing a massive increase in dogs being drugged as a management strategy, when all the dog needs is to be trained in an appropriate way. Do not get a Hungarian Vizsla and then complain when you need to take (very) long walks every single day. That's what you signed up for! Do not get a Dutch Herder if you object to the word *no*, and do not get a Border Collie when you have ten cats and five toddlers and live smack-bang in the middle of a noisy city, with no garden or quiet environment for walks.

Drugging these dogs so they have no energy, personality or enthusiasm for their lives is not the answer. Sure, they may no longer chew the baseboards, bark and chase bicycles, but they are not happy, contented dogs, having their needs adequately met. All drugs have side effects, and your dog cannot tell you what they are. If your force-free trainer has persuaded you to get your veterinarian to prescribe a sedative such as gabapentin, research the human side effects[15] as well as those suspected to occur in dogs.[16] Speak to humans who could not tolerate the drug and ask yourself, Is this how my dog is feeling? All because "no" is considered a dirty word?

Sadly, we do not see owners thoroughly researching the drugs they are told to give their dogs like gravy bones. Instead, the typical owner thinks everything is going swimmingly. Her dog is popping so many pills that he rattles, and he is so calm she can even give him regular "days off" from being walked, each and every week of the year, just as her friends do with their drugged pets. Why should they walk their dogs every day? They deserve some "me time," don't they? The poor chumps that are called "dogs" are expected to just vegetate in their houses, often for days on end, with no walking, no running free, no checking their neighborhood for scent marks (the equivalent of our e-mails). You know, call me rude, but maybe a soft, plush animal toy would be a better idea if you dislike making the effort to walk your dog even once per day?

I rarely go onto internet forums, but when I do, I see this suggested more and more often. Stop walking your dog! Walking is bad for your dog! Your dog will be happier at home! Really? Scatter a bit of kibble for environment enrichment and all will be fine? Management strategies are not a substitute for a dog living life as a dog, and if he's being that aggressive, maybe he needs a good boot up the backside and be told to behave. Oops, that was politically incorrect. My bad! Obviously I am not endorsing kicking any dog, other than if under attack, but if I did not laugh, I would cry.

This is where I fear we are headed: increased use of sedatives, more management and dumbing down dogs into creatures that never misbehave because they are dead behind the eyes. Then we will see an increase in the banning of large breeds, building on existing dangerous-dogs legislation, as would that not be convenient? A few amendments here and there, a few thousand dollars in lawyer fees and boom, big dogs banned. Small-breed Doodle and Poo owners would give a big sigh of relief.

But they shouldn't relax just yet. The dumbing down of high-drive small dogs will soon come to be added to the agenda, as who wants those nasty Jack Russell Terriers about, with their snappy, pointy teeth and their yippity-yapping? Is that really what we want, what force-free trainers want? Taking away small working breeds and to be left only with curly-haired teddy-bear look-alikes? To be in the position Ukraine was in several years ago, when over eighty dog breeds were banned, including

Chapter Four. Corrections and Management 99

Jack Russell Terriers?[17] Labradors too. Don't be smug. It may be your dog's breed next.

After all, they are already starting to come for certain small breeds, primarily on health grounds, including in the UK.[18] The Netherlands has banned the breeding of Pugs[19] in addition to Affenpinschers, Boston Terriers, English Bulldogs, French Bulldogs, Griffon Belge, Griffon Bruxellois, Petit Brabancons, Japanese Chins, King Charles Spaniels, Pekingese and Shih Tzus. Are any of your favorite breeds on this list? Do you want to be told you cannot own one of these gorgeous little dogs? I don't. By all means, put pressure on breeders to only breed with health-tested stock, to do away with extremes, to outcross, but don't ban these lovely dogs as the Netherlands and other EU countries have now done.

Those of you who watched with impunity, or even applauded as breed-specific legislation was implemented and large dog breeds banned may not now be feeling so smug. You are also in a pickle. No longer is being small and cute a get-out-of-jail-free card. Your little brachycephalic princess, your breed that requires "assistance" to reproduce are in the sights of the animal welfare campaigners. They are not content with outcrossing, introducing more healthy genes and a better structure into these dogs. They are banning them, just as they have done with large, high-drive breeds. Thankfully that day has not yet come in the U.S.—but what you Americans do have to contend with is owners just ditching their badly behaved dogs.

Rehoming and euthanasia are often the management strategy of last resort for frustrated dog owners who have a dog they neither like nor love and that is residing in their home like a roommate who raids the fridge, steals your Netflix password, and never pays the rent on time. There is a building sense of horror and despair among those who work in animal rescue. We all expected a massive influx of "COVID puppies" when working from home was discontinued and kids went back to school. What I suspect many rescue workers did not expect were some of the reasons for rehoming. Spaniel Aid UK reported that in the first six months of 2022 they received 552 requests from people who wanted to surrender their dogs. Out of those 552 dogs, 230 had a history of biting humans, and 250 displayed resource guarding.[20]

Spaniels are not a breed that most people would immediately think of as being surrendered for biting people. XL Bullies maybe, but Spaniels not so much, and yet here we are. We do see rage syndrome in golden and red Cocker Spaniels,[21] but 34.7 percent of the dogs with requests to surrender were working Cocker Spaniels,[22] which, unless they come from back yard breeders and have parents that never actually worked, do not tend to be full of rage, otherwise they could not effectively do their job. Which, of course, is the entire point. Working Cocker Spaniels were far and away the largest percentage surrendered, with English Springer Spaniels coming in next at 18.3 percent and Sprockers (Springer Spaniel × Cocker Spaniel) following at 12.6 percent.[23]

As I mentioned previously, many high-drive breeds are being let down by force-free trainers who will not give them rules or outlets for their energy and drive. Spaniels should not be racking up human bite histories. I do not believe there is suddenly a massive amount of genetically defective, fearful Spaniels in circulation, but when a dog's needs are not met, and when a high-drive dog is not properly trained and becomes frustrated, this is what happens, irrespective of how inherently good-natured and kind the breed actually is.

Euthanasia is the last resort when a shelter cannot be found and the family in question may love their dog but do not like him, and just cannot put up with his behavior any longer. This trend is rising, as any vet will tell you. The dogs at the greatest risk for rehoming or euthanasia are heavier-weight dogs and those with aggression issues, including biting, both within the family and toward strangers.[24]

Yes, girls and boys, these are the dogs that force-free trainers cannot cope with. Thirty-four percent of owners say they would consider euthanasia before rehoming their dog, which may or may not be justified, we can't tell. But it's alarming nevertheless, and I suspect it involves the demonization of too many dogs that *could* be helped. It's also worth noting that a 2022 article stated there are approximately six thousand "kill shelters" in the UK, describing such shelters as being set up to kill animals for profit.[25] Kill shelters are also common in the U.S., but most UK owners are not aware that they exist, and that the snappy, nervous dog they got tired of and dumped may end up in one.

It's an incredibly sad state of affairs when a dog that is not a "bad dog," as we discussed in Chapter Three, suffers this fate. How tragic when the dog could be saved and rehomed, or his behavior changed enough so he could stay in his current home if only he was trained in a balanced manner with boundaries and consequences for bad behavior. Referring a dog to a decent, balanced trainer or a good reward-based trainer who uses some corrections is preferable to euthanizing him, but it goes against the ethos of extreme force-free trainers, who maintain that no force must ever be used, even to save a dog's life. Really? I have no words. Did you get "dog trainer" confused with "state executioner"?

As we have seen, all force-free trainers *are* using corrections and tools, it's just that the corrections and tools they are prepared to use vary significantly. When their methods fail, the inexperienced and inept among them use very unethical management strategies, drugs and then surgery,

Chapter Four. Corrections and Management

to try to do what a balanced trainer or a good reward-based trainer can perhaps do without having to resort to such extreme measures. Why are extremists clinging to this force-free agenda when dogs' lives are being lost? For some, yes, it's simply a marketing strategy, but for others it's an ethos they've bought into and really believe, the mantra of "death before discomfort" being one they live by and ultimately see as more important than the dogs in their care.

Chapter Five

More on Training Tools and Equipment

What are the choices for dealing with a dog that suddenly lunges when he spots something he *really* wants to ~~kill~~ investigate, such as a squirrel? You can be hypervigilant on walks and try to redirect him first, but there is always a time when you miss something. Pulling hard and suddenly into a flat collar risks damage to the trachea, particularly for small dogs. Letting go of the dog entirely because he is too strong may allow him to run onto a road. But he needs *something* to control him, or to not be walked anywhere there are trees, which may not be realistic.

Most force-free trainers will use a flat collar or a harness, depending on the owner's preference. On rare occasions some will use a slip lead to issue a correction, not just to prevent a dog's disappearing over the horizon. I have seen force-free trainers who work their dogs in IGP reluctantly admit they use slip leads while training protection, as it gives the dog more clarity while he is in drive and hence in a high state of excitement. So, when it's convenient...

If you need to use a slip lead, then use one. Some dogs learn that they can slip their collar, and then what do you do? Some harnesses can be slipped out of, as can head collars, particularly by dogs that are close to brachycephalic. I have never known a Rottweiler that cannot easily slip out of a head collar. A well-fitted slip lead, though, is not so easy to get out of. Better that a dog is kept safe and is not able to panic and run off. As ever, train the dog that is in front of you. I am not saying to put genuinely brachycephalic dogs on a slip lead; such dogs require a comfortable, well-fitting harness and are not capable of pulling you behind them, whereas a Pugweiler can. With ease.

A variation on a slip lead (a slip lead being a collar and lead in one) is a martingale collar. A martingale tends to be made of thick nylon or leather, along with a metal chain that will tighten around the dog's neck

Chapter Five. More on Training Tools and Equipment 103

if he pulls. There are also choke chains, which are made all of metal, and fur savers, which are all-metal collars with big links (like a chain) that are generally used on large dogs. Slip leads, martingale collars and fur savers can be used with a "dead link" so they can only close a certain amount and will *not* actually choke the dog. Or they can be set to continually tighten. It depends on your needs.

Since a slip lead is all in one, I always carry a light cord model to catch stray dogs or help break up a dog fight. It can be very quickly and easily slipped on and off, and can be useful alongside a collar that stays on during the whole walk and carries a dog's ID. A lead can easily be put on and taken off martingale and fur saver collars as desired. As these collars can tighten if required, they provide clearer communication to a dog than a flat collar. Dogs often pull hard and choke themselves in flat collars, so collars such as martingales, at worst, are no different in action to an incorrectly used flat collar that the owner has been told not to remove. At best, they are all that is required to stop the dog pulling—always along with proper training, which includes the dog learning engagement with his owner.

Yanking and pulling on the lead is one of the most commonly requested issues that trainers are asked to advise on. A flat collar may be fine, depending on the dog. With most small dogs that have low to moderate drive, this is all that is needed. The dog learns pressure and release correctly. The owner learns how to engage her dog (keep his interest and get him excited about training), use rewards properly, and issue fair lead corrections. Everyone is happy. Or a harness may be used if this is more comfortable and appropriate for the dog in question. Most people can pick small dogs up if they give any trouble. However, they generally don't once they understand behavior.

For a bigger and/or stronger dog there are additional choices, again depending on the dog and on the owner's preferences. A slip lead or martingale collar may work well, along with training in the same way as with a small dog. Do not buy into the marketing claim that head collars and front-pull harnesses do not involve force and are inherently kinder than a slip lead or martingale. They may be right for you and your dog or they may not, but irrespective, they use force and discomfort to ensure compliance.

I find head collars too aversive and front-pull harnesses to be ineffective and overcomplicated to use. Getting the timing right when pulling various straps whenever your dog is excited and going full steam ahead is beyond most owners, myself included. However, some trainers and owners love these tools and I have seen them used very effectively. If either of them work for you, then go for it! Unfortunately, both of these tools are commonly used *just* as a restraint by inexperienced trainers of all ilks, without teaching engagement, reward, corrections, and pressure and release. This approach may work, but when it does the effect tends to be temporary, the dog becoming habituated to the discomfort of the head collar/front-pull harness, and ultimately any tool used in this way acts merely as a Band-Aid.

Head collars are the mainstay of many force-free trainers in this type of pulling/lunging on the lead scenario. If a flat collar does not work, then a head-collar is reached for, slip leads and martingale collars being considered abusive. Other trainers will reach for a front-pull harness first, though I would say a head collar is the more popular option, particularly for dogs bigger than a Spaniel.

When the dog is not engaged and does not understand pressure and release, or if a head collar is just wrong for the dog, it can cause quite nasty sores, particularly when the owner is told this is the only option left and to persist in its use even when the dog is being rubbed and is clearly uncomfortable. Most head collars are made of nylon, and even soft, padded webbing can rub and injure the thin skin on a dog's face. Head collars are hated by many dogs, who desperately try to get them off their head no matter how long a trainer takes to try and desensitize the dog to wearing one. Ladies, they are like putting a tight bra with spaghetti-thin straps on double D boobs. The pain never goes away.

Unless fitted and worn very loose, head collars exert constant pressure, pressing on the nerves and fascia of a dog's head. If tight, they will do this even when not in active use. The fascia is the connective tissue that holds blood vessels, nerves, muscles, etc., in place. A dog's head is pretty bony and has only a light covering of muscle and skin in most places. There is very little cushioning between the head collar and the nerves and fascia it is sitting on top of. A head collar does not just pull the dog's head toward the handler and give her leverage, it can also be used to cause extreme discomfort. Not so force-free or positive now, is it?

Large breeds with short noses, such as the Rottweiler, Dogue de Bordeaux, and Mastiff, will remove most head collars in seconds, which could leave you in a sticky situation. Head collars, and pinch collars as well, should have a safety strap, a short line that links to a normal flat collar. These tools very rarely fail or come off, but as it is not unheard of, better to be safe than sorry.

Other reasons I dislike head collars? Clamping a dog's mouth shut is not just uncomfortable for him, it also takes away his primary defenses, being his teeth. This makes some dogs feel insecure and fearful while on walks with other dogs running around them. Some dogs just give up and become shut down. As with a sleeve muzzle, a head collar which sits tight around a dog's nose will prevent his mouth from opening fully, restricting

Chapter Five. More on Training Tools and Equipment

his ability to pant and preventing him from cooling down in hot weather. This is incorrect use. A head collar should *not* be fitted this tightly over the nose. If you need to have it this tight to prevent pulling and lunging, then a head collar is not the right tool for your dog. Many head collars will continue to tighten around the nose and cannot be properly adjusted, so if you are going to use one, buy a more expensive model that you can avoid tightening fully on the muzzle.

In addition to removing his defenses, strapping a dog's mouth shut is just not polite. Dogs do not appreciate it. Could you damage your relationship with your dog by clamping his mouth shut and forcing him into a device which is always uncomfortable, constantly putting pressure on his facial nerves? You might. It's a helluva rude way to treat your dog. And this is considered more positive than a martingale collar? a slip lead? Really?

As with any tool, when recommending a head collar the trainer should explain to the client that it may work well or it may not be the answer. If the dog suddenly stops pulling and his tail and ears go down, and he trudges glassy-eyed beside his owner, then the collar is acting as an aversive as opposed to providing the trainer with a useful tool. If the dog has always been allowed to goof around, then this is understandable. I would be a bit depressed if suddenly I had no option but to behave. The glumness should not persist when the dog understands what is required and is not pulling, though.

Maybe this is what the client wants, a dog that is obedient but despondent—many do, sadly. But this sort of reaction from a dog cannot be said to be positive. Some dogs will recover their good spirits, becoming habituated to the pressure of a head collar, but the control can start to wane as the discomfort no longer bothers them so much. Other dogs understand what is required, and how to switch off the pressure and return to their happy, tail-wagging selves. If so, all is well. Job done! Or the dog may remain suppressed and unhappy, but obedient on the walks he no longer looks forward to.

I have no objection to force-free trainers, or any other trainer, suggesting a head collar. Head collars work well for a great many people and their dogs, even though I personally would recommend going through other options and tools first, as this particular tool is not really for me, in the same way that a pinch collar may not be the thing for other trainers. We all have our preferences. I respect that. It should be all about the dog and the client, *not* about the trainer.

I don't deal in absolutes, and where people do, I see it as a red flag. If I am prepared to accept that a head collar is a good, appropriate tool for many dogs, then why is my right to use a pinch collar being petitioned to be removed? Both may be experienced as an aversive if used incorrectly or on the wrong dog. There is no single solution for every dog. Taking away my tools leaves me with no effective way to communicate and work with the dogs I own and train, while the force-free trainer merrily abuses dogs, shutting them down or leaving them out of control when a pinch collar or even a simple martingale or slip lead may be ideal for them. Sorry not sorry. That does not work for me.

We know that anything that tightens around the neck is out of bounds for the vast majority of force-free trainers, so what else is in their arsenal for dogs that a head collar will not prevent from pulling, or that will not wear one? It's funny that sores never seem to be a deterrent to their continued use. But if a client kicks up a fuss about her scarred, miserable dog, then usually the answer is now a front-pull harness. Similar to a head collar, a front-pull harness works via discomfort and, at times, pain, and it also can cause cuts and muscle pulls. I have heard it said it can cause arthritis if used long enough incorrectly, but I have never seen this personally. At least when not in use, a front-pull harness should be very comfortable for the dog to wear, which is a big bonus compared to the majority of head collars.

The front-pull harness works by preventing the dog from being able to move one of his front legs forward. The harness has a strap which fits vertically between the dog's front legs, with one or more rings at the center of the chest or, for more leverage, placed on a strap that goes across the chest. One end of the lead is attached to this front ring, and the other end is attached to a ring on the top of the harness, on the dog's back. The lead therefore forms a loop between the two rings.

When the dog pulls, the end of the lead attached to the chest is yanked toward the handler, so that it presses against the inside of the dog's leg which is closest to her. This pressure stops the correct gait of the dog, preventing the leg from moving forward and even pulling him off balance if applied strongly enough. When the dog walks on a loose lead, the main pressure felt from the lead is via the ring that sits on the part of the harness on top of his back.

A dog that ignores the action on his leg can pull his leg muscles; cheaper harnesses may cut into the leg, causing sores. Many big, strong dogs ignore the pain and can get their legs moving forward enough to yank back on their leads, and a tug of war ensues. The harness is doing little good, and the dog is still towing his owner about wherever he wants. Clients can also find it hard to fiddle about with the two ends of the lead, swapping which part they pull on depending on how well the dog is walking.

So, what tools do balanced trainers use that are considered cruel and unnecessary by the force-free brigade? The most self-righteous will

Chapter Five. More on Training Tools and Equipment

condemn anything but a flat collar. Some will be OK with a head collar or front-pull harness, and a very small minority will use a slip lead. What they will not advocate are pinch collars and e-collars. But with the right dog, and provided they are used correctly—and remember, any tool can be abused—these can be excellent tools.

When you use any tool or method of communication with a dog, you and the dog should be working in partnership with each other. A pinch collar used on a trained dog who understands what is being asked of him allows a trainer to use an extremely light touch, as the dog is fully aware that if he ignores the trainer, the action of the collar will have unpleasant consequences for him. This is particularly useful when the dog is in a highly aroused state and is tempted to ignore the trainer and instead do his own thing.

Many dog owners look at pinch collars and think they look like barbaric torture devices, and they are right! They *don't* look particularly appealing. I personally don't like the look of them, no matter how many years I have used them. But they suit certain dogs, and I am not going to put a visual distaste of mine over a dog's welfare. In the same way people imagine a scalpel being so sharp that if they just touched it, it would cut right through to the bone, they imagine that if they put a pinch collar on their dog he will whimper and whine in pain as his neck is torn apart. In both cases, this is untrue.

A pinch collar is not going to hurt your dog when it is correctly used. Unlike a head collar, a pinch collar is comfortable for your dog until it is in use. Some dogs, even when properly trained, will still pull hard into a pinch collar on occasion—it is not *that* aversive—but the majority of dogs will give it a good degree of respect. It is a communication tool, nothing more, nothing less. Some say its prongs mimic the teeth of another dog, one reason many dogs immediately understand the correction it provides.

Every dog owner knows there are many instances where a dog would prefer to do his own thing and ignores his trainer. This is where the pinch collar can be used to give a lead pop. No longer is the trainer asking the dog to work with her, rather she is *telling* the dog to obey her commands, the pinch collar reinforcing to the dog that although he still has choices, it is very much in his best interests to do as he is told. There is nothing wrong with telling a dog what to do. He. Is. A. Dog. The use of a pinch collar in this way allows the trainer to open a fair, easily understood line of communication with the dog, while retaining the ability to work with a light touch. She does not have to yank and crank on the pinch collar; a small pop is generally sufficient.

The pinch collar, like any tool, is only abusive when it is misused. The trainer should be capable of clearly showing the dog what is required of him, including the consequences of ignoring commands, so that there is no misunderstanding between them. In the wrong hands, a pinch collar can be abusive, as can a flat collar, as can a trainer's voice. Shouting and yelling at a dog can be emotionally abusive in a way that is harsher than any punishment from a tool such as a pinch collar. After all, shouting at a dog is personal and can ruin a good relationship and bonds of trust, whereas a lead correction does not have to have that personal aspect to it when used alone, with no voice.

I like to think of a pinch collar like a knife. If I'm cutting cake, I don't need any special sort of fancy chef's knife that is made in Japan by Samurai. A fairly dull one from Walmart will do just fine. For a low-drive, compliant dog that is keen to please and rarely exerts his own will once he understands what is being asked of him, a flat collar, aka a dull knife, is all that is required to cleanly and easily cut the cake and get nice heelwork, achieving a pleasing result with minimal effort.

However, if the dog is a high-drive working line German Shepherd, the task is more akin to cutting a steak. A dull knife may do the job, but it's hard work and the end result looks messy. Yes, the steak is cut, but not in an optimal way. In this scenario, a very sharp knife allows me to cleanly and safely cut the meat with a small amount of effort, without tearing or damaging it. Of course, like a sharp knife, a pinch collar is not for the inexperienced and should only be used by trainers who understand how to fairly communicate with and train a dog.

Pinch collars are also called **prong collars**, as the action is different from that of a flat collar or a standard collar that tightens, such as a martingale or a slip lead. Most pinch collars also tighten, but the action is a pinching one, not choking, the pressure being distributed evenly around the neck and not just on the trachea (windpipe). This is one reason many dogs find communication clearer with a pinch collar than with a standard collar, where the pressure is concentrated on a small area.

Dog owners and trainers should always use the tool appropriate to the job and in line with their skills. Just as a three-year-old child would not be asked to prepare Wagyu steak with a sharp knife, an inexperienced dog owner should not buy a working line German Shepherd Dog, a Belgian Malinois, a Rottweiler, nor any other high-drive breed that is typically "too much dog" for the average person. However, an experienced handler of these breeds can effectively use a pinch collar and create a work of art: a well-behaved dog that is a pleasure to own and watch work. An inexperienced owner, with the advice and coaching of a good balanced trainer, can learn how to do this too.

One of the criticisms many force-free trainers have is that some of the tools a balanced trainer may use, such as a pinch collar, are totally

Chapter Five. More on Training Tools and Equipment   109

unnecessary, and that as *they* don't use these tools (and since they consider them cruel, never having seen a pinch collar in real life, never mind used one), no one should get to use them. They don't point to the dogs they have failed, that now never go for walks or that are drugged. Nope. Those dogs are conveniently swept under the carpet.

"We must be the only arbiters of all things good and bad, and we will ban everything we don't agree with," seems to be the way they roll. Why don't they use their cash to prosecute heinous dog abusers under the current laws, instead of pouring money into inventing new and unnecessary laws? They won't, though. They seem to believe they are Judge Dredd. Maybe in their dreams they are bellowing out, "I am the law!"

Will the average low-drive, eager to please, show line Labrador require a pinch collar on his daily walks? No, generally he will not. Usually a martingale collar, slip lead, or, if the owner desires, head collar or front-pull harness will do the job nicely. Will the average high-drive, eager to please (himself) Dutch Herder require one? Yes, maybe he will, in order to handle him with a light touch in challenging situations, a pinch collar (unlike a head collar) not being brought into action 99 percent of the time.

Correctly using a pinch collar is not shutting a dog down, suppressing his behaviors, hurting him, or causing him to redirect on his handler out of pain and fear. Sure, he may temporarily look a bit glum the first time it is used to enforce control, as I explained previously, but that's not being shut down. Aren't you a bit upset when you don't get your own way? No wonder your Dutch Herder is shocked when for the first time in his entire privileged life he is walking along at *your* pace instead of his own. Call his name, though, and he will look up and make eye contact with you, his tail twirling like a helicopter propeller. A shut-down dog does not behave this way, happily engaging when asked.

Loose lead walking is a reasonable request for any dog, aside from those with extreme fear or requiring other advanced behavioral modification work. Setting boundaries and rules for a dog takes any confusion away from him. In the case of a pinch collar used to enforce loose lead walking, pulling hard into the collar is not a good life choice for him, nor is eliciting a lead pop from his handler. Large, high-drive dogs can learn to walk nicely on lead without being shouted at, jerked about, emotionally traumatized, or whatever else the general public is told will happen if they go to a balanced trainer. When we know what our realistic choices are, life is generally happier and we are more content than when we are pining for something we *may* get away with occasionally and at other times will get us into big trouble.

In addition to pinch collars, many balanced trainers use e-collars. Now, there are a fair number of ways to use an e-collar, and the way most of us are familiar with is as a positive correction, to stop a dog from doing something bad. This can be enforcing a recall, stopping a dog from chasing cars and bicycles, or in behavioral modification for a wide range of issues.

However, many trainers these days also use e-collars in an extremely sophisticated way, as the mainstay of their training. E-collars can be used as negative reinforcement, using pressure and release, a light stimulation, as a means of *communication*. This is in no way aversive, and in fact some trainers will turn this light stimulation into a conditioned response. Bart and Michael Bellon, with their NePoPo system,[1] are some of the trainers who utilize e-collars in this manner, with solid scientific theory underpinning what they are doing. It may have become a bit of a dog-training cult, but in many ways a good one!

E-collars have the advantage that the dog does not have to be physically close to the trainer, or indeed on-lead, in order for the trainer to give him a correction. This provides a trainer who uses e-collars correctly with a massive advantage. As with anything in life, you must select carefully among balanced trainers who use e-collars to find one who has sufficient knowledge and is right for you. E-collar training generally takes time, as does all good training. In addition to the training itself, the dog needs to go through several training sessions, perhaps longer, where he is taught what the e-collar stimulation *means* and *how to take the pressure off*. He is not learning any new behaviors at this point, just how the e-collar works. This type of work is very much about educating the dog, *not* zapping him and causing pain. Some trainers disagree and think e-collars require no introduction and should be used as a positive correction with a high stimulation.

It never pays to buy a cheap e-collar, and the very best ones are about five times my monthly rent! Totally unaffordable, but in life you often get what you pay for. Thankfully good, more affordable models are avaliable. Another limitation is that the device requires a remote control, which some dogs can become savvy about, watching to see if an inexperienced owner has forgotten his remote or if the collar is turned on and has power. Plus, in an emergency, grabbing and using a remote control may not come naturally to many people. However, if the dog is introduced to the e-collar correctly, it will almost never have to be actually used, and many emergencies will be avoided, the dog choosing to make good decisions with no prompting.

I would not want to rely solely on an e-collar for my everyday walks with my own dogs, given that it is soon to be banned where I live, with such bans spreading all over Europe and soon, I am sure, in the U.S.[2] This is a travesty, and will prevent many dogs living their best lives, as e-collars are amazing tools, helping dogs that would otherwise lead very unhappy "managed" lives. Sadly, I find many of the e-collar fanatics to be as bad as

Chapter Five. More on Training Tools and Equipment

the force-free extremists, with lots of arguments over which is the best way to use them, attacking each other with vitriol.

Even if you don't want to use an e-collar to train obedience with negative reinforcement but just want a good recall when on walks, the dog must be taught what the e-collar stimulation means. Some trainers will "charge" an e-collar as a first step, in the same way we talked about **charging a clicker** or marker word in Chapter Two. Before anything else, we want to find the lowest level where the dog *feels* the stimulation so we can ascertain what is going to be a good working level for training. In order to do this, some trainers use a super-light stimulation paired with food, and a conditioned response is created. When the dog's back is turned and he cannot see the trainer, she will press the button, giving him a stimulation; if he turns to her, looking for food, then she knows he feels it, and she can work from there depending on what she wants to train. If he does nothing, she knows he does not feel it, and she can turn the stimulation up a tiny amount and repeat the process until he does react and come for a food reward on feeling the stimulation.

Other trainers will find a dog's working level by increasing the stimulation until she sees the dog react in some way, possibly by twitching an ear, shaking their head or neck or looking around. If the dog jumps in surprise, vocalizes or looks anxious, these are all signs that the stimulation is already too high. There are merits to using both of these techniques, and much will depend on the individual trainer, the training she seeks to achieve, the dog in question and the trainers expereince using e-collars.

Although most people use an e-collar *just* to enforce recall or stop poor behaviors, it can be so much more. Recall in and of itself depends on good engagement which *must* come first, the e-collar ensuring that the dog gives the handler his attention, which can prevent the unwanted behavior of running off, acting as an invisible lead. Having a dog come to you when you ask is mainly down to engagement, rather than using the threat of force. However, an e-collar can be used to let the dog know that what you say goes. If you ask for a recall, then he must come back to you, though if good engagement is not there, the recall will invariably be slow and reluctant.

The e-collar can be used for many other behaviors, not just to enforce rules by the handler but to trick the dog into thinking a certain behavior is not advisable for him irrespective of the handler's presence. Used in this way, the correction comes from what the dog is doing at the time he receives a stimulation, though great care must be taken to ensure the timing is 100 percent accurate and the dog associates the correction with the right thing. This can be used for dogs that chase cars, for example, or raid bins, both of which he needs to understand will have bad consequences for him, even if his owner is not there.

An e-collar used to stop dangerous behavior usually *is* used in the manner of an aversive, ideally as a one-time "this will hurt, so don't ever do it again" type of deal, in order to prevent the dog from doing something which could get himself killed, a scenario which is often set up by the trainer. As I said, a great deal of skill is needed to effectively use an e-collar in such a situation, and yes, it does involve force and possibly pain. So what? Much better that a dog gets a short, sharp shock and now believes biting car tires is a bad idea than to get run over. Also better that he learn to recall on command than to chase another dog out of the park and onto a road, getting both of them flattened by a truck.

Don't get me wrong, *great care* needs to be taken when applying any tool in a genuinely aversive manner. This is why finding a good, experienced trainer is so essential. If a dog chases cars, say, and the trainer just whips a cheap e-collar on him and zaps him at the highest setting when he runs up to a car, which has now braked and is at a standstill, chances are the dog will become terrified of cars. He may never want to go near a car again and shy away from them as his owner is walking him along the pavement. To make the correct association, of *chasing* cars with an aversive, is not so easy.

As well as stopping bad behaviors with e-collars, more and more trainers are using them to *teach behaviors* with negative reinforcement backed up by positive reinforcement. There are *so* many behaviors you can teach and back up with an e-collar: it is not just for corrections. Not everyone is into trick training, or training at all, and most people just want a well-behaved dog they know will recall when on walks; an e-collar can help train dogs in such behaviors. E-collars are for everyone, not just elite trick trainers and people with large, out-of-control dogs.

You can see, then, that an e-collar used as a negative reinforcer can be a very effective tool in dog training, can you not? It is just aversive enough to be irritating and encourage a good behavior, more a communication tool than an actual aversive, and in some cases ruling out a harsher positive correction at all. So why do force-free trainers not use e-collars?

Sadly, most force-free trainers have drunk the Kool-Aid and believe the old, debunked studies in which e-collars were used in an abusive way and which should never have passed an ethics committee review. No, their solution for high-drive dogs, which tend to be medium-sized or small dogs, is to reach for much harsher aversives that they *do* like and approve of, such as head collars attached to a long line, which, if they work—a big "if"—often end up shutting down the dog, since a head collar's action cannot be turned off and so it is a constant negative reinforcer and an occasional negative correction, whereas an e-collar only has an action when required. Which may be once or twice a year. The refusal to

Chapter Five. More on Training Tools and Equipment 113

use e-collars makes no logical sense. The baby is being thrown out with the bathwater.

An e-collar does not have to be used with an electrical stimulation; it can also be used with a vibration, just as your phone or electric toothbrush vibrates. In general, though, dogs do not like a vibration and actually prefer a very light stimulation. Many collars can also be set only to give a beep, or to give beeps followed by a stimulation if the dog does not listen to the initial beep as a warning.

Taking away the ability of trainers to use e-collars does a massive disservice to many dogs, including deaf dogs, which rely on a small stimulation to get their attention so their owner can give them hand signals. Without an e-collar, these deaf dogs would not be able to run and play off-lead; they would be kept permanently on-lead, trapped in gardens or at best have a once-a-week exercise session in a fenced-off area, which may simply not be enough off-lead running for the dog in question.

It is also the case that in countries where e-collars have been banned, such as Wales, there have been disastrous consequences, both for livestock[3] and the great many dogs that have been shot while giving chase to their wooly peers. When a pregnant sheep is chased, even if she is not caught and bitten by the dog, she very often will have a spontaneous abortion, losing her lambs. Having their sheep chased has massive financial and emotional consequences for farmers, some of whom have had to deal with finding a field full of aborted lambs.

Should these dogs with an unreliable recall have been on-lead? Yes, of course they should, but it might be that an owner thinks her dog has a good recall or has been fine around livestock before, so she takes a risk and gets into trouble. Or she may walk with her dog through a field which has never contained livestock in the past, and suddenly there they are. What Brit can forget the video of Fenton the dog chasing deer in London's Richmond Park?[4] Fenton was a failed guide dog for the blind, and I hope he previously had a really good recall. I'm sure he did, that is, until he didn't. If Fenton's owner wanted to regularly walk him in the park, then some e-collar training would possibly have stood him in good stead when he knew his dog had a pre-existing problem with ignoring him.

Unfortunately, people thought this lack of recall and chasing deer—including chasing them onto a road—was funny. A children's book of Fenton's escapades called *Find Fenton* was even written.[5] This sort of behavior is not funny. The deer were not laughing, and neither was Fenton's owner. Fenton would not have been laughing if he had been shot or hit by a car.

Guide dogs used to be some of the best-trained service dogs out there, but since the force-free narrative has been taken up by Guide Dogs for the Blind, the UK charity which trains the majority of them, guide dogs are now some of the worst-trained service dogs around (in my opinion). I wanted to find a reference for Fenton's being an ex-guide dog and truthfully, having now read some articles on him and seen pictures of him lunging at other dogs, I am quite horrified by how badly trained he was.[6]

I'm not necessarily attributing blame to his owner for this, nor may it have been the fault of his trainers, who were limited in the tools and training methodologies they could use on him. Some dogs are simply stronger-willed than others and absolutely will do their own thing unless they are very firmly informed it is not a good life choice for them. Given the thousands of dollars it costs to breed, raise and then train a guide dog, what a waste of money that was if Fenton could simply have been given a firm "no" and told to get his act together and behave himself instead of being launched into internet fame.

How could a reputable charity rehome a dog that could not even walk on a lead without lunging at other dogs or jumping up at people, and that had no recall? Many blind people I have talked to have received such badly behaved dogs and were expected to rely on them. Surely Fenton should have received basic training before being passed on, whether he was suitable to be a guide dog or not. Yes, we all have dogs who disobey at times, and, truth be told, I feel a bit sorry for Fenton's owner, in that he was given a large dog that was "trained" (and I use that term loosely) using a methodology the dog clearly did not understand and that did not suit him.

Wales currently has a ban on e-collars, with the government intent on implementing it across the rest of the UK, which is causing a lot of unrest with farmers' groups and gamekeepers.[7] Also bear in mind that the nation's Department of Environment, Food & Rural Affairs (DEFRA), which supports the ban, sponsored the debunked University of Lincoln e-collar studies, which are still being put forward as a reason for a ban despite their being the laughingstock of legitimate dog trainers and animal behaviorists everywhere.[8]

In this debate, we have arrogant dog trainers who have achieved little more than TV fame and a healthy salary on the back of the force-free training movement versus trainers who repeatedly title at world-championship level dog sport and have happy, active, high-drive dogs.[9] I know who I believe, and we will delve deep into e-collar studies and what goes on behind the scenes in the next chapter.

Unfortunately, where there is money there is a desire to throw others under the bus provided your own interests are protected, and many e-collar users have formed a cult similar to that of force-free trainers, putting forward that pinch collars are more abusive than e-collars and would be the better collar to be banned, so e-collars can stay. Again, why are trainers turning on each other instead of pulling together to help dogs?

Chapter Five. More on Training Tools and Equipment 115

The High Court Case involving e-collar manufacturers and the government[10] makes for interesting reading in this and many other regards, with, quite frankly, an expected amount of subterfuge from the government, plus an astounding reliance by the court on the outdated, biased research of the University of Lincoln in England,[11] when there has been much better research, both before and since, which counters those findings and for some reason did not seem to have been permitted to be used as evidence.

Ultimately the court accepted as factual that there are dogs that cannot be helped to behave appropriately by positive reinforcement and food treats, yet this did not appear to be a concern for them, optics being more important. It appeared that, provided the general public wanted a ban—despite the fact that the majority of respondents to the consultation did not want a ban!—then a ban would be permitted.[12] This can hardly be said to be democracy.

It must be remembered that the big animal charities were pushing the government for an e-collar ban, and where there is money, there is influence, no matter what the general public thinks, nor what will happen to the dogs that will be adversely affected. It seems that keeping dogs in charity kennels, and the dollars coming in to support them, are more important than retraining them and placing them in loving homes. According to these campaigners for animal welfare, better the dogs stay put and the coffers fill up, or, when they become inconvenient enough, they be sent to the in-house veterinarian for the big sleep.

The last tools I want to discuss are voice and body language. I am not an advocate of shouting at and berating dogs, using threatening body language to make them think they are going to be punished. Yelling at a weak-nerved, anxious dog can be extremely emotionally abusive. Using a fair tool as a correction is not. Owners who have been told never to correct their dog, just to ignore all bad behavior, can get extremely frustrated. Their dog is not getting better and they inadvertently display very threatening body language, towering over their dog and scaring him. This is deeply unkind. Much better for both dog and owner for the owner to just tell the dog what the rules are via a fair, well-understood correction that is not personal.

I use differences in tone when training my dogs: a high-pitched voice can generate a lot of enthusiasm and arousal in a dog; a low pitch can enforce commands. I use variations in body language and facial expressions too, which can help establish good communication with a well-trained, experienced dog—icing on the cake, as it were.

For example, I often use different body language in obedience training. For a straight recall, which means come directly up to me as fast as possible without stopping, I will stand with my legs at hip width when I call my dog. However, when there *may* be a need for an emergency "down" in the middle of the recall, I stand with closed legs. The dog knows via my closed body language that I may ask for a "down" and that he must be prepared, so he is listening very closely for that instruction instead of rushing up to me, breaking the sound barrier in the process.

Why beat around the bush? We live in the real world and there may be times when we need to use "force" to allow our dogs to have happy, fulfilling lives and at the same time to be safe, under control and not put in the path of danger. Telling me I cannot use a pinch collar, a tool that is appropriate for a high-drive Rottweiler, German Shepherd Dog or Belgian Malinois, while you merrily torture your low-drive Labrador with a head collar? Sorry. Not acceptable. Who are you to tell me what tools I can use when you won't train a high-drive dog, you won't put a pinch collar or e-collar on yourself to see what it feels like, you have no idea how to correctly use them, and you're reaching for a more physically and psychologically harmful tool, which is ineffective to boot—on *your* say-so as to what is appropriate or not?

Governments thrive on public opinion, and sadly, when it comes to animals they care about as much for them as they do for their poorest constituents. The Dangerous Dogs Act 1991 in the UK was a terrible, badly thought-out, knee-jerk reaction to satisfy the public, which the press had wound up into believing our streets were populated by massive, snarling dogs, saliva dripping from their jaws as they went on the hunt for pensioners and babies. I have a feeling XL Bullies will be added to the banned list before long. We will just have to wait and see.

The same is happening with e-collar bans, and in time we will see bans on pinch collars, martingales and slip leads. That is the time I will stop owning and training dogs. I love handbag dogs, but I do not want to own one, nor spend my life training only them. High-drive dogs are being expected to live unnaturally restricted lives, just so owners of low-drive dogs can treat their pets like stuffed toys, not walking them if it's wet outside, or if they pull or are otherwise annoying. This is not ethical.

What will happen to the 300,000 or so dogs trained with e-collars in the UK[13] when the ban comes into effect? I wonder if, behind closed doors, the government is promising to give financial aid to the charities, to help euthanize the thousands of large dogs that will end up in shelters. Would that not be convenient for the shelters that campaign so tirelessly for the ban?

Chapter Six

The Science

The war cry of force-free trainers everywhere is that using positive reinforcement *only* is the most effective and humane way to train dogs, and that science has proved this. Is this true? No, quite the contrary. There are more than enough studies that prove corrections are effective when training dogs,[1] and of course all force-free trainers use corrections anyway. It is simply a matter of which corrections they prefer, thinking they have the divine right to tell everyone else which types of dogs they should own, what activities they should do with them, and consequently the corrections it is acceptable to use.

I cannot list every scientific study which backs up my assertions in this chapter, otherwise I would be writing an entire book just on research literature. This is a book on force-free dog training, not on curing insomnia and inducing a good night's sleep. On the whole, I have tried to limit myself to one example per point I make, though where I think it adds value I have referenced several research papers. I have also tried my best to cite studies which are freely available for you to read online and which you do not need to purchase if you want to examine them in their entirety, which I would encourage you to do. Many of these papers have interesting nuances, plus you should not just blindly take my word for things. We all have bias, yes, even me—perhaps particularly me, given that this is my book in defense of my own and my dogs' way of life. Read the papers which interest you, and make up your own mind as to which are reliable and valid, and which are not.

Research on Corrections and Rewards

Corrections are not the devil in ~~Prada~~ steel-toe capped boots, just ready and waiting to give your dog a good kicking for being a tad disobedient, as force-free trainers would have you believe. In the same way that positive reinforcement is essential in dog training, so are corrections. The problem with most scientific research is that it tends to be absolutist. Life is not like that. You cannot say that in all circumstances only one technique and one technique only will work and will be effective on all dogs, in all situations, and is suitable for all owners. Often, however, this is the argument made by force-free extremists. Why not? It works, with tools having been banned on their say-so, even though there is *no hard science whatsoever* to back their claims up, just emotion and tugging on people's heartstrings.

Sadly, there is not that much well conducted research that does not have holes in it which either side can pick apart, particularly when it comes to issues such as training new behaviors, which every force-free trainer will state with absolute authority is best done in a purely positive way. I disagree. I have already set out why kind, informative corrections can benefit a confused, frustrated dog, and I do not need to do so again.

Studies that compare the speeds of learning different new behaviors will typically focus on one group of dogs that receives positive reinforcement only, one group that receives harsh corrections only, and a final group that receives positive reinforcement combined with harsh corrections. This is also a common tactic in studies which examine the use of "cruel" training tools.[2] Please note, there is no group in which positive reinforcement is combined with kind, helpful corrections or the correct use of the tools in question. Hence there is extreme bias. The study invariably shows that using positive reinforcement only is the best way to teach new behaviors and that corrections are unnecessary and, more often than not, abusive. On the face of it, I would agree, but when I look at the way the tools and corrections have been used, which is in a harsh, abusive way that no balanced trainer would endorse, then I see the study for what it is.

Now, one-sided research of this type would not be a problem if it was offered as an opinion, which actually is correct in what it puts forward, as far as it goes. I am all for the extensive use of rewards in training, and I totally agree that we should *not* be using compulsion training or misusing tools such as pinch collars and e-collars. However, nowhere do these research papers say that the way the tools were used is incorrect, and that when used in the right way they are good options for many dogs. These very important facts are left out, and the research is then used as a basis for the extremists to convince people that all corrections are unnecessary and that tools such as e-collars and pinch collars are always harmful for dogs and must be banned.

When it comes to stopping poor behaviors, the scientific studies available to review become more numerous, though they are not as clear-cut as common sense would dictate, since the extremists still have a position to uphold and an underlying agenda to protect. The study design is often biased, commonly including only overly harsh corrections[3] while the scientists claim they are just implementing industry best practice,[4] even though their methods are thirty years out of date. If they are not aware of the fact that they are abusing the equipment, then they jolly well should be. The use of overly harsh corrections means that even where they are shown to be more effective than force-free training, the corrections can be discounted as being unethical.[5]

As usual, common sense and science tell us that the use of corrections, more often than not in combination with positive reinforcement for good behavior, is both quicker and more effective than positive reinforcement alone when we seek to stop bad behaviors. Redirection may be nice in theory when using force-free methodology, and may work well and indeed be a good option, if not the best option, when dealing with certain dogs. This is often the case when the competing reinforcer is weak, and the dog is nervous. However, it is not the whole story.

We cannot keep bending over backwards to pretend all dogs are trembling, delicate little flowers, easily influenced and willing to be redirected away from the object of their desire with a small piece of kibble. Many dogs are brimming with self-confidence, and they want what they want. This is not necessarily what *you* want. Cookies alone will not cut it, though cookies combined with an appropriate correction will. It is also the case that there are some behaviors which must be nipped in the bud so that the dog does not even consider performing the action ever again, including when the owner is not there to redirect him. This would include counter surfing, raiding bins and predatory behaviors, where a dog goes out to kill an appealing moving object, which could be wildlife, cats, other dogs, cyclists or whatever is most pleasing to him.

Despite the constant hollering of "science says," there are *no* studies, legitimate or otherwise, proving positive reinforcement alone can prevent or stop predation in dogs. Not one. Nada. Nothing. Zilch. There *are* studies to the contrary, which prove that corrections *do* work to stop predation, such as the New Zealand study[6] on the use of e-collars to aid in the conservation of the Kiwi.[7] E-collar training all but eliminated predation in the dogs that participated in the study, being effective in 87 percent (48 out of 55), with such training remaining effective one year after the study ended, including when the dogs were not wearing an e-collar, were off-lead, and not necessarily under the direct supervision of their owner. (After all, who has not had a dog temporarily disappear behind a bush or a tree while out on a walk?)

In general, the force-free studies which have set out to look at predation and the effectiveness of positive-reinforcement-only training, usually in comparison to e-collars, fail miserably. This would be expected by anyone who has ever owned a high-drive dog. Or just any dog with a pulse. The scientists have to publish something for their grant money, hence the study invariably morphs into a paper which is not on dog training but on ethics, usually ranting about how abusive e-collars are.[8] If you read the study carefully, however, grudging admissions can often be found, hidden away in a dense block of text, along the lines that "hard" corrections with tools such as e-collars *have no have negative long-term side effects.*[9]

Research papers comparing e-collar-trained dogs to force-free-trained dogs try to divert readers from the fact that the e-collar-trained dogs did not slaughter any livestock during the trial, even when off-lead and close to animals dogs like to chase, such as sheep.[10] In addition, they gloss over the fact that the purely-positive-trained dogs never even got to a stage of training where it was safe to let them off-lead. Their trainers were well aware that had they not been forcibly restrained, they would have gone on a killing spree the likes of which Stalin would have approved of.

Having stated that all training tools are evil and immoral, force-free predation studies will proceed to claim it is not possible to prevent a high-drive dog from chasing other animals when off-lead, or at least not unless he is zapped into a pile of smoking cinders, as if a victim of spontaneous human—well, canine—combustion.[11] I can just imagine the dog's little paws sitting there on the grass, his body having been vaporized by the high e-collar stimulus, a patent leather collar complete with diamanté studs sadly glittering in the sunlight just between where the front legs would have been.

The force-free extremists then turn to management techniques, claiming all high-drive dogs (meaning the ones that cannot be adequately drugged) must be kept permanently on-lead unless exercised in a controlled setting. This is unrealistic,[12] a research paper on wildlife conservation stating "there is a prevalent culture of off-leash dogs, with complaints that leashing imposes a significant burden...."[13]

The force-free-backed studies end up no longer being genuine studies on predation. Why they are still being touted as proof that positive reinforcement works better than corrections to stop bad behavior and predation is beyond me. In essence, the uneducated force-free fanatics who have never actually read or understood the studies they quote keep insisting "science says, science says," like an old-style record player with the needle stuck in the groove. These are now coming back into fashion, wouldn't you know? Just shows that the cables in your kitchen junk drawer may actually come in handy one day. Resist all urges to throw them out!

If positive reinforcement only is so good at stopping predation, why is it that a bounty of $55,000 went untouched? As I mentioned earlier, this money was put up as part of a challenge by Jamie Penrith and others for a force-free trainer to retrain a dog to stop predatory behavior using positive reinforcement only.[14] There was not a single taker. If positive reinforcement is *so* much better at stopping a dog from chasing and killing livestock, Jamie should have been inundated by the world's top force-free trainers, pushing, shoving and elbowing each other out of the way in order to be first in line to enter the contest and claim the prize. Yet not a single, solitary force-free trainer was up for it. I wonder why that would be?

Ethics remain the only valid(ish) argument against corrections, and these are really down to the exact circumstances of the training in question and what the trainer is trying to achieve, in addition to personal viewpoint. Ethics are subjective by their very nature and differ by generation, as we will discuss in Chapter Ten. Any tool or training technique can be abused, and any trainer can be abusive, including force-free trainers who base all of their training sessions around flat collars, cookies and negative corrections, which as we know can be incredibly frustrating and confusing for many dogs. When such a trainer practices excessive food withholding to force compliance, it can turn to outright abuse, and all the while the trainer is singing from the purely-positive hymn sheet to her clients. Hardly ethical now, is it?

How Is the "Science" Conducted?

The fact is, scientists are not impartial and show confirmation bias[15] when designing experiments, doing their best to prove what they already believe. We all demonstrate confirmation bias to some degree, including myself. I mean, I tend to focus on the research papers which prove corrections are effective and humane. In an effort to be fair, I have also quoted from biased studies which were designed to reach the opposite conclusion but then turned out to support corrections, though the researchers were effective at diverting readers from this with their smoke and mirrors.[16]

Confirmation bias is simply the tendency to notice evidence that matches your own beliefs and assign it much greater value than any evidence to the contrary. This is in addition to dismissing or simply not seeing anything which contradicts your point of view. When conducting scientific studies, we devise experiments in order to arrive at the objective truth, though when dealing with dog training, which is inherently subjective, this is difficult. Usually a question is posed, for which the study aims to find the answer. This could be, for example, "Can e-collar training stop predatory behavior in dogs?"

Next a hypothesis is put forward.[17] This is a tentative answer to the question which often demonstrates the researcher's confirmation bias. So, for our question, the hypothesis might be, "We expect to find that e-collars are effective in stopping predatory behavior in dogs and have no adverse effects on dog welfare, either short-term or long-term." This is a hypothesis which may show bias but is at least dog-centric, putting the dog first. Any study should have protocols to call off the work if animal welfare is in question.

An example of a poor hypothesis would be, "We were interested especially in finding occurrences of pain, fear, avoidance, pain-induced aggression and submission." This is from an actual study.[18] If you are a person with ethics who claims you love dogs and ardently believe in force-free training, then why on Earth would you design a study to *deliberately* cause a dog pain and fear during training? I mean, you're admitting this is what you are setting out to do.

It's like slaughtering a pig you've raised as a pet just to prove that pigs will squeal in fear, pain and confusion when you cut their throat. Is this a case of the end justifying the means, or did the scientific team have so little confidence that force-free training works that they had to torture dogs with extreme corrections in order to prove their point? And this is the objective "science" we are supposed to rely on when banning tools?

After the question and hypothesis have been settled but before any experiments can be done, the proposed research must pass the review of an ethics committee and, more often than not, depending on the country in question, win government approval. This is done to ensure that animal welfare is not compromised, and scientific journals will generally not publish research that has not been properly approved, both by the university in question and by any national legislative requirements. In the UK, most scientific experiments on dogs, including studies on dog training, require a Home Office license, as specified by the Animals (Scientific Procedures) Act 1986. Journals should also ask for a statement that there is no conflict of interest on the part of the researchers, though this seems to have a very loose interpretation by the people involved in such studies, as we will discuss in due course.

Once all of these steps have been completed, which generally takes six months or more, the experiment can be conducted and the hypothesis tested to see if what the scientists suspect is indeed true. The data collected from the study is analyzed and a research paper written, a draft of which is submitted to an appropriate scientific journal for peer review.[19] The peer review process is designed to catch any glaring holes in the paper, which can then be revised, resubmitted, and finally published. Peer review does not guarantee that a paper is not biased or inaccurate—particularly with dog training, given that it's so subjective and political—but it does help. If a truly poor paper is published, other scientists may pipe up and refute the results, as happened with the Lincoln e-collar studies, which have been greatly criticized.[20] Not all journals provide this opportunity, though, and the peer review process at those that do may be conducted by people with a similar political agenda, rendering it about as useful as a cat flap on a submarine.

An important part of engaging in science is recognizing that we all have our own prejudices and that we must try to be impartial, ignore our confirmation bias, and, if our hypothesis turns out to be wrong, accept it and say so. Unfortunately, this does not always happen,[21] and some scientists double down and defend their mistakes, quite frankly making fools of themselves.[22] There have been many studies on dog training which would be amusing in their absurdity if it were not for the fact that they are being used to push government policy and advance the agenda of individual politicians.[23]

When evaluating scientific studies, we also have to be careful to consider sample size. There is a big difference between a study that involves thousands of dogs, such as the New Zealand study on the predation of native birds by dogs, which had 1,156 dogs participating,[24] and studies that involve fewer than 100 dogs, such as the Lincoln studies, which had only 63 participants.[25]

Corruption and How It Influences Science

What was particularly annoying about the Lincoln researchers was that they deliberately did a bait-and-switch regarding the application and point of the research of the two studies[26] which greatly influenced how the dogs were trained with the e-collars, with the second study being especially disingenuous.[27] That study got the most criticism from other researchers,[28] one of whom said the work was "very seriously flawed and should not be relied on,"[29] and the paper was replied to with other commentary as well.[30] The subsequent response from Lincoln was unprofessional and, simply put, pathetic, with no points of substance.[31]

Changing the parameters and purpose of the second Lincoln study[32] may have fooled the general public and politicians, but, quite frankly, it was a sneaky, desperate move. This is little consolation given that it seems the researchers have achieved their goal of political manipulation,[33] with e-collars now set to be banned in the whole of the UK following the Court of Appeal dismissing the case brought by the Electronic Collar Manufacturers Association and PetSafe Ltd. in 2021, which challenged DEFRA's decision to ban e-collars.[34]

The court based its decision solely on the University of Lincoln's research, which is ludicrous given how widely it has been debunked by more prestigious researchers and universities.[35] Considering how biased the Lincoln studies were, and the number of serious errors they made in scientific method,[36] not to mention their disregard of plain common sense, this is a travesty of the court and political system. It should be noted that the research was sponsored by DEFRA,[37] a UK governmental body, so the process can hardly be said to have been impartial. Lincoln received £69,925 in 2010 from DEFRA,[38] the equivalent of approximately £99,400 in 2022[39] ($112,465).[40] It also received funding from various other sources, the total coming to a whopping £538,000[41] ($596,828).[42] That's a sum not to be sneezed at for a five-day experiment with 63 dogs.

The UK has a history of government corruption and interference in research when it comes to dogs, having paid Medical Detection Dogs, a charity that formerly had close ties to the University of Lincoln and the e-collar research team, £500,000 in May 2020[43] ($557,345).[44] This was ostensibly for COVID-19 research and to train six dogs, though all that happened for several years was photo shoots with the Queen Consort, the charity's patron, and lots of unfulfilled promises to the general public as to when the dogs would be trained for operational work (hint: they never were).

The COVID study was not opened to tender per UK competition law rules, the money simply being handed over via the back door, no questions asked. Some if not all of the dogs were selected from shelters for their cute looks and marketability so as to get more donations from the general public, not for their working ability—no doubt a reason why the study was such a dismal failure. It took over two years to achieve what multiple overseas teams did in six weeks, the study finally being published in a relatively unknown journal with no fanfare or publicity in May 2022.[45] This was quite unlike when the charity was begging for public cash by prostituting itself on every media outlet available, the £84,000 ($83,630)[46] per dog thrown at it by the government seemingly not enough. Publishing the research in 2022 when COVID was all but a bad dream and everyone was glad to see the back of it was very convenient for Medical Detection Dogs, effectively brushing its embarrassing "research" under the carpet. Nice work if you can get it.

Science is like any other profession, with high stakes, fat salaries and a lot of subterfuge involved. It is often tied to politics and large sums of grant money. As we saw, DEFRA literally paid the Lincoln researchers to give it the results it desired so that a ban on e-collars could be pushed through on the basis of "research." Science is important for the force-free activists, as it's the weapon they use to persuade governments that the tools they dislike, most commonly e-collars and pinch collars, must be banned and that public opinion supports them, and few (though not all)[47] politicians want to come across as supporting animal abuse. Many scientists who conduct the research own dogs themselves, are dog trainers (of sorts), or are members of force-free dog training organizations, and hence are not impartial. Some are even campaigners for bans on e-collars, yet state that their work is unbiased and declare no conflict of interest when submitting their papers for peer review.[48] Tut-tut.

To my knowledge, there have been no moves by force-free campaigners to ban head collars, even in Sweden, where crates are banned.[49] This seems odd to me, given how aversive head collars are, even when simply sitting on the dog's head and not in use, but there you go. What is good for the goose seems not to be good for the gander. The "force" that people see as acceptable will always be a matter of opinion. I am not going to petition to ban head collars, as they suit some dogs, just not my own. If those other dogs like them and have a better life wearing them, then I am all for it. Why spoil it for someone else when the matter does not concern you?

We already have legislation to prevent animal abuse, and all animal lovers want such practices stamped out. Well, almost all. There are government ministers in the UK who want the ban on fox hunting repealed, one of whom was recently battling for the position of prime minister[50] and, if he had been successful, would have repealed the ban in a jiffy, despite a newspaper poll showing 84 percent of the general public would oppose such a move. Like the force-free campaigners, who also have political support within the government, he did not care and would happily have put his own agenda and interests first. Tearing hundreds of foxes to pieces while still alive—fine by him and his wealthy cronies. Giving two e-collar corrections per year to stop a little dog from being similarly ripped apart by a big one, well, that is considered cruel. Logical? No. Politics should play no part in legislation designed to protect animals, but sadly, in the UK at least, this is what is happening.

Those hundreds of thousands of pounds of funding would have been better spent breaking up dogfighting rings or tightening up legislation on animal abuse. Have politicians and researchers been spending too much time in the parliamentary bar, I wonder? Or have they been lurking in the dungeon, testing e-collars and pinch collars out on each other? Strictly in the name of scientific research, you understand.

Bias in E-Collar Studies

One of the things that always concerns me about e-collar studies is the willingness of scientists to cause pain and fear in dogs, on the basis that the ends justify the means. This includes not only treating dogs unfairly on purpose, but also using bad science.[51] I mentioned one such study above, where the hypothesis was, "We were interested especially in finding occurrences of pain, fear, avoidance, pain-induced aggression and submission."[52] An e-collar used correctly in this type of study should not elicit a single occurrence of pain, fear, etc., so clearly these researchers set it up to deliberately produce these results, and yet they call themselves dog lovers? Scientists? Ethically and morally superior to me and other trainers and owners who keep their dogs safe and use training tools judiciously?

This was a study[53] on the short- and long-term effects of e-collar use and involved 32 guard dogs: a mix of Belgian Malinois and their crosses, plus German Shepherd Dogs and one Rottweiler. The dogs received 107 shocks which were high enough to make them vocalize in pain, all in the name of "training." This was *not* a study on predation, where a short, sharp shock is used to save the life of another living creature, and in which it is permissible to use a high e-collar stimulation. There was no emergency which required a dog to stop dead in his tracks to prevent injury to a person or another animal. Therefore, it could fairly be said to be abuse. Saying you're doing it in the name of science is not a get-out-of-jail-free card, as far as I am concerned.

This study concerned the training of guard dogs, both in obedience and protection. News flash: If you're using a pinch collar/e-collar stimulation high enough for the dogs to vocalize from pain, in an ordinary training session including heelwork,[54] where 33 shocks are administered for the crime of simply forging ahead of the handler, well, that says it all, and there's a special place in hell for you. There was no mention of any praise given to the dogs, no engagement work or play with them, no food rewards. In short, no positive reinforcement at all was provided to the dogs during the training. Wrong. Wrong. Wrong.

When a dog is trained correctly with an e-collar—which, in obedience work, uses low stimulations and there are no vocalizations of pain. You may administer a stimulation sufficient to cause pain in an emergency, where the dog requires a "hand of God" correction, but that's it. Same with a pinch collar. A dog should not be vocalizing in pain, nor flinching. Sure, his ears may momentarily flatten and his tail go down when corrected, but that's normal when he strongly wants to do something but is prevented from proceeding. If the dog has been enjoying the work, he immediately reverts back to his happy self after being corrected. It is no big deal.

In real-world training, corrections are not strong enough to cause pain or fear, just at a level sufficient to communicate with the dog and to reinforce to him that he must be obedient. Pain and fear are not required to do this. If a dog is ignoring his trainer and needs to be corrected constantly at a level high enough to cause yelping, there is clearly a serious training issue, and the dog should be removed from the situation and the trainer as well. The dog is not ready for that sort of work yet, and the trainer is not competent to use the tool in question.

The problem with this study,[55] therefore, was the poor standard of training of the dogs, both in relation to what was being asked of them and in the way the e-collars and pinch collars were introduced and were being used. The study was conducted by compulsion trainers, about 30 years out of date, not balanced trainers. In obedience training, the corrections should in part be used as negative reinforcers, with pressure and release to build drive and enthusiasm, in conjunction with positive reinforcement and, at times, positive corrections. That is the way dogs are trained in modern obedience and protection work (also known as bitework).

During "manwork," as they so endearingly call protection work in this study,[56] dogs were being abused. Perhaps "manwork" is a poor translation, as this was a study from the Netherlands. Nevertheless, the term provides a clue as to the old-school way in which e-collars were used in this study, given that "manwork" was more common in the 1970s, when the use of corrections was admittedly unsophisticated and did utilize pain in training. During protection work, or "manwork" (bless their little cotton socks), dogs are highly aroused, and a harder correction may be needed to ensure compliance than the ones used in obedience. However, the dogs should have been made very familiar with the exercise, and if in order to be obedient around a **decoy** or helper they needed such hard corrections that they yelped, the foundation and basic training required for such work were sorely lacking. Clearly, the dogs were being trained using e-collars and pinch collars in ways which went out with the Ark, making the study unethical and not a true reflection of the correct use of such tools. The project did not seem to train the dogs in a meaningful and fair way, but was rather intended to cause them pain and hence to prove a point and confirm the scientists' hypothesis.

The study states the protection work was highly rewarding for the dogs, but was it? No other rewards were used in the training. A dog with high defensive drive can still be fearful and not really enjoy protection work, but nevertheless he will try to do his best in the training, mainly acting from instinct. If the dogs were being subjected to harsh corrections and given no other reward, I doubt very much they were enjoying their training. Plus, the paper states, "handlers of non-shocked dogs admitted that they use prong collars, and that their dogs experienced beatings and other harsh punishments, such as kicks or choke collar corrections."[57]

Yes, you read that right. Beatings. Kicks. The study should have been canceled then and there on ethical grounds, and the "trainers" reported to the police. The researchers too for standing by and watching. Yes, during protection work you may shove a dog, or push him with your legs to raise his drive. This does not hurt, and indeed is fun for the dog, building his confidence, as he gets to fight you and he always wins. It is not a punishment, or designed to be uncomfortable, never mind painful. What you do *not* do to a dog, ever (unless he is trying to rip your face off), is kick him or beat him.

Was winning and being right so important to these scientists that they had to unfairly punish dogs by lighting them up with e-collars for doing virtually nothing wrong? For pulling against pinch collars? The scientists knew these dogs were being beaten and kicked, yet did nothing. And you, the force-free trainers who support these studies, say you are the ethical ones and are on the dogs' side? These were compulsion trainers, abusive trainers, beating dogs with the researchers standing by and doing nothing, yet you dare equate them with modern, balanced trainers in order to serve your force-free agenda and get e-collars and pinch collars banned? Shouldn't a prosecution for kicking and beating a dog come higher on your agenda, given that there are animal welfare laws to prevent this sort of abuse?

Although actively looking for harm to the dogs, the researchers did say, "We have not proved that the long-term welfare of the shocked dogs is hampered…"[58]—which is something, but it is clear that their short-term welfare was compromised, as the dogs were yelping in pain. Of course they were suffering! They were being kicked and beaten, in addition to being electrocuted, as if they had broken into ZIP Code 90210 and were about to eat Prince Harry and Meghan Markle's offspring. The study was designed so there could be no other conclusion than that e-collars and pinch collars are wrong and unethical.

I am all for getting rid of compulsion trainers, but don't you dare tell lies and pretend that modern, balanced trainers use e-collars and pinch collars in this way, and that they beat the stuffing out of their dogs. This study condoned, even encouraged these dogs' abuse, all to prove a hypothesis. I have no words. Also, how exactly was this study not shut down when it became apparent how the dogs were being treated? Why did a scientific journal, *Applied Animal Behaviour Science*, accept it, given that the abuse of dogs was admittedly carried out, which was against the law?

I am totally and utterly disgusted. As the old saying goes, "Lie down with dogs and you'll catch fleas." Or as one commentator on the paper stated, "The authors appear to hold a certain view of the issue and significant parts of the discussion appear to focus on reinforcing this opinion with extrapolation from what appears more limited information."[59] This

Chapter Six. The Science

was never about science or finding out the best way to train dogs, it was only about the researchers proving their own biased hypothesis.

Now let us move on to our friends at the University of Lincoln, who are as sneaky and ruthless as KGB operatives regarding the science surrounding e-collars. The university, in the East Midlands region of England, conducted two studies, the first from October 2010 to June 2011,[60] published in 2014,[61] and the second, written by a master of science candidate who cherry-picked aspects of the video footage from the first study, published in 2020.[62]

ARDO (the Association of Responsible Dog Owners) has a far better breakdown and criticism of the Lincoln studies than I could ever produce. Please go to their website if you want to see their analysis of the "science" in these studies,[63] not to mention links to other commentators' articles debunking it.[64] There are some additional points I would like to bring up, however, that no one else has really covered in much depth, which I will get on with without further ado.

Just as an experiment, what if I copied the government and the Lincoln researchers and did something similar, twisting the research to fit my own agenda and political objectives? It's not beyond me to create a biased study, starting with a seemingly innocuous question and hypothesis and changing the circumstances to suit myself as and when I please. Then, when we look at the final results, I shall take my cue from Shakespeare's "The lady doth protest too much" and loudly insist that the study is in no way a farce. No, it could not be predestined that the results would all go my way. Never in a month of Sundays! Shall we copy the experts and invent our own little corrupt, I mean magnificent, study for fun? I rather think we must.

To start, would it be A-OK if I whisper to the ethics committee that there might be some mild animal discomfort, when all the while I have murder in mind? I mean, Lincoln had the audacity to say the e-collar stimulations would be benign.[65] If dogs are yelping in pain, that is not a benign stimulus, is it? However, given that their research was originally supposed to be about stopping predation, high stimuli were to be expected, and might have been appropriate in the circumstances. There was some obedience involved in the study, but it was considered as ancillary to the main point, the prevention of predation. Yet at the end of the day, obedience was what was analyzed and deemed of importance, not the dogs' ability to resist chasing and ripping apart sheep, as the e-collar trainers were told was the purpose of the study.[66] If I was a sheep, I would be more concerned with life and limb myself, but no, it seems that sitting your bare bottom down on snow quickly (which was one of the behaviors asked for) is the epitome of how to judge a dog's training.

As perhaps should have been expected, the plan for the second Lincoln study made no mention of eliminating predatory behavior,[67] instead concentrating on obedience, recall and basic positions such as "sit." Now, do we use high e-collar stimuli to teach a dog obedience? No. No, we do not. A dog that has just been trained with high stimuli looks like he has swallowed a murder hornet and had it come out the other end—alive. High stimuli are used specifically to stop predatory behavior. And the e-collar trainers focused on what they were told to do: train for preventing predation, not for enthusiastic recall and quick obedience. They did not even have sufficient time to form a bond with their dogs, and therefore achieve engagement with them, before commencing the training. Switching objectives in this way was a sneaky move on the part of Lincoln, and there was yet more subterfuge, as I will attempt to replicate in our experiment.

Having sailed through the ethics committee, I would tell both groups of trainers in the study that this is the research question: "Is positive reinforcement better than e-collar corrections to stop dogs from ~~salivating over~~ looking at bunnies in the distance?" The force-free trainers think, "We can do that," as do the balanced trainers. My hypothesis is, "All the bunnies in the force-free training group will die a horrible death," but I do not share this. I mix the rules up a little bit, and oopsy-daisy, did I forget to say the dogs would be off-lead and that "distance" is a relative term, the bunnies being several feet away behind a low fence, one the dogs can easily jump over? I am so naughty, tee-hee-hee!

Like Lincoln, in order to be objective, we must be able to tell which group is which so we can ascertain which dogs look stressed and which are happy. For the force-free group, I select a bunch of petite female trainers, 98 pounds or under when soaking wet, all of whom use only cookies and flat collars as tools. No lead pressure allowed; you must run after the dog if he pulls! (The dogs will be off-lead when they are introduced to the bunnies, but let's keep that a pleasant surprise for now. I suspect some of the dogs may even slip their loosely fitted flat collars before the lead is taken off. What fun!) Meanwhile, my balanced training group is all big, burly men, just so there is no confusion. Large men vs. small women—it's easy to know which group is which. A bit like how Lincoln did it.[68] Well, they do say imitation is the best form of flattery.

Just to spice things up, the women in the force-free group train their dogs in the spring, while the bunnies are joyously bouncing about in the sunlight, hoppity-hop-hop-hop! All training is done at a distance, just as I promised. But 100 meters, 10 meters, 1 meter? Surely it's all relative and distance does not matter to a force-free-trained dog that is only interested in cookies, does it? When testing time comes, it seems a few of the dogs go crazy and slip their collars, chasing after and dispatching the poor bunnies with ruthless efficiency, before we even get to the big reveal where the leads are removed. One of the force-free trainers actually flings her lead at her dog while he is harassing a bunny. That is not a purely positive way to do things, is it? I'm shaking my head and tutting contemptuously as I sit here typing. What brutal force! How can we condone such behavior?

About the male trainers in the balanced e-collar group, well, what can I say? I want it to be fair, so I decide they should train their dogs in the winter. During their test, it's snowing, so the bunnies are all snug in their cute little hutches, out of sight and out of mind, munching their carrots and kale. Off-lead, the e-collar-trained dogs walk right past the enclosure with the hutches in it, not even trying to peer inside, let alone massacre the bunnies like the force-free-trained dogs did. Whoever would have thought *that* would happen? I took my lead (ha!) from Lincoln, which trained the e-collar group in the snow[69] and the force-free group in the spring sunshine,[70] then had the audacity to criticize the e-collar dogs[71] for being slow to obey when asked to sit on the cold, wet, snowy ground. I mean, a dog is just as happy to sit on snow as he is on warm spring grass, isn't he? If not, I think we can fairly say the Lincoln study was biased.

In order to make my study as fair as fair can be, both groups have spent a week training just with cookies. Then the e-collar dogs were given four weeks to learn that the e-collar stimulus means good behaviors are always rewarded with lots and lots of cookies and that poor choices have consequences. So, the force-free gals got one week to train their dogs and the balanced trainers a total of five weeks, as we want to keep everything fair and above board. I mean, everyone needs to have an equal chance at getting their dogs to understand what is being asked of them and what the tools mean, before any sort of testing starts.

In my hypothetical experiment using the methodology the University of Lincoln seems to have used, in the positive-reinforcement-only group things go—well, let's be blunt here, they go to pieces. While on-lead, the dogs ignore the cookies, a few pull the trainers down, and a couple slip their loose flat collars, jump the fence, and kill some bunnies. When off-lead, all the dogs run away and kill the remaining bunnies. But the e-collar dogs, after five weeks of training, look like they are ready to strut their stuff at the Westminster Kennel Club.

My hypothesis is proved, and I am able to confidently state that positive-reinforcement-only training is extremely dangerous and unethical, as next time it could be a child killed, not a bunny. The study is presented to the government as a basis for banning flat collars and insisting all dogs must now wear slip leads, choke chains or martingales, ideally pinch collars or e-collars, as so many of the trainers were pulled right over. It's clear to see: every dog in the land, large or small, must receive e-collar training before going out in public—you know, to keep everyone safe. It's only ethical given that none of the cookie trainers had any control whatsoever over their dogs, either on- or off-lead, and all of the bunnies in their part of the study ended up dead. R.I.P., bunnies. Your sacrifice in the name of science will never be forgotten.

Does this sound far-fetched? Was my scientific study well designed and fair? Or did I set the force-free trainers up to fail, and set the balanced trainers up for success? It's not as if there was any difference whatsoever in the physical conditions the groups worked in, or any prejudice in what was expected to be trained, or the appropriateness of the time scales provided for the tasks concerned, was there? All I did was attempt to replicate the way our erstwhile colleagues at Lincoln designed and then conducted their studies, so I can't be said to have done anything wrong. After all, the Lincoln studies were so good they led to e-collars being banned in the UK,[72] so the science must have been good too, right?

When Lincoln was challenged on the way their e-collars were used,[73] including the time allowed for training, they doubled down on their mistakes, refusing to take responsibility for their own study design, claiming everything was done as recommended by the e-collar "experts."[74] In so doing, they demonstrated little to no understanding of how e-collars are used correctly in practice by dog trainers. Surely as scientists it should have been their absolute priority to conduct the study in a way which was ethical and fair to the dogs in question, even before considering scientific merit. If the "experts" had said the dogs had to be taught to do the Macarena first, or jump off a cliff and wait until rigor mortis set in, would Lincoln have dumbly went along with that too?

It was Lincoln's study. They laid down the study conditions, design, parameters, objectives, and time scale for training. Ultimately, Lincoln was supposed to be the experts, taking responsibility for making sure the tools were used correctly and the dogs did not suffer pain or fear. Why did they think they could slither out of this and blame other people[75] when the study was so clearly flawed? I would have more respect for them if they had admitted they got it wrong, but of course they would not do that, as the whole point of the research was to get e-collars banned.

The "experts" Lincoln referred to[76] are the Electronic Collar Manufacturers Association, a European organization of businesses, not a body of expert dog trainers. With all due respect, trade associations are concerned with selling the greatest number of their products and making profits for their shareholders, *not* with the most sophisticated use of their products. Does ECMA know trainers who buy lots of their products? Yes. Are those the very best trainers? They may be, but on the other hand they may simply be the trainers that buy the most e-collars from them.

Ask yourself this: If you have a rotten tooth, do you ask a manufacturer of fillings to recommend a dentist for you? No, of course not. You find the very best dentist you can afford. I have a feeling that the majority of dog trainers who are experts with e-collars wanted nothing whatsoever to do with this research project once they knew the conditions set out for the training, which were clearly inadequate. The project set the e-collar trainers up to fail, though in fact they did succeed in what they originally set out do, deterring predation, before the goal posts of the study were oh so conveniently moved.

I am of the opinion that the Lincoln studies are unreliable and should be discounted, or at the very least removed from the scientific journals in question, due to the conflicts of interest and prejudice of the scientists involved. You cannot rely on science that has been conducted by biased researchers. It is immoral, if not illegal, to sign a conflict of interest statement when a member of the scientific team has, prior to the research, written a personal letter to the study sponsor (DEFRA) calling for e-collars to be banned.[77] Nor is it acceptable for people on the study team to be members of a dog training organization which vilifies e-collars and similar tools.[78] A conflict of interest does not have to be financial; it can also exist when there are strong emotions or personal beliefs involved, as was clearly the case with the Lincoln research team.

Lincoln got criticism it was not happy with, then started to cry "fake news." The e-collar-trained dogs were supposed to be trembling wrecks, since unethical training methods had been used on them. Was that the case? Even using poor training methodology, the dogs in Lincoln's e-collar group showed no significant difference in cortisol level,[79] and indeed over the longer term there were no negative effects on the e-collar-trained dogs at all, as confirmed by DEFRA, which stated in their final report, "Activities that might be associated with aversion or anxiety were rare and there were no significant behavioral differences between treatment groups. There were no differences between treatment groups in cognitive bias scores, nor in measures of temperament. None of these measures had changed from the pre-treatment assessments."[80] They went on to admit, "There were, however, a number of behavioral differences between the groups observed during training. Some of these appeared to relate to trainer related factors, rather than the use of e-collars."[81] Maybe the differences in results also related to some dogs not wanting cold snow on their backside, yet others being quite happy to plonk themselves down on warm spring grass,[82] don't you think?

So concerned were the Lincoln researchers that they were not going to get the results they desired, which was the dogs demonstrating high levels of stress, that they discontinued measurements relating to heart rate, concentrating instead on the collection of salivary and urinary cortisol, both more intrusive tests. Given that a stethoscope is less distressing and easier to use with a dog than taking mouth swabs or collecting urine, why were heart rate measurements *really* discontinued halfway through the study?[83] I doubt it was for reasons of scientific merit.

E-Collars as Positive Tools During Training

This is not a new use of ε-collars, IGP trainers having employed such techniques for years. E-collars were an integral part of a behavioral modification program for extremely aggressive dogs carried out by Daniel Tortora as far back as 1983.[84] The e-collars were used not to suppress the dogs or to create learned helplessness, but rather to provide them with confidence, a sense of security and an understanding of how they could control the environment which was frightening them and so make themselves feel safe via appropriate behaviors. The methodology used in the study appears to be of particular use where routine counter-conditioning has failed.

The study described the e-collar stimulus as "a challenge the dog has to overcome"[85] rather than a punishment, helping the dog develop self-confidence and a sense of safety. Although the sample size was small, the training resulted in "complete and permanent elimination of aggression in all of the 36 dogs tested. In addition, it produced extremely extinction-resistant prosocial avoidance responses, [and] significant increases in the dogs' emotional stability…."[86] This study has flown somewhat under the radar and is well worth reading if you have the time.

The Science of Stress and Learning

All of us undergo stress in our day-to-day lives. Your dog is no different. Stress is a fact of life, and indeed humans and animals alike were designed to cope with stress, particularly in the short term, with one research paper stating, "Short-term stress enhances innate/primary, adaptive/secondary, vaccine-induced and anti-tumor immune responses, and post-surgical recovery."[87]

Putting pressure on a dog over a short period, when appropriate for the dog in question and beneficial to his training and long-term welfare, will not cause lasting side effects. Indeed, it will enhance cognitive ability and learning.[88] Force-free trainers insist corrections always cause fear and will break the bond you have with your dog, causing him to move away from your side. And it is true that a poorly timed, overly harsh correction *will* do so, particularly when the dog has no real engagement with you—which says a lot about the skills of such trainers if this is the type of response they get from the dogs they correct.

But dogs' minds and bodies were designed to be able to deal with short bursts of stress—with, for example, the immediate adrenaline and cortisol release that occurs in a stressful situation.[89] Most hard, one-off corrections in a training session, provided they are well understood, fair and appropriate, do not cause undue stress. However, a session that is overly long and full of hard corrections, oft repeated and not well understood, is not good training. Sadly, this is the type of training session that scientists who wish to prove that corrections are harmful, or to ban certain tools, will typically conduct. How ethical are such scientists in creating a training session that sets a dog up to fail and receive multiple harsh corrections, over and over, as the session drags on? Not very ethical, in my opinion. Or, let's be honest, not at all.

Many of us enjoy the rush of hormones we get from a short-term stressful situation, whether that stress is mental, physical or both. Some people love adventure sports, or even the death-defying roller coaster at the amusement park. I like horror movies, myself. Yet other people go further and live for contact sports such as martial arts. Now, these activities are not the same as a trainer administering a correction. But if short-term stress, physically and psychologically, *was* harmful to mammals, then martial arts would be banned, as would theme parks, and all we would have on TV would be romcoms. Oh, and we would all be dead.

On the other hand, long-term stress and, in particular, the long-term effects of the hormone cortisol have been demonstrated to be very harmful indeed.[90] When a dog has a behavioral problem and management is not working out, tackling the issue in as short a time as possible is preferable for the sake of the dog. For example, a big, excitable dog that pulls hard on the lead and subsequently is never exercised, staying locked in his crate all day since when the Kraken is released[91] he goes on a rampage, is living in a permanently high state of stress, and that is a serious welfare issue.

When the issues on the lead are not due to fear or anxiety, and the dog fully understands what is expected but is bigger, stronger and more determined than his owner (and knows it!), with a fundamental lack of respect for her outside the home or training room when distractions are present, then there is no point messing around with boundaries and cookies for a year or more, hoping he will calm down but getting nowhere. In such a situation, several training sessions with a pinch collar or e-collar can turn that dog's life around.

Yes, he must be trained to have engagement, and he must understand leash pressure, how to have an **off switch** so he can settle down and exhibit good behavior in the home, and not be so excited that he is working over threshold. However, some of these dogs already check all those boxes; they simply have no respect for a flat collar and never will. A pinch collar is not a miracle worker—it is just a tool, and the right training must be instilled in the dog first—but in some circumstances it can provide appropriate consequences for pulling. No yanking and cranking is required, just some direction. Taking that pinch collar away from an owner in favor of imprisoning the dog—sorry, "managing" him—does no one any favors. Certainly not the dog.

I am vehemently against using violence on dogs, such as kicking them in a temper or beating them up in the name of training. Compulsion training: not my thing. We should never want to cause dogs any sort of discomfort with no purpose: that is abuse and does not contribute to a dog's learning experience. However, one short, sharp shock with a hard lead pop, though it may be visually unappealing, can cause *much* less discomfort overall than months and months of cumulative collar pressure, which in some dogs results in a damaged trachea. Or, alternatively, the sky-high cortisol levels that come with being crated 24/7.

I fear that where tools such as e-collars and pinch collars are banned, the more unethical trainers will take their dogs behind the scenes for a good hiding, turning back to compulsion-based training. It's easy for trainers in the U.S. to smirk at the situation in Europe, telling us to keep using e-collars and pinch collars in private. But this is not workable. If trainers who also have a boarding kennel or breeding business, types of activities typically licensed by local government, are caught with an e-collar or pinch collar, they could have the majority of their livelihood taken away in one fell swoop, as their licenses to run their other businesses would be revoked along with their permission to train. People are spiteful and will report trainers they dislike, calling the police and animal welfare authorities to perform an unannounced inspection. What are trainers supposed to do, hide their e-collars and pinch collars in their toilet tank and plant pots?

Is this what the force-free people want, reformed compulsion trainers who have started to use more rewards going back to their old ways of giving a dog beating as their tools are now gone? A "hard" dog is one with determination and that will not respond to a mild correction, and yes, giving such a dog a kick so he becomes a little fearful of his trainer will improve his attitude no end. But is this ethical? No. I, for one, don't want to see it. But it will start to happen more often as we increasingly ban tools that trainers depend on. I would much rather such a "hard" dog gets a fair correction from an e-collar or pinch collar than is smacked about with a two-by-four.

Banning things people use and rely on never works. Did Prohibition work in the 1920s?[92] Does banning drugs work today? If it does, then why are more and more states legalizing cannabis? Why do force-free extremists think banning pinch collars and e-collars will work? All it will do is drive good trainers underground and turn them into criminals, letting down the dogs that need their help in the process. Some will give up, and the severe behavioral cases they would have tackled will instead be sent straight to the veterinarian for the ol' blue juice.

Some trainers will take the risk of being shut down and continue to use the tools they need to best train difficult dogs. The less ethical will get over-rough with their dogs, and yet others will choose between getting rid of the breeds they love or dumbing them down. Most will end up choosing show lines, training low-drive dogs that are easier to handle. We have seen this in the IGP world, where these days the more sensitive dog is favored over the badass dog that strikes fear into the heart of the toughest competitor. With bans on e-collars and pinch collars increasingly commonplace in Europe, there are more and more "soft" dogs in the sport that could not do a real day's work in the police or military. These are the types of dogs that force-free IGP trainers own yet still fail to win trials at the top level with, using slip leads and cookies. How strange is that?

Leadership and Dominance

Whenever a balanced trainer says a dog needs a leader, the force-free brigade will pipe up that the early studies on wolves carried out by Rudolf Schenkel in the 1940s through those of David Mech in the 1970s are totally outdated, incorrect and have been thoroughly disproven.[93] They will crow that wolf packs do not have alphas and therefore no one should show "dominance" over a dog or give him "leadership," since these are outdated concepts. Recent studies have indeed shown that in a natural setting, wolf packs consist of parents and offspring—mom, dad, and kids, not alphas and betas. And as with any good family, they do not constantly fight to gain control,[94] as arguments are hardly conducive to "happy wife, happy life."

Nevertheless, when unrelated wolves are thrown together in captivity in an old-style zoo, where the area is too small and the resources scarce, the behaviors noted by early researchers such as Schenkel once again raise their ugly heads.[95] Fights break out as the wolves try to form some sort of hierarchy, with each wolf in it for him or herself. The conclusions of Schenkel and his successors may not be reflected as anticipated, but that does not make their observations invalid in an artificial setting.

How does that relate to dogs? Well, for starters, they are *dogs*, not wolves, and a great many wolf behaviors have simply been bred out of them. Dogs are not afraid of humans in the way wolves are; they look to us for guidance, including responding to the direction in which a person is pointing or gazing.[96] Wolves do not respond in the same way and neither do chimpanzees, though, interestingly enough, cats do! Most dog breeds have been designed to live with people in a family unit, within the same home, rather than outside in groups with other dogs. However, there are behaviors they do retain which would be essential to survive in the wild or in the event of a zombie apocalypse, such as prey drive and the ability to hunt. These are low in some dogs, high in others. When the end of days arrives, I will be well provisioned, my own dogs being excellent hunters.

Dogs that come to live with us in our small homes are placed into an artificially constructed "pack" (if that is a term you like), just as Schenkel's wolves were. They do not have the option to leave when they reach sexual maturity, as would a wild wolf, in order to find a mate and form a breeding pair. Indeed, many dogs have their natural hormonal urges surgically curtailed. However, in the vast majority of homes with pets there is harmony, our dogs happy to remain in a somewhat juvenile state and content to take direction and leadership from us, just a wolf pup does from its parents. With more confident breeds, however, in the absence of a good human leader, a dog may take the job on for himself, since nature abhors a vacuum.

When we do not adequately step into the leadership role, including when outside the home, our dogs are condemned to live fearful lives. No one has their back, and the world is a scary place. Such a dog may show defensive aggression, barking and lunging at other dogs, at people, and at anything unusual, particularly when on-lead and he cannot move away. Unfortunately, many people proudly say such a dog is protecting them. He is not. This is a scared dog, not a dog that is acting from a place of love, as these owners like to think. If this is your dog, you have let him down. When and if you step up and act as a good leader should, he will relax and live a far happier life, no longer forced to make decisions out of fear, which he is not well placed to do.

As humans, we dictate the amount of space our dogs have to live in and where they are free to move within our homes. We give or take away their ability to exercise. We control access to essential resources such as food, play, and mates. In short, whether we like it or not, we have to take on the role of a parent, since we are in the business of preventing natural behaviors and restricting resources. Our dogs are entirely dependent on us for those resources, and if we do not meet their need for leadership, it can and will cause conflict. A parent's role is to provide guidance, discipline and enforcement of boundaries. It is not handing out cookies for simply breathing.

Most force-free extremists are not well educated. They cannot name Schenkel or the other scientists they look down their noses at. They do not understand why some of the facts from the early wolf studies were disproven and why some remain relevant and are indeed applicable to the dogs that live with us in our homes. In general, dogs will try to advance their position in life, even if only in small ways. Unless we tell them which behaviors are not acceptable, they will readily engage in counter surfing, protecting their seat on the sofa, etc., as why would they not? Unless we give them boundaries, which come from corrections, management or a combination of both, they absolutely will take as much advantage of us as they can. Schenkel's science was not all bad, and if viewed correctly it shows that dogs do require leadership in order to live in harmony with us, and that they will otherwise fight and squabble for resources in the artificial environment and thrown-together pack of our homes and families.

So, that is that on the subject of "science says." What have we found out? Well, mainly that science is contradictory and actually says very little. It can say anything we want it to, really. We certainly should not be banning tools on the basis of flawed science that was designed to satisfy a political agenda, with the researchers having serious conflicts of interest they do not bother to declare. But this is where we are. Having established that science does not say all corrections are inherently evil and all force-free training is good, we must look at the ethics of dog training and examine who the real winners and losers are when purely positive training is mandated. I don't think you need me to tell you, it is not the dogs who are the winners. But first let's look at how dogs are put together.

Chapter Seven

The Innate Drives of Dogs: Brain Structure and Physiology

Force-free trainers like to compare correcting a dog to corporal punishment in schools or parents smacking their children, both of which have been banned in many countries. They say any correction which causes pain, discomfort or fear—and all corrections do this except for their own, of course—are unethical. Instead, they promote "errorless learning," whereby the dog is trained in a distraction-free environment, each move carefully controlled by the trainer, the aim being that the dog never makes a mistake. This sounds great, but in reality dogs learn less quickly[1] and typically grow bored with constant rewards for little effort, causing them to lose motivation. Worse, when faced with the real world outside the training room, where all dogs must eventually go, more sensitive dogs can fall into a state of learned helplessness as they cannot cope with failure and uncertainty, only being comfortable in an environment entirely controlled and manipulated by their trainer.

Just as making life as perfect as possible does not work as intended with dogs, every parent will attest to the fact it does not work well with children either. Our instinct as parents is to protect and nurture, yet some kids who are constantly supervised and assisted or are never allowed to make mistakes sometimes have an ingrained sense of entitlement and deal poorly with authority. We humans have a tendency to claim that all generations subsequent to our own are rude and badly behaved, and, putting on my tin-foil hat, I think they have a point. Some of today's kids are the most open-minded, beautiful souls imaginable, but others are undisciplined, entitled, and rude, with very little respect for anyone. When it comes to humans, it may be fair to say violence begets violence, but we know this is not how dogs live. They do not have the concept of being disrespected when their owner says "no."

Dogs are not humans. Dogs are dogs. Their physiology and brain structure are similar to that of humans, but there are notable differences in how developed these structures are. For this reason, we cannot expect dogs to use logic and behave as we do, even if they are raised in our homes and treated as human children from day one. It is deeply unfair to expect such behavior from our dogs; rather, we must strive to respect them for the amazing species they are. Breeding, over hundreds if not thousands of years, has changed the physical and mental characteristics of dogs from those of their ancestor the wolf, creating different breeds which all have unique characteristics and charm.

Breed Differences

Force-free trainers will tell you that all dogs can be trained the exact same way, using the same methodology, as they are inherently all the same and respond to training, which must be via positive reinforcement only, in the same manner. Now, I do agree that positive reinforcement should be the *basis* of all dog training. However, it is a mistake to think that all dogs have the same mental and physical characteristics and abilities. It is also a grave mistake to believe that dogs do not require corrections and guidance regarding which behaviors we, as humans, consider good and which are undesirable to us.

Neither should it be thought that all dogs have the same likes and dislikes in life. Quite simply, they do not, and it's important to adapt our training to each individual dog, and what that dog considers a reward and what he considers a correction. I mean, do you like chocolate? Cake? Cookies? What if you were given a plate of Brussels sprouts for dinner, with a garnish of lettuce? Some of you would be ecstatic, others not so much. As humans we have our preferences, ranging from the people we enjoy spending time with and the food we like to the sports we participate in, and so on. Dogs are the same. If I gave a vegan a piece of beef jerky, she would not be impressed.

Let's take several breeds of dogs and compare them, thinking about what they commonly do and do not like, and taking into account their genetics and morphology. Let's start with the Pekingese[2] and the Saluki.[3] It should be clear that they are very different dogs, both visually and temperamentally, even though both are ancient breeds, both are stunningly beautiful, and both were bred to be the dogs of kings and queens, albeit for very different purposes.

The Pekingese is a toy breed that was designed to be a good pet and lapdog, while the Saluki is a hound, bred to be an exceptional hunter. Of course, good hunters can also make excellent pets even if they are rather large for lapdogs, the mantra "if I fitz I sitz" being quite common with many large breeds, including my precious Rottweilers. However, stout, vertically challenged lapdogs with short legs tend not to be the best of hunters. (I will now be expecting enraged toy dog owners to send me pictures of their dog's thousands of kills and championship wins in Barn Hunt, stomping terriers into the dirt as he displays his hunting prowess.)

A Pekingese is very small, hairy, adorable butterball, weighing up to about 13 pounds.[4] Bred by monks to live in the royal court in Imperial China,[5] the Peke is loyal and brave, but he is not the fastest mover on the planet, being rather sedate, "built for comfort, not for speed," as the saying goes. By contrast, the regal Saluki, a dog that towers over the Pekingese, is tall, slim, and incredibly fast and agile, with a massive amount of prey drive.[6] Bred to hunt,[7] this amazing hound was a favorite of the Egyptian Pharaohs, right through to today, when they are still greatly prized in the Middle East as hunting dogs.[8]

As a hunter, the Saluki likes to chase (and kill) small animals. He just does. This is not the Saluki being cruel or having a malicious streak, it is simply what he was bred to do for thousands of years and something he excels at. Indeed, you would be hard-pressed to find a gentler, kinder, more intelligent dog than the Saluki, though I would not trust him as far as I could throw him (hint: not very far) with my small dog or cat.

On the other hand, the Pekingese has zero interest in giving chase to animals smaller (or larger) than himself, such as mice and rats. He has low prey drive and would far rather be snuggled up on his owner's lap enjoying delicacies than engage in a seek-and-kill mission. Think of Tricki Woo in *All Creatures Great and Small*.[9] The Pekingese and Saluki's brains are wired very differently, and the instinct to give chase and hunt has been bred out of the Pekingese, whereas it has been enhanced in the Saluki.

Both the Pekingese and the Saluki should be trained using *lots* of positive reinforcement, but it would be unwise to put them into similar circumstances and expect the same result. For example, if you take both these dogs to a dog park and let them off-lead around other dogs, you should not expect the same behaviors. Every dog's inherent level of drive and the traits, instincts and personality of his breed should always be respected in order for that dog to live his best life. We should never set our dogs up for failure, and you should always pick a dog that will suit your lifestyle. On the subject of dog parks, they are a bit like crack cocaine: it may initially seem like fun, until it all ends in tears. Just say "no." No good comes of dog parks. By all means, find some doggy mates for your pup, but make sure their play is under control and that you can always recall your dog and have him come back to you.

During training, play or when out and about, as we discussed in

Chapter Seven. The Innate Drives of Dogs

Chapter Three, dogs can go over threshold, where they have an emotional response above and beyond what they can cope with and cannot use their brain to work out what we are asking of them. When they are in such a state, it's unfair to use what would, to the dog, feel like punitive measures in order to control them. I am not going to take a Saluki to a dog park full of sprinting, high-velocity small dogs and start blasting him with an e-collar to try to stop him from chasing them when he becomes extremely aroused. That would be cruel. A typical sighthound will have an inherently high level of drive around small furries (dogs, not humans) which cannot be trained out of him using punishments. Rather, we have to implement management strategies with such dogs, taking into account their genetics, which simply means to use common sense and not take your Saluki to "play" with small dogs at the dog park.

That does not mean your Saluki cannot be trained to be good with small dogs or even cats in his own household, given time and patience. Similarly, he may very well enjoy playing with other dogs which are a similar size to him, strange or not, and which he does not view as prey. This of course depends on his own and the other dogs' respective dispositions. Not all dogs like every other dog they meet, and not all dogs want "friends" of their own species. As I said above, visiting a dog park, aka "flea- and virus-infested doggy fight club," is asking for trouble with any breed of dog, but if you choose to take your chances, one day you will no doubt learn the hard way.

In addition to the majestic Saluki, there are other very high-drive dogs that do not easily go over threshold and jump from zero to one hundred in an instant, instead retaining the ability to think and be trained because their arousal level rises more gradually. Such dogs have been bred to be capable of working with humans and taking direction while in this state. One such breed is the Belgian Malinois,[10] which like the Saluki is extremely high-drive but has emotional control and greater trainability. We *can* gradually train the Malinois not to go running off to kill small dogs or cats he may spy on an off-lead walk in the park, though e-collar training may be one of the best ways to do this in order to keep everyone safe, especially when the dog has a gastronomical interest in small animals.

Even dogs from within the same Kennel Club grouping can have very different personalities and types of drive. The stunning Saluki is a sighthound, bred to hunt using his acute eyesight to spot prey, then to catch it using short bursts of great speed. By contrast, let's take another hound, the beautiful Beagle,[11] also an ancient breed kept by royalty and the English aristocracy, although unlike the Saluki, this breed has amazing endurance and hunts using his nose rather than his eyes. Docile and calm, the Beagle is not at all bothered about pursuing sprinting terriers, though he has a tendency to put his nose to the ground and become temporarily deaf, heading off after interesting scents while impervious to the entreaties of his pursuing owner. We have looked at three ancient breeds, then, the Pekingese, the Saluki and the Beagle, all with royal links, yet all three very different in personality, innate drive, and purpose.

Looking at all four dogs overall, the Pekingese, the Saluki, the Beagle and the Belgian Malinois, and given their inherent drives and typical personalities, would I have different expectations and train them differently? Yes, I would. All dogs I train get masses and masses of rewards, but what the dog considers a reward will differ with each dog and what I am training him to do at the time. I might be training a behavior that involves some enthusiasm and movement on the part of the dog, such as agility or obedience, or doing training whose sole purpose is for the dog to learn to act calmly and relax, such as a place command.

A Saluki will enjoy a flirt pole, as will a Belgian Malinois. A bite pad or wedge will be enthusiastically grabbed by the Mali in a game of tug, all quite instinctively, whereas the other three breeds would be totally "meh" if this was offered to them as a reward. All four breeds tend to be over the moon about food rewards, though the canine trash can, I mean Beagle, will gobble up pretty much any type of food offered, whereas the Pekingese and Saluki have much more refined tastes.

When it comes to food rewards, many Malinois get maximum enjoyment when the reward is given to them with some snappy movements and bouncing about on the part of the handler, rather her gently placing the food directly into their mouth, as you would do with most Pekingese. So, not only are the rewards each breed enjoys different, even the method of delivery can be drastically different to give a dog maximum enjoyment, which, when rewarding a dog, is our aim.

Rewards are easy to figure out, but what about corrections? Would an e-collar or pinch collar be an appropriate type of correction for each of these breeds if they displayed the same behavioral problem, say, being kept under control on a trail walk? Well, the Pekingese needs neither. He is an agreeable little chap, and if you let him off-lead on a trail walk he would probably not stray far from you. If he did, and refused to recall, most able-bodied adults would have no problem catching up with him and gently restraining him. On-lead, he will most likely wear a comfortable harness as he trundles merrily beside you, little tongue poking adoringly out. The Pekingese was bred to be an easy and compliant pet and that is what he is, though being brachycephalic he would struggle with a long trail walk unless he had done a lot of fitness work beforehand.

The Saluki is similar. He does not need an e-collar or a pinch collar. However, I would not let him off-lead in the wild, as his temptation to

Chapter Seven. The Innate Drives of Dogs

chase a small dog or a startled rabbit is high. For on-lead walking he needs a hound collar, which is a collar designed for his slender neck. He may jump and pull hard if he sees a fast-moving small animal, and his owner should consider the type of environment she places him in. Dog parks and trails with lots of rabbits here, there and everywhere may not make for the most enjoyable walk for either dog or owner. If you want to walk your dog off-lead daily on rabbit-strewn trails and not have to be hypervigilant about losing him unless you commit to e-collar training with a skilled trainer, a Saluki is not for you.

Many trainers have successfully trained Salukis and other sighthounds with e-collars. There is no inherent reason not to use an e-collar with the right dog, the right owner, and in the right circumstances. However, you do have to consider what is fair to the individual dog given his innate drives and the difficulty of finding a genuinely skilled trainer in this area. Without avoidance training, many dogs will go over threshold incredibly quickly, and once a dog is there, the harshest correction will do nothing to dampen his arousal. This is totally and utterly unfair to the dog, and neither is it fair to the smaller dog, cat, rabbit or other critter he has chased and killed. Buy a dog that will suit your lifestyle, and if you can't or won't change to accommodate a dog that *doesn't* suit you, finding a more suitable home for that dog is a bit like an amicable divorce and better for all parties concerned.

The Beagle, unlike the Saluki or the Peke, can go pretty much anywhere and will greatly relish a long, energetic walk on a trail. On-lead, he will not need much more than a well-fitting harness or a flat collar, perhaps a slip lead or martingale for some young dogs that may get overexcited at all the delicious smells which abound. Would I let a beagle off-lead on a trail without an exceptionally good recall already in place? No, I would not. On a typical trail, depending on the terrain, there will be a multitude of attractive smells which are much more interesting than his handler. E-collar training can be a great option for a Beagle that likes to disappear into the sunset. Unlike the Saluki, Beagles do not go from 0 to 100 in an instant, and their focus on a scent can be interrupted with the equivalent of a firm tap on the shoulder using an e-collar. Or they can be kept on a long line, though this can ruin the walk somewhat, particularly if traversing woods.

A Belgian Malinois on a trail may benefit from an e-collar if he does not have a great, immediate recall and likes heading off, invested in his own devices. As a very trainable breed, many Malinois have exceptional recall and handler focus, so much depends on the dog, the type of trail, wildlife and livestock which may be about, and the risks present in that environment. Some handlers like e-collars as an emergency backup with such a high-drive dog. Similarly, some Malinois benefit from wearing a pinch collar while on-lead, which like the e-collar may be rarely if ever used, but when it is, it stops the handler from being pulled over and keeps the dog under control using a light touch. Or he may be just fine on a flat collar. Much depends on the individual dog.

Before moving on, I will repeat what I have said earlier in the book in case you have been chapter hopping: *Training and the dog's emotional state is the basis of everything.* An e-collar is simply a tool. Alone, it will do nothing to improve a dog's recall or prevent him from legging it after livestock when on a trail walk. Alone, it will make things worse. First the dog must be trained to recall and conditioned to the e-collar, to *want* to be with you, which involves lots and lots of goodies, whether they be food or games. Some breeds see other animals as more attractive than you, and for this, e-collar training can allow you to better control your dog and allow him freedom he would otherwise not enjoy, but it *only* works if the recall is already there and the dog respects his handler and has been well trained to understand what the e-collar stimulus means. Without correct training, using an e-collar is unfair to your dog.

Different Dogs, Different Drives

Dogs have different types of drive.[12] Not all types of drive are the same in their intensity, and even the same type of drive will differ between different breeds, and between individual dogs within one breed. Dogs must be respected for their genetics and what they were bred to do, and this very much includes the type of drive(s) they have, and in which proportion. Now, each and every dog is an individual, and there are differences within breeds, particularly between show and working lines. However, if you buy a Pekingese as a watchdog (as his Kennel Club profile says he is), expecting him to pursue, bite and take intruders to the ground, you will be sorely disappointed. Unless it's the Golden Girls breaking in and an ankle bite would suffice. Even then, the average Pekingese would not be able to survive the shade thrown at him by Dorothy.[13] But then, to be fair, neither would I.

Prey Drive

When we think of drive in dogs, we mostly think of prey drive,[14] though some trainers believe there are up to fifteen types of drive in dogs.[15] There are even different types and intensities of prey drive. Prey drive is hardwired into every dog as an instinctual behavior, and it can elicit very high emotions, though not every breed has a high prey drive. As with the Peke, we have bred the prey drive out of certain dogs, and we have increased it in others.

Chapter Seven. The Innate Drives of Dogs

At its most basic, prey drive is the instinct to survive by killing another animal. It involves scent, sight, stalking, chasing, pouncing, and darting in to nip, as well as grabbing hold of animals, shaking them, suffocating them, and, in fighting large animals, teamwork to bring down prey. Prey drive has been adapted as humans have bred dogs for our own purposes, and we now have dogs that herd, that point at game, that retrieve, that chase and take down criminals, that detect drugs and explosives. All of these behaviors started with prey drive and were modified to suit our own ends.

A dog with a high prey drive is a big responsibility, whether he is large or small. A large dog chasing a small dog in play, a behavior which could be said to be practice for hunting, can easily turn into something more sinister as his prey drive kicks in and the game becomes much less fun for the weaker dog. Dogs in play have very different body language from dogs in true prey drive.

Play Drive

Play drive involves ebb and flow, with different postures such as "play bows" that indicate the dog is indeed playing. Other behaviors such as reverse sneezing, first by one dog, then another, can break up play which is getting too intense and remind the dogs that this is only a game. A lot of loud growling can take place during play, depending on the breed. Rottweilers, for example, can be very loud and fierce during play, and with my own dogs I am fine with it unless it reaches a level where I think the play is getting too intense. It is then my job to tell them to either stop playing or just to pause the game, let them calm down, and then allow them to resume play, which they will do immediately. If you cannot recognize when your dogs are getting carried away and split them up, you risk having a fight on your hands.

We can indulge the play drive during training as a reward, and the excitement and arousal elicited during play can enhance the speed of learning and the fun of the training session for both human and dog. Some dogs will prefer food as a motivator, and some play. Unless they are very hungry, most dogs with a high drive to play can be amped up more with play than with food. This can be useful when we want to work the dog in an increasingly high state of excitement in the training room, getting him accustomed to being obedient when in a state of arousal. This then helps in the real world, where his impulse control has improved to the extent that he is able to control his emotions and remain obedient around high-level distractions.

Food Drive

Food drive is one drive which we dog trainers take full advantage of. Some breeds are notorious for having a very high food drive; these include the Labrador Retriever, a dog that could be described as a canine trash can. Other breeds behave more like a cat, turning their nose up at anything other than imported raw Swedish meatballs for their dinner. These dogs do not respond to treats during training, requiring some other sort of motivation, usually play, as they do genuinely enjoy owner approval and affection. This may coincide with a break from training, and is often a good approach with small, low-drive toy breeds.

When a dog goes *over threshold* in his training, his food and play drives will often decrease or become nonexistent, and this can be an indicator to the trainer to take it down a notch or two, particularly when working with a dog that has fear-based behavioral issues. Other dogs may not be fearful, simply overexcited, or just too goal-oriented and focused on the task at hand to accept a reward offered by the trainer. I have one dog that loves tracking and is incredibly goal-oriented. She misses a lot of chances for food on her tracks, as she is concentrating hard on detecting scents. Once the track is complete, she is her usual greedy self.

Social Drive or Pack Drive

Social drive or pack drive in a dog is the need to live with other dogs or humans, or, in the case of livestock guardian breeds, to take other animals under their wing and into their protection. Some breeds, including the Beagle and Foxhound, like to live in packs with other dogs. Indeed, I have heard it said by a laboratory worker that one of the reasons Beagles are so popular in animal research experiments is their strong pack drive and ability to live happily around other dogs without the need for human affection, making the researchers feel less bad about the atrocities they are carrying out on sentient beings. This may be an old wives' tale, but it is true that although Beagles love their humans, they were originally bred to live in large packs in kennels, not in our homes. They are also medium-sized, have easy-to-care-for coats, and are docile and good-natured, so unlikely to bite when stressed.[16]

Defensive Drive

Defensive drive is basically protecting what is yours when challenged for it. I have split this drive into four behaviors: fight, flight, fawn and faint. When challenged or threatened, most animals have one of these reactions.

Chapter Seven. The Innate Drives of Dogs

Species which are lower down on the food chain or are herbivores have a tendency to run away (horses), though others within the same family will stand and fight (donkeys). Other animals will faint and play dead (possums) and yet others will fawn and try to appease their aggressor (many humans and dogs). Dogs are unusual in this respect, as I have seen all four of these behaviors with dogs, as I'm sure we all have with humans.

A dog with a strong defensive drive, one that comes forward and attacks a human, wanting to *fight* when scared, under pressure or just protecting what is his, is a dangerous dog indeed, particularly if he is big and strong. In the UK we have had a lot of attacks by XL Bullies,[17] many of which have been bred for color and not for temperament, ending up weak-nerved and easily startled. Not good in such a big strong dog, particularly when he has a mixture of fear and defensiveness, in which case he will have more of a tendency to commit to the bite and retain it,[18] as opposed to darting in and out for a quick nip and not hanging around to be kicked back, as the majority of dogs will do.

Dogs can be defensive about protecting their space, their food, their toys, their offspring, etc. This behavior tends to stem from fear in some way, even though it may not seem like it, despite the fact that it may not seem reasonable to us humans. We can understand a bitch threatening to bite a stranger who comes close to her puppies, or a dog upset at having a bone taken away from him. However, at other times it's less understandable for a dog to be defensive, such as when "Prince Charming" the Patterdale Terrier threatens Grandma's guests when they want to sit on "his" embroidered cushion on the sofa.

When a dog displays defensive drive around toys, food, etc., it's important to work with him so his fear of being "robbed blind" decreases and he knows that if you ask for his coveted, favorite toy, your intention is to swap it for something of *much* higher value. Say his toy is a boring plastic bone, then he may be happy to have it swapped for a Kong filled with liver. Similarly, a dog that is prepared to protect "his" space needs to have his privileges on sofas and beds removed and be given a safe place of his very own such as a crate, where he knows he can relax and retreat and will not be disturbed by anyone. We all need our man cave.

Force-free trainers will tell you that displays of defensive drive always come from fear, but in my experience, though fear is a factor 90 percent of the time, there are dogs that are not fearful and are just bullies, plain and simple, which is more a case of *offensive* drive, which I will briefly discuss before moving on to the other types of defensive drive. A dog with offensive drive will actively look for a fight. He enjoys it. It's fun, in the same way some people like boxing or full-contact martial arts. A dog with high offensive drive that is not corrected for bad behavior does not necessarily live a comfortable life, as he is always questioning himself about what is and is not reasonable for his human to ask of him. When a dog is prepared to threaten people to get his own way, including throwing away the need for bite inhibition, he is a *very* dangerous dog and not a pet for an inexperienced amateur. Professional trainers generally don't like to be bitten by such dogs either.

These types of dogs may only be aggressive toward humans, but my view is that he will also not be good around other dogs, but always on the lookout for a fight. While many dogs will pick on dogs that are not challenging them in any way but are submissive, small and defenseless,[19] this dog will not care. Any other dog is fair game. Owners of such offensive-drive dogs must be responsible and have established an exceptional recall, keeping the dog on-lead around other dogs and muzzled when they cannot guarantee that recall. However, a big dog in a muzzle can inflict a lot of blunt force trauma on a small dog.

Now, there are dogs that will start fights with other dogs but that have no aggressive proclivities toward people. Such a dog may be incredibly nice to live with, having no offensive or defensive characteristics. He simply does not like other dogs. Plain old dog aggression, particularly when defensive and acting out of fear, and aggression toward people rarely go hand in hand in the way portrayed in the media. After a dogfight, when you hear someone screech, "It will be a child next, lock up your kiddiewinks, the devil dog is coming!" you should know it's a patent lie and highly unusual for the vast majority of dogs who engage in fights with other dogs. Dog aggression *does not* equal human aggression.

However, we do have to recognize that there are some ~~deranged~~ not-nice dogs out there. This is the type of dog that will terrorize his family, moving them around the house as he wishes, telling them where they can sit and which rooms they can safely enter without feeling the wrath of his teeth. Such a dog may very well redirect a bite onto you if you try to tell him "no," not because he is frightened, but because he finds it unacceptable for a mere human to tell him what to do.

When a dog is showing defensive or offensive aggression, I always check for pain, fear or other causes first, but do not discount that your beloved dog may simply be a spoiled brat. It happens. Sadly, trainers are seeing an increase in this type of behavior from the most mild and amenable of dog breeds, such as Spaniels,[20] because when a dog has no structure, boundaries and rules in his life, he will step in to fill the vacuum and make his own rules. An otherwise good-natured dog of a docile breed that has become a bit aggressive due to never having been told "no" can be an easy fix once he realizes the rules have changed and his owner is now in charge. The dog will quickly become submissive and keen to please.

Chapter Seven. The Innate Drives of Dogs 151

But confident breeds known to have a lot of offensive characteristics will not be so keen to back down, and need an expert hand. There is no shame in calling in a trainer. Many pet owners live too long in fear and misery, as they are ashamed to admit that in their house the dog calls the shots. Such a person may have used force-free techniques which have failed miserably, or have been told to euthanize her dog, and so will not seek any more help. Do not be that person. Having a trainer is a good thing. A professional trainer, that is. Even competitors in top-level dog sport almost always work with their own trainers, no matter how many years' experience or world championship titles they have. If you have a problem, even if you think no one else can help, take a deep breath and go look for the "A-Team" of trainers.

Back to the different kinds of defensive drive. A *flight* reaction is typical for a great many dogs. We all want to survive and not get hurt, right? Most dogs are bred as family pets, and this is a normal response when threatened. Unfortunately, we are seeing more and more dogs bred by back yard breeders that are nervous and fearful even in normal, everyday situations. Sadly, more care is often given to producing cute puppies with curly locks and a teddy bear smile that blow up on Insta and sell for $$$$$ than producing dogs with robust, friendly temperaments that can cope with most aspects of day-to-day existence. Some dogs will run far away when scared and off-lead, in the direction of home if they do not trust their owner to be able to sort the situation out for them. Others will instinctively run to their owner, which is a massive relief.

However, beware! When cornered and with nowhere to run to, dogs with a solid flight response may become scared enough to bite. There will be plenty of warning via body language and growling, but often such a dog will be too scared to even growl. A person who misses these signals will often claim the dog has attacked "out of nowhere" and "without warning," even though he has given very clear signs of fear and distress. Do not ignore a scared, cornered dog. He has teeth and will use them when scared enough. Sometimes you can diffuse a situation, and sometimes you can't and have to try to avoid snapping teeth. Ask any vet tech.

A dog that bites from fear when his escape routes are cut off, such as during a medical examination, must be treated with a lot of patience when at all possible. If you have a dog that is a fear biter when restrained, please be fair to your veterinarian. Explain the situation in advance and either book a double appointment so there is time for the veterinarian to make friends and build a little trust with your dog, or muzzle train your dog at home so he is used to being muzzled and does not see it as an additional stressor, so everyone is kept safe. Veterinarians will often give their time for free to make friends with a scared dog, and if this is offered to you, take advantage of it. Some dogs (often small brachycephalic dogs) cannot wear a muzzle or be safely examined while stressed, and if this is your dog, it is your responsibility to put the time in to make veterinary examinations pleasant for him and the staff at your veterinarian's office.

A *faint* reaction is less common in dogs, or at least not a full-on faint as you would see with a species such as a possum,[21] complete with full-on death smell. There are a few different types of death faking, including tonic immobility or "playing possum"; the particular behavior observed depends on the species and why the animal is reacting in this way. A terrified dog may simply become immobile and totally submissive. He will still have muscle tension, though, as opposed to an animal that has a genuine faint reaction and goes fully limp.

Fawning is another reaction some dogs may display, often when being given a punishment or a harsh correction. Very often we may also see it when we provide a fair correction which was unexpected on the part of the dog. I will give an example. One of my young Rottweilers decided to try her luck and bully another one of my other bitches. I saw what may have become a fight start to kick off and firmly told the aggressor, "That's enough." She ignored me. I then recalled her, starting off nice(ish), before telling her that if she did not recall immediately I would turn her into one of those furry hats with the little earflaps. Still no recall. Now, my number one house rule is "no bullying," and ignoring three fair, understood, commands is not allowed in my home. I bellowed "NO!" and threw my book at her, hitting her squarely and hard on her naughty behind. She did not expect this.

Instead of running away in fear and cowering, my dog understood what was a fair correction under the circumstances, since she is well aware that she must not bully or annoy other inhabitants of the house and that yes, she must *always* recall when asked. She was not emotionally traumatized, distraught or terrified by being corrected, as force-free trainers will tell you she would have been, though she was extremely keen to regain my approval and displayed a fawning reaction. I didn't need to attempt another recall, as she immediately came up to me very submissively, tail wagging off her bottom, and asked politely if she could come onto the sofa with me. I said "yes," and we spent the afternoon snuggling.

This young bitch learned a very important lesson about discipline that day, and discovered that even if I am lying down reading and may not be in a position to get up and immediately correct her, it is still my house, my rules, and there are always consequences for bad behavior. There is an old saying that goes, "Dogs fight for the right to breed, bitches fight for the right to breathe," which is very true. Few things are as vicious as a bitch fight, and I was not prepared to let any sort of antagonism build up between my bitches.

Now, I am not advocating that you routinely use a book or any other household object as a tool for disciplining your dog. That is not appropriate. Did I physically use something to strike my dog? Yes. Was this appropriate under the circumstances? Yes again. In a situation which could go south very quickly—and believe me, a full-on fight between two grown Rottweiler bitches is one of those—you *must* be in control, and it's better to be proactive and nip trouble in the bud. Sometimes you have to use what is at hand, no matter how unorthodox. I would not have had to do this to defuse a situation between two small, submissive dogs, but with two "Type A" personality working dogs, yes, it was necessary.

I have seen trainers and other people lose the use of a hand or arm due to a severe dog bite, and a dog can accidentally redirect onto you, his beloved owner, without meaning to during a fight. Indeed, prosecutions against the police are increasing for nerve damage done by police dogs, particularly when the dog will not "out" and release the subject. I did not want to end up in a hospital getting stitched up, nor did I want either of my dogs in that situation at the veterinarian's, not to mention the inevitable ongoing antagonism between them if they had had a serious fight.

Is that the police knocking at my door, or is it the sound of all the force-free enthusiasts raising enough red flags to fill Tiananmen Square and Red Square combined? When they start chanting "Onward, Christian Soldiers" while marching to my home, I will start to get worried. Or maybe brew a nice pot of tea. No offense intended to Christians, the Chinese and Russians, Communists of whatever flavor, or anyone else. To add fuel to the fire, I once threw a bucket of water over a horse that was trying to flatten me like a pancake against the wall of a stable (this also worked well). But that is another story for another day—and perhaps another book?

The Brain

We now come to the brain, the dog's brain, to be precise. Well, mainly. Dogs have a brain very much like our own, with the same basic structure as in the vast majority of mammals, as we know from the complex representations of magnetic resonance imaging (MRI), which has only increased in popularity in the last twenty years or so,[22] though slice and dice doctors have existed for a very long time.

Every species is different, and their brains tend to be adapted to help them survive and indeed thrive in their particular environment. Dolphins have a high encephalization quotient (EQ, or brain to body weight ratio), second only to humans[23] (sorry, dogs), and minds no less complex than a human's, with some brain structures more developed than ours, just like a dog's. Dolphins not only have a well-developed auditory cortex, since they are marine chatterboxes and require good hearing, but an additional paralimbic part of the brain relating to social behaviors and emotions which even humans do not possess.[24] On the other hand, they have little to no sense of smell, with only vestigial olfactory bulbs in newborns[25] which quickly fade away to nothing. This is in direct contrast with dogs, which have an excellent sense of smell, the olfactory apparatus taking up as much as 2 percent of the dog's brain, whereas in humans it only accounts for a dismal 0.03 percent.[26]

Where dogs do not do so well is in the cerebral cortex, the cortex not being a standalone structure but rather the outer layer of the brain. It's the bit we use for problem solving, learning and memory, but it's also linked to our emotions.[27] You know in a horror movie where the bad guy takes a chainsaw and…? Well, when the brain is sitting on his platter, glistening in all its glory, the cerebral cortex is the wrinkly, folded layers we see on the outside. In a human, the cerebral cortex makes up about 50 percent of the mass of the brain,[28] whereas in a dog this percentage is much smaller, the cortex having fewer folds and hence less surface area.

It will come as no real surprise that primates and cetaceans (dolphins, whales, etc.) have more convoluted brains and hence a more powerful cerebral cortex than dogs, but what may be surprising is that this also applies to even-toed ungulates (Artiodactyla), which includes pigs and cows.[29] We all know pigs are bright—but, er, cows? Yes, cows. Cows are also even-toed ungulates. It has indeed been shown that the brains of carnivores have fewer folds than brains of a similar mass belonging to mammals in the order Cetartiodactyla (Artiodactyla and cetaceans) and, of course, primates.[30] Other studies say cortical size is similar in carnivores and herbivores (including cows), though after we get past an animal the size of a Golden Retriever, the smaller the animal, the more cortical neurons it will have.[31] Interestingly, raccoons have as much cortical density as primates. Go, Team Raccoon! There are a lot of factors to consider: brain mass, overall brain size, EQ, the size of individual brain parts, the density of neurons in the cerebral cortex, etc., etc. Corvids (crows, jays, magpies) show cognitive abilities and performance similar to primates in terms of the number of cerebral cortical neurons.[32] Which any lover of horror movies knows well. Ravens rock!

This is all very interesting, but what does it tell us except for a few fun facts to help us win the local pub quiz? (My team is the Sean Bean Appreciation Society.) Not so much, really. I mean, it's been shown when conducting an MRI on a dog's brain that the caudate nucleus, part of the brain's reward system, responds equally *or greater* to human praise than it does to food.[33] Toys were not used as a reward for this part of the experiment,

Chapter Seven. The Innate Drives of Dogs

presumably as the dogs needed to be kept as still as possible. But will dogs learn tasks better and more quickly with human praise than with food and toys? Does praise give as much of a dopamine hit as food or toys? In my experience as a trainer, I would respond with a resolute "no" to both of these questions.

Most dogs find praise meaningful, but as an aid to learning it does not have the clarity of communication of using a clicker/marker word backed up by whatever the dog's beating little heart desires most, food or play. We've discussed drives and seen that both the food drive and play drive were necessary for dogs to survive during their evolution (and we have developed or decreased these drives in different breeds). Today, as domesticated animals, the ability to please us and hence be given praise is also important for dogs' survival, though few humans would starve or mistreat a dog for not being "good." They might leave him tied up outside a rescue center, though, which is a more certain death for many dogs.

The experiments we've been looking at also showed some very interesting brain activity in relation to language, and indeed there has been a trend in "teaching dogs to talk" using programmable buttons which a dog presses to indicate his needs. When a button is pressed, a word such as "food" is burped out. This can be used for a dog to alert his owner of simple needs including "toilet" or "walk" in the same way as a dog ringing a bell attached to the garden door does.

However, dogs cannot form complex sentences in the way many of the owners of these devices perceive them to, most dogs coming up with gibberish and others simply learning to link steps, as they can be trained to do with any behavior. My service dog will give a medical alert, go to the kitchen, open the cupboard door, take my medicine bag in her mouth, and bring it to me. This is a series of linked steps, as is pressing buttons in a certain sequence. My dog understands (to an extent, I am sure) that I am unwell and that she will be generously rewarded for this series of behaviors, but she has no comprehension of pharmacology. Similarly, a dog forming basic sentences has no comprehension of their actual meaning[34] (no shade on the gorgeous, smart dog and her owner in the video).

It's not for me to criticize people who say their dogs can speak English, Mandarin or Hungarian, forming complex sentences in each language, but have a look on YouTube yourself and make up your own mind. In the notes I have provided a link to one channel I find particularly good,[35] featuring a very endearing, sweet little dog, and it shows how useful and how much fun training of this type can be for both you and your dog. There's lots we can do inside the home to train our dogs and stimulate their minds, even in a small home.

Consider the species you are working with and respect its unique abilities. Intelligence is not just one thing and one thing alone. I could not survive by myself if dumped in the wild, or if there was a zombie apocalypse. Neither could my dogs (but I think you'd find my cats could, even though many dog lovers put cats down as stubborn and stupid, despite the fact that very little research has been done on cat intelligence). However, we don't need a brain scan to tell us that dogs are smart and have an extraordinary sense of smell. If you want a conveniently sized living hot water bottle for cold weather, pick a cat, but if you want to sniff out drugs, a dog would be a better choice.

All of us have our favorite species which we enjoy working and living with, whether it's a pig, horse, dog or cat. Maybe even a raccoon or raven. If I ever get my own desert island, I would build a sea pen to rehabilitate orcas and dolphins that have been in captivity. I would also provide a haven for those rescue dogs that can never be safely rehomed, and I would retrain suitable canine candidates to be service dogs for the disabled, ideally also teaching disabled, out-of-work individuals to be dog trainers themselves, in order to give them a meaningful new career in animal welfare. Elon, Warren, King Charles III, get out your wallets. My book sales will not pay for the island. What are you waiting for?

Chapter Eight

Balanced Training versus Force-Free Training

If all of us, owners and trainers alike, are using a degree of force when living with and training our dogs, then why should it really matter how a trainer brands herself for marketing purposes? All dog trainers, if we're being honest, know we use force of some sort during training, even if that force is the smallest degree of "hard" body language or a difference in voice tone that confers our displeasure to the dog, acting as a correction. With some diehard force-free trainers, this may even be inadvertent.

I Want to Believe...

I want to believe that life with my dog can be all peace and harmony, with not a bad word or emotion between us. I want to believe, but I can't. Force-free dog training is a myth. Purely positive trainers use force, even when preaching otherwise. Is it the case, then, that dog owners know this, understanding that force in some form is always used, and the amount of forceful techniques and tools employed is simply a matter of degree? Force-free trainers insist that everyone knows they use force of some sort and there's no harm in their marketing themselves as force-free to get a competitive edge, even when they're lying. It doesn't harm anyone. Right? The answer is, "Wrong." It harms dogs, and as dog trainers, dog owners and dog lovers, we should ultimately aim not to be harming dogs.

Unfortunately, a great many dog owners believe what they are told in social media posts and the like, which is where they get the vast majority of their information on dog training these days, whether they are on their first dog or have owned several. Increasingly, they are led to believe that corrections of any sort are *always wrong* and that no force at all must be used in dog training. It's the modern way, the scientific way, the *kind* way. If a trainer suggests that her clients so much as say "no" to their thug of a dog, she's branded as a monster and will get the nickname "Dahmer the damned dog trainer" in her local community, her lovingly homemade treats that dogs go crazy over viewed with the utmost suspicion.

Sadly, many dog owners never question the legitimacy of what they are being told, even if it defies common sense, nor do they hire or even speak to a dog trainer if they are having problems with their dog. In fact, such pet parents never do anything with their dog at all other than sigh over him, since they are too embarrassed to leave the house with their precious little darling in tow, knowing full well that exposing adorable Gizmo to sunlight would be ... unfortunate. As would getting him wet or, heaven forbid, feeding him after midnight.[1]

Online Training Courses

Well, online dog training content, to be precise. Keeping dogs restricted to the home, not even attending training classes to try to mend their errant ways, is being encouraged more and more by force-free trainers, many of whom sell online courses which tell owners to keep their troublesome pooches behind closed doors and far away from the stresses of the outside world.

In my experience only a very tiny minority of dogs genuinely benefit from never being walked or taken outside their house and garden, certainly not the millions of dogs we are being hypnotized into thinking will live their best life this way. It's the owners who are benefiting, though clearly not their legs, glutes and heart, dog walking being good exercise and all that. Should unethical force-free trainers be gleefully liberating the bank accounts of naive dog owners for easy money, with not a word said by their peers? To my mind, no.

Online training courses, promoted as providing dog owners with peace and tranquility, are booming. I can't turn on my computer without being bombarded with sponsored advertisements for "calming crate games" and "household hobbies for dogs," which are snapped up by desperate owners who just want five minutes of peace and quiet before the onslaught of yapping and barking starts up again. Just. Five. Minutes. Anyone with kids has been there. Often. I agree, constant commotion is a given with toddlers and puppies: it simply goes with the territory. An adult dog has no such excuse. Your pet does not need to bark at every passerby, leaf, plastic bag or molecule of air just to live a fulfilled life. Crate games can actually be pretty good, though I have yet to find a video that can show my dog how to do the ironing.

Chapter Eight. Balanced Training versus Force-Free Training

Increasingly, force-free trainers push the agenda that badly behaved dogs will be more fulfilled and happier if they never have to face their fears or be confronted with anything that triggers bad behavior, whether inside the home or out. With many dogs, running riot is seen as acceptable. The horrors of the outside world can be anything from terrifying traffic traumas to demon dogs of the downtown, people pushing prams in the park, the trials and tribulations of trails and tracks, and other such tongue-twisters which should not be read out loud after a gin and tonic.

Now, there is nothing wrong with online training videos and tutorials, and there are some genuinely excellent ones out there, created by force-free and balanced trainers alike. Many trainers provide teasers on YouTube, and if my wallet and bank account were not deflated like a tween's face when his first TikTok video has zero views save for Mom, Dad and Gramps, I would subscribe to many of these courses myself. I would learn a great deal from them and be a very happy camper indeed.

In the main, these online training courses have the most value when the owner has some training experience and a well-behaved dog and is seeking to improve her knowledge in a certain defined area such as clicker training, trick training, obedience, scent work, etc. Such an owner will have already nailed good timing when giving rewards and corrections, in addition to understanding how dogs learn and process information. Mostly, when training a new behavior, few corrections other than helpful, enthusiastic guidance are necessary, and there is very little that can go wrong when using these courses to teach an old dog, or indeed a young one, new tricks.

The danger comes when a course creator (a) tells owners that a few indoor games, taking five minutes per day, will fulfill all of their dog's wants and needs, so no walking or other interaction with "real life" will be necessary; (b) provides videos for advanced behavioral modification but markets them to novice dog owners; and (c) provides no communication or follow-up, and will not reply to requests for clarification or advice regarding their videos' contents.

Some trainers will back up their online courses with monitored forums and chatrooms, regular Q&A sessions for subscribers, and perhaps a limited number of one-to-one Zoom or telephone chats. In this way, dog owners are able to find support both from the trainers themselves and from other owners who may be going through similar issues. This can be of immense value. It's a lonely job owning a disobedient dog, particularly a large one, since everyone in the neighborhood invariably crosses the road to avoid you, and the gossip and criticism is never-ending. You've all seen it: the church garage sale goes silent when the wayward dog owner enters, in the same manner as when the Satanists from number 666 come in to try to find a dybbuk box or two.[2]

Often, unless we have another pair of eyes watching what we are doing when training our dogs, we never work out precisely what we are doing wrong, no matter how high the quality of the online content. As I've said before, all top trainers have their own trainer, even if just to provide a second pair of eyes.

Let's take, for example, an online course on competitive obedience. Your dog is already a lovely, well-trained family pet, but you would like to venture into formal obedience. However, you do not have a suitable trainer you can train with in the real world and who is within easy traveling distance. Now you can watch a video and faithfully follow all of the suggested steps—but end up perplexed at why your dog is just not getting it "right."

In training a behavior like focused heelwork, doing something as simple as slightly turning your head and shoulders in order to look down at your dog, to see if he is in the correct position, will invariably throw him *off* position. Without another trainer (or helpful friend, spouse or non-fur child) present who can tell you when the dog is positioned correctly and hence when to mark and reward, it's so, so hard to get a young dog working at your side accurately, with power and precision. This is something I battle with myself, as I have no one to rope in to assist me on a day-to-day basis.

If you can set up a tripod or find a good place to balance your phone, being able to send footage to your content creator, or even post on a forum they run, can be fantastic and nip in the bud a lot of problems you might accidentally be creating in your training. All dogs are different, and a creator cannot cover absolutely everything in one video. Some dogs need to calm down before you can go for more precision, and others need to be more dynamic. These factors can affect the choice of reward you use, and even the way you offer that reward. Often, to ramp up a dog's drive, it's necessary to play the fool a bit and be overly expressive, which many people are not comfortable with, underestimating just how boring a training session can be to a dog, rewards notwithstanding.

Novice trainers who buy a standalone video often will not get that much out of it, since they have no one to ask when things go wrong. The saying "you get what you pay for" very much applies, and taking online courses may not be any cheaper in the long run than hiring a trainer face to face, as you must often buy multiple courses on the same topic to get to where you need to be. And why not? We all have to make a living, dog trainers included. When buying online content, bear in mind that there will be no refund if you don't like it, it's low-quality, or it has been misdescribed, and consider whether you are getting good value for your money.

Chapter Eight. Balanced Training versus Force-Free Training

Most importantly, what additional resources and support are available from the creator?

The force-free mantra—that if a dog's behavior is not improving, it's not the methodology or training course that's at fault, but rather a failure on the part of the dog or the owner—is distasteful to me. Yes, it may be the owner's fault, but people need help, education, and encouragement, and not be guilt-tripped into buying additional expensive videos in a desperate attempt to do right by their dog. I mean, I would buy them, if I had bought into the theory that the method was right and the fault was all mine. Having invested in a certain course because "science says" it is the only way to train dogs and that balanced trainers are out of date and abusive, then of course a loving pet owner just spends more and more money or simply gives up, neither of which benefits the dog.

The courses I feel are most unfair to dog owners, particularly new owners who lack experience, are the ones where the creators are peddling a lie to line their own pockets. This would include courses that tell potential purchasers they can cure their dog of severe behavioral problems all on their own, or that their dog can be content to be locked in a crate 23 hours a day while the owner works double shifts. No, the dog doesn't need exercise, just five minutes of intellectual stimulation via crate games, with some sedatives mixed in with his food. Now, a plush toy can be pretty content with this lifestyle, for sure, leaving the owner to gulp down the sedatives. But a living, breathing dog that requires love and company? Not so much.

In addition to their hawking of online courses, you will find the worst of the grifters telling dog owners they need some additional tools for maximum success. This typically means their own brand of front-pull harness, head collar and clicker, all of which are essential, as are their super-duper training belts for holding cookies, not to mention the cookies themselves, which, ounce for ounce, are quadruple the price of gold. All these items are for sale in the content creator's shop and may be conveniently added to your purchase automatically at checkout. I mean, it will all be discounted by 25 percent, provided you buy everything within the hour. You'd be crazy not to take advantage of such a wonderful deal, which is not made available to other people you know, just an offer especially for you, you wonderful person, you!

As a side note, never trust someone who wears too much hair gel or has lips the average Mallard would be envious of. Get worried should your online content creator resemble your boy/girl band crush from the 1990s and has seemingly had an unfortunate accident with a wind tunnel. Avoid like fleas anyone who behaves like an aluminum siding salesman, putting pressure on you for a quick, discounted purchase.

Would I Lie to You?

One of my bugbears is trainers who market themselves as force-free and produce online content that is either full of corrections which they insist are not corrections or which feature "force-free-trained dogs" about which even the most trusting people would have their suspicions. These very same dogs can sometimes be seen if you cunningly use the Wayback Machine website[3] to peruse old photographs and videos from previous *balanced-training* incarnations of these trainers' websites, since Dalmatians don't change their spots. It is not uncommon for money-hungry trainers to switch sides and jump on the force-free bandwagon as a marketing gimmick, as that's what's selling best these days.

Everyone needs clothes on their back, food in their mouth, and the odd gold plated-toilet and bidet in their home. Even so, there are some trainers I want to slather, naked, in royal jelly. In a nonsexual way, that is, just so we're clear. I would then put them in a crate with a terribly hungry Honey Badger.[4] Why? Well, there is just way too much deceit in the dog training industry. One force-free dog trainer recently posted one of her training sessions on YouTube, and it is an interesting video, to say the least. Bear in mind, this trainer is very vocal against balanced trainers, constantly tweeting (quacking? I am old, you know) that any trainer who is not entirely force-free is a cruel, reprehensible excuse for a human being. Pretty offensive for a "be kind" advocate.

Anyways, this trainer is adamant that she is *entirely* force-free and uses positive reinforcement *only*, with all dogs in her care obliged to wear a flat collar and nothing else. How intriguing, then, that one of the dogs in her video is walking beautifully on a loose lead and wearing what looks like, wait for it, either a pinch collar or a grossly overtight, ill-fitted martingale collar. I mean, this collar is *tight tight tight* and sitting suspiciously high up on the dog's neck, just below the ears. While he is on a loose lead. This is exactly where a pinch collar typically sits. It is not where a martingale collar generally sits when the lead is slack and the collar is not in use, as is the case in the video; however, the higher the collar, the more control you have, so it could be a martingale.

The dog in question is a long-haired German Shepherd, and all that really can be seen of the collar through the hair are the small metal-chain links on the top of the dog's neck, plus the ring the lead is attached to. But as I said, these links are stretched tight. If this is a pinch collar and the trainer was clear that she uses such equipment, then absolutely fine. I would have no issue with it, and the dog is walking beautifully to heel around other dogs, on a constantly loose lead, tail happily wagging. Fantastic. I'm all for it. But this is not a balanced trainer, this is a force-free extremist. She says so herself.

Chapter Eight. Balanced Training versus Force-Free Training 163

When kindly queried about the dog wearing anything but a flat collar, as she has made very, very clear is the only acceptable collar to use, both in her videos and on her website, the trainer doubled down. No apology for misleading her fans or anything like that. Instead, she scathingly retorted that if people had been following this dog's progress, they would know he was prone to slipping his collar and therefore needed a martingale to stop him from going AWOL when scared. Not to control him, or to train him with corrections, or anything abusive like that. Just for safety. She ranted on about how even though the dog was *wearing* a martingale collar, it was not aversive because she was not *using* it, and that because she never uses corrections on any dog, just cookies to cajole and encourage them, she found the comment that she was *using* a martingale collar to be exceptionally hurtful.

Well, the dog was not in a flat collar, was he? Even the best-trained dog can lose concentration and abruptly stop to sniff something, at which point the lead will not retain its slack, causing the martingale—or, let's be honest, the pinch—to tighten about his neck. I am 100 percent for safety and using a collar a dog cannot slip out of, but if you live by the sword you die by the sword. This is a trainer who regularly curses out other trainers for using slip leads, martingale collars, etc. She can't have it both ways. If the dog loves his cookies so much and has total trust in his handler, why would he ever get so scared that he would attempt to slip his collar and escape in the first place? Or is this a case of the force-free trainer's old chestnut "anything goes in an emergency" coming around? That in itself is dubious given that the dog was being trained in an enclosed field with high fencing, so what emergency could there possibly be? He certainly could not escape.

Now, some dogs will get scared and their "go-to" behavior is to try to run away. This can be genetic, and a dog with this sort of flight reaction is absolutely no reflection on the quality of the trainer or the bond he has with such trainer. It is what it is. If you are a force-free trainer with this type of dog, you could be in a quandary, and I have no criticism if you opt to keep that dog safe even if it means going against your fundamental principles. Just eat a bit of humble pie! I will support you in the principle that safety always comes first, but admit that with some dogs there is a place for tools other than a flat collar. If you can use a martingale on a dog that slips his lead, I can use a pinch to reinforce respect for lead pressure.

This dog had in fact been trained by this school from an eight-week-old puppy, so if their force-free-training ethos is superior to every other training method in the universe, as they claim, he should have had such total faith in his handler that he would have trusted her to sort out any scary situation and not slip his collar, leave her side and run. Never mind why such a behavior had become so established and commonplace anyway that the trainer felt that all of her beliefs regarding abusive equipment had to be jettisoned and the dog must wear a collar he cannot slip, all while being trained in a totally safe, enclosed space. To me, these circumstances say the dog was not fearful, just disobedient, and at times had better things to do with his life than eat cookies. I believe that the dog had been sold and was in his final stages of training as a service dog, and it was decided that his issues around respecting commands had to be sorted out once and for all. With corrections.

Now, a service dog should not be flighty or nervous. That is the primary disqualifying factor for such a dog, particularly a big breed that could pull a disabled owner over if he took fright and strained at his lead. He should be neutral around other dogs, not jump up at people, and not try to pursue moving objects such as cyclists, no matter how enticing and figure-hugging the Lycra. I am going to trust that this trainer was not selling an unsuitable dog and putting a disabled person's life at risk, simply a dog with which her force-free methods were proving unsuccessful, and the hand-over date to the new owner was looming.

It was not my place at the time to point out that this dog was almost certainly in a pinch collar, not a martingale as was stated. It was not my business, and although I may have gnarly feet and hookity toenails (just wait until you are old), I am not a troll and I don't believe in starting online fights. The video has since been deleted, as you would expect. Many force-free trainers who have previously been balanced trainers, or even compulsion trainers, either hide their past or claim to have seen the light, rebrand themselves and then go on doing exactly what they have always done in the past. In my opinion, this trainer doth protest too much about balanced trainers. She was foolish and forgot herself. So common and accepted was the use of a badly fitted, super-tight martingale or well-fitted pinch collar in her day-to-day work that she totally forgot who her client base now was and posted a video she would prefer had never seen the light of day.

Everyone knows that videos can be doctored or become outdated, so sometimes multiple complaints are needed before any investigations are carried out. But for the purely positive crowd, using a pinch collar is blasphemy of the highest order, and if this trainer's force-free training org ever gets wind of the fact that she is using a martingale collar that is way too tight, never mind a pinch collar, then according to their rules she would be excommunicated, and run out of town with firebrands and pitchforks. She would probably not even get a warning. What does this say about such dog training orgs, the vast majority of which now force their members to take an oath of allegiance to the purely positive philosophy? Do they really believe in what they are doing, or is it just window dressing to make dog training an increasingly profitable enterprise?

Progress of the Highest Order

Let's be clear, society has changed greatly in the last twenty years, in many ways for the better. In the world of dog training, I'm glad the compulsion trainers have largely gone, though we have now come full circle. It's now the case that any type of raised voice or physical correction, such as a hard "no" or lead pressure, has people clutching their pearls. What else? Corrections are seen as unpalatable to the majority of millennials and their kids, many of whom want to treat their dog like a low-maintenance child at best or a stuffed fluffy toy at worst. Do we use physical corrections on human children these days? No, and rightly so, but a dog is not a child. Human kids bite and have tantrums for a couple of years, which we ignore with patience, waiting for when they grow out of it, whereupon they can be gradually taught why such behavior is wrong and how to self-regulate their emotions. This does not work with dogs, which have neither the language capabilities nor the understanding of ethical and moral concepts that we humans do. What does work for dogs—which will otherwise nip and throw toddler-like tantrums all their lives if allowed to—are corrections.

The orgs I talked about above are against the use of any force whatsoever, all training mandated to be purely positive, and they quite correctly tell people that puppies must stay with their mothers until they are an absolute minimum of eight weeks old. Both mom and a puppy's littermates have important lessons to teach him, lessons that we as mere humans are not well equipped to impart. I agree. The lessons being taught are psychological ones relating to what is and what is not acceptable behavior, and no one does this as well, and in such an effective way, as the puppy's mother.

Puppies start being weaned once they have teeth, as early as three to four weeks of age.[5] They are physically ready to be on their own well before eight weeks, but we keep them with their family so that mom and their siblings can teach them important lessons. With mom, this comes mainly in the form of appropriate corrections, which involve growling and pressure, from both body language and physical restraint.[6]

Why, then, is it fine for a mother dog to teach her puppies with verbal and physical corrections, but once a puppy leaves his canine family he suddenly becomes incapable of learning boundaries and appropriate behavior via corrections, as this now delicate hothouse flower will wilt and lose the will to live should rules be put in place? Now, your job with a young puppy *absolutely* is to build a bond of trust and love, and much behavior that we would not tolerate from an adult or adolescent dog is overlooked in a puppy. Many people stop treating their puppy as a puppy way too early, expecting too much from a five- or six-month-old dog. However, you can use gentle redirections and mild, appropriate corrections even with a very young puppy. Corrections are not punishments, nor are they aversive. Stopping play with a boisterous puppy that is getting carried away, overexcited, rude and nippy acts as a correction to him. This correction is fine and appropriate.

Trainers who alpha roll puppies and adult dogs get bitten. They deserve to, and I would wish more of them got bitten harder if it would not result in euthanasia for the dog in question, which sadly it would. An alpha roll is when you force your dog onto his side or back to show him that you're the boss. Like biting a dog for biting you, this method is outdated and, quite frankly, stupid. We are not dogs, and we cannot issue the same corrections that dogs can. Similar corrections, yes, for example a hard "no" instead of a growl, but we do not have expressive ears and tails to help us communicate with our dogs, or sharp teeth to correct them with. As humans, we use our brains, our voice, our body language, and the tools we have made. A collar. A lead. A crate. It is illogical to say that once a dog leaves his mom, for the rest of his life he can only be bribed into behaving with cookies, not given rules and boundaries via appropriate corrections, whether verbal or physical?

Millennials, I am not throwing shade at you. However, you have been singled out for brainwashing by the various dog training orgs, animal charities and so forth, as you are of an age to be these groups' most reliable client base going forward, born as you were between 1981 and 1996.[7] The Gen X-ers and Boomers are aging out or dying off, and their dog training wisdom, gathered over many years, can simply be ignored. You, my Millennial friends, are our future.

My question is, why this effort to make Millennials drink the Kool-Aid? Why is the truth not considered good enough for you by the great and the good? We teach a dog to do things we want by using incentives, and we use corrections to stop him from doing things that we know are dangerous for him or just not appreciated by the human world. It's as simple as that. Rules and boundaries exist in life—they have to—and in training our dogs to observe them we can do so kindly, with fairness and compassion, by using the same basic principles that dogs use in correcting each other. We can use our voice, body language, physical restraint and pressure, and we can ignore a misbehaving dog or place him in a safe place, just as his mom does.

It's You, Not the Dog

So, we have established that we have balanced trainers masquerading as force-free trainers, slapping a pinch collar on dogs at their training center while presenting themselves as holier-than-thou online. If a trainer is lying about how she lives her life and conducts her business, would you trust her with your dog, particularly behind closed doors? It's very, very wrong to lie, and these trainers need to be made to refund their clients' hard-earned money if they are preaching the purely positive gospel but shoving a pinch on a dog to get quick, effective results. I don't respect the force-free ethos, but I have even less respect for trainers who ignore their clients' wishes.

In the same vein as trainers who are economical with the truth, I have seen some worrying videos put out by similarly vehement "force-free" trainers who are attempting behavioral modification but in so doing are putting others in danger: the dog being trained, the strange dog he encounters, and anyone that may step in to stop a spat between them.

These are trainers who have mildly reactive dogs with no real fear or aggression but that are simply noisy and rude, becoming overexcited on spotting another dog. However, these trainers will not tell the dog that any audible excesses, such as loud whining or barking, is wrong. Nor will they correct any pulling or lunging on the lead, and they may even allow the dog to pull them toward strange dogs, all the while barking, howling and yelping, since it's not allowed to put pressure on his delicate neck. If the dog won't turn and go in another direction when offered cookies, then they will follow the dog's lead. Such trainers rarely have a **stooge dog** to use, so they go to parks and use any strange dog they encounter as an aid to training, which to me is sheer insanity.

In this scenario, the dog is ostensibly worked using thresholds, but not in a particularly meaningful way. Often the threshold training is in name only, as the dog never gets any better, since no alternative behaviors or corrections are ever used. The dog just keeps on being rude. He knows no different, and his excited barking often gives him a rewarding adrenaline rush. In some cases, a year or more passes and, as the dog moves through adolescence and matures, never having been allowed to play with other dogs, some of his excitability around them decreases on its own. He no longer gets a buzz from barking at them, and he settles down. This is more a matter of extinguishing a behavior than threshold training, but in any event the dog is pronounced "cured" without any force having been used.

Now, if that suits you as an owner, letting the passage of time train your dog to get over any slight reactivity, that's fine. We are all different. However, you will often be viewed as a pest in your local community, as indeed you are. Do you want to be that person who is inconsiderate to everyone around them, while all the time asking them to "be nice?" OK, so your dog's reactivity should not be enough of a trigger to seriously dampen anyone's day, provided you have enough control to keep him away from other dogs, but not everyone does. Pavements are narrow, and blind corners exist. That young mother walking her puppy while pushing a stroller in the park doesn't want your lunging, howling dog getting right in her face. If I was her, I would whip out my pepper spray from underneath my baby's blanket and ensure your dog thinks twice about mobbing mine ever again. I'm nice like that.

In particular, it's not OK when trainers allow a reactive dog under their tutelage to drag them toward another dog without first knowing that strange dog or asking the owner if they can let the dogs interact. That is simply not acceptable, as it's incredibly dangerous. How rude when a trainer lets a barking, reactive dog pull her up to a polite on-lead dog, or indeed to an off-lead dog minding his own business, whose owner will recall him if she has any sense, though that's not easy when the canine thug has placed himself between her and her dog. All for the convenience of the trainer.

The dog coming up to your dog may not like other dogs. He may be scared of them. He may be a puppy going through a fear period. He may be half the size of your dog. He may be old, or have had recent surgery and not be allowed to jump or bounce around. You don't know. He may even be very dog aggressive, and will kill your dog. Muzzles are not infallible, and many people with seriously aggressive dogs don't see the need for them, provided their dog is on lead and under control, since other dogs should not be getting up close and personal.

Some force-free trainers who allow a degree of lead pressure, or as much force as is required in an emergency, wink wink, nudge nudge, will take on more problematic behavioral cases, on the assumption that they can turn and walk away if they see another dog coming. Avoiding other dogs when and if required is common in behavioral modification using thresholds, and I do it too. In fact, it tends to be done more by reward-based trainers, who may well have their own stooge dog to use, than by force-free trainers. Many trainers offer reactive dog classes in a controlled environment and under close supervision, which to my mind can be the best place for owners to learn how to handle their reactive dog.

It's great to say you'll turn and walk away when you see another dog coming too close. Pretty much every trainer does so during the training process, but you *must* have control over your dog if things go terribly wrong. What if you turn to evade an approaching dog and another dog and his owner are suddenly right in front of you? If your dog is being walked on a flat collar he does not respect, and he is stronger and more

Chapter Eight. Balanced Training versus Force-Free Training

powerful than you, with greater determination, blood can very easily be spilled—yours, your dog's, the other dogs', their owners', passersby's. Not a situation you want to be in, just because you have been told that anything but a flat collar is cruel. Keeping your dog safe, whether on a slip lead, a martingale, or a pinch collar—whichever he respects enough to be kept under control but which does not evoke pain or fear—is a sensible choice. Better to have an adequate tool and never have to use it than find yourself in the middle of a dogfight, and I'm not talking about *Top Gun*.

Now, we already know a little about threshold training. Many trainers, of whatever ilk, use it over an extended period of time. However, in lots of cases this is mainly for the owner's benefit rather than the dog's. Even dogs that have been involved in a fight will often bounce back fairly quickly. If jollied along in a brisk way, given encouragement and confidence by their handler rather than everyone getting tense about it, they do not become insanely fearful of other dogs. As always, much depends on the dog's genetics and propensity for fearfulness, but animals were designed to be able to quickly get over non-life-threatening traumas. It is we humans who overthink things.

If you put your hand on a hot stove as a kid, old enough to know that stoves can hurt you, and you receive a minor burn, the injury would not come as a total and utter shock. It would be painful, and there would be tears, but you would be unlikely to be petrified of the stove and refuse to enter the kitchen ever again. However, if you touched the stove and were electrocuted, thrown across the kitchen and spending the next month in the hospital, you may have PTSD and be too scared to enter the kitchen for a while. Your mom would be sympathetic but would probably tell you to man (or woman) up and not serve you hand and foot, getting drinks from the refrigerator for you as you are "too scared" to leave the sofa and go past the stove to get them yourself.

Dogs are similar. They are not necessarily traumatized by a minor spat where no blood is drawn, or just a little bit of fur flies. Many dogs, particularly if of a confident breed, will just shrug it off. Although such a dog might understandably be a little wary about strange dogs, or those that approach with poor body language, or that are reactive and barking, he is not stricken with terror unless his owner does something to reinforce the fear, making the dog question whether he should be scared.

When our dog has been attacked and injured, even if only mildly, we as owners understandably become fearful of the same thing happening again, and this rubs off onto our dog. We see another dog in the distance and immediately tense up, tightening the lead and making it uncomfortable for our dog, holding him close to us, if not picking him up and squeezing him. This is a triple whammy for the dog: (1) another dog is coming, (2) his owner is scared—which he can clearly smell coming off his owner in waves, and (3) his leash has him in a stranglehold or he is being crushed in his owner's arms. In these sorts of situations, the threshold training is for the owner's benefit.

With a dog that does not have deep-rooted behavioral issues stemming from a deep fear or trauma, but rather politeness issues or a slight lack of confidence, most balanced trainers will not make extensive use of thresholds. They know they are in command and can control the situation, keeping the dog safe, and this transmits to the dog. After some preliminary training to make friends and build trust, including basic obedience training using rewards and corrections, the dog is introduced to being trained around other dogs, where he is expected to behave and concentrate on his handler. Many dogs will not go over threshold, and indeed are on threshold on day one of their training. Some genuinely have never been aware that pulling on the lead and vocalizing is wrong. Once this is understood, the dog just accepts the new rules and gets on with life.

Some trainers are skilled at training people as well as dogs and are able to get dog and owner working together in a few brief training sessions, often moving them into an obedience class or one specifically tailored for reactive dogs. This is preferable, as the dog can very quickly learn to be walked safely and comfortably by his owner in public, greatly improving the quality of life for both of them. Of course the dog must be on threshold and not suppressed in his behavior, but it is surprising how there can be a 360 degree turnaround in some mildly fearful and reactive dogs in only one or two sessions when a skilled trainer steps in to help. The trainer's confidence and leadership allow both dog and owner to relax. The dog's basic obedience, engagement and bond with his owner improve, and he comes to know that his owner will protect him and make decisions for their partnership, instead of his having to cope with his fears on his own or, at worst, having them magnified by his owner.

When a dog has had a bad fight with another dog or has a genetically fearful nature, things must be taken slowly and carefully with both dog and owner. The same goes for a problem that has existed for a long time, such as a dog that is not well-mannered or under control at home. We must also take longer with dogs that get overexcited and aroused extremely quickly and easily, as keeping them on threshold takes patience as well as skill, and the dog's self-control needs to be allowed to develop, which can take time.

Great care must always be taken with very strong, powerful dogs. Even small dogs can pull their owners over if they do not have good lead manners and have never been told they must not pull on the lead, or that lunging unexpectedly will have negative consequences for them. It must

Chapter Eight. Balanced Training versus Force-Free Training

always be remembered that puppies have fear periods and that under a year of age, *puppies will be puppies*. People often want to shove a pinch collar on their five-month-old large working breed when he pulls on the lead around other dogs, showing excitement and vocalizing. With many breeds this behavior should be considered the norm and dealt with via redirection, encouraging the dog past distractions, not by yelling at him and yanking and cranking, creating fear, confusion and the possibility of genuine problems in the future.

As we can see, there are problems with force-free trainers giving unsafe advice, just as there are problems with bad balanced trainers who do the same. To be avoided at all costs are compulsion trainers and the militant purely positive cults. Force-free training does not equal risk-free training, as so many people think. It is surprising how many of these force-free jokers there are about, and how much money they make from total and utter nonsense, particularly when they put dogs at risk and into unsafe situations. I'm good with slow training if the client is happy. Ineffective training, well, that's a shame for the client who's paying for no results and the dog that ends up locked indoors. When force-free training fails and clients are told there is no other way to turn except drugging or even euthanizing their dog, that is unforgivable.

I have recently seen an increasing number of force-free trainers give advice that is perplexing, to say the least. For example, recommending that dogs learn to use a cat scratching post to "wear their nails down" so they don't need to be trimmed. Helpful hint: you will be a skeleton before one solitary nail is adequately shortened in this manner, not to mention that even if there was an alternate universe where it did wear them down, the middle two nails would be short but the side nails would remain untouched. Plus, how exactly does a dog learn to trim the nails on his back paws? If I paid $100 for a course that told me it would end all my nail trimming woes, just to see a video of a dog dragging his paw over a cat scratching post in a desultory fashion, I would be fuming.

Why not just, I don't know, teach your dog to sit quietly while his nails are cut or Dremelled? Positive training with plenty of rewards is a great way to do this. However, dogs' paws have a lot of nerve endings, and for some dogs with very sensitive nails the inducement of cookies is not enough. Such dogs just have to be told it is not an option to struggle and nip, even though we can sympathize that it's uncomfortable for them. It is medically necessary to trim a dog's nails; leaving them alone is not an option. Better that a dog becomes accustomed to having his nails trimmed without fuss than think that getting into a fight with his owner about it is a good idea.

These days, it's not just genuine dog trainers putting themselves out there online, there are also plenty of social media influencers who promote themselves as dog trainers and who make an extremely good living lecturing owners to be force-free, promoting a supposedly harmonious lifestyle that dog owners should aspire to. It is a mirage. It is not real. Do you think that force-free or any types of dog training influencers are telling the truth about how their dogs behave when the camera is turned off, or about the corrections they really use? No. They are promoting a certain brand and putting their best foot forward. Always. Anyone who has worked in the media will tell you that in real life, people are not always how they appear on camera. The nicest, wittiest and kindest celebrity can be the very devil herself behind the scenes.[8]

Who Cares?

So why does this all matter? Well, for many of us, our dog is our ride or die. We want the best for them, and being given misleading information can be deeply upsetting, especially when you've drained your finances in trying to do the best by your dog, not using what the force-free mafia consider abusive techniques, such as a firm "no" and a basic lead correction, and not making any progress as a result. It's fine to be a positive dog trainer; in fact, it's more than fine, it's admirable, preferable. After all, I consider myself to be one, even though my young dog sometimes wears a pinch collar. I would say that most balanced trainers are really reward-based, though it is a spectrum. What is not OK is to lie and, on top of that, throw serious shade at people who do not agree with you, all to get dollars in your piggy bank. This is the reality of the force-free extremists; they don't let their training do the talking, instead they go all out to shut down anyone who disagrees with them.

We are increasingly seeing laws enacted to ban the use of e-collars, pinch collars and anything else the force-free extremists dislike. Why? Well, follow the money, honey. Dog training is big business, with many dog trainers and influencers becoming multi-millionaires, all on the basis of preaching "be kind" in dog training. The optics of a dog lovingly taking a cookie from your hand are much nicer than seeing a large, snarling, growling dog being given a harsh correction for seriously bad behavior.

Eighty-three percent of people in the U.S. today live in urban areas, not in the countryside.[9] An increasing proportion of the dog-owning population wants small, easy to manage, biddable dogs that require only short walks (if any, certainly not daily or in inclement weather) and that rarely assert their own will. The American Kennel Club list of the most popular dog breeds of 2021[10] includes in its top ten breeds seven that I would

Chapter Eight. Balanced Training versus Force-Free Training

consider mild and/or small breeds, including French Bulldogs, Poodles, Labradors and Golden Retrievers. The only two exceptions were the German Shepherd dog at number four and the Rottweiler at number eight, with the German Shorthaired Pointer at number nine. Bearing in mind that the German Shepherd and Rottie are primarily show lines, not working lines, the difference between those breeds and the others on the list is similar to the difference between acetaminophen and crack cocaine. Both have their uses. Different ones, but uses nonetheless.

Many owners of small or mild dogs are scared when they see a bigger, tougher dog coming their way. I don't blame them. I often am uneasy myself when I see an out-of-control, badly behaved dog approaching, barking its head off on the end of its Flexi-lead. Other dog owners (not me!) have little control over their dog, and they fear the big dog approaching in case its owner has the same low level of control and will not be able to stop their angel from being eaten. (Lucifer was an angel too, just a fallen one, but let's not go there.)

Taking away the tools that owners of large, high-drive working breeds use will make it harder to continue to own those breeds and give them a decent quality of life. Soon it will no longer be pleasurable to own a big dog with an even bigger personality, and people will move to small or mild-mannered breeds. Or working breed show lines will be further manipulated to be more amenable, with no drive, happy to inhale cookies instead of running and playing energetically as a working breed of dog should. This is not a world I want to live in. I would rather have no dog than a "Notweiler," and put a leash on my cat.

I am sure you are asking, Why is the canine establishment so keen to shake everything up? Yes, small, docile breeds are easy to train with a hard look, no force required, but why does it matter so much to the force-free training orgs that big, working dogs go the way of the Dodo? I mean, the majority of force-free trainers make their money from handbag dogs, so what's the big deal financially if balanced trainers work with the bigger ones? Well, it's not just dog trainers, there's a far larger, very lucrative market which prefers small, easy-to-handle dogs, and that's the charity sector, both in terms of rescues and, to an extent, service dogs. These charities are an incredibly big business but surprisingly secretive about the precise state of their finances. Over the last few years, almost all of these charities have jumped onto the force-free bandwagon, despite having used corrections for years in their dogs training and rehabilitation. Why? you may ask. Why indeed, and in Chapter Ten, we will delve into the winners and losers in the dog training industry. But first, let's take a look at some legal issues.

Chapter Nine

Legal Beagles

In this chapter I'm going to look at the types of legislative changes that are increasingly affecting dog training and ownership. I will mainly stay on my side of the pond, simply because politics, and consequently legislation, have been more effectively hijacked by force-free activists in the UK and Europe. But do not be complacent, those of you who live in the U.S. These days, common sense cannot be relied upon to prevail, and you will not remain safe from the lunatic fringe only by virtue of your Constitution, which is something the UK and many other European countries do not have. Bans on certain tools and training techniques, not to mention breeds, plus battles over other animal welfare issues such as tail docking and ear cropping, are very much coming your way. Fight and protect your rights now while you still have the chance.

You Shall Not Pass (Over Our Border)

In the UK, I have found that legislative change regarding dogs tends to occur in one of two ways: (1) there is a public outcry in reaction to certain closely spaced events, and as a consequence badly thought out legislation is hurriedly pushed through Parliament in order to appease the great unwashed (as our uber-wealthy politicians see the general public); or (2) there is slow and gradual petitioning and ~~bribing~~ wooing of politicians behind the scenes over a long period of time by certain action groups, which may lead to some form of public consultation, but in general the result is predetermined according to what will best line the pockets and interests of the politicians and action groups in question. In both cases, there is no real care or consideration for actual animal welfare; rather, politicians will do what politicians do: look after number one.

The Dangerous Dogs Act 1991 (DDA) was a badly written, ill-thought-out piece of UK legislation which even the government now admits only came about due to press hysteria regarding dog attacks.[1] Journalists were telling the public that American Pit Bull Terriers, amped up to the max, were running around neighborhoods eating babies and the like. Such reports were published all in order to sell more newspapers, not due to any altruistic concern for children, nor a particular love for babies, who typically do not spend money purchasing the local rag. In the view of politicians and journalists alike, babies are only of real interest to dangle on the knee for photo ops and for scandalous articles claiming they are being eviscerated and consumed alive. By dogs. It seems I am not a fan of politicians or journalists. Who could tell?

The result of the DDA was that four breeds of dog were banned: the Japanese Tosa, the Dogo Argentino, the Fila Brasileiro and the Pit Bull Terrier or dogs of that type, as Pit Bulls are not considered a breed in the UK, but rather a type of dog. The ban was justified by describing all of these dogs as bred to participate in dogfights and not to be pets. As dogfighting has been banned in the UK since 1835,[2] it is highly unlikely that reputable breeders were breeding dogs for fighting over multiple generations. Rather, these were easy breeds to pick on.

People who do breed dogs for the purpose of dogfighting are criminals, pure and simple. They tend not to be upstanding citizens who pay their taxes and refrain from public littering. These guys don't pay an awful lot of attention to the law. Any law. Complying with the DDA would not have entered their tiny skull cavity, never mind pierced the one brain cell lurking there all alone, pining for company. They just kept their fighting dogs "out of sight, out of mind" as they always did, and it was business as usual.

The dogs which were affected were the numerous dogs unfairly seized by the police for being the "Pit Bull type." These were often friendly, sociable dogs that had done nothing wrong and just looked the wrong way, perhaps reported by someone who had a grudge against their owner. Many of these dogs were crossbreeds and more often than not had no Pit Bull in them, rather they contained a lot of Staffordshire Bull Terrier plus a little bit of something else that provided enough deviation from standard Staffy size and dimensions to make the police suspicious and provide the grounds to seize them.

Kept in "approved" kennels with little to no human interaction, many of these dogs ended up traumatized, languishing for years while their owners fought desperately in court to have them returned. Those were the lucky ones. Some owners signed papers authorizing the police to destroy their dog if he measured up as a Pit Bull, not realizing what they had done. I mean, not many people fully read terms and conditions when in handcuffs, threatened with arrest and a body cavity search unless they sign on the dotted line. The vast majority of people would be signing that document with their toes. If you're a fan of horror stories, plus some happy endings, the "Save Our Seized Dogs—Put BSL to Sleep UK" Facebook page may be for you.[3] ("BSL" stands for breed-specific legislation.)

I will leave you to look up the exact details of the DDA restrictions in full, should you be interested,[4] but essentially the breeding and importation of the aforementioned four breeds was prohibited, with further restrictions placed on the dogs' living conditions, including that they must be leashed and muzzled in public, neutered/spayed, micro-chipped, insured, and only owned and walked by a fit and proper person.

After the DDA in the UK, more and more breed-specific legislation was passed in other countries in Europe and beyond, setting a precedent which resulted in the death of many innocent, well-behaved dogs. Politicians went about banning or placing restrictions on whatever breeds they had a personal grudge against. Even now, as I am writing this, many European countries still have breed-specific legislation,[5] most notably the Republic of Ireland, Romania, Portugal, Iceland, and Spain, with bans and restrictions in other counties worldwide, including Israel, Singapore, Malaysia, and the UAE, and of course there are bans on pit bulls in many parts of the USA.

In 2003 China followed suit, jumping on the breed restriction bandwagon, but they had to take it one step further, as befits a government with a competitive personality. The city of Beijing ended up banning even more breeds than Ukraine, since any dog over 35 centimeters tall (just under 14 inches) was banned from the center of the city.[6] This would exclude any dog taller than a small Beagle.[7]

As originally written, the ban simply applied to dogs that were "large and vicious."[8] Could it be, given that "large" is a matter of opinion, that some small breeds with the tendency to be nippy—otherwise known as "vicious"—were also intended to be banned? I'm looking at you, Mr. Jack Russell and Ms. Chihuahua.[9] Presumably the ban, if read as intended, would have left a Pug free to loiter around on his own. But that was unclear.

So, a couple of days before the rule came into force, a clarification was made.[10] Large dogs were once more stated as being banned, but "large" was now defined as being 13.8 inches tall or more, which is clear enough. In case you're struggling to envisage the height restriction, if a French Bulldog grew so much as one inch over his normal height, 13 inches being the maximum for the breed,[11] he too would be banned. Watch out, folks, your ankles and knees are at risk from rampaging French Bulldogs. Better ban them!

Vicious dogs were also still not welcome, though what constitutes vicious is really down to the individual dog in question. Or so you would think, but no. A list of foreign breeds, all of which were considered to be vicious, was provided, a list with no rhyme or reason at all, no doubt prepared by an administrator with access only to a censored internet, given that this was 2003 Communist China.

Every dog on the list was too tall to be permitted anyway, if they conformed to breed standard, with many, such as the Great Dane, far above the height restriction.[12] Many of the breeds, including the Saint Bernard and Bernese Mountain Dog, were meek and mild, even though tall. Retrievers were not banned as a group, though Setters were. Terriers as a group were safe. Had the administrator never met the average ~~terrorist~~ Terrier that was hangry, one ponders? I think not. The Kerry Blue and Bedlington Terriers did make the banned list, along with the British Bulldog, all of which I would trust over the average Dachshund, which, despite his diminutive height, has very powerful jaws and teeth, being bred to hunt Badgers.[13] He was also found to be the most aggressive dog breed overall in a 2008 study,[14] with honorable mentions to the Jack Russell Terrier and the Chihuahua, all three breeds displaying serious aggression, not just to strangers but to their owners too. Ouch. Talk about biting the hand that feeds you. Yes, I know there are wonderful Jack Russells, Chihuahuas and Daxis: I have trained all of them, lived with two of them, and am very fond of them in general! I do not create the scientific studies we are seeing so much of in this book.

I suspect the list of banned breeds in Beijing was mainly political, intended to stop people from importing foreign breeds of dog. Listing specific breeds meant it would not be possible for budding entrepreneurs to deliberately create mini-me versions of popular overseas breeds in order to slip them in under the height restriction. No Chinese breed was included on the list, not even the Tibetan Terrier,[15] which standing at 14 to 17 inches, *should* have been banned on height alone. They may not be true Terriers,[16] given that they are quite docile and have little prey drive, but they can take a bit of a pop at strangers, both canine and human. Most are adorable little dogs, but they were originally bred as watchdogs, giving them some defensive aggression, unfortunately combined with nervousness. Never a good combination. Similarly, the Tibetan Mastiff was not listed, nor was the Shar Pei, neither breed, even if scaled down, the epitome of a safe, non-vicious dog that has no protective instinct whatsoever and would never consider such an uncouth action as biting a human or another dog.

The legislation in China and also in Ukraine demonstrates the absurdity of breed-specific legislation. You cannot list all of the breeds in the world, and putting in height, weight or type restrictions does not work either. Even within breeds that have a well-deserved reputation for aggression, there are individual dogs that are simply delightful. Limiting the breeds of dog that people can own seems to me a severe restriction on personal freedom. History tells us that once a government limits the freedoms of even a small group of citizens, it never ends well.

There are many rare breeds and local crossbreeds that are never banned but that typically have far more aggressive tendencies—mainly toward other dogs—than breeds such as the German Shepherd Dog and the Rottweiler, which always show up on banned lists and yet which remain, year in year out, very popular as pets.[17] Some of these rare breeds, for example the Bully Kutta[18] from Pakistan, are still bred for dogfighting. Import a top dog of a certain variant as a stud, and he may well come with a list of confirmed kills. Despite their inherent poor temperament and unsuitability to be kept as a pet in an area with a high density of other dogs, Bully Kuttas can be imported with gay abandon into most countries, including the UK. Meanwhile, more visible dog breeds that have done nothing worse than catch the attention of journalists and raise the blood pressure of politicians (sadly, not fatally) are banned. You simply cannot list all of the dogs that you feel are dangerous. Another breed will always pop up.

If you have never heard of a Bully Kutta, envisage a Pit Bull in your mind. Now ask a mad scientist to call Jurassic Park to get some Velociraptor genes for drive, plus a bit of T. Rex for size. Add a sprinkling of trenbolone to give some edge, and you have your modern variant of the Bully Kutta. There are reportedly fewer than twenty Bully Kuttas in the UK, and I could not find the breed listed on the American Kennel Club's list of most popular breeds in 2021.

I'll be honest, I almost crashed my car when I saw my first Bully Kutta in the flesh, just, you know, taking his owner out for a run. I considered asking if I could hire him as my personal coach. His owner had an upper body which would be the envy of any football player, as deciding to stop running when tired out would not be an option when "walking" him. Or him walking me. Training me, even? He was a dog I would not object to being trained by. Within a month of daily sessions, I would fit into the dress I wore to prom aged eighteen.

In the U.S. you have similar problems to Europe, at least on a local level, with breed-specific bans, particularly with regard to Pit Bull Terriers. But if you want a Bully Kutta in the UK or U.S., OK. Not a breed on anyone's radar, even though some varieties are still being bred for dogfighting in Pakistan, so a dog killer (sad but accurate) may not be more than a generation away from the dog you buy on U.S. soil. This is simply a fact, not to throw shade on the dog, which can be the right one for the right handler who has the right environment to keep him in.

All is not yet lost in the U.S., as in many places dog lovers have been fighting back. Successfully. It can be done. On September 19, 2022 in

Minot, North Dakota, the city council voted to repeal the ban on Pit Bulls which had stood for decades.[19] We need more of this, and we need to start standing up to the preliminary probing of force-free trainers who want to introduce bans on tools such as pinch and e-collars.

If all of us do not stand up for Pit Bulls and other large, high-drive dogs, both in terms of fighting breed-specific legislation *and* supporting the tools most often used with such dogs fairly, safely and well, they will decline. Such breeds are not fun to live with when the owner cannot put in place effective rules and boundaries which her dog understands and responds well to in training, and it must *always* be remembered that actual training is the key.

E-collars and pinch collars, yes, even flat collars, keep a dog at our side by restricting his movement through force. Balanced training, via plenty of engagement and appropriate corrections, produces a loose lead and a neutral dog. Just be careful, is all I'm saying, otherwise, before you know it, all that will be left are small, low-drive dogs, which may very well suit you. For now. They will be next to be petitioned against, given time. Then when you're my age and need a service dog—and no one is more than a car crash away from needing one—they will be banned too, the thought of a dog doing a day's work being considered a disgrace.

By and by, more breeds of dog will be included in breed-specific legislation, and they will not be the ones you may suspect. In fact, the force-free trainers among you may be appalled, as much of your client base is set to disappear if the U.S. copies Europe. Those veterinary groups you managed to convince that corrections are cruel and unnecessary, and that Lucifer himself sits and makes pinch collars and e-collars in his spare time, the American College of Veterinary Behaviorists being one of them, well, they are not always going to be your friends. They may have bought into your force-free agenda and currently be promoting it heavily,[20] but don't be fooled. Once you've served your purpose as mere dog trainers, they will drop you like a malfunctioning e-cig[21] when they call for a ban on breeding the small dogs many of you depend on for your livelihood.

In Europe veterinarians started a campaign, Vets Against Brachycephalism,[22] which now represents 66 countries, 82 professionals, and 81 organizations and practices, and yes, the U.S. is represented among these veterinarians who want small brachycephalic dogs banned. By the time you force-free trainers recognize the fact that brachycephalic breeds are in danger of being banned in the U.S. too, on the say-so of veterinarians who are fighting with the same gusto that enabled you to get Pit Bulls banned, with bans on pinch collars and e-collars under discussion, it will be too late to complain. You will have made your bed and will have to lie in it. Let's discuss this some more, shall we?

Bye-Bye, Puggle

In Europe we are in the middle of a war. Attention has turned from banning large breeds to banning small ones. The target is brachycephalic dogs, which often live short, painful, miserable lives, all for the sake of being cute.[23] If you are a force-free trainer, how can you look yourself in the mirror when you train and promote the ownership of brachycephalic dogs? These dogs are in pain every day, often every minute of every day, literally, as they cannot sleep properly[24] and suffer from a host of medical conditions.[25] By specializing in working with these dogs, by featuring these dogs on your website and in your advertising (which may well be in breach of your country's veterinary advertising regulations),[26] you are promoting the breeding and keeping of dogs that live in pain. A balanced trainer may give an e-collar correction to a dog twice a year and you feel that correction should be banned, but the dog breeds that live in pain every day should be encouraged? No. That's called being a hypocrite.

Now, the law may not even have to be amended at all regarding some brachycephalic breeds, since existing animal welfare laws may be sufficient. On January 31, 2022, the Oslo District Court ruled that breeding Cavalier King Charles Spaniels and English Bulldogs was illegal.[27] The very act of being born, given that 50 percent of British Bulldog mothers require a cesarean section and both breeds have multiple health issues, inflicts harm on these dogs, in breach of Norwegian animal welfare laws.[28] Remember, these are two very popular breeds, Bulldogs coming in sixth on the list of the most popular breeds in the U.S. in 2021, with the Cavalier King Charles Spaniel placing at number 15.[29]

In addition to the existing laws, there are other means to decrease the popularity of a breed. In the Netherlands, despite legislation prohibiting the breeding of animals where the health of the parent or offspring is harmed, the law was being ignored,[30] as in Norway. The Dutch Kennel Club even made a fitness test, including a 1-km walk, mandatory for Bulldogs. Without avail. Now the club lists twelve brachycephalic breeds it will no longer register unless its breeding criteria are met.[31] The list includes the second most popular breed in the U.S., the French Bulldog.[32] The full list comprises the Affenpinscher, Boston Terrier, Bulldog, French Bulldog, Griffon Belge, Griffon Bruxellois, Japanese Chin, King Charles Spaniel, Pekingese, Petit Brabancon, Pug and Shih Tzu.[33]

Many people, no matter where they live, want to have a pedigree dog that is health-tested, is registered with a kennel club, and can be shown and participate in club-sanctioned events. It may seem that crossbreed dogs such as Doodles and Poos are seeking world domination, but a UK survey conducted by Blue Cross in 2022[34] found that only 24 percent of

Chapter Nine. Legal Beagles 181

dogs were mixed breed (19 percent of respondents admitted their dog was a mutt, with a special Cockapoo category of 5 percent, which I have added together in some amazing mental gymnastics). Interestingly, on the list of the ten most popular dogs there were no brachycephalic dogs, even though 41 percent of respondents said they purchased their dog from a breeder. In a similar survey by Dogs Trust, the UK's largest dog welfare charity, only the Shih Tzu was mentioned among the most popular breeds.[35]

These statistics are, shall we say, "suspicious," given that 6,122 Pug puppies,[36] 2,337 Shih Tzu puppies,[37] and a whopping 54,074 French Bulldog puppies[38] were registered in the same period, 2021. More than fifty-four thousand Frenchies in one year. To give context, in the Blue Cross top ten, Golden Retrievers ranked number two behind crossbreeds, with 11 percent ownership, yet only 11,808 Golden Retriever puppies were registered.[39] In the same year, 54,074 French Bulldogs were registered, yet French Bulldogs don't make the most popular list for either Blue Cross or Dogs Trust. Hmm.

In fact, the only dog that beat the French Bulldog on either the Blue Cross or Dogs Trust list was the Labrador Retriever, with a massive, world-beating 61,559 puppies registered in 2021.[40] Admittedly, many of those dogs could have come from back yard breeders. Not over fifty-four thousand of them, though. Both of these charities push small and medium-sized dogs, particularly the Jack Russell Terrier, which only had 355 registrations and are renowned snapmeisters.[41] Now, who are the members of Vets Against Brachycephalism, I wonder? Oh yes, Blue Cross (number six on their list),[42] and though Dogs Trust may not be among their members, you can bet the reason for that is political, to keep those pennies rolling in. Cowards. Can I say that and not be sued? It's my opinion, after all. So, we have lies about the most popular breeds in order to push an agenda, just as force-free trainers lie about only using positive reinforcement. Funny, isn't it?

I don't stand on a soapbox and call for death to Pugs, and for Frenchies to be banned. I don't go onto Japanese Chin forums and rant about how cruel it is to keep such dogs. I loved my long-backed Dachshund cross, even if her father had intervertebral disc disease and more allergies than you could shake a stick at. I would like to see breeders of dogs with inherent health problems be given incentives to breed healthier dogs, ones which do not need BOAS (brachycephalic obstructive airway syndrome) surgery to be able to get a good night's sleep or a C-section to give birth. I would not ban these dogs, though. Why, if you force-free fanatics are so passionate about animal welfare, do you apply prohibitions to tools that actually help dogs, such as pinch collars and e-collars, but at the same time are happy to advertise your services with a French Bulldog on your website?

I mean, even the Association of Pet Dog Trainers in the UK has unhealthy breeds pictured, and thus promoted, on their website. These breeds include Dachshunds[43] and cute Australian Shepherd/Border Collie puppies with the merle gene, ironically on the site's "Choosing a Puppy" page.[44] Yes, the merle gene, the one that causes deafness and blindness when it is doubled up,[45] as back yard breeders are wont to do. If in doubt, *don't* promote breeds that have such serious health issues unless extreme care in breeder selection is exercised. I mean, up to 24 percent of Dachshunds have intervertebral disc disease in their lifetime,[46] and it's a breed promoted on your website? Particularly don't do this when lecturing other people that they are cruel and misguided. Better a deaf or crippled dog than a well-behaved dog in a pinch collar, you think? I don't.

Now, I could not find any calls for an absolute ban on e-collars or pinch collars on the Association of Pet Dog Trainers' website, though they are very much in favor of positive reinforcement, as am I. However, they are members of the Animal Behaviour and Training Council, which is very much against pinch and e-collars. In an interview with the BBC about e-collars, Jane Williams, their secretary, is quoted as saying, "Using unethical methods is a breach of dog welfare."[47]

The Animal Behaviour and Training Council also has merle puppies on its website.[48] Even worse, these puppies look like they have white hair on their ears, and we know what that is associated with in breeds that carry the merle gene, having been good boys and girls and read the article I linked to above. Yes, bad things. I quote: "White markings on or around the ears are associated with ... deafness and the same mechanism causes deafness in double merles but with a different genetic base."[49]

Am I saying these puppies have the double merle gene and are potentially deaf or blind? No. Am I saying they *look* like they might have this doubled up gene, given the white on their ears? Yes. Have a look at confirmed double merle puppies,[50] then compare. Very similar. If your organization is going to say that users of e-collars and, by implication, pinch collars, including myself, "breach dog welfare"[51] and are "using unethical methods,"[52] then don't you *dare* put photographs on your website encouraging the purchase of puppies based on fancy colors rather than temperament and health and then claim the upper hand over balanced trainers. Don't. You. Dare.

Now, am I being horrible to these two organizations? Some will say yes, and some of those who say yes will be happy and claim it's about time they were called out for their hypocrisy. They are, after all, bodies that publicly call me and other balanced trainers nasty names.[53] The Animal Behaviour and Training Council is a charity, and so should be accountable for any unethical practices.

Promoting the breeding of merle dogs by highlighting them on one's website is surely unethical. It has been proven time and again that back yard breeders do not health-test and happily churn out deaf and blind dogs, just to get more money for a pretty color. These two orgs work both publicly and behind the scenes to take away my freedoms, that is, to own and train the breeds I love. Well, then, for once I am going to bite back and point out that they have been reckless and unethical in promoting breeds that have the merle gene.

The Truth, the Whole Truth, and Nothing but the Truth, So Help Me Dog

Do not think for one second that force-free trainers are paragons of kindness and that they practice what they preach. Oh, and that they are totally honest, and with no agenda to be pushed at all costs. Many do not fit this mold. Indeed, now that much of the training industry is advertising itself as force-free, these trainers are turning on themselves with the ferocity of a Bully Kutta on steroids that has just taken a dragon-sized dose of crystal meth. Recently, I have seen a great many online posts in which factions of the force-free community are attacking each other in an attempt to stand out from the pack, since they all have the same marketing shtick and are desperate for clients.

On one conversation on an online dog forum, a Neapolitan Mastiff owner was looking for a boarding kennel that is familiar with "big, strong dogs who pull on the lead." As expected, force-free trainers jumped in and claimed the dog needs a "behaviorist" to care for him, and that the owner must avoid balanced trainers like a decomposing raccoon under the porch. This little lamb must be terribly scared to pull so hard on the lead in order to escape his frightening house and get to the safety of the park. He must be gently counter-conditioned into walking nicely for cookies, packets of the stuff rammed into his mouth when he sees the park pathway so he no longer bolts in terror toward the park gates.

The force-free trainers were adamant that the dog's home must be a frightening place and that he needs some sort of behavioral modification given that he is so keen to get to the park. You know the drill. All dogs are puddles of fear, surrounded by a miasma of low self-esteem. It could not be possible that a big, strong, confident dog could have preferences in life, such as enjoying a walk in the park, meaning he heads there at a pace faster than his owner's legs can manage.

There was immediate agreement that only force-free trainers can call themselves behaviorists since they are science-based and, yes, you know what comes next, "science says" positive reinforcement is the best indeed, the only humane way to train dogs. These trainers use lots of negative corrections in their training and will boot a dog up the backside in an emergency, but let's gloss over that. Now, however, the argument got heated. Other force-free trainers chimed in, all indignant, insisting that *the law* says only force-free trainers with *a degree* can call themselves behaviorists. (This is untrue.) Others countered that only members of the Animal Behaviour and Training Council and the Association of Pet Dog Trainers can call themselves behaviorists. The only consensus was that balanced trainers cannot be behaviorists.

In the UK, as in the U.S., dog training is a largely unregulated industry. Now, in both countries there are certain terms that describe very specific professions, such as "veterinary behaviorist,"[54] and "board-certified veterinary behaviorist,"[55] which only people with the right qualifications can legally use. The licensing that allows people to use such terms is governed by legislation relating to veterinarians. This situation applies to all professions, including law, dentistry and medicine. But the word *behaviorist* by itself has no legal restrictions in the UK, no matter what force-free trainers with a degree in animal behavior will claim. These trainers were lying when they said that balanced trainers cannot use the term, and also when they said that only force-free trainers with degrees can use the term; hence the fight.

Other quite amusing food fights among force-free trainers recently have been between the extremist faction and the more moderate faction, those who admit they give their dogs boundaries and rules and use tools such as head collars, just never use corrections. Ahem, I think your pants are on fire.[56] Anyways, there was a massively indignant post vilifying trainers who use luring with food rewards. What is wrong with luring, you may be wondering, scratching your head. Well, apparently it equates with dog abuse, since it coaxes dogs to perform "inhumane" actions, such as walking to heel on the lead, when this must always be the *dog*'s choice. If your dog wants to pull on his lead, say the extremists, you must sprint after him so his neck is not hurt.

Heaven forbid that there should exist well-behaved, happy dogs that have had lures used to teach them how to walk close to their owner's side on a loose leash. Those dogs may have a wagging tail, but they've been traumatized, girl! Apparently the trainer who wrote the post has performed multiple behavioral consults with dogs that, when they see the treat pouch come out, sprint fearfully to their safe space in the back of their crates, all because they have been trained using lures. Guess this trainer does not know crates are considered cruel by her extremist mates in Sweden and Finland. Oh, the horror!

This trainer recommends that dogs have autonomy in all aspects of their daily life. Should a dog design to leave his crate (or "his" place on the sofa or bed) and interact with the family, he may. When he feels like a walk—which will involve tugging and dragging his owner about at random, not to mention barking at other dogs—he can suggest it and must be obeyed. Even if the Super Bowl final is on. If rain is forecast, then under no circumstances must he be lured to come outside with treats so he can quickly do his business and then go back inside. No! No, no, no. Cruel! Well, is his name Gizmo, I wonder? Maybe if it's after midnight, she has a point, as we covered in a previous chapter. But no. Absolutely not. Even if he is just a dog, luring him to come outside with treats is evil, and he *must* be permitted to toilet in the house. I am not making this up. I am not going to include a screenshot or link, as that would be unfair to certain individuals' privacy, but I genuinely am not making this up.

In fact, to show I am not making this sort of thing up, let's look at an article from the magazine *Psychology Today* in which one force-free advocate lays into some others.[57] My intention is not to bully the person who wrote this article, but if you put something in a magazine, saying it is the entire truth and criticizing those who disagree, including trainers like me, then it is going to be critiqued. To be honest, I suspect she is exaggerating to put her point across, but hey, you never know. It is her methodology I am discussing, not her integrity as a dog owner, behaviorist or person.

Here we see an extremist force-free trainer reprimand the trainers at what is clearly a more middle-of-the-road force-free training facility. She starts by agreeing with me, saying that in her view the facility she dislikes is not really force-free, that it is using the term for marketing but not living the life. Why does she say this? Drumroll, shock, horror: the trainers use verbal and lead corrections to influence dogs. They also seem to use some very strange techniques I have never heard of in almost fifty years of training dogs, or maybe these were made-up examples. I mean, who backs a dog into a corner in order to get him to sit? Weird.

The author claims that her reactive, barking dog was not treated right (not like a princess, she no doubt thinks) in a group training class. Yet what person on God's green earth takes a fearful, nervous dog that flares up at other dogs and people to a busy dog training class, just so she can practice counter-conditioning? Narcissism at its finest. Other people's dogs are not there to be barked at by your dog. They just aren't. Then, when the trainer of the class says he does not want her dog there, the author throws her weight about and argues that she knows best. She admits her dog was over threshold in the class, barking and backing away in fear from strange people and dogs he did not know, so why did she not leave? Why did she return to attend another class, traumatizing her dog further, and then moan that she could not get a refund? Is money more important than her dog? She set her dog up for failure and then refused to take responsibility for her own actions. You could not make this up.

Her description of counter-conditioning being the action of pushing hot dogs into her dog's face is deeply troubling. You can't and should not try to force a scared dog that is over threshold to stay around what scares him. That's more akin to **flooding**, not counter-conditioning. Forcing food on a dog that is too scared to think and respond to basic commands he is familiar with, can poison the reinforcer, making the dog avoid food rewards, since when they are around, he's learned that something very scary may be about to happen to him, and he will be forced into a situation that terrifies him and where there is no escape, and no support from his owner. This is the opposite of counter-conditioning. Did the trainer with the treat-pouch-terrified dogs have a point? She would have if luring was attempted in this scenario, that's for sure.

Counter-conditioning alone does nothing for scared, reactive dogs. A dog needs to have an alternative behavior he understands and be on threshold, in an emotional state where he is not so scared that he cannot think clearly. He needs to trust that his handler will not force him into a situation where he is terrified. A dog that can think, and that trusts his handler to have his back, can not only be convinced that the thing that scares him is not so bad, but also be taught appropriate behaviors to replace those he used to display when scared.[58]

A dog can be given counter-conditioning, but he also must be given guidance, in the form of corrections, since appropriate, mild corrections are guidance, nothing more, nothing less. They do not increase fear; they do not cause redirections onto the handler, instead they provide clarity and security. A dog can be guided with either negative reinforcement or positive correction, as there can be very little difference between the two in practice.

This article was propaganda, a story designed to get a list of predetermined points across and push an extreme force-free agenda. The author even got the "I saw the light" line in, to make herself seem more human, apologizing to her past dogs on which she apparently used pinch collars. Nice try, but your description of counter-conditioning is truly awful. People should *not* be following your lead, putting frightened and reactive dogs into a small, indoor group class setting where they are constantly over threshold and unable to escape their fears. Holding such a frightened dog in place while ramming hot dogs in his face is only making matters worse. Come on, how force-free is that?

Police Dogs

The day will soon come when police dogs are no more. A friend of mine who is in the Scottish police said that in Scotland it has already been decided that police dogs are to be phased out in years to come. I could find no proof of this, yet I would not be surprised, since in more litigious countries such as the U.S. there is increasing legal action over injuries that suspects have sustained while being arrested. We have touched on this already, but it bears repeating. We live in a worrying world where police dogs are being banned simply because they can no longer be trained effectively. Plus, finding dogs with the right genetics and that have the heart to work is becoming harder and harder. When we go force-free in our training and cannot put pressure on a dog, he consequently cannot learn to deal with pressure. The dog has no resilience. We never gave him a chance to develop any.

There are different types of police dog, the first being those that do general purpose work. These are dogs which can track a suspect using their nose, then take on the suspect and detain him. Many can also find drugs. Such dogs tend to be German Shepherds and Belgian Malinois, with some forces still using Rottweilers, though they are more common in the military than in the police. These police dogs can bite and hold that bite, and to do this they must have a confident temperament and a personality that can withstand pressure from a suspect.

Then there are dogs that concentrate on more specialized scent-work, often the same breeds but other breeds too, mainly Spaniels and Labradors, with the odd Pointer or Bloodhound. These dogs may do anything from search and rescue to finding cadavers and locating USB sticks, a favorite with criminals for storing evidence. In scent-work a lot of rewards are used, but also corrections which guide the dog and encourage him to find the scent. Force-free trainers say to never correct a dog, but a correction can be guidance, it can hurry up the training process, and, very importantly, it can make the training more fun for the dog, as he is working *with* his partner and not just left to flounder around.

In training a dog to apprehend a criminal, he must be taught to put himself in danger by taking hold of the criminal and holding on, even if he is being kicked or hit. This is not a natural thing for a dog to do. Dogs typically do not want to start fights with humans, who they are well aware can hurt them physically. Most *people*, never mind dogs, will want to get the hell out of there if they are being punched or kicked. Training in bitework is always about building the dog's confidence, raising the pressure gradually, and the dog's genetics play a massive part in this.

If we train a dog in bitework using force-free methods, we have two problems. First, if the dog is never put under the pressure of receiving a strike during his training, what will be his reaction when that happens to him in real life? He will be shocked, that's what. He will be scared and not know what to do. Such a dog may refuse to engage with the suspect and back away, looking for a more attractive target (since bitework is a game for the dog), which creates a dangerous situation for the handler and anyone else in the vicinity.

Second, when the dog is having fun and wants to continue his favorite pastime, which is biting people, he may not release the bite when commanded to do so. If the handler has not been able to establish a consequence for this failure to let go, there is a stalemate, often leading to the suspect being injured and thrashing about in pain. If the dog is pulled off while still hanging onto the suspect, flesh has a tendency to tear. Now, you can select genetically weaker dogs that let go with minimal intervention when asked to politely, but then we are back to problem one: what happens if the dog is kicked or other pressure is put on him? A dog that is happy to let go anyway will drop a suspect like a scalding cup of coffee should a drug-addled suspect put up any sort of a fight. Force-free training does not work for general purpose police dogs. Period.

What about specialized scent dogs? We teach scent-work in a very simple way, using a dog's superpower and plenty of rewards. Let me give you an example of how these rewards work. One fine day I call you over to my house and show you a big yellow painting. Solid yellow. "Oh, that's lovely," you say, wanting to be nice but having little interest in abstract modern art. I wave a $50 bill just above the canvas, tempting you to grab it. I give you the fifty when your hand is just where I want it, pointing to the big yellow painting.

"More cash?" I ask. You point to the yellow painting again, and I give you another $50. This goes on until you have $5,000. You are ecstatic. The next day, we do the same thing. Soon you are knocking at my door before I have even woken up, demanding to be let in to play the point-at-the-painting game. After a while, I can show you a painting that has just a tiny bit of yellow, the size of a pinhead, and you will find it and point to it, knowing you will get $50. This is how we teach a dog scent-work. Well, more or less.

But what if you get confused and point to colors similar to yellow, such as orange? Or if I only want you to point to bright canary yellow and will no longer reward you for pointing to banana yellow, but won't help show you the difference? This is where the kind correction comes in. You point to orange and I say "no" kindly. You already understand a harsher "no" for gobbling up my protein bar with raisins (good thing you're not a dog, as raisins are poisonous to dogs),[59] but my tone now is encouraging, so you're not frightened or put off, and you understand that a kind "no" is a correction which gives guidance. Soon, you learn only to point to canary yellow, and you learn this much more quickly than if I had given

Chapter Nine. Legal Beagles

no guidance to you regarding the wrong colors. Corrections do not have to be harsh. They can stop frustration, aid learning, and make learning more fun.

It's worth noting that I use money examples in this book since most people like money and, as with dogs, the reward has to be worthwhile. But if I wanted to reward an old, vain multi-millionairess who is very greedy (most multi-millionairesses are—how do you think they got rich?), $50 would not cut it. On the other hand, if I offer her a next-day appointment with the world's top plastic surgeon, who usually has a one-year wait list for Botox treatments, irrespective of wealth or celebrity, I think that would do very nicely as a reward.

So, we can train scent dogs with very kind corrections or (only to an extent, obviously) force-free, but they still need to learn to be reliable enough to work in the real world. Some breeds, as we know, are very sensitive to their handler and to pressure, so when working we can use almost invisible corrections, such as a hard look or a sharp tone of voice. However, dogs with such a degree of sensitivity generally do not cope well in public.

Similarly, a dog that has a great nose for scent-work but that would rather run up to people and pose for an Insta pic will not be a good drugs dog if he cannot be corrected for that behavior in a way that is meaningful to him. When we go entirely force-free in our training, our scent dogs learn more slowly and end up like low-drive Spaniels and Labradors, given that only light corrections are permitted. Such dogs tend to be too docile, and too uninterested in working hard to find a scent, to be terribly good at the job.

General purpose dogs that also do bitework, or that need different corrections if they are to be meaningful to them, will die out when we ban tools such as martingales and pinch collars, even more so when we ban any corrections at all. Scent dogs will also go, since with no corrections allowed, they will be low-drive and lazy, and artificial noses will eventually be designed that surpass their abilities.

From police dogs being phased out, as practically seen already in Germany with a ban on pulling collars and half of Berlin's police dogs suddenly retiring, it's a small step to banning every other working dog. I mean, if you're a guide dog, what seems better to you, some kibble from your owner or a piece of steak in the grocery display, right under your very nose and eyes? I am thinking the steak. With no effective corrections for bad behavior, or even just to show the dog what is right and wrong, why would he not pick up the steak and eat it? Sadly, UK–trained guide dogs can and do.

Banned Tools

Banned books tend to be books that are disapproved of in school libraries; banned training tools come with legislation passed to fine or jail any dog owner who uses them. You do not want to go down the road of banning tools as we have done in Europe.

In the UK, the government has stated they are banning e-collars, and I have no doubt they will move on to pinch collars and martingales shortly. What is interesting regarding the e-collar ban is that it seems not to apply to the wealthy. When you have a beautiful lakeside home and you install a tear-inducing invisible fence (tear-inducing in terms of the zap provided to the dog and the cost to you) in order to preserve your view, in addition to controlling your dog, well then, *of course* you don't need to obey some law on e-collars. Don't be silly! It's perfectly fine to light up your dog like an umbrella struck by lightning during a storm,[60] as it's *his choice* to electrocute himself. Or walk in the rain.

Let me play devil's advocate. Why do e-collar bans never seem to include invisible fences, other than in countries such as Sweden, which also bans crates? Why? I mean, the dog must give himself a very harsh shock in order to learn that the fence line should not be crossed. The owner does not start off with a mild stimulation—no, the dog is totally and utterly fried. Why is this acceptable to the government, but using an e-collar humanely as a positive reinforcer is not?

If I had a deaf dog and I used a mild stimulation as a positive reinforcer to replace a verbal cue, to enable my dog to go safely off-lead, I would be furious. Some bans only apply to e-collars with a static charge, others also apply to those with a vibration, which is fair enough since many dogs hate a vibration, much preferring a charge, though I do not think this is the rationale.

If it is fine for a dog to learn to stay away from an invisible fence via a harsh correction from an e-collar—no, not just a correction, a harsh punishment—then why should a skilled trainer not use an e-collar? Such a trainer may use it in the same way, with good timing, to give a one-off, short, sharp shock to stop a dog from doing something dangerous. She may use it as a reinforcer, or as a very mild correction that is more of an instruction. You could say that once a dog has been introduced to an e-collar and trained so he knows that disobedience has consequences, it is his choice whether to be disobedient and receive a correction for it. As for me, I think it's safer for a trainer to administer a fair correction that is well-thought-out and adjusted to the circumstance at hand than for a machine to blast a dog at a nonvariable setting.

Why is the pleasant view of a rich person considered more important than dog welfare? Are the invisible fence manufacturers lobbying politicians, or do the politicians have lots of wealthy friends with invisible fences? If you insist an e-collar is not needed in training, OK, fine—but a nice view is not needed either. Build an ordinary wooden fence. That will contain your dog, and he will never, ever have to receive a nasty electric shock.

It should be noted, many dogs learn that if they run fast enough, they will not get a shock from an invisible fence. As do horses with thick blankets—well, small ponies—that learn to crawl "under" electric fences. Horse owners, unsurprisingly, tend to be wealthy people, and their animals are not subject to the same rules as dogs. Who would have thought? Well, actually, horse owners are generally not wealthy in practice, as the horse is an animal which eats money and spends his days plotting the best, most costly way to injure and/or kill himself. But you get my point. There is one rule for the wealthy and one for the man in the street who cannot afford a house with a view, nor a horse.

Since animal welfare laws were amended to ban pulling collars for police dogs in Germany, then why have spurs and bits not been banned there for horses? Roweled spurs can cause wounds—yes, actual wounds— on a thin-skinned, clipped horse, yet this is considered fine and dandy. Just a bit of blood, use a towel to wipe the horse's sides in public, no harm no foul. No. Just no. If you ban pinch collars, you must also ban roweled spurs, tools that look exactly the same, both being made of metal and having prongs. I am not for bans, I am all for training the person using the tool instead, but I do not like hypocrisy. Could it be that horse sport is such big business in Germany that bans on spurs and bits will not be passed in the same way that pulling collars and e-collars have been banned for dogs?

Even most non-riders know that a bit—yes a piece of metal—goes into a horse's mouth, but in addition to the bit, there is a strap called a noseband which goes around the nose. Often this noseband is fastened so tightly that the horse is in severe discomfort, particularly when the bit moves into an uncomfortable place in his mouth. With his jaw strapped shut by the noseband, the horse cannot rectify the uncomfortable position of the bit. There have been many instances in competitions where a horse's tongue has been seen to go blue and flop out of the side of his mouth, all circulation cut off. If you have ever crossed your legs and had one leg "fall asleep," you know how painful this can be. Why is it fine to use a noseband to strap a horse's mouth shut, the horse feeling the pressure all of the time, but a dog cannot wear a martingale collar, which only applies pressure when he pulls against it?

If we are going to go down the road of bans, we have to look at all species of animal, not just a chosen few. Real thought must be given to bans and what their objectives actually are. We must follow the money trail, both in terms of which animals will be affected and who will benefit, not just in the here and now, but in five or ten years.

Do we want a world where all the dogs we have left in existence are small, low-drive, non-brachycephalic dogs, our wonderful working dog breeds having become extinct or dumbed down so much that they are dead behind the eyes? No Pugs, no Frenchies, no dogs that have any sort of health issues, as more and more will be banned. As genetic diversity decreases, we will have no purebred dogs and end up with crossbreeds and not much else. Many people want this and think it would be for the best, preaching "adopt, don't shop." Force-free trainers may see a beautiful world of easy-to-handle Doodles and Poos, but I see those Doodles and Poos in scary-clown costumes. Your dream is my nightmare.

Dogs as well as horses are beloved by their owners, the vast majority of whom do not set out to harm them when training or knowingly buy a dog with health issues. Rather than ban tools, let's improve the standard of education for trainers and owners alike and get rid of back yard breeders who churn out nervous, sick, miserable dogs. I do not want to see "cookie monsters"—dogs that will not comply when the offered cookies run out or when they are not as attractive as a competing reinforcer—locked away like Rapunzel, never allowed out of their towers to see the light of day ever again.

CHAPTER TEN

Cults

Currently in Europe, we balanced trainers have allowed ourselves to be backed into a corner by the force-free extremists, with bans on dog breeds and tools flying about left, right and center, totally out of control. We watched the force-free mafia manipulate the media, and we sat by and did diddly-squat. I'm sure a great many of us never thought it would come to this, that outright lies would be told and believed, and that the general public would lap it all up like a puddle of antifreeze, sickly sweet on the tongue but oh so very deadly. In Europe we are losing our working dogs, our small dogs, our training tools, our dog sports—in short, our very way of life. Other countries take heed: fight for your rights before it is too late.

The Cult of the Broken Dog

Force-free training organizations use much the same tactics that the average cult uses on its members.[1] Their truth is the only truth, which is that all dogs can be trained to do *everything* using only cookies and positive reinforcement. All corrections are evil—well, other people's corrections, that is (not their own, obviously)—and science has proven that the corrections balanced trainers use cause pain, fear and suffering. Always. Now, this is not true, but it is "the law" of the force-free training mob. A head collar? Fine. A slip lead? Why, that's a travesty against the God (Dog?) of Love and Peace.

The force-free extremists start out nicely, playing on the emotions of the general public, before moving on to persuade dog trainers, often of many years' experience, that they too have been doing it wrong all along. Everyone adores their dog, after all, and who wants to use a correction when it's not required? This is particularly true when we're told that corrections will cause our dogs pain and distress, turning them against us, making them scared and distrustful, maybe even biting the ogre that stands before them in sheer terror for their lives. All this from saying the word *no* for counter surfing. I don't want to hurt my dog or cause him any distress, but what I do want is a dog that can have a good quality of life.

The force-free mafia are persuasive and use love bombing as part of their strategy, treating possible converts as the most special, smartest people *ever*.[2] How intelligent you must be, they say, to understand that force-free training is led by science and that balanced training is out of date, its methods disproven and unethical. As we saw in Chapter Six, their claims about science are totally untrue, based on cherry-picking from bad science which was biased to begin with. However, as humans we are *all* in danger of being taken in by a cult, given the right circumstances.[3] As a species we are intrinsically trusting, not to mention susceptible to flattery and open to being manipulated by individuals with skills in that area.[4]

When people state they want dogs to be treated ethically and kindly, that must be a good thing, right? Would such people, who have pocketsful of delicious cookies, be liars and frauds? "No," we say to ourselves, and many of us believe what we are told. These are learned men and women, scientists, they know best and have authority over us. We must believe them and do as they say.[5] It does not matter that our dog is obedient and well-behaved, walking nicely in his pinch collar. Off it must come, and if the dog no longer walks well, ignoring the proffered cookies, he must be managed or medicated instead.

Don't believe me? Then look to past experiments on humans, which prove just how suggestible we really are, particularly at the hands of people in positions of authority. Psychologist Stanley Milgram and his experimenters, for example, persuaded participants to administer what they believed were real electric shocks to other people.[6] Participants turned up the current at the request of a scientist in a white lab coat until they heard the people they thought they were shocking start to scream. Then they turned it up yet more until the screaming stopped. Was the person dead or unconscious? In a similar way force-free extremists get the general public to accept their viewpoint, convincing people—including politicians—that their way is the only way, that their science is king, and that they *must* be obeyed.

Social media, which is addictive,[7] plays on our natural inclination to trust and obey authority figures. Massive groups have gathered online, comprising fundamentally decent, good people brought together on a global scale, to promote the very best for the dogs they love. At first it is fun, but, as time goes by, leaders emerge from within the group, very often people who do not like to be contradicted, and members become frightened to show any dissent lest they be ostracized.[8] As humans, we are hard-wired to live together in groups,[9] as we are safest in a community (a bit like dogs), and this is particularly true if we are part of the ruling majority.[10] Members feel a sense of community in these online groups. Their feelings are validated and they stay, even when they feel increasingly uncomfortable about the message which is being preached.

If you're on Facebook, TikTok, YouTube, or any other social media platform, it will come as no surprise that the videos and posts which are suggested to you, many of which are paid-for advertisements, are targeted to your interests.[11] In a competitive industry such as dog training, this type of marketing is key. As force-free training became the norm in Europe, dog owners started to be targeted with advertisements promoting the force free cult. Before long, it was all we saw on social media, and many dog owners came to believe that it was the norm, that using purely positive training methods was the only ethical way to train dogs.

People could be forgiven, then, for believing these extremist force-free trainers when they told them that balanced training was dead, abusive, and that they needed to see the light. After all, most members of the public had never seen any balanced trainers on their social media feeds, just a plethora of force-free trainers, all backing each other up, convincing them that they must convert in order to be safe. To be loved. To be kind, ethical dog guardians. The force-free mafia were the first to take advantage of social media, leaving balanced trainers far behind, like so many sloths. Now, of course, the gloves are off and force-free trainers are turning on each other in droves, but by now they have almost taken over the entire dog training industry in Europe, with bans on e-collars and pinch collars abounding.

A small number of the force-free mafia might admit that corrections *can* stop a bad behavior, but they will come back at you with the "fact" that it has been scientifically proven that offering cookies stops bad behaviors faster and more effectively. Really? What about restraining a dog with a collar and lead, since that is a correction? Are you suggesting that a high-drive, off-lead dog that has never been issued any corrections in his life will not run off after a squirrel when he sees one? Can I have some of whatever is making you high? Pretty pretty please? Or is restraining the dog with a head collar suddenly fine and dandy in this scenario?

If you ask for legitimate scientific studies and hard facts regarding the assertion that cookies stop bad behaviors better than corrections, none will be forthcoming. All you will be given is an opinion article with no references to any science, not even the Lincoln e-collar studies. When asked, "What if there is a competing reinforcer?" the force-free trainers, provided they know what the term *competing reinforcer* means, will reluctantly admit that if cookies alone do not work, then management techniques should be used instead of corrections. They will claim that a correction harsh enough to stop a bad behavior must, by its very nature, cause pain and distress.

Therefore, by their logic, it is unethical to use corrections on any dog, no matter the circumstances. Again, due to these trainers' presumed authority, the majority of people accept this argument without question.

And it sounds compelling at first, doesn't it? People can stop correcting their dogs, and we should all buy shares in cookie companies—we'll be rich! The meanies with big dogs must be forced to manage them at home, where they cannot respond back to your small dog's incessant barking and lunging, making him feel threatened. No, you cannot tell your yap-on-a-strap that his behavior is wrong, since such a heinous act would cause him to experience fear and emotional trauma. Better that a wayward dog grows fat on the sofa with a few sedatives in his dinner than learn to be neutral around other dogs, people, cyclists or whatever else he finds exciting and interesting. Or tasty.

Once they've hooked people with kindness and flattery, the extremists become not so nice if any one of their number dissents or asks questions.[12] Members of the cult must not only convert to an entirely force-free methodology with their own dogs, they must join the force-free army, pushing the ethos onto everyone else, since conversion of the masses and making changes in the law is the ultimate goal. A member who does not want to be one of the group's flying monkeys and go on the offensive against balanced trainers will be ostracized, and suddenly "be nice" is out the window. Having initially been love bombed, then isolated from her dog-owning friends who are not force-free, this cold shoulder is hard to bear,[13] and the dissenter quickly gets back into line.

Everyone is susceptible to manipulation,[14] and the force-free extremists have big money behind them to help make it happen. They spend millions on the sponsorship of "scientific studies," and I use the term loosely, since these studies are mandated to say what the extremists want them to say. This includes scientific research sponsored by the state, which is ostensibly objective but which is conducted by biased researchers and is then used to ban training tools, as we saw in Chapter Six. The extremists spend even more on politics, buying votes. They hire top advertising agencies to push their agenda on social media, creating a worldview that if you are not force-free, you are an animal abuser.

What also concerns me are the young dog trainers who have been targeted and misled by the force-free mafia. From their earliest days online—which, let's face it, was before they even started school—they have had it pushed on them that all dogs must be trained without force, using only positive reinforcement. These young trainers bought into this, never knowing any different. The majority have trained very few dogs, and those they have trained are mainly low-drive, small or medium-sized breeds, their idea of an ultra-high-drive dog being a Terrier or Spaniel.

Chapter Ten. Cults

Indeed, these breeds have plenty of drive, but Spaniels in particular can be "soft" and easily intimidated, not committing to a bad behavior when enough pressure is put on them by a trainer. Dogs that are a bit tougher and more opinionated, like the majority of ~~terrorists~~ Terriers, more often than not can just be picked up and carried away if need be. But these young trainers believe all dogs are created equal, that it's "all how you raise them," having no grasp of genetics and the various drives of the working breeds. They genuinely believe that a handful of kibble will stop a large, high-drive dog in his tracks like it stops their show-line, obese Labrador Retriever, aka the walking dustbin.

Full of passion, these junior trainers are on a mission to bully and intimidate anyone who disagrees with them, displaying a religious zeal that would intimidate the Witchfinder General, or indeed the Wicked Witch of the West. Proclaiming "Be kind," these young trainers ruin lives and businesses, denouncing as cruel tools they have not touched with their own pure hands, never mind seen in use. They have dogs drugged and put down on their say-so, their egos bolstered by their peer group, when the truth is they simply do not have any experience relating to the problems the dogs in question were experiencing.

All *good* trainers, whether they call themselves balanced, force-free, purely positive or whatever else, are actually on the same side. It's frustrating that we do not all work together. Trainers in various schools may have different client bases, but force-free trainers should support the effective training of dogs that they do not have the skill set to help themselves. Some do, but many do not, increasingly putting all of their trust in the force-free methodology even when it is not working for a particular dog. If a trainer does not understand a training technique or tool, why not spend time with a trainer who does, in order to learn its proper application, instead of criticizing something they have no actual knowledge of, in some cases condemning a dog to live half a life, if he lives one at all?

Force-free trainers can be a vicious lot when it comes to protecting their interests, which are primarily financial. The most prominent force-free trainers have massive online followings and are multi-millionaires, as I will detail later in this chapter. However, the less successful among them are struggling to pay their bills, maybe running one or two classes per week and that's it. Trying to keep their heads above water, they routinely send out their die-hard supporters to bully and intimidate balanced trainers. I have had to call the police over online death threats that I received simply because I am a balanced trainer. Once, a head-collar salesperson sent me hundreds of abusive messages and texts because I had politely declined to buy her products, which she offered to me at a discount(!), in favor of continuing to use pinch collars.

With the growth of social media, force-free training extremists have been able to expand their empire. Charities jumped on board, aware that increased donations result from pulling on people's heartstrings. Veterinarians and other professionals with degrees, very much with their own agenda, also rushed in, setting themselves up as behaviorists. Some of these professionals are hands-on, but others, particularly veterinary behaviorists, do not even train dogs at all, simply giving advice. They spout a lot of babble about how we must always understand a dog's motivations, his history, and every small detail about him in order to help him behave well. Now, it's true that emotions drive behavior, but do we need an extensive life history to tell us that the dog standing in front of us is scared, or excited? Let's discuss.

The Dark Side of Behaviorists

Many behaviorists, whether they are dual-qualified as veterinary surgeons, have a degree in animal behavior, or are plain old dog trainers, often work directly with insurance companies. Indeed, it is common for behaviorists/veterinarians to set up financial deals that suit both themselves and the insurance companies, and this is particularly true of the big corporate veterinary group practices, which are owned not by veterinarians but by investment banks and therefore have profit as a priority, not animal care.[15]

These large corporate practices, working together with insurance companies and drug companies, are dictating the cost of products and services. In the UK, many small family-owned practices have been priced out by the big corporates, which then raise prices even further once they have a monopoly, increasing the cost of common drugs by as much as 40 percent, seemingly overnight.[16] The long tentacles of such companies extend not only to veterinary care but also to behavioral work.

Insurance companies will often state that only members of certain behavioral or dog training organizations can be used if clients want to file a claim for behavioral consults under their policy. This may or may not be evident in the small print when the policy is taken out. While these organizations are not necessarily force-free, neither are they neutral, being prejudiced toward certain trainers. For example, the code of ethics of the Canine and Feline Behaviour Association in the UK,[17] under "Termination of Membership" at point 12, states:

> Applicants whose main experience, qualifications and/or services proffered to the public are more than 50% security type work/protection dog work are not eligible to join the CFBA unless an exception is made by the directors of

the CFBA because they have canine behaviour skills/qualifications above the joining CFBA requirements.[18]

How is this of benefit to a Belgian Malinois that has severe behavioral issues which require an experienced trainer who is very familiar with the breed and their inclination to bite, who trains such dogs day in, day out, and is not fazed by aggression? Is it better that this dog be taken to a "full member" of the Canine and Feline Behaviour Association, possibly (I presume, since I could not find the criteria) a recent graduate with four years of dog training under her belt as part of a degree in animal behavior but who has never worked with such a dog? Or would the dog be better off going to a trainer such as Ivan Balabanov, who is an extremely skilled behaviorist[19] but whom, it appears, is a person this organization would not approve of?

I may sound like a prude, but one of this organization's full members is pictured on its website wearing a massive nose ring, the like of which Sinbad the Sailor would covet. Any large dog in the habit of jumping up would have that ring ripped out in a millisecond. Although I don't care what your personal style is, and nose rings can look cool on bulls and humans alike, when working with animals safety *must* come first. Perhaps she takes it out every morning before going to work, and simply put it in for the photograph. Let's hope so. If anyone turned up to work with any of my dogs wearing such a large nose ring, nice as it may look, I would ask them to remove it, not relishing screams, blood and a trip to the emergency room.

It may (or may not) surprise you to know that a great many veterinary behaviorists do not even see their client's dog in the flesh. The dog is in one room, safely out of the way, and the owner and the behaviorist are in another room. The behaviors displayed by the dog are never observed firsthand, let alone the behaviorist taking hold of the lead and working with the dog. All that is provided to the client is a chat about learning theory. In the U.S., the veterinary behaviorist will almost certainly be a member of the American Veterinary Society of Animal Behavior, which is a group of force-free extremists. All the client gets is theoretical advice on how to offer cookies, management techniques, and a list of favored medications when the positive-only training methods invariably fail.

If a behaviorist, of whatever ilk, does not watch the dog interact with the owner and look at the problems and emotions being experienced firsthand, how can she give meaningful help and advice? In my view, she cannot. There are many times when the client is negatively influencing the dog and as soon as the behaviorist or trainer takes the lead, the reactivity melts away. Such a client needs to recognize her own fears and insecurities regarding the dog and might ideally be referred to a psychologist, strange as that may sound. If the veterinary behaviorist only has a chat with the client, how can they ever really get to the bottom of what is going on? Yet many poor clients who have been paying through the nose for expensive pet insurance policies may have no option but to depend on force-free, hands-off "behaviorists."

Of course, veterinary behaviorists have an advantage in that they are also veterinarians, having qualified into a field which requires a high degree of intelligence and many years of study, but is this necessary? In my opinion, no. Any good dog trainer or behaviorist should have a basic knowledge of canine anatomy and internal medicine and thus be able to see if a dog is in pain. If in any doubt, a behaviorist who is not a veterinarian can and should work with the dog's regular veterinarian in order to ascertain whether there could be a physical cause for the dog's behaviors. Conditions such as hypothyroidism, blindness, arthritis, and a whole host of other aliments can cause pain or discomfort, and so influence behavior.

Some insurance companies are more liberal than others regarding the professionals they will work with, so it always pays to carefully check your policy. But some will only allow consults with trainers and behaviorists who are members of force-free training organizations such as the American Veterinary Society of Animal Behavior, and it would be foolish to believe that no backroom deals were done to facilitate this.

TV Shows

In the game of dog training—and for many trainers it is very much a game, a lucrative game—there are winners and there are losers. Make no mistake, fortunes are made, and at times lost, such as in the case of the "Dog Whisperer," César Millan.[20] One day his star was on the ascent, the next he was being ridiculed and called out as the personification of Lucifer, albeit a version who was always seen brandishing a choke chain.

Were all of César's methods good? No, absolutely not, and the "do not try this at home" klaxon must sound now. Loudly. Alpha rolls? Not advised unless you want to end up with half a face. However, some of his methods are the exact same ones that force-free trainers use, particularly in relation to using food to teach impulse control. No difference. Plus, he saved the lives of a great many dogs who would otherwise have been euthanized, and for that he has my deepest respect irrespective of the mistakes he made while training dogs, and we have all made them. Mistakes that is. I'm all for the dog, and he *did* help a lot of dogs.

Once again, this comes back to an ethical dilemma: Do the ends justify the means? When César was setting up, it was at a time when many

Chapter Ten. Cults 201

people *had a problem* and seemingly *no one else could help*,[21] and though *Dog Whisperer* first aired in 2004,[22] I think it had enough of an '80s retro vibe for you to know how this goes without me reciting any more of the *A-Team* intro. Will I be sending any dog of mine to stay with César anytime soon for training? No, but it cannot be disputed he's helped more dogs and their owners than I have. How many of you can say you have helped more dogs than César? It's easy to jump on the bandwagon of condemning everything he has done, but like everyone on this planet, he was not all bad.[23]

Also remember this was a TV show, and to a great extent César was hamming it up for the camera. Good TV is not taking a dog and sympathetically training him slowly and patiently over several weeks, or indeed months. Provoking a dog to bark and be aggressive, even to bite the trainer,[24] is far more entertaining, and for this the general public must take some responsibility. Who was it that had an appetite for watching such staged, reality-type dog training shows? If there was no demand, the show would have been canceled after the pilot, not run for nine seasons.[25]

These days the shows have changed, but not as much as they should have, because otherwise it's ... boorrriiiinnnnnggg. Just boring. We still see self-professed force-free trainers putting dogs in unfair situations, strapping them down in head collars and subjecting them to a lot of stress, none of which is necessary to evaluate or train them. It is all done to generate viewing figures, not for the benefit of the dogs. Like many others, I have encountered dogs that have been on these types of reality TV shows and came away as badly behaved as before, with the owner no farther along in having a well-trained dog. Dogs and their owners need time and the work put in day in, day out for training to progress, not a trainer swooping in for 48 hours, no matter how charming and pleasant they are.

Most of the trainers on today's dog training shows call themselves force-free, though "balanced trainer" would be more accurate for the majority, since they do indeed use force and plenty of it, including tools such as head collars and no-pull harnesses. Victoria Stilwell, with her series *It's Me or the Dog*, is a good example of such a trainer. Her website promotes that she uses positive reinforcement and avoids intimidation, physical punishment and fear,[26] yet she frequently uses head collars, which many dogs find aversive. She has also designed and sells her own no-pull harness.[27]

Victoria is another trainer who has enjoyed great success, some well-deserved, some not so much. Like César Millan, she has made a very good living out of training dogs, and why not? We all need to keep our dogs well supplied with cookies. However, to compare the caliber of dangerous dog that Victoria deals with in her series to those featured by a trainer such as César, well, it's like comparing the graphics of *Pac-Man* to *Grand Theft Auto*.

Often in Victoria's shows, the dog is set up to look very dangerous indeed, but look carefully at the footage of the episode "Lives Are at Risk Around This 'Weapon on a Leash'": would a truly dangerous dog be introduced off-lead to strangers and a camera crew in the dog's own home territory?[28] The answer is a resounding "no." Do you think the production company would take on such a legal liability? Of course not. If this dog had severe issues with human aggression, or defensive aggression around his space, he would never, ever have been introduced in this way. It makes for good TV, though, seeing a big dog run into a room with threatening music in the background. Quite simply, it's good viewing.

In this episode *It's Me or the Dog*,[29] featuring an aggressive Presa Canario, we see a dog wearing a pinch collar. This is not the dog that was introduced to Victoria, but one being used as a demo dog in bitework by the K9-1 company,[30] which has excellent trainers and is a good source of information if you want to dump Netflix and cozy up with YouTube for the weekend.

Surely promoting a dog trainer who, horror of horrors, uses pinch collars would be the antithesis of everything Victoria stands for? Well, it is, yet there she is doing it, watching the dog in the pinch collar work with a decoy and calling the demonstration, and I quote, "impressive."[31] Yes, the dog is in a pinch collar, and Victoria Stilwell, queen of positive reinforcement, states that the dog's training is "impressive."[32]

I will give Victoria a thumbs-up for the fact that at least in *this* episode, she understands that some dogs need a tool which is different from cookies and a head collar. Indeed, if we watch a podcast with the K9-1 trainer who worked with Victoria on this episode,[33] it would appear that behind the scenes Victoria admits that force-free training is a marketing strategy, no more, no less. She maintains her force-free, purely positive ethos not for the benefit of dogs, but rather because her sponsors require it.[34] I don't know who Victoria's sponsors are or if the K9-1 trainer is being truthful, but I am inclined to believe him.

The truth about reality TV, or indeed any TV show or movie, is that what we see as the finished product is a far cry from what actually goes on behind the scenes. TV is not about education, it's about making money by creating programs that appeal to the masses, that the most people will pay for. Do not believe everything you see, whether it be a show with César Millan or Victoria Stilwell. I mean, if you have Victoria Stilwell essentially endorsing pinch collars, given that a dog wearing one appeared on her TV series[35] and not a thing was said other than that the dog worked in an "impressive" way, then what and whom can you trust?

Money

As always, we need to follow the money. As I have said, dog training is a lucrative business. Let's see just how lucrative, shall we? Now, I could not find all the details I was looking for, but still, this gives us a rough idea of how much money the dog training industry is worth. Here goes:

Victoria Stilwell: net worth of $20 million in 2021[36]
César Millan: net worth of $20 million in 2022[37]
Ian Dunbar: net worth of $14 million (date unknown)[38]
Karen Pryor: net worth of $1 to $3 million in 2021[39]
Jean Donaldson: net worth of $950,000 (date unknown)[40]

Well, it would appear that making a successful TV series is the best way to make money in the dog world, not primarily writing books about dogs, like Pryor and Donaldson. Sadly, I don't have the legs for high-heeled boots, nor do I give out an S&M vibe, so I doubt I would make a big splash on TV. But with my ever-thirsty bank account, I would not turn down $1, never mind $1 million. "Could I be in the wrong career?" I ask myself. "Yes, probably," I hear myself reply. Maybe there should be more questions, along the lines of "Why am I talking to myself?" but perhaps it's best to just leave it there.

In addition to the force-free dog trainers, whether they write books, make TV series, give real-life lessons, or promote online courses, who else benefits from force-free training? Well, dog charities and shelters, but also dog behavioral organizations, which promote the force-free ethos and charge high membership fees. Also benefiting are the manufacturers of force-free dog training equipment, such as those that produce head collars and front-pull harnesses, all of which make a pretty penny from the force-free agenda, despite these tools not being remotely force-free.

Let's take the organization American Humane as an example. The CEO earned $548,382 in 2022.[41] I would be happy with that, wouldn't you? An Auditor of Companion Animal Behavior, which would appear to be a role that includes an element of dog training (though I could be wrong), only earned $95,882,[42] however, well below the average salary of $133,043. So, how is this group funded? Well, it has celebrity supporters, including Victoria Stilwell, Betty White (R.I.P), Hugh Jackman, Whoopi Goldberg and a variety of, err, celebrity dogs such as Giggy, Lisa Vanderpump's late Pomeranian.[43] Total revenue for 2021 was $21,274,306, with 72.4 percent ($15,396,030) from contributions.[44] Over and above this income, the group had net assets of $21,324,945.[45]

This is not a lesson in economics, but as you can see, being a charity is profitable. Very profitable indeed, and charities are increasingly hanging their hat on the force-free philosophy, as that gains more donations, pure and simple. We all want to see cute, abused puppies being given cuddles and cookies, with no corrections necessary, do we not? It feels good. We get all warm and fuzzy inside. However, this is not real life, and the losers are the dogs. Now, American Humane does not seem to promote itself as force-free, its website referencing pinch collars in the same sentence as head collars, in that neither should be left on a dog when he is unattended.[46] However, a great many charities *do* brand themselves as force-free, particularly in Europe, which is a trend set to spread to the USA.

In the UK, Dogs Trust had an income of £111,100,000 ($125,495,074.94)[47] in 2019.[48] Donations, in addition to legacies from the deceased, amounted to £100,200,000 ($113,141,129.77),[49] with £1,800,000 ($2,032,179.40)[50] raised from adoption fees and £7,400,000 ($8,354,515.33)[51] from trading activity (excluding investments).[52] All this to re-home 15,000 dogs.[53] What is trading activity, you may ask? Well, Dogs Trust sells training courses, a virtual session for £55 ($61.95)[54] and an in-person session for £70 ($78.48).[55,56]

What do you really learn in a Zoom training session? Very little, unless you're an experienced trainer brushing up on skills and fine-tuning a dog, or an established client learning new skills or tricks with your dog in a controlled environment. As a trainer you cannot take hold of the lead virtually, nor can you teach clients good timing very well on Zoom. You can give them theory, but not a real-life training session, which is what many of them are paying for. When dealing with issues such as dog reactivity or aggression, you need one-on-one sessions, often with a stooge dog, and it's no quick fix. It is not something you should attempt virtually, and yet here we are, with Dogs Trust earning £7,400,000 ($8,354,515.33)[57] in 2019 from trading activity.[58] And £1,800,000 ($2,032,179.40)[59] raised from adoption fees[60] is not to be sneezed at either.

Dogs Trust is an organization which promotes force-free dog training. It is all about positive reinforcement, which is fantastic. I am all for positive reinforcement, but in their website's menu of videos,[61] do we see *anywhere* how to correct bad behaviors? No. We do not. Yet it is preventing bad behaviors that most owners struggle with. Of course, before you tell a dog he is doing wrong and correct him, you must always first teach him what you want him to do, using positive reinforcement. But when the day comes that the dog turns to you and says, "No, I have better things to do with my time" and does whatever he pleases, then you must know what *you* should do. Hint: throwing cookies at his disappearing backside is not the answer.

Giving only one side of the story is like providing instructions on how to drive a car but only detailing how the gas pedal is used, with no mention whatsoever of the brakes. Brakes? What brakes? If you have a dog, or a car, or even a bicycle, you need brakes. Now, common sense tells us that the brakes fitted to a bicycle are different from those fitted to a semi-truck. Similarly, an elderly Pug is best suited to a nice, comfortable, well-fitted harness, but an aggressive two-year-old Dutch Shepherd needs the canine equivalent of air brakes (generally an e-collar or a pinch collar) to keep everyone safe on the roads. Or at the local park, as the case may be.

Adoption is also big business, whether it's the big boys such as Dogs Trust and American Humane or a smaller rescue group that may make a fortune fundraising off a once-in-a-lifetime event. In 2007, forty-seven "fighting dogs," aka Pit Bull Terriers, were rescued from the "care" of Michael Vick, an NFL quarterback.[62] Best Friends Animal Society took twenty-two of these dogs,[63] the rest being placed in foster care. Best Friends has been quoted as saying they raised tens of millions of dollars,[64] and indeed their 2020 tax filing shows a total revenue of $106,903,525.[65] Yes, over one hundred million dollars for a charity which does not cover the entire U.S. and which most of you may never have heard of. In 2007 their net assets were $27,634,966,[66] so since this incident they have done very well. Did they expand mostly around the time they took in these dogs? I'm not an investigative journalist, so I don't know. I'm not criticizing this charity, as they seem great from a quick scan from where I sit in the UK. This is just a demonstration of how animal charities are big business. In Europe, charities now must be force-free to raise the most cash, and if you want to save your U.S. charities you must act to stop training tools from being banned, as that is the thin edge of the wedge for charities and dog trainers alike.

The Losers

OK, we know who the winners are, but who are the losers? Sadly, the dogs. It's no secret that record numbers of dogs are languishing in rescues, with others euthanized due to behavioral problems or the shelter in question simply not having sufficient space. Hand on heart, I cannot say that those still in rescue are the lucky ones. Some are shut away in crates, often for years, too dangerous to live a normal life or be re-homed, yet their well-meaning shelter refuses to euthanize them.

COVID-19 was responsible for thousands of people, tens of thousands even, going out and buying a puppy.[67] The kids were at home and bored, and how easy was it to go to a back yard breeder and play the genetic lottery, picking up a puppy covered in cute fluff? Or even have it home delivered, like a Lagotto Romagnolo pizza? Good breeders often have waiting lists which are years long. They do not churn out litter after litter, but only conduct very well-thought-out breedings after extensive health and temperament testing, in addition to considering show wins and working titles.

As many as 40 percent of those new puppy buyers had no experience with dogs,[68] all at a time when dog trainers and behaviorists were unable to conduct face-to-face consults. The consequences are now being seen far and wide. Where I live, dog ownership is becoming a bit more of a misery from day to day. There are swarms of what I can only describe as badly behaved young dogs running amok, many with behavioral issues. This is me describing the situation as a dog lover. Imagine how bad it is for people just visiting the park or the beach with their kids.

In one week recently, I counted five different off-lead dogs running up to my on-lead Rottweilers in the park, two of which were not friendly and would have had a pop at my dogs if I had not stepped in front of them and made it clear that I was a *much* bigger badass than they were. Out of these five dogs, only one had an owner who even attempted a recall, calling to her dog once, then just doing nothing as she knew he was not coming back anytime soon. I had to lead three of them back to their owner so they could collect their recalcitrant pooch, which trailed behind me trying to annoy my dogs.

This may all seem like fun and games, but what if any of these dogs had ran up to the (illegal) Pit Bull that frequented the park and that was juiced to the max (with trazadone, most likely), in addition to being as strung out as a hen in a hurricane? This was a mutt with big D energy (D for demonic, not dog). This dog put the Terminator to shame with his muscular, shredded body, and with his cool, calm approach to violence he seemed to be channeling the spirit of Jeffrey Dahmer. Not good. This dog was a regular in the park for about a week, until his owners moved on, no doubt due to complaints. It's a posh area, don't you know. Anyways, if those five dogs had run up to this dog instead of mine, the encounter would not have ended well. A few of these dogs' owners had young children with them, who no doubt would have been deeply traumatized to see their four-legged friend being ripped apart, if not consumed.

This is not a dig at all Pit Bulls, but more than fifty years of training dogs, including in bitework, told me that this dog was *not* nice around other dogs—or people, given that he redirected a few times onto his owner when confronted with basic commands he did not want to comply with. No blood drawn that I could see (though I was not getting close), but a definite growl, and contact made by the dog's muzzle, if not his teeth. Now, there are some dogfighting rings known to be not too far away from where I live, and from this dog's energy and appetite for a brawl (and yes, he was at times off-lead) my guess is he was a game-bred Pit Bull, though in my experience most Pit Bulls are handler-friendly except when their drive kicks in—then all bets are off.[69] In my opinion, if that dog had been seized by police, given his attitude, he would have been deleted: "101 page dog not found."

However, those five dogs got off with being threatened by me, which sent a couple scooting back to their owners, tail between their legs. The rest, as I said, I had to return to their owners. From their expressions, the owners seemed to be sucking on lemons, but better their dog encountered an apparently menopausal, rage-filled lady than turned into a hashtag by the Pit Bull. Something like #mydeaddarlingdog.

The owners were all seemingly unaware of the dangers of allowing their rude dog to run up to any random dog he does not know and try to cause chaos. It is *extremely* poor etiquette to let an off-lead dog run up to an on-lead dog *at all*, never mind to then try to jump on top of them. That is a recipe for a fight. Dogs in parks that allow off-lead walking tend to be on-lead for a reason. Maybe they are reactive. Some are old. Yet others may have recently had surgery. The point is, you just do not know why they are on-lead. No on-lead dog should be subjected to unwanted attention.

My dogs are both friendly, neutral, and under control, but I never forget that they are Rottweilers. If the two aggressive dogs had started a fight, or even if the playful dogs had gotten too amorous, my older bitch would have delighted in teaching them a lesson. Pack mentality then kicks in, and if my younger dog had joined in, well, who are you going to bet on? My dogs may be under control and on-lead, but if a fight breaks out between them and a third, off-lead dog, that is more than one person can split up. Two fit, adult, working Rottweilers versus an overweight Patterdale Terrier with a bad attitude? It's not going to end well for the Patterdale, let's put it that way.

There are other kinds of losers too. At the time of writing, we are in the middle of a perfect storm. I see more and more first-time dog owners who have had no access to trainers of any sort for a year or more and whose dog has poor genetics, which in the majority of cases manifests as neurotic and nervous behaviors, often leading to fear-based aggression. When the dog is a large breed, the house is essentially inhabited by an AK-47 with a pulse. Now the dog is not so much fun for the family. They do not have time to properly exercise and train him and he has become a real liability, with behavioral issues they do not know how to cope with. Sadly, in many cases, this is a dog they no longer want in their lives, and some of these dogs may not be the powerful meatheads that you suspect.

What To Do?

What to do indeed. As we have already discussed above, you will see many force-free trainers who insist that there *are* formal certifications for dog trainers and that these are for purely positive trainers only. In the UK and the U.S., this statement is a steaming pile of doggy doo-doo. And I am being polite. Other than for some narrowly defined positions within the veterinary profession, this is not the case, and many of the "formal certifications" the force-free trainers refer to are issued by private businesses which create their own qualification requirements and certificates, a bit like Trump University. This is not to say that many of their courses are not excellent, but they do not give graduates the right to say that they alone are qualified to train dogs and the right to say what is right and what is wrong.

Now, I would be all for setting up a system of formal qualifications if all things were equal, but they're not. The main problem which arises, aside from cost, is the fact that the people with the most political clout will be the ones put in charge, *not* the best behaviorists and dog trainers, given that there are two sets of polar opposites fighting for power. In Europe the extremists have already won and have had many training tools banned. They would be delighted to create a syllabus and set of qualifications which would drive balanced trainers out of business completely.

Any set of qualifications should be designed to accommodate everyone, from owners of pet handbag dogs to departments with police dogs, from owners who just want their dogs to learn basic obedience to people who are looking for advanced trick training. If we are going to create such a system, in Europe at least, we need to do so quickly, as the experienced trainers who can work with severe behavioral issues, including human aggression, are getting old. When these trainers retire, many of their skills will be lost.

When we lose certain skill sets, we let down the difficult dogs that are just as deserving of help as any other dog with a problem, and if current moves to turn all dog training force-free succeed in Europe, the next port of call for the extremists will be the U.S., as we can already see in New York and California. Personally, I think any curriculum should force trainers slightly out of their comfort zone, enabling them to see a different side to dog training and perhaps helping them realize that there are great similarities between the different schools of dog training along with the important differences.

I have seen force free trainers go to pieces when wearing a bite sleeve and acting as a decoy with a dog performing a bark and hold. This is an exercise where the dog pins a decoy in a "hide" (a structure with a single entrance/exit) and stands and barks at her,[70] though many dogs will also jump up close to the decoy's face. When the decoy moves toward the entrance/exit, the dog grasps the bite sleeve to stop her from exiting the hide. If a trainer experienced in bitework is too scared to do this exercise with a trained dog in a controlled environment, how can she possibly hope to perform behavioral consults genuinely aggressive dogs whose bark cannot be said to be worse than their bite?

Gathering insight into different aspects of dog training can change a young (or old) trainer's view on what she is able to cope with herself and when she should refer a client to someone who uses different tools and techniques. Some trainers, however, will blame the dog[71] and only consider using force-free management, medication, or euthanasia, refusing to admit that all dogs must be treated as individuals. A good curriculum can also show trainers the appropriateness of certain balanced-training tools, given that such tools can make the difference between a person or dog being bitten and a safely structured training session that is fair to the dog, who learns and benefits from the experience. For example, some commentators estimate that a pinch collar reduces a dog's pulling by 50 percent and requires 90 percent less force from a correction,[72] making it a subtle tool and a safe one with a determined, powerful dog, and it can be surprising how quickly force-free extremists will reach for such a tool in an emergency.[73]

This goes both ways, of course. I have zero interest in trick training, barn hunt, dock diving, agility, or hoops, but it would do me no harm to learn a bit about them and even have a go at them with my dogs. I guarantee I would come away having learned some neat new training techniques. There are many force-free-training extremists whom I will admit I could no doubt learn valuable lessons from. Many are masters of skills such as free shaping, and I think you can learn something from everyone you meet, even if it is just tolerance, patience, and reflecting that being sent to jail for murder is just not for you.

Should force-free trainers who blatantly lie to clients be referred to a fair trade commission[74] or similar body that regulates advertisements and business practices? After all, if a trainer insists to a client that she is force-free and that their dog will be trained using positive reinforcement *only*, then surely that is what should happen. We all know that a flat collar and lead uses force, but what if the trainer tells the client their dog needs a head collar to stop him from pulling? This tool is very aversive for many dogs, so such a trainer is hardly being truthful when she says she is force-free. She is, rather, utilizing false advertising in order to gain a business advantage.

Of course, no trainer can guarantee a specific result with a living creature, but what if a force-free trainer confidently says she can stop a high-prey-drive dog from pulling on the lead around distractions such as squirrels, by using no force or corrections whatsoever, just cookies. We know this is simply not going to happen anytime soon with no corrections, as does the force-free trainer if she is being honest. Should she be able to advertise herself as force-free, without penalty, while continually telling the client it will take more time, more time, more time?

One year later, when the client asks how much longer the training is going to take, the trainer invariably tells her that her dog is defective. There's nothing wrong with the force-free training methodology, but her dog is going to need to be permanently managed or sedated just so he can walk past the squirrel tree on the way to the park without pulling his owner flat onto her face. Bear in mind that the trainer will have no doubt charged the client $50–$100 per week for all of that time. Ethically, and from a business viewpoint, is this acceptable?

Well, if I was the client and refused to drug my dog or restrict the routes we walk, and then found a reputable, balanced trainer and hey presto, my dog is loose-lead-walking around distractions after just a few sessions, I would be angry. Very angry. Yes, the dog may have learned good engagement from the force-free trainer, which would have given the balanced trainer a flying start, but with the force-free trainer only half of the equation was ever going to be put in place. Without being taught the concept of pressure and release on the lead, and therefore consequences for bad behavior, there is nothing to stop the dog from pulling when he sees a squirrel. Cookies are no match for a live, scurrying squirrel.

I could never get back the time I had wasted if I was the client, but I would want a refund for the $50–$100 per week I had paid for the last year of "training." Wouldn't you? However, we all know this money would not be forthcoming if I asked for a refund. I could take legal action, but it would be expensive, and it's unlikely I would get anywhere. So, never mind taking business away from other trainers, should protections not be put in place for clients, to prevent force-free trainers from making promises they cannot realistically ever keep?

Ethics

There is no easy answer, but it is inevitable that what we consider to be the ethical treatment of dogs will change over time. Rules and boundaries imposed using corrections are a necessary part of training, in order to teach our dogs how to live with us in society as well-behaved canine citizens. When we restrict the ability of trainers to use corrections, not because they do not work but because management, medication and

Chapter Ten. Cults

finally euthanasia are touted as being the only solutions, then ultimately we are left with ethics to defend our viewpoint.

If we decide it is not ethical for an animal to ever feel any discomfort, no matter how fleeting, and that dogs must be autonomous and make all of their own life choices, including running free and breeding whenever they want(!), then logically we can no longer keep pets.[75] However my sciatica is telling me loud and clear that discomfort, pain even, is part and parcel of life, and that no one gets to "run free" so why should dogs?

Most so-called force-free trainers just want to use the kinds of force they like and approve of, and traditionally such trainers were happy to let balanced trainers do their own thing. They had little interest in training protection dogs, sports dogs, police dogs or large, high-drive breeds with an attitude. But increasingly these days, at least in Europe, the extremists within the force-free movement are taking charge, and they want to dictate how all dogs are trained, even in areas where they have no experience. Eventually, the moderate force-free trainers who use corrections in addition to potentially aversive tools such as head collars and no-pull harnesses, will be seen as compulsion trainers. That day is not that far off. What then?

There will be no pure-bred dogs left, since the "adopt, don't shop" agenda will be imposed absolutely.[76] Genetics are important, and with no pure-bred dogs, which are bred for very specific purposes, there will be no more working dogs. Domestication should never have happened, we are told,[77] and therefore we will have no service dogs, no police dogs, no hunting dogs. Ordinary pet owners will be described as exploitative abusers who keep dogs as property, as commodities—monsters who dare to dictate how dogs, cats and other animals must live.[78] The pitchforks and torches will not come out, rather our rights will be removed by stealth, the aggressors all the while insisting they are peace-loving folk, working for the greater good, and that every human and animal must have the right to live an authentic life. Just not those of us who would like to own dogs, in whatever capacity.

Conclusion

What do you want in life when it comes to your dog? Personally, I want a dog I both love *and* like. A dog that is a dream about the home, can be trusted not to raid bins or counter surf, and does not have to be put away when guests come over. A dog the postman looks forward to saying hello to. A dog that snuggles up on the sofa beside me, then spoons in bed later (the TMI klaxon is now sounding, but it's extremely cold where I live).

I want a dog that is also good outside the home, one with a fantastic recall that is easy to handle around reactive dogs, traffic, kids with balls, etc., and that I can walk safely and comfortably in normal circumstances without the use of lots of tools. Those are my ultimate goals. I am lucky: I have two dogs like this, for which massive thanks must go to their respective breeders, but I also had to put in the work, though I very much started with a hand stacked in my favor.

In days gone by, the sort of behavior that I describe above was considered a normal expectation for any family dog. Yes, a dog may have problems and go through various difficult phases during puppyhood and adolescence; that is to be expected, and my family's dogs were not exempt in that regard. Nevertheless, by the age of two, most dogs from my childhood were happy, well-adjusted members of society. Sadly, these days, despite more access than ever to good dog trainers and excellent free instructional videos by virtue of the internet, such a family dog is becoming a rarity.

You may think the majority of dogs are great, since those you see out and about in public are friendly and well socialized. A bit of lead pulling here and there, a few squabbles at the dog park, but nothing major. However, many of these nice dogs have bad manners at home, such as raiding bins and eating dish towels. Not to mention, like the bottom of an iceberg, there are a great many dogs that never go outside their yard, or if they do, it's after dark, when it's quiet and there are fewer people and other dogs about.

Conclusion

Where have we gone wrong? Well, I hope this book has shown that the force-free training movement has a lot to answer for, and that in reality, no dog is trained without force and corrections of some sort. It is merely a matter of degree. The force-free training activists started off with the very best of intentions, to move people away from compulsion training, not to avoid corrections altogether. But we have now come full circle and more people than ever cohabit with dogs they really do not like very much at all—a chore to endure rather than a pleasure to live with.

I recently visited an online reward-based service dog training forum, not to troll, but because there are extremely good trainers there, with excellent skills in very specific areas of service dog training. I am disabled and have a service dog myself, so these forums are of great interest to me, even though some of the trainers there are ~~ranting lunatics~~ force-free extremists. They insist they use no force at all, yet their profile pics show their own dog wearing a head collar. Go figure. A few of these trainers turn out nicely trained service dogs that help people, so while they may be untruthful in claiming that they are "force-free," at least the dogs they train are safe and do their job.

Anyways, in a survey of dog owners on the site, one question asked what their service dog-in-training's main personality traits are, and every checkbox described dogs that are nervous, fearful or have behavioral issues such as resource guarding. So I created two additional checkboxes, one for happy, confident, and well-adjusted dogs and one for excitable, over-enthusiastic dogs, thinking that ordinary dogs particulalrly those in adolescence had been overlooked. No one else on the site ticked off either of these boxes.

I find this incredibly sad and extremely worrying, particularly given that these were *service dogs* in training. Now, you could say people join a forum to get help with their troublesome dogs, which is true, but not one confident dog? Not one, apart from mine? There were no excitable, friendly goofballs going through adolescence, just scared, nervous dogs. This is not normal, and fearful dogs absolutely should not be unfairly pressurized into service dog work.

On one hand we have force-free trainers telling people their big, strong dog cannot be helped with loose-lead walking if he won't respond to cookies, and on the other hand that their small, scared dog can make a wonderful service dog with enough counter-conditioning, insisting that it's the norm for adult dogs to be scared of loud noises, strange people, other animals, and so forth. Just spend every day stuffing your dog's face with food in the name of "training" they preach.

I am getting old. I don't want to carry a backpack containing an entire day's food ration around with me, just to get my dog to pay attention and do as I ask. Nor do I want to have to turn around and go home simply because I left the e-collar remote control on my bedside table. I want a dog that can be taken out and enjoyed on an average walk without packing the same amount of baggage a newborn baby requires.

If I was going to have my dog off-lead while walking a trail up a mountain, where there is a small chance there might be sheep, would he be wearing his e-collar if he had in the past *ever* shown a tendency or even a vague interest in chasing livestock? Yes, he would be wearing it. Even if he had never shown an interest in sheep, he would still be wearing it. In fact, he would also be kept on-lead until I was absolutely sure there was no livestock in the area.

If I was going to a very different venue, say a church bazaar, where I know there will be out-of-control dogs and even more unruly children charging about, what would I do? Would I put a, heaven forbid, pinch collar on my highly confident, excitable young dog that is prone to bouncing around like a cat that got into the magic mushrooms instead of the catnip? Yep. You bet I would. I mean, it's a church bazaar, so with a bit of luck I'd be forgiven and not lynched.

In both cases, I would also have plentiful rewards with me. Just as I always carry poop bags in my training jacket pockets, so do I carry high-value food rewards and a ball on a rope. The jacket makes me look like a character in a documentary on homelessness, as if I've been pulled through a hedge backwards. Repeatedly. Nevertheless, I wear it everywhere. Ultimately, however, I want a dog that does not sulk and refuse to behave if I forget the cookies one day. In my opinion, that is how dog ownership should be, training for the best but preparing for the worst, and not being blind to the dog you actually own. Dogs are dogs, and they cannot be relied upon to behave beautifully all of the time, even the best trained of service dogs. They have off days and make mistakes in their work just like we do.

Many of us aspire to owning the perfect dog, whether as a pet, a show dog, a service dog or a sports dog, yet the best laid plans often go astray. I have had two dogs in a row with serious orthopedic issues, the first dogs I have ever had with such complaints one from sheer bad luck, the other from genetic factors, despite her parents' excelllent health tests. That's life. We don't always get what we want, or what we need, and perhaps it's for the best. People involved in dog sports are either Beelzebub incarnate, ghosting, gossiping and bullying their way through life and generally the biggest bunch of [insert the worst expletive you can think of] around, or, at the other end of the scale, the nicest, most generous, kindest people you ever will meet. There seems to be little in between.

I adore my dogs, and along with my cats they mean more to me than anything in this world. We take the dog we end up with, and we love and do our best for that dog, even if that means using tools we never envisaged we may need. Or, ultimately, we can place that dog into a better home that can offer him the things we can't. A bit like an amicable divorce. What we should not do is "manage" the dog into living a miserable life, or drug him into oblivion, or euthanize him, simply as he does not fit the mold of the ethos we have bought into. He is a dog, not a human. He does not care about your commitment to only using a flat collar. It is not a hill he would die on if he had the choice.

Despite the force-free takeover of the dog training industry, more dogs than ever are in shelters for behavioral issues, and those that are not are likely being managed or medicated. Treating a dog as an entitled toddler with full bodily autonomy, not to mention choice over all things in his life, does him no favors. Your dog is not autistic, nor does he have "special needs," and by saying these things you greatly disrespect disabled people who live with these very real medical conditions each and every day of their lives. If your dog cannot leave your house or yard because he is too unruly, excitable, pulls too hard on the lead, is too reactive to people and other dogs, or whatever else the problem is, he is a perfectly normal dog. A difficult dog perhaps, but normal. Don't give up on him on the say-so of a bunch of extremists.

In my opinion, most people who sit at either extreme in the dog training industry have a limited education and skill base, which is why they themselves are limited: limited in the kinds of dogs they can train, limited in the tools and training techniques they use, limited in their knowledge of dog training and behavior. When trainers tell you that they cannot help your dog and he must never leave your home and yard or be allowed off-lead in public ever again, believe them. Your dog cannot be helped by *them*, or by their version of how a dog is to be trained. It does not mean you and your dog are failures, as the force-free ethos suggests; rather you need training tools and techniques which suit you, your dog and the specific problems you are experiencing. A "one size fits all" solution, saying every dog must be on a flat collar and respond to recall for part of his daily food ration, does not fly in the real world. A Siberian Husky is not the same beast as a Yorkshire Terrier.

I see vicious fighting from extremists on both sides, force-free activists and compulsion trainers, with little representation from those balanced trainers who sit squarely in the middle and use both corrections and rewards with the dogs they train. Everyone wants to produce well-trained, happy dogs, and most people involved with dogs professionally in one way or another just want to make a decent living without being bitten. There's nothing wrong with that. Every trainer has a type of dog they prefer to train, and some specialize in certain problems. I am old, with bad knees, crippled hands, and sciatica. I prefer to train big, confident dogs that can easily reach my hand for rewards. I do not enjoy waddling like a duck on my haunches, bum almost on the ground, in order to lure vertically challenged dogs, as if trapped in my own training session nightmare. Don't get me wrong, I love small dogs, and much training can be done without lures or food given directly from the hand. But in a play on the song lyrics, "I like big dogs and I will not lie." I think I got that right. How can song lyrics be so hard to remember?[1]

When balanced trainers do speak up, too many of them are large, hairy men with even larger, hairier dogs who are campaigning to retain the tools they rely on.[2] This is not relatable for the vast majority of dog owners, many of whom own a small to medium-sized dog that lacks confidence, has low drive, and is not particularly strong-willed. Most of these dogs will never need a pinch collar, though an e-collar would not be a bad idea. Similarly, women don't need a lot of guys mansplaining to them why their Fifi is a horror. They are certainly well aware ~~that they need an exorcist~~ why they are shunned by all and sundry as their yipping, yapping terror proceeds down the road, motorists looking twice to make sure its head is not rotating 360 degrees.

We need more women trainers to stand up and be counted, to become more of a presence online, to join in the podcasts and overall conversation. I look at the most popular online dog trainers, and they are mostly men.[3] More often than not, the trainers they interview and collaborate with are also men. Are women reluctant to be interviewed, or are they never invited, as it's still an old boys' club? After all, there are many female world champions in IGP, trick training, doggy dancing, competitive obedience, agility, dock diving, or whatever dog sport you can think of, dog sport (along with equestrian sport) being one of the few sports where men and women compete on equal terms. There are also a great many women behaviorists doing an outstanding job, often with very difficult dogs, and yet others breaking the boundaries of what was seen as possible in training, in both competitive sports and, for want of a better word, experimental dog training outside the lab.[4]

Part of the problem, as I see it, is online bullying and hatred. Many women (and men) who are balanced dog trainers don't want any part of cancel culture and bullying; they just want to mind their own business and to train dogs. The force-free extremists, on the other hand, seem only too happy to stalk and harass those they do not approve of, doxing them shamelessly. This is odd given that they are the ones screaming about ethics and morality.

Why is discomfort, no matter how momentary and beneficial to the

Conclusion

dog's long-term health, well-being, happiness and lifestyle, seen as unacceptable during training? Discomfort, pain even, like death and taxes, is an unavoidable part of life, and dog training holds no special place in the universe where such concepts do not exist. Why is it that giving a dog a correction, even a mild one, is considered so very wrong these days?

Over the last ten years or so, the vast majority of the general public and a great many trainers have said they do not support the use of training techniques, tools or equipment that involve harsh, punitive corrections or cause the dog fear. I absolutely agree. I train with an abundance of rewards, and though I certainly give corrections, as we cannot get around the fact that corrections in some form are required, they are neither harsh nor punitive. Rather, when I correct a dog, the correction is fair, well-thought-out, and appropriate for the dog in question. It will not harm him, either short- or long-term. He will not dissolve into a pool of self-pity, though he may regret his actions momentarily and just maybe will make a face like someone with a soundly slapped posterior, as he would prefer to continue to get his own way. Do the prongs of a pinch collar (and the sight of a temporarily sulking dog) look great? No. Is it the best tool for many dogs? Yes.

The *dog* must ultimately be the one to show whether a tool or training technique acts as an aversive for him or as a useful addition to his training, enhancing his understanding and keeping him safe and under control in his everyday life. Taking a helpful tool away from a dog and therefore limiting his freedom and ability to live his best life is not acceptable. Why are we giving dogs the choice to say "no" to being groomed and to having their nails trimmed, both actions necessary for their basic health? Is it really in a dog's best interest to have zero recall and to think it's permissible to bark and growl at other dogs, and even people, that they meet when out on walks, never mind throwing their weight around in the home? If a training tool works for a dog, it should not be taken from him, removing his ability to enjoy walks with his owner simply because the optics of wearing a pinch collar are not great.

The general public, and also young, inexperienced dog trainers, are making arbitrary value judgments about tools they have *never* used themselves and do not understand the correct use of. They have not seen an e-collar being used correctly, or the difference it makes to the lives of a high drive dog and his owner when he is finally able to be safely walked off-lead. These judgments are based on the migraine-inducing shrieks of "Abuse!" by force-free extremists who say they are "science-based" trainers and who offer "management solutions" and medications as alternatives to the e-collar, pinch collar, slip lead, martingale and choke chain. They do not explain that "management" in many cases means never allowing the dog out of the owner's tiny yard. Or he can be driven once a week to a high-fenced exercise area where he can dash around the perimeter while his owner ignores him and plays with her phone.

These are the suggested solutions for dogs that have worn a pinch collar, e-collar, etc., for years, and that have consequently been out and about in the real world for years with no issues, living their best life. Remove the tools, and the suggested solution is no more walks or freedom, just incarceration. Now, the e-collar may only be used as a correction once or twice a year, as once a dog is well-trained with such a tool (other than when training advanced obedience), it doesn't really need to come into play. It's a similar story with the pinch collar. Well-trained dogs that understand lead pressure but ignore the action of milder collars will walk very nicely at heel after an introduction to the pinch. The dog chooses not to pull into it and receive a correction. He is not shut down, scared or suppressed, simply making good life choices with an appropriate tool that suits him.

But, and it's a big but, dogs are not stupid. Training is never quite at an end, so banning and removing tools, even if they are rarely used, will still have negative consequences. A dog may only be corrected infrequently with an e-collar, but it keeps him safe. If he misbehaves once and gets away with it, then very soon, if he is a smart dog, he will try to push his luck again. This is not poor training, it is a dog being a dog. With his owner no longer having any way to give him corrections off-lead, a strong-willed dog will start to do whatever he pleases and subsequently become out of control. The dog which the local community once loved, which was a problem to no one, is now limited to the house, the yard, and the fenced-off, expensive training area his owner can only afford once a week. How is removing the e-collar benefiting the dog? It is not. Offering him "crate games" twice a day as an alternative to his daily off-lead walks simply does not wash.

Not everyone has a big, strong dog, or even a dog with any drive, determination or confidence. More and more people own nervous, anxious dogs that prefer to never wander far from their owner's legs and are happy with "at home" days when they are not walked, should the weather be inclement. In time, these dogs, if they are brachycephalic[5] or long-backed,[6] will become banned breeds. Maybe merles[7] will too, as irresponsible back yard breeders continue to churn out Australian Shepherds and Border Collies without health testing, invariably breeding two carriers together. *You* may then be searching for another breed, as like me (with my love for large dogs), you find that your heart dog is no longer acceptable in society on the basis of ethics and morality, just for slightly different reasons. Even when specific dog breeds are not banned and tools are banned instead, it still affects all dog owners, as they have less and less control over their dogs natural, but at times unwanted, behaviors.

People are increasingly lacking common sense around dogs. I don't know if it's because a TikTok video went viral, but dog owners in my local park recently started to participate in a strange sort of "game." On an almost daily basis, an increasing number of people have thrown balls directly over the heads of my dogs, using a plastic ball launcher. This was no accident. There's an entire park out there, but no, these people snuck up behind us and threw their dog's ball over our heads, just to see what would happen. All the while, I suspect, recording the scene on their phones.

My dogs tend to amble slightly in front of me when walking in the park, and a ball suddenly and unexpectedly soaring over our heads is an incentive for them to go after that ball. They don't know if *I* have thrown the ball for them. They are dogs. They have high prey drive and like nothing better than to chase a ball, in addition to which both my dogs are trained in heelwork with a ball being thrown as a reward. Your small dog rushing past my dogs (one crashing into my legs, almost kneecapping me) does not help.

If my dogs are on-lead, the most that happens is that they instinctively start after the ball and then stop when told not to or they come to the end of their lead, dashing the would-be cinematographer's hopes that I would be pulled over and dragged along the ground. No matter that I'm disabled with a clearly labeled service dog, as long as they have their fun. However, if my dogs are off-lead, then the tears start to flow when one of my dogs is the fastest and steals the other dog's ball. After all, there's no ball as good as a stolen ball. "It's new, I want it back before it's chewed up," they invariably whine, as my dogs gleefully run about with their new toy and the defeated small dog slinks back to his owner.

Now, this is a public park, there for all to enjoy. It's absolutely my responsibility to have full control of my dogs at all times. If you want to nominate your dog for a Darwin Award,[8] then stupid as that is, it's your prerogative. I'm not going to start rolling my eyes, jab my finger in your face and say, "Let me educate you" in the most passive-aggressive, patronizing way possible. However, I will say this: On multiple occasions, had it not been for both of my dogs having been trained with a pinch collar and therefore respecting lead pressure, not to mention both of them possessing an outstanding recall due to e-collar training, there would be three dogs going for the same ball every time you pull this stunt. This is not a fight your small dog can win on his own should he take umbrage at my Rottweilers stealing his ball.

My dogs are friendly with other dogs. They wear appropriate collars on walks and are under my control, but not all dogs are the same as mine.

Rottweilers rarely start fights, but they won't back down from a fight that another dog starts with them. When your dog attacks another dog over his ball, since you find it funny to see owners of big dogs struggling to keep hold of their dogs when you antagonize them deliberately, or to see two dogs go for the same ball, one day it will backfire on you. This will particularly be the case when tools such as pinch collars, martingale collars and e-collars are banned and dogs know they can pull hard into a collar, or run away and not recall, with no consequences.

A large, high-drive dog that sees a ball, forgets his manners and just runs may pull his owner right over, injuring her. Or, as this prank is most often done from behind and the owner is not ready for her dog to unexpectedly lunge, the lead may be yanked from her hands. If you're lucky when you pull this stunt, the dogs won't fight over the ball and you can strut about yelling that the big dog should be under control and muzzled since he chases other dogs' balls. But one day the large dog won't be a friendly one, and the ball will not be the object of his desire; it will be your small dog as he sprints past. Possibly within reach of the aggressive dog, even if he is on-lead. When you're sobbing and holding a dead dog in your arms, it doesn't matter if you're "in the right." You still have a dead dog.

There are a great many Spaniels, Retrievers, Labradors, Collies, Terriers, etc., that are dog-aggressive; it's not just the large guarding breeds. I have seen plenty of owners of such medium and small-sized dogs who have no consideration for other dog owners, thinking their extremely aggressive dog has the right not to wear a muzzle on walks, as any dog running up to them is clearly out of control. When their dog is on-lead, it's the off-lead dog that is always at fault. Are they wrong? No. Not in a perfect world. No dog should *ever* ignore a recall and run up to an on-lead dog, though it happens. Frequently. But do you really want a visit from the police, not to mention another dog's death on your conscience, just because the approaching dog was a puppy, or had an irresponsible owner who could not be bothered to teach a recall, or was a good dog that one day simply made a mistake? When e-collars are banned, there will be many, many more such mistakes.

More often than not an aggressive Spaniel will get a level of leniency that would not be afforded to a Staffordshire Bull Terrier, so it's not necessarily the large, powerful on-lead dogs that are the biggest risk. That Labrador walking on a loose lead may become the very devil himself if he goes for your dog's ball. Or, if your dog whizzes too close to that Springer Spaniel, whether on-lead or off-lead, he may get nailed. A dogfight is a nasty business, no matter the size of the dogs involved, so please, for the love of all things holy, don't use ball chuckers to throw balls directly over the heads of other dogs, or right beside them. It's bad manners, and you could

Conclusion

be responsible for your own dog's death or serious injury. Why? Because you thought it was a funny prank to see the owners of dogs you dislike struggle when you antagonize their dogs.

Having let off steam with my rant, let me repeat, as I have said throughout this book, that *the majority of small, low-drive pet dogs DO NOT need prong collars or e-collars in order to lead happy lives.* However, we have a dog population of 13 million in the UK, and it is estimated that up to 300,000 dogs would be affected by an e-collar or prong collar ban.[9] Who are *you* to say to 300,000 dogs that they can no longer go for walks? That they must be "managed" or rendered brain-dead with drugs? Do you think the management technique of being left in a fenced yard to vegetate with the cucumbers is fair? Or should such a dog be re-homed, as his loving owner does not have the sort of money and financial privilege to afford a home with extensive grounds? Fine for the wealthy to have an invisible electric fence as a border, but not for a trainer to use an e-collar for recall or training? How very odd.

Force-free extremists should not get to make that decision. Surely as animal lovers it is for us to ensure that all dogs have a high quality of life. *All* dogs, not just small handbag dogs, not just low-drive dogs, not just dogs scared of their own shadow and that would rather stay in the house. We also need to consider the dogs that are large, powerful, and have a high prey drive, and which a pinch collar or an e-collar suits, ensuring they can live a happy life, walking nicely at their owner's side before they are let off-lead in the park, on farmland or wherever else they are walked, their owner safe in the knowledge their dog will recall no matter the distractions.

A trainer or dog owner saying they do all of their training in a force-free way, with no corrections whatsoever, is like someone saying they have never broken the law. Balderdash! (Now, there's a strong word which is not a crude expletive.) I have never met anyone who has never broken a single, solitary law in their entire life. It is impossible. Drivers, who among you has not exceeded the speed limit by so much as 1 mph? Pedestrians, have you truly never crossed a road where it was not a designated crossing place? Or stepped into the road a millisecond before the crossing light turned green? Anyone who claims they have never broken a law has not lived, and anyone who claims they have used only positive reinforcement has never trained a dog.

Sadly, the extremists cannot accept that not everyone is like them. It seems to insult their very existence, and instead of accepting that we all, including dogs, have different wants and needs in life, they take it upon themselves to interfere in matters in which they have no knowledge or experience. Like any well-meaning bigot, they believe that all others must conform to their viewpoint and that if this cannot be achieved voluntarily, it must be enforced via a combination of vicious smear campaigns, political pressure and bribes, not to mention financial support to dubious "scientists," leading to changes in legislation.

These force-free owners and trainers are entitled, yet deeply unhappy and unfulfilled in their lives. They do not work on themselves and their own demons but instead target others, so as to bring everyone else down to their level. They seek out well-meaning dog owners and recruit them into the force-free cult, projecting their emptiness and rage at their own inadequacies as trainers onto the very dogs they profess to care about and want to save from pain and fear, claiming that any dog that cannot be trained with a pocketful of cookies and a head collar has autism or mental health problems and must be euthanized, managed or medicated for his own good, as heaven forbid their training methods and ethos could be at fault.

"Think of the dog's autonomy," they preach. "Corrections always cause pain and fear. Just ignore any bad behavior and reward the good." They are unable to understand that in the real world, the good things in life cannot be appreciated or experienced fully without negatives existing too, that not everyone has acres of fenced yard with which to manage their "challenging" (that is to say, normal) dog. "Death before discomfort" has become an alarming reality recommended for a great many dogs that won't conform and become something they are not.

If one of these dogs is lucky and is not shipped to the kill shelter, he can be consigned to the utopia that befits every plush toy, lying glassy-eyed on the sofa for 23 hours a day, his drug cabinet fuller than the average downtown pharmacy, a dog walker occasionally hired to trundle him around the block on his front-pull harness. Satisfied that their own misery has been imposed on the dogs in their care, the extremists get a brief thrill from the control they have exerted over these poor souls, once vibrant, now placid and depressed. Of course, this is all validated by people online who say, "Well done, we don't need to see those nasty big dogs out on walks in public anyway."

Make no mistake, this is a cult-like environment. The Ant Hill Kids[10] had nothing on the force-free mafia, and the Borg[11] would pale at the viciousness and speed with which they have assimilated the lonely, the impressionable, the sad, and the ill-informed. Dog owners struggling with a rude or scared dog join the movement and become flying monkeys, turning into the worst type of "be kind'" internet trolls. Secret social media pages are set up with the aim to destroy the life and livelihood of anyone who does not drink the force-free Kool-Aid, organizing stalking campaigns with military precision. Behind them, pulling the strings, are

Conclusion 223

powerful people with an additional agenda, which is generally making money off the dogs we love, in any way they can.

I look into the beautiful, deep, trusting brown eyes of my dogs as they snuggle beside me on my sofa where I am writing, and it sickens me that the force-free brigade would rather drug or kill my gorgeous girls than say the word *no* to them. With the pinch collar in the bin, my young, excitable dog would be free to turn into a badly behaved, ill-disciplined lout, whom if she spotted a discarded chicken bone on the pavement would see no reason not to haul me along behind her and make a grab for it. Should I just watch her gobble it down? Heaven forbid I utter the word "no," backed up by a pop on the lead (attached to her pinch collar). No amount of offering cookies, or hours of practice swapping out rubber bones at home, can compete with a half-eaten KFC to a **green dog**, not yet at maturity.

How did we get to this total and utter lunacy, where the force-free fanatics have taken over entire countries, getting certain collars, and even crates, banned? Their inflexibility and refusal to think logically or consider any situation but their own, their entitlement, callousness, and sheer spite is mind-blowing. How effortlessly they project their feelings of inadequacy, powerlessness, anger and frustration onto people like me and dogs like my own, demanding we submit to a miserable existence so they can crow that they know what is best for us, despite never having met us nor seen how much happier my dogs are than their scared, drugged-up, sad parodies of dogs, which are "managed" in their gilded training rooms, never venturing into the real world to breathe fresh, pine-scented air in the forest or go crabbing in rock pools on the beach.

I feel desperately sorry for these dogs owned by force-free extremists. Even so, they are not my dogs and I cannot fully understand their lives or the circumstances they live in, nor their past traumas. Therefore, it would by hypocritical and wrong of me to insist that the tools, medications and management techniques used on them be removed in favor of trying what works for me and the dogs I train. I take it on trust that these dogs are loved and that their owners are genuinely doing what they think is best for them.

So why, then, do force-free extremists not return the favor, trusting me to do the very best for the dogs under my care? Why are they so insistent on interfering in my life? There is a genuine lack of compassion and remorse over the dogs' lives that are being cut short by the extremists. It seems that as long as the absolutist agenda of their mafia brothers and sisters is satisfied, anything goes, and the welfare of individual dogs is not their concern. We hear the word *narcissism* a lot in today's society, used to describe anyone from an annoying "Karen"[12] to a serial killer like Ted Bundy,[13] yet it also describes the extremist force-free mafia to a T.

Where did my generation go wrong in raising such a nasty bunch of entitled bullies who think they can rewrite the laws of science and nature to suit themselves? Not every dog is a weak and trembling wreck, jumping at his own shadow and preferring to stay inside his home. It's wrong to impose on my dogs the management and medication that you require to keep your own dogs under control. On the face of it, I'm desperately sorry for your dogs, but if you have created a happy, yet limited life for them, the best life possible given the circumstances, then good for you. I won't dispute that you have done your very best, even though you are trying to destroy me and my dogs, not to mention our way of life.

Just stop and think for a moment. If I can forgive, and see you may be in a tight spot but are doing your best, then why can't you? The sadness you feel for your dogs, your inability to train them to overcome their behavioral issues and genetic fearfulness so they can enjoy life and walks in the real world, does not give you an excuse to punish my dogs for being healthy and well-adjusted. Yes, they require corrections and consequences for poor behavior: they are dogs. It is not required often, but when it is, I do not hesitate. They also receive abundant praise for doing the right thing, and I am satisfied they are living their best lives. Why do you want to take this from us? From thousands, if not millions of dogs and their owners? Look deep into your heart and ask yourself, "Why are the lives of these dogs so worthless to you?"

Leave. Us. Alone. Serve your cult leaders as you wish, drink gallons of their Kool-Aid, but stop spreading propaganda based on smoke and mirrors, on outright lies. You do not have the backing of "science." I am not going to starve my dogs for days on end as a "humane method of training" to deal with a competing reinforcer when a simple "no" and a small lead pop does the job. Neither am I prepared to have my dogs "managed" and never leave my home again should the drugs not work or have unacceptable side effects. Their "poor little necks" are the size of my thigh, and I am not one to turn away from a slice of cake. Or three. OK, the entire damn cake. Rottweilers were bred for well over a hundred years to be confident dogs that are emotionally resilient and can take direction, including corrections.

Not all dogs are bred to be docile companions, and they need to be kept and loved as the individuals they are, not forced to conform to what you want a dog to be, compliant and shut down, or a hothoused, nervous trickmaster that must be managed and not allowed outside around distractions. I will not subject my dogs to frustration-based training as you do, making them plead with me to guide them and give kind corrections and leadership. Turning my back on them in that way is unfair and cruel. Neither will I deprive my dogs of essential resources for long periods of time, forcing them to grovel and be compliant just to survive and be fed. I want them to work with me as in a team because it's fun for both of us, not because they are bribed or bullied with food withholding. In a team, there is a leader, which is me. "Leader" is not a dirty word.

You do what you think is best for you and your dogs, but I will not be copying you, with your management and medication. I will give up dogs entirely before I own Rottweilers that are so brain-dead they are content to sit on a sofa 24 hours a day. Like your purely-positive-trained dogs, my dogs also get play, love, and plentiful rewards. In fact, I would bet my dogs receive far more rewards than yours, both in frequency and intensity, and far fewer corrections, given the surplus of negative punishment you dole out and the emotional trauma your dogs go through as a result. Am I being fair? No, but the force-free mafia are not fair either, and it's time to fight fire with fire and expose who and what they are, including their debunked, biased "science" and the damage they are doing to so many dogs.

How much better it is to kindly and clearly teach dogs right from wrong and see their tails wag and ears perk up as they enjoy being trained and going for structured walks, not simply turned loose in a fenced yard to amuse themselves alone before being stuck in their crate in the utility room, given that they can't be trusted to be unsupervised in the house. Better watch out: once crates are banned, that utility room may need extending and a new window put in, to meet the sunlight regulations. I am not like you, though. I will not watch the joy leave the eyes of my dogs, no matter what bans you seek to force through the legislative process.

Force-free extremists, why don't you turn your attention to real cruelty, to fox hunting and badger baiting, to grouse shooting and animal experimentation, to the very worst of factory farming, or would that displease your betters who are laughing at you all the way to the bank? What about bits in horses' mouths, spurs that dig into their sides? Your indignant squawking as I use 99 percent rewards and, horror of horrors, 1 percent corrections is unfair to my dogs. You want the world to stop revolving in order to accommodate and normalize how you train? Tough. I hope the U.S. stands up to your nonsense, as we have been unable to do in Europe. I desperately wish someone would teach you how to help your own dogs live a better life. I don't hold your dogs accountable for your ethos and propaganda. They may belong to bigots, but that is hardly their fault.

Owners with problem dogs, why not provide your dog with direction and be a fair, confident leader within your team of two, instead of avoiding his problems? You cannot hide from the world forever. The lies you have been fed, that your dog cannot be helped with his excitement or reactivity or whatever else, may simply be incorrect. Look for a good balanced trainer. A good play-based trainer. A good reward-based trainer. Just any good trainer that will give your dog boundaries and use appropriate corrections, whatever they may be.

Possibly your dog can't improve; this may totally be the case. But unlike your force-free trainer, and as a trainer myself, I aim to be flexible. I am more than willing to listen to what another trainer has to say to me regarding the training they have already done with a dog they have given up on or think they cannot help any further. If you have not tried a certain tool or training technique, never explored all the options or seen the tools in use which you have been told to demonize, you will never know what might be achieved with the dog that is too much for you.

Yes, an argument can be made that you don't need to actually lie on a bed of nails to know you won't sleep well on it, but that's not the case for everyone when it comes to trying unfamiliar tools and methods. Why are you taking it on yourself to side with people who have seduced you with the beautiful lie that corrections are not required, and who say that if a dog will not respond to cookies, well, it's the dog's fault, and better he is euthanized than suffer discomfort during training? Isn't that too easy a way out, to blame the dog and his owner? Ask yourself, why are you so keen to join their cult? Is the Kool-Aid that tasty? Why does everyone have to be forced to agree with you? Are you really so lonely that the online validation of strangers keeps you toeing the force-free line, even when in your heart of hearts you know you are letting dogs down?

Force-free enthusiasts, by now it must be obvious that I am not you. You may not like me, but what if the shoe was on the other foot? What if I was insisting that all dogs have e-collar training? No, not using humane, modern training techniques, but rather the methodology the various e-collar researchers deemed to be ethical when they conducted their studies. Would you be happy? Do you think training a dog over a short time period while using no positive reinforcement and instead lighting him up like a Christmas tree for the slightest disobedience is scientific and will provide a genuine comparison of training methodologies? Well, do you? This is the "science" you squawk about. I rather think you would not be so keen on that, would you?

I will never try to ram my training techniques and tools down the throat of force-free owners and trainers; I like dogs too much. I also like freedom of choice too much. People, no, not so much. But you are entitled to your views, and even though I personally believe that a lot of what you do to your dogs with your management, medication and deluded training is both unethical and deeply unkind, the choice has to be yours to make, from your own free will. If you do not want to help your dog live his best life and do not want to make an informed choice since your mind has already been made up, then I cannot stop you from wearing your blinkers.

Conclusion

You will open your mind and learn, or you will not. All that matters is the dog, and if he is genuinely living his best life, then good on you. If not, shame on you.

Your dog ended up with you, the force-free enthusiast, and that might or might not turn out to be quite tragic for him. I'm sure your intentions are pure. However, I also assume the vast majority of readers in the force-free community are outraged that I dare to challenge their cult and tear down their "science says" propaganda, showing it for the biased, illogical lie that it really is. Angry at me? Well, maybe *The Anarchist Cookbook* is still available online. Take care not to get added to a watch list, though, won't you?

Writing this book has taken six months of my life. There have been times I have looked up from my work at the clock and it is midnight, and my dogs are patiently sitting, giving me puppy-dog eyes, waiting for their last walk of the day around the woods. They don't get "at home" days imposed on them for my convenience, so on go my boots, jacket, gloves and hat and we enjoy a walk together under the moonlight. In the pouring rain. Or hail. Well, it is England, after all.

I hope that after reading this book, dog owners can see that possibilities exist for their dogs, ones which go beyond management and medication. That a pinch collar is not Lucifer manifest in physical form, nor is an e-collar Perun, the Slavic god of thunder and lightning.[14] No matter what a force-free trainer has told you, your dog may not be beyond redemption. Corrections, used with good timing, judiciously, and in an appropriate way for the dog in question, are guidance, not punishment, as you have no doubt been led to believe. Have you enjoyed this book? You can say "no," and if you say it nicely, I will not wilt into a puddle of bruised ego and decimated self-esteem. Your dog is the same.

Love your dog. Reward him often, with enthusiasm and joy. Play with him each and every day. Make his emotional wellbeing a priority. Bake him a liver cake for his birthday. Just love him, but understand that part of loving him is being a good leader, setting boundaries, and enforcing those boundaries via fair, consistent corrections. Actually, scratch the bit about the liver cake. I forgot my young dog's birthday yesterday, and to add insult to injury, I clipped her nails. I fear I will be excommunicated as a pet guardian. Jokes aside, don't struggle alone with your dog's problems, OK? Seek advice from a good trainer, no matter what she calls herself, provided she will love and respect your dog for the wonderful being he is. If just one reader approaches a good balanced trainer and her dog is saved a life of medication and misery, then the blood, sweat and tears involved in writing this book, plus the late-night walks in the pouring rain, will have all been worth it.

Good luck and happy training.

Glossary

active submission—Not an adult party game, but a dog lowering his ears and tail, submissive to his owner.

aversive—Something a dog does not like *at all*, and that, if well administered, tends to be sufficiently severe to stop a behavior very quickly. See Chapter One for more details.

back yard breeder—Think up your own desired expletive, ideally a very crude, descriptive one. Go for it. Make those sailors blush. BYBs are "breeders" who exploit animals for profit. The dogs they use for breeding are not tested for health and temperament, and have no working or show titles. They are kept in inhumane conditions and abandoned or shot when they are no longer of use. Repeat after me: "I do not buy from back yard breeders."

balanced dog training—A methodology that uses both rewards and corrections, more often than not utilizing all four operant conditioning quadrants. See Chapter One for more details.

barrier frustration—This occurs when a dog is upset at being restrained in some way. It may be when he sees another dog but cannot reach him, as behind a fence, or when he is on-lead on a walk. It generally manifests with the dog barking, whining or yodeling, loudly singing the song of his people. Depending on the barrier, he may also lunge or pull on the lead, jump up at a fence, or run up and down the fenceline. Barrier frustration may look like aggression, but it is usually due to excitement, either at the thought of a potential playmate or stemming from insecurity.

BOAS (brachycephalic obstructive airway syndrome)—The veterinary term for the problems brachycephalic dogs suffer from, including an elongated soft palate.

charging a clicker—A clicker is charged so it has power, a bit like a battery. A clicker (or marker word) helps train your dog, both motivating him and providing clarity, as he learns that when he hears a click, it means a reward is forthcoming. The click can then be paired with a desired behavior to teach the dog what we want from him and increase the incidence of this behavior occurring. A clicker is "charged" by clicking, then immediately rewarding the dog. Initially this is done for repetition after repetition, which could be 50 times or more, depending on the dog. To see if a clicker is indeed charged and the dog understands that a click means food is coming, wait until he does not have his attention on you, then click. If he turns around and immediately looks to you for a reward, you know he has paired the noise of the click with a reward, and the clicker is now charged. If he does not look to you, more repetitions are required.

choke chain—A collar made from metal links, which can be small or large (in which case the collar is often called a fur-saver). The collar tightens around the dog's neck if he pulls. With some models, the amount of constriction can be limited so it never becomes too tight.

clicker—A small mechanical device which makes a distinct "click" sound and is used to mark correct behaviors. See "charging a clicker."

competing reinforcer (distractions)—Simply something which acts as a reward for the dog and which he *may* prefer to the reward you are offering him, creating conflict. Does he choose the competing reinforcer, or does he choose you? A competing reinforcer can be anything from a scent to an opportunity to play with another dog or chasing a squirrel. Extreme force-free training, using only positive reinforcement breaks down when we take the dog out of the training room, where there are no distractions, and into the real world, where there are many. To be obedient in any situation, a dog requires consequences for ignoring his handler whenever a competing reinforcer comes along.

compulsion trainer—A trainer who uses little to no positive reinforcement or rewards in their training, relying only on the dog feeling compelled to obey, least he be punished by the trainer. See Chapter One for more details.

cookies—Food treats given to dogs.

correction—Giving a dog a correction is simply telling him that a behavior he has just performed or is currently engaging in, is incorrect. It can be conveyed as a bit of friendly advice or as a firm reprimand. A dressing-down in the manner of an angry drill sergeant tends to be a correction which acts as an aversive. See Chapter One for more details.

counter-conditioning—Used primarily with fearful or anxious dogs to change their emotional response to a certain stimulus from negative to neutral, or even positive. To effectively perform counter-conditioning, firstly an alternative behavior we want must be taught to the dog must be well established, then the dog's threshold needs to be ascertained. Counter-conditioning takes skill, and is not a matter of simply trying to stuff hot dogs down the dog's throat when he is around whatever upsets him. Confident, excited dogs may get more excited, and terrified dogs more scared if the trainer is flooding the dog in this way.

decoy—A man or woman in a bite suit, working with police dogs or sports dogs. A decoy is often also called a helper, depending on the dog sport/activity in question.

direct reward—A lure used to create the behavior we want, such as sitting. There are no additional steps, and nothing stands between the dog and the reward. We hover our hand (containing a food reward) above the dog's head and slightly behind, and the dog consequently follows it, sitting down. We immediately mark him for this correct behavior, and give him the reward from our hand, which is now conveniently just above his muzzle.

ditch the bowl—A methodology where the dog does not receive his meals in a bowl but instead is given his daily food allocation in the form of rewards while he is being trained. This can greatly increase a dog's motivation to be obedient and can be extremely effective, particularly for training in a controlled environment. If the dog does not comply with what the trainer is asking, he goes hungry until the next training session, which could be the next day, or even the day after that, and on and so forth.

e-collar—A collar which uses electricity to provide a beep, vibration, electric stimulation (similar to a TENS machine), or a combination of all of the above. The trainer controls the stimulus given to the dog with a remote control or, depending on the model, an app on her phone. It is mainly used as negative reinforcement, or to give positive corrections.

emotional dog training—A method generally used by the force-free community and balanced trainers which works with the emotions of both the dog *and* his owner to influence the direction of the training session. Understanding and accounting for emotions is extremely important on both ends of the lead, since emotions in turn drive behaviors. However, sometimes we must face our fears in order to live our best lives, and if used by a force free trainer this method of dog training has a tendency to concentrate on management techniques, with the dog never moving further forward in his training, permanently remaining in the sanctity of his home and garden.

engagement—Throw out your diamond rings, ladies—the most loving, true, lasting engagement comes from your dog! A dog has good engagement when he is concentrating absolutely, hanging on his handler's every breath and heartbeat. You know that look of laser focus your dog gets sometimes, often when he spots a squirrel? He is so still and focused that he even closes his mouth, not even panting any more. Well, that is the type of engagement we ideally want from our dogs when we are training them.

flooding—A training technique whereby a dog is exposed to a stimulus he is afraid of and is kept in that situation until he stops reacting. Flooding can result in suppression of behaviors, and also learned helplessness. It tends to increase fear, not decrease it. Flooding is extremely stressful, and is not a technique I would ever personally use for behavioral modification.

force-free/purely positive dog training—An ideology based on the lies that no force whatsoever is used while training dogs in this way, only rewards and positive reinforcement. But these dogs are wearing collars, are kept in houses, etc., so, you know…

free shaping—Often used to teach dogs behaviors indirectly. Lures are not involved, rather the dog performs a behavior on his own initiative and is then marked and rewarded. Free shaping can be carried out at a distance from the dog, and it is often used to create complex behaviors by linking together a series of individual behaviors.

green dog—A young dog, more often than not of a working breed, that is physically reaching maturity but lacks any formal training. He may have learned the very basics of obedience and, if we are lucky, have had exposure to different environmental stimuli. This is a dog that is ready to start being trained for a job.

gut villi—Finger-like projections on the wall of the dog's small intestine that absorb chyme, a liquid mixture of broken-down, partially digested food and stomach acid. Chyme leaves the stomach and enters the small intestine so its nutrients can be absorbed by the projections, which give the gut villi a large surface area. Villi die off relatively quickly when a dog is starved, altering the rate of food absorption. This is why food withholding, when carried on for too long in order to force compliance, can be physically damaging to your dog.

head collar—A device which is fastened onto a dog's head, a bit like the halter used on horses. It has a loop which goes around the back of the head and one which sits around the muzzle. In general, it is the nose loop which tightens most when the dog pulls. Head collars are not force-free, as they cause discomfort to dissuade the dog from pulling on the lead. When the head collar tightens, it puts pressure directly on the sensitive nerves and fascia which sit just under the surface of the thin skin of the face.

IGP (Internationale Gebrauchshund Pruefung, formerly IPO or Schutzhund)—A dog sport which comprises three phases: obedience, tracking and protection. Dogs work though levels IGP1, IGP2 and IGP3.

indirect reward—Using free shaping to create the behavior we want. The dog performs the desired behavior, and we immediately mark him for it, then give him a reward. The dog *offers* the behavior, as opposed to being lured into performing it, which causes the reward to follow.

jack-potting—Giving a dog a large quantity of food piece by piece as a reward, either for a particularly good performance to cement in the dog's head that this is what we want, or at random, as a surprise to raise dopamine expectation.

kibble—Small balls of dry, processed dog food, often used by ditch-the-bowl trainers as a reward.

Koehler method—Providing consequences for bad behavior so that the dog will choose to behave well instead of receiving that kind of unwanted attention.

leadership—Most dogs do not want to navigate the world alone, making all the decisions for themselves and their owner. It is not a comfortable or safe position for a dog to be in, resulting in his feeling anxious and uncertain, which often manifests as reactivity. Your dog needs you to be his leader. A good leader gives her dog confidence, as she keeps him safe. She is not a tyrant or a bully, but neither is she a pushover. Rather, she is fair and kind, working with her dog as part of a team, even delegating when necessary, such as trusting her dog in scent-work.

learned helplessness—This occurs when a dog has been pushed to the point that he feels he has no choices and gives up hope of ever escaping a painful or frightening situation. Even if the dog is not restrained, he will not try to run away or defend himself if a person hits or otherwise abuses him.

LIMA (least intrusive, minimally aversive)—Ethical trainers and owners alike use this principle whenever they can, both with dogs and other animals.

luring—Using a reward, usually food, to get the dog to follow the direction of your hand (or a target stick) with his nose and mouth, ready to be marked and given the reward.

marker word—Instead of using a clicker, many trainers use a marker word, which can be any word you like, as long as the *sound* is unique (and consistent). I use "yes!" in a high-pitched, excited tone, so it can be easily differentiated from my usual speech patterns. "Chip!" is also popular and lends itself well to being used in this way.

marking a behavior—Using a clicker or marker word to tell the dog that the behavior he has offered to the trainer is correct, and that he will consistently be rewarded for it.

martingale collar—A collar that is partially made of material or leather, and partially with a chain that tightens around the dog's neck. A martingale can be used in a way where it continues to tighten until pressure is released, or where it only tightens to a certain extent, then stops, meaning it can be adjusted so it will not over-tighten. If the "dead rings" are used, it will not tighten at all, making it a flexible tool.

off switch—The dog's ability to settle down in the home, quietly sleeping or amusing himself without constantly looking for human attention or running amok.

partial reward—A partial reward schedule is where the reward is not given each time the dog successfully performs a behavior, but is rather provided after a certain time period or after a certain number of repetitions.

pinch (prong) collar—Looks can be deceiving. Made of metal and with blunt prongs (often tipped with rubber) which contact a dog's neck, and usually with a chain that tightens the collar, at first glance pinch collars look like they should be donated to your local S&M dungeon and never allowed near a dog. However, when used correctly, the pinch collar is far from aversive and certainly not cruel. It's designed to give the dog a fair, easily understood correction, since when it tightens, pressure is distributed evenly around the dog's neck instead of putting all the pressure on one small area. This action allows fingertip control of the dog using clarity, *not* pain or extreme discomfort.

play-based dog training—Dogs are not fans of Scrabble, Snakes and Ladders, or Monopoly, tending to prefer scent work, playing tug, chasing a flirt pole, retrieving a ball, etc. Play-based training has the benefit of being a *lot* of fun for both you and your dog, enhancing engagement and also the bond you share. At the same time, rules and boundaries can effectively be laid down, as all games have rules. During play, when the dog's prey drive is properly utilized, he is in a much higher state of arousal and excitement than when being trained using only food rewards. This allows the trainer to make herself appear to be the best thing since wireless high-speed internet, meaning competing reinforcers are of *much* less value to the dog than they usually are, which can be a very important element in the training process. I play with all of my dogs daily without fail, including when I was on crutches, mostly lying on my sofa. If you get anything out of this book, I hope it is that you decide to give play-based training a shot if you have not yet done so.

positive dog training—A technique that works on the basis of LIMA. A great deal of positive reinforcement is used, and for many dogs this may be as much as 99 percent positive reinforcement. However, corrections and all the operant conditioning quadrants are also used.

Premack principle—This basically states that you can use something your dog really likes in order to reinforce something he doesn't like doing very much. For example, if I have a dog that is not a natural retriever, I can train him to retrieve objects for me provided I give him a big enough reward to make it worth his while; in this way, the disliked activity of retrieving becomes more common.

random reward—A reward that is given entirely at random, not according to any sort of schedule based on how much time has passed or the number of repetitions of a behavior.

reward—Simply something the dog likes. All dogs are different, and it's important to find out what your own dog finds rewarding, and exactly how rewarding. What we as humans think will be rewarding may not tally with what a dog considers rewarding. The most commonly used rewards in dog training are food, play, toys, and affection/praise. Some trainers will have high-, medium- and low-value food rewards, using high-value food when they want to really motivate the dog or when teaching a new skill, with lower-value rewards used for confirming behaviors the dog knows well. Other trainers only use one type of food reward, often as part of the dog's daily allocation of food.

service dog—A dog trained to mitigate the disabilities of a disabled person. This is the term used in the U.S. and many other countries, though in some parts of Europe a service dog is called an assistance dog.

slip lead—A collar and lead combined, usually made from cord or leather. It comprises a loop which is placed over the dog's head onto his neck and which tightens if he pulls. With some models, the amount of constriction can be limited so it never becomes too tight.

stooge dog—Used during behavioral modification to help train dogs that have reactivity issues around other dogs, such as dog aggression, barrier frustration, etc. A stooge dog allows the trainer to determine the reactive dog's thresholds, to perform counter-conditioning, and simply to get the reactive dog used to seeing, and being trained around, another dog. The stooge dog must be highly obedient and have the utmost confidence in the ability of his handler to keep him safe at all times, in all situations. He needs to have very neutral (or friendly) body language and the ability to not react or become upset when he is lunged at, barked at, or just generally threatened by another dog that may well be bigger than he is.

suppression—This has become a dirty word in dog training, and although in general it is not ideal, sometimes it is necessary. When training a dog, we want his emotions to be positive ones. In particular, we do not want to suppress the emotions of a scared or anxious dog; rather, we want to use techniques such as counter-conditioning in order to change those emotions from bad to good. However, some emotions we cannot change. A dog that has a strong dislike of other dogs and that is aggressive toward them, not out of fear or a bad experience but due to his genetics, is not going to become a lovebug, no matter how much counter-conditioning he receives. We need him to behave in a neutral manner around other dogs, and therefore we may have to suppress those bad behaviors which stem from dislike. Such a dog is never to be trusted around other dogs, as under the surface he is always in the same place emotionally, his dislike suppressed but unchanged.

Chapter Notes

In putting together the chapter notes, I tried to link primarily to sources that are freely accessible to everyone online and which do not require payment or a subscription. I have also linked to some visual sources, as so much of dog training is practical and is better observed than read about. Many eminent scientists, dog trainers and other experts have channels on YouTube where they speak about their field of interest; therefore, where possible, I have included links to such platforms.

Introduction

1. Cambridge Dictionary online, definition of "parent," accessed 27 June 2022, https://dictionary.cambridge.org/dictionary/english/parent.
2. Collins Dictionary online, definition of "pet parent," accessed 22 June 2022, https://www.collinsdictionary.com/dictionary/english/pet-parent.
3. "Randall" (Christopher Gordon), "The Crazy Nastyass Honey Badger," CZG123 YouTube channel, 18 January 2011, accessed 21 September 2022, https://www.youtube.com/watch?v=4r7wHMg5Yjg.
4. Robby Berman, "Dogs, cats, other pets: would they eat you if you died?" Big Think, 26 June 2017, accessed 4 July 2022, https://bigthink.com/sex-relationships/ever-wonder-if-your-beloved-dog-or-cat-would-eat-you-if-you-died/?utm_medium=Social&utm_source=Facebook&fbclid=IwAR3zge8IsV18oG7I243xAJLSHaTj-xt5PiUH_yD8_lx9UkHkFv_D7c7II90#Echobox=1656898152.
5. "DEFRA's research on dog e-collars is 'very seriously flawed and should not be relied on,'" National Gamekeepers Organisation Official Blog, 7 December 2020, accessed 1 September 2022, https://gamekeepersblog.com/2020/12/07/defras-research-on-dog-e-collars-is-very-seriously-flawed-and-should-not-be-relied-on/.
6. Ibid.
7. Ibid.
8. "Prong Collar, Animal Cruelty and the Police in Switzerland," Robert Cabral YouTube channel, 25 October 2022, accessed 15 August 2023, https://www.youtube.com/watch?v=Els2sRMlDHc&ab_channel=RobertCabral.
9. Kate Connolly, "German police dogs sent off duty after ban on 'pulling collars,'" *Guardian,* 6 January 2022, accessed 4 July 2022, https://www.theguardian.com/world/2022/jan/06/german-police-dogs-sent-off-duty-after-ban-on-pulling-collars.
10. "The Animal Welfare (Electronic Collars) (Wales) Regulations 2010," Legislation.gov.uk, 2010, accessed 4 July 2022, https://www.legislation.gov.uk/wsi/2010/943/contents/made.
11. Rasa Žiema, "Crate training. Why is it illegal in Sweden and Finland?" Dogo, 3 November 2020, accessed 4 July 2022, https://dogo.app/crate-training-why-is-it-illegal-in-sweden-and-finland/.
12. A. Zabarylo, "About the approval

of the Rules for keeping and handling animals in the city of Lviv," Ukraine, Lviv City Council, 17 March 2016, accessed on 4 July 2022, https://www8.city-adm.lviv.ua/inteam/uhvaly.nsf/a19074bb3a9b23eac2256ac40046fcb4/63aa8786c99c5aabc2257f8000546480?OpenDocument.

13. Patricia B. McConnell, "Dog Laws Around the World," The Other End of the Leash, 6 October 2011, accessed 4 July 2022, https://www.patriciamcconnell.com/theotherendoftheleash/dog-laws-around-the-world.

14. Earthling Ed (Ed Winters), "Have You Ever Thought About This? The Ethics of Pet Ownership," Earthling Ed YouTube channel, 25 May 2019, accessed 25 October 2022, https://www.youtube.com/watch?v=hrwG1BHdHIk.

15. Ibid.; Chris Hines, "The Ethics of Keeping Pets," Chris Hines YouTube channel, 10 July 2016, accessed 25 October 2022, https://www.youtube.com/watch?v=L42lFtzN5i4.

16. Kate Barrington, "What is a Landrace breed?" PetGuide.com, 17 July 2018, accessed 31 October 2022, https://www.petguide.com/blog/dog/what-is-a-landrace-breed/.

17. Winters, "Have You Ever Thought About This?"; Hines, "The Ethics of Keeping Pets."

18. "I own a German shepherd; will my dog be regulated next?" Breed-Specific Legislation: FAQ, DogsBite.org, accessed 31 October 2022, https://www.dogsbite.org/legislating-dangerous-dogs-bsl-faq.php#feartactics.

19. Ibid.

Chapter One

1. Cambridge Dictionary online, definition of "reward," accessed 18 July 2022, https://dictionary.cambridge.org/dictionary/english/reward.

2. Cambridge Dictionary online, definition of "relief," accessed 18 July 2022, https://dictionary.cambridge.org/dictionary/english/relief.

3. Natalie Bucklar, "Ditch the Bowl," Pawsitive Thinking, 19 May 2020, accessed 31 October 2022, https://www.pawsitivethinking.co.uk/dogs/ditch-the-bowl/.

4. Howard E. LeWine, M.D., "Oxytocin: the Love Hormone," Harvard Health Publishing, accessed 31 October 2022, https://www.health.harvard.edu/mind-and-mood/oxytocin-the-love-hormone.

5. Cambridge Dictionary online, definition of "aversive," accessed 18 July 2022, https://dictionary.cambridge.org/dictionary/english/aversive.

6. Cambridge Dictionary online, definition of "punishment," accessed 18 July 2022, https://dictionary.cambridge.org/dictionary/english/punishment.

7. "Skinner's Operant Conditioning: Rewards & Punishments," Sprouts YouTube channel, accessed 31 October 2022, https://www.youtube.com/watch?v=ne6o-uPJarA.

8. Margaret E. Gruen, Philip White & Brian Hare, "Do dog breeds differ in pain sensitivity? Veterinarians and the public believe they do," National Library of Medicine, 17 March 2020, accessed 31 August 2022, https://www.ncbi.nlm.nih.gov/pmc/articles/PMC7077843/.

9. Anton Lyadov, "On the USA–Russia border: How people live in the most remote region of Russia, The People YouTube channel, 23 August 2022, accessed 31 August 2022, https://www.youtube.com/watch?v=d99vm9gXWv4.

10. Katrina Gulliver, "Semiotics of Dogs," Aeon, 4 August 2022, accessed 31 October 2022, https://aeon.co/essays/dogs-are-symbolic-containers-of-human-hopes-desires-and-vices.

11. Patricia B. McConnell, "The Model-Rival Method," The Other End of the Leash, 26 January 2011, accessed 31 October 2022, https://www.patriciamcconnell.com/theotherendoftheleash/the-model-rival-method.

12. Saul McLeod, "Pavlov's Dogs Experiment and Pavlovian Conditioning Response," Simply Psychology, accessed 31 August 2022, https://www.simplypsychology.org/pavlov.html#:~:text=Pavlov%20showed%20that%20dogs%20could,an%20unconditioned%20(innate)%20response.

13. Pavlov's Dog Game, Nobel Prize website, accessed 31 August 2022, https://educationalgames.nobelprize.org/educational/medicine/pavlov/pavlov.html.

14. Michael Domjan, "Thorndike and the Law of Effect," Learning and Behavior: Key Concepts by M. Domjan YouTube channel, 15 July 2020, accessed 31

August 2022, https://www.youtube.com/watch?v=VTuwMCJjslc.

15. Saul McLeod, "Operant Conditioning: What It Is, How It Works, and Examples," Simply Psychology, accessed 31 August 2022, https://www.simplypsychology.org/operant-conditioning.html.

16. Saul McLeod, "Little Albert Experiment: Watson & Rayner," Simply Psychology, accessed 31 August 2022, https://www.simplypsychology.org/little-albert.html#:~:text=The%20Little%20Albert%20Experiment%20demonstrated,become%20afraid%20of%20a%20rat.

17. Michael Domjan, "The Premack Principle and Response Theories of Reinforcement," Learning and Behavior: Key Concepts by M. Domjan YouTube channel, 23 July 2020, accessed 31 August 2022, https://www.youtube.com/watch?v=6FxRj_DvkD4.

18. Karen Pryor, "History of Clicker Training I," Karen Pryor Clicker Training, 24 September 2013, accessed 31 August 2022, https://www.clickertraining.com/node/153#:~:text=What%20the%20dog%20trainers%20are,where%20I%20learned%20it%20myself.

19. "'Alpha' Wolves?" Eduweb YouTube Channel, 15 February 2008, accessed 31 August 2022, https://www.youtube.com/watch?v=tNtFgdwTsbU.

20. Anita Wolff, "Three Pioneer Observers of Animal Behaviour," Encyclopedia Britannica, accessed 30 September 2022, https://www.britannica.com/explore/savingearth/three-pioneer-observers-of-animal-behaviour.

21. *Ibid.*

Chapter Two

1. Saul McLeod, "Operant Conditioning: What It Is, How It Works, and Examples," Simply Psychology, accessed 31 August 2022, https://www.simplypsychology.org/operant-conditioning.html.

2. Saul McLeod, "Pavlov's Dogs Experiment and Pavlovian Conditioning Response," Simply Psychology, accessed 31 August 2022, https://www.simplypsychology.org/pavlov.html#:~:text=Pavlov%20showed%20that%20dogs%20could,an%20unconditioned%20(innate)%20response.

3. "The Seat Belt Analogy and Negative Reinforcement," Training Without Conflict, 21 September 2022, accessed 31 October 2022, https://www.youtube.com/watch?v=XzJdC2QZZXw.

4. Bart Bellon website, accessed 1 September 2022, https://www.nepopotraining.com/en/about-bart-bellon.

5. Training Without Conflict website, accessed 31 October 2022, https://www.trainingwithoutconflict.com/.

6. *Ibid.*

7. *Ibid.*

8. J.A. Anguera et al., "Video game training enhances cognitive control in older adults," National Library of Medicine, 10 April 2014, accessed 2 September 2022, https://www.ncbi.nlm.nih.gov/pmc/articles/PMC3983066/.

9. Jose Gomes, "Schedules of reinforcement in animal training," Train Me Please, 1 February 2018, accessed 2 September 2022, http://www.trainmeplease.com.au/blog/schedules-of-reinforcement-in-animal-training.

10. *Ibid.*

11. *Ibid.*

12. Robert Sapolsky, "Dopamine Jackpot! Sapolsky on the Science of Pleasure," FORA.tv, 2 March 2011, accessed 4 July 2022, https://www.youtube.com/watch?v=axrywDP9Ii0.

13. Robert C. Wilson et al., "The Eighty Five Percent Rule for optimal learning," Nature Communications, 5 November 2019, accessed 1 July 2022, https://www.nature.com/articles/s41467-019-12552-4.

14. Sapolsky, "Dopamine Jackpot!"

15. Hope Cristol, "What Is Dopamine?" WebMD, accessed 31 October 2022, https://www.webmd.com/mental-health/what-is-dopamine.

16. Gomes, "Schedules of reinforcement in animal training."

17. *Ibid.*

18. *Ibid.*

19. *Ibid.*

20. Adrienne Farricelli, "Using Jackpots of Treats in Dog Training," PetHelpful, 5 March 2014, accessed 31 October 2022, https://pethelpful.com/dogs/Using-Jackpots-of-Treats-in-Dog-Training.

21. McLeod, "Pavlov's Dogs Experiment..."

22. *Ibid.*

Chapter Three

1. *America's Top Dog*, "Border Collie Takes Down Police K9 to Win Competition," | A&E. 28 July 21, accessed 19 August 2022, https://www.youtube.com/watch?v=vsnaixx_TZg.
2. Kumar Mehta, "A Harvard psychologist says humans have 8 types of intelligence. Which ones do you score the highest in?" CNBC Make It, 10 March 2021, accessed 17 August 2022, https://www.cnbc.com/2021/03/10/harvard-psychologist-types-of-intelligence-where-do-you-score-highest-in.html.
3. Manpreet Singh, "What Are the 12 Types of Intelligence?" Number Dyslexia, 4 March 2022, accessed 17 August 2022, https://numberdyslexia.com/12-types-of-intelligence/.
4. "Caucasian Shepherd Dog," American Kennel Club, accessed 18 August 2022, https://www.akc.org/dog-breeds/caucasian-shepherd-dog/.
5. "Border Collie," American Kennel Club, accessed 18 August 2022, https://www.akc.org/dog-breeds/border-collie/.
6. S.A. Saganuwan, "Modified formulas for calculation of encephalization quotient in dogs," National Library of Medicine, 3 June 2021, accessed 17 August 2022, https://www.ncbi.nlm.nih.gov/pmc/articles/PMC8176606/.
7. Ibid.
8. Ibid.
9. "Belgian Malinois," American Kennel Club, accessed 18 August 2022, https://www.akc.org/dog-breeds/belgian-malinois/.
10. "Border Collie."
11. "German Shepherd Dog," American Kennel Club, accessed 18 August 2022, https://www.akc.org/dog-breeds/german-shepherd-dog/.
12. "Rottweiler," American Kennel Club, accessed 18 August 2022, https://www.akc.org/dog-breeds/rottweiler/.
13. "Border Collie."
14. "Belgian Malinois."
15. Kate Connolly, "German police dogs sent off duty after ban on 'pulling collars,'" *Guardian*, 6 January 2022, accessed 4 July 2022, https://www.theguardian.com/world/2022/jan/06/german-police-dogs-sent-off-duty-after-ban-on-pulling-collars.
16. Kevin Maimann, "Time to Cancel Police Dogs, Experts Say," Vice.com, 6 July 2021, accessed 18 August 2022, https://www.vice.com/en/article/z3xqzy/time-to-cancel-police-dogs-experts-say.
17. "An Offer to ALL Force Free Dog Trainers ($55,000)," Jamie Penrith Dog Training, 12 September 2021, accessed 18 August 2022, https://www.youtube.com/watch?v=TeMeeaEqzXY.
18. Author's veterinarian school notes.
19. "Barbara Woodhouse," Wikipedia, accessed 15 September 2023, https://en.wikipedia.org/wiki/Barbara_Woodhouse.
20. Libby Brooks, "Kennel owner dies after attack by rescue dog near Dundee," *Guardian*, 24 December 2021, accessed 18 July 2022, https://www.theguardian.com/uk-news/2021/dec/24/kennel-owner-dies-after-attack-by-rescue-dog-near-dundee.
21. "2017 Dog Bite Fatality: Rescue Pit Bull Attacks, Kills Elderly Woman in Virginia Beach Hours After Being Adopted," DogsBite.org, 1 June 2017, accessed 18 July 2022, https://blog.dogsbite.org/2017/06/dog-bite-fatality-adopted-out-pit-bull-kills-virginia-beach.html.
22. "Pet Health," Parsemus Foundation, accessed 28 July 2022, https://www.parsemus.org/pethealth.
23. Gretel Torres de la Riva, et al., "Neutering Dogs: Effects on Joint Disorders and Cancers in Golden Retrievers," PLOS ONE, 13 February 2013, accessed 18 August 2022, https://journals.plos.org/plosone/article?id=10.1371/journal.pone.0055937.
24. Dr. Tom Mitchell, "To Castrate or Not to Castrate!" 10 December 2020, accessed 7 August 2022, https://www.facebook.com/behavet/posts/pfbid02emyUEFEyTDRz4zkpJUx6yYpuXZ96J1rRWrkKkdcr6dYkCH5SD7FkQFfRhgPuw2qql.
25. Benjamin L. Hart et al., "Assisting Decision-Making on Age of Neutering for 35 Breeds of Dogs: Associated Joint Disorders, Cancers, and Urinary Incontinence," Frontiers in Veterinary Science, 7 July 2020, accessed 19 August 2022, https://www.frontiersin.org/articles/10.3389/fvets.2020.00388/full.
26. Marcelina Kriese et al., "Reasons for and Behavioral Consequences of Male Dog Castration—A Questionnaire Study in Poland," MDPI, 23 July 2022, accessed 28 July 2022, https://www.mdpi.com/2076-2615/12/15/1883.
27. "Dr. Robert Sapolsky: Science of Stress, Testosterone & Free Will,"

Huberman Lab Podcast #35, 30 August 2021, accessed 28 July 2022, https://www.youtube.com/watch?v=DtmwtjOoSYU.

28. "An Offer to ALL Force Free Dog Trainers ($55,000)"; "Barbara Woodhouse"; Brooks, "Kennel owner dies after attack by rescue dog near Dundee"; "2017 Dog Bite Fatality."

29. Kriese et al., "Reasons for and Behavioral Consequences of Male Dog Castration."

30. Ibid.

31. "'I'm not a cat' says lawyer during Zoom filter mishap," Global News, 9 February 2021, accessed 30 July 2022, https://www.youtube.com/watch?v=w6TpsWhQMTQ.

32. "Why Did Nikola Tesla Say That the Numbers 369 Are the Key to the Universe?" Future Unity, 28 October 2022, accessed 2 November 2022, https://www.youtube.com/watch?v=eYFw4ICJNK0.

Chapter Four

1. John Whittaker, "Ban on Dog Shock Collar Sales Proposed in State," *Post-Journal*, 20 September 2022, accessed 31 October 2022, https://www.post-journal.com/news/local-news/2022/09/ban-on-dog-shock-collar-sales-proposed-in-state/#:~:text=Shock%20collars%20for%20dogs%20may,the%20sale%20of%20the%20devices.

2. "Our Mission," Shock Free San Francisco, accessed 31 October 2022, https://www.sf-shockfree.org/mission.

3. "Official Supporters," Shock Free San Francisco, accessed 31 October 2022, https://www.sf-shockfree.org/supporters.

4. Azzura Lalani, "Toronto dog collar ban barks up the wrong tree, dog lovers say," *Toronto Star*, 12 March 2017, accessed 31 October 2022, https://www.thestar.com/news/gta/2017/03/12/toronto-dog-collar-ban-barks-up-the-wrong-tree-dog-lovers-say.html.

5. Jennifer Pagliaro, "Toronto city council overturns ban on pronged dog collars, choke chains," *Toronto Star*, 29 March 2017, accessed 31 October 2022, https://www.thestar.com/news/city_hall/2017/03/29/toronto-city-council-overturns-ban-on-pronged-dog-collars-choke-chains.html#:~:text=Just%20weeks%20after%20 it%20came,the%20public%20on%20their%20use.

6. *Blackfish* website, accessed 2 November 2022, https://www.blackfishmovie.com/.

7. Alex Bellotti, "'Psychotic' life of SeaWorld orca Tilikum—'forced drugs,' bullied and deadly games," *The Mirror*, 20 May 2021, accessed 28 July 2022, https://www.mirror.co.uk/news/us-news/psychotic-life-seaworld-orca-tilikum-24149594.

8. "*Blackfish* in about 15 minutes (Short Version)," Janardhan Pokala YouTube channel, accessed 28 July 2022, https: https://www.youtube.com/watch?v=MEUmG4hRV4o.

9. *Blackfish* website.

10. Ibid.

11. Patricia B. McConnell, "The Model-Rival Method," The Other End of the Leash, 26 January 2011, accessed 31 October 2022, https://www.patriciamcconnell.com/theotherendoftheleash/the-model-rival-method.

12. Bellotti, "'Psychotic' life of SeaWorld orca Tilikum."

13. *Blackfish* website.

14. Harriet Meyers, "OCD in Dogs: Can It Happen?" American Kennel Club, 13 October 2020, accessed 29 July 2022, https://www.akc.org/expert-advice/health/obsessive-compulsive-disorder-dog-behavior/#:~:text=Obsessive%20Compulsive%20Disorder%20(OCD)%20in,the%20dog's%20ability%20to%20function.

15. "Side effects of gabapentin," NHS, accessed 2 November 2022, https://www.nhs.uk/medicines/gabapentin/side-effects-of-gabapentin/.

16. Rania Gollakner, "Gabapentin," VCA Animal Hospitals, accessed 2 November 2022, https://vcahospitals.com/know-your-pet/gabapentin#:~:text=The%20most%20common%20side%20effects,with%20liver%20or%20kidney%20disease.

17. "About the approval of the Rules for keeping and handling animals in the city of Lviv," Lviv City Council, Ukraine, 17 March 2016, accessed 4 July 2022, https://www8.city-adm.lviv.ua/inteam/uhvaly.nsf/a19074bb3a9b23eac2256ac40046fcb4/63aa8786c99c5aabc2257f8000546480?OpenDocument.

18. Malvika Padin, "Will pugs and French bulldogs be banned in UK?

Breeds face urgent health crackdown," *The Mirror*, 14 April 2022, accessed 29 July 2022, https://www.mirror.co.uk/news/uk-news/pugs-french-bulldogs-banned-uk-26711608.

19. "Irish Pug Dog Club Statement—May 2020," Irish Pug Dog Club, accessed 29 July 2022, http://www.irishpugdogclub.com/statement-on-dutch-pug-ban.html.

20. Twitter feed of Spaniel Aid UK, 1 July 2022.

21. Jennifer Viegas, "Golden spaniels like to play rough, rough," ABC News (Australian Broadcasting Corporation), 14 December 2006, accessed 28 July 2022, https://www.abc.net.au/science/news/stories/2006/1811539.htm.

22. Twitter feed of Spaniel Aid UK.

23. *Ibid*.

24. Carlo Siracusa et al., "Dog- and owner-related risk factors for consideration of euthanasia or rehoming before a referral behavioral consultation and for euthanizing or rehoming the dog after the consultation" (*Journal of Veterinary Behaviour* 22, Nov.–Dec. 2017), ScienceDirect, accessed 28 July 2022, https://www.sciencedirect.com/science/article/abs/pii/S1558787817300436.

25. Nicole Cosgrove, "11 UK Animal Shelter Statistics & Facts to Know in 2022: Benefits, Facts & More," PetKeen, accessed 28 July 2022, https://petkeen.com/animal-shelter-statistics-uk/#:~:text=How%20many%20kill%20shelters%20are,to%20kill%20animals%20for%20profit.

Chapter Five

1. Bart Bellon website, accessed 1 September 2022, https://www.bartbellon.com/.

2. "Ban on Dog Shock Collar Sales Proposed in State," *Post-Journal*, accessed 31 October 2022, https://www.post-journal.com/news/local-news/2022/09/ban-on-dog-shock-collar-sales-proposed-in-state/#:~:text=Shock%20collars%20for%20dogs%20may,the%20sale%20of%20the%20devices; "Our Mission," Shock Free San Francisco, accessed 31 October 2022, https://www.sf-shockfree.org/mission.

3. Hayley Dixon, "Electric dog collar ban will lead to 'animal welfare disaster,' warn farmers," *Telegraph*, 3 September 2022, https://www.telegraph.co.uk/news/2022/09/03/electric-dog-collar-ban-will-lead-animal-welfare-disaster-warns/?fbclid=IwAR3I48plKVAYFEDoIsTOIifpvfleNbuK_EsgAEUiasygTxj0b7MR5hoDjuE.

4. "Fenton the dog chasing deer on news," Nigel Reed YouTube channel, 30 November 2011, accessed 1 September 2022, https://www.youtube.com/watch?v=HgNUzVx1PgU.

5. "Fenton's official book—*Find Fenton!*" JAGGL113 YouTube channel, 20 September 2012, accessed 1 August 2022, https://www.youtube.com/watch?v=sjcwIrUpnlo.

6. Stephen Moyes, "Fenton! Deer-chasing dog Fenton steps out on a tight leash—as he is tracked down by *The Sun*," *The Sun*, 28 November 2011, accessed 1 August 2022, https://www.thesun.co.uk/news/938257/fenton/.

7. Dixon, "Electric dog collar ban will lead to 'animal welfare disaster,' warn farmers."

8. "DEFRA's research on dog e-collars is 'very seriously flawed and should not be relied on.'" National Gamekeepers Organisation Official Blog, 7 December 2020. Accessed on 1 September 2022 at https://gamekeepersblog.com/2020/12/07/defras-research-on-dog-e-collars-is-very-seriously-flawed-and-should-not-be-relied-on/.

9. "The Truth about E-collars in Dog Training: Ivan Balabanov debunks the myths surrounding e-collars," Ivan Balabanov YouTube channel, 5 October 2020, accessed 1 September 2022, https://www.youtube.com/watch?v=F4hiy7IVkeY.

10. High Court Case regarding banning e-collars in the UK, Royal Courts of Justice, 24 October 2019, accessed 1 September 2022, http://www.landmarkchambers.co.uk/wp-content/uploads/2019/10/Electronic-Collar-Manufacturers-v-SS-for-Environment-24-Oct-2019.pdf.

11. "DEFRA's research on dog e-collars is "very seriously flawed and should not be relied on," National Gamekeepers Organisation Official Blog.

12. High Court Case regarding banning e-collars in the UK.

13. Dixon, "Electric dog collar ban will lead to 'animal welfare disaster,' warn farmers."

Chapter Six

1. Arnja R. Dale, Christopher A. Podlesnik, and Douglas Elliffe, "Evaluation of an aversion-based program designed to reduce predation of native birds by dogs: An analysis of training records for 1156 dogs," *Applied Animal Behaviour Science* 191 (June 2017), accessed 5 October 2022, https://www.sciencedirect.com/science/article/abs/pii/S0168159117300746.

2. Yasemin Salgirli, "Comparison of Stress and Learning Effects of Three Different Training Methods: Electronic Training Collar, Pinch Collar and Quitting Signal," Ph.D. thesis, University of Veterinary Medicine Hannover, 2008, accessed 5 October 2022, https://leerburg.com/pdf/comparingecollarprongandquittingsignal.pdf.

3. *Ibid.*

4. Jonathan J. Cooper, Daniel S. Mills, and Lucy China, "Response: Commentary: Remote Electronic Training Aids; Efficacy at Deterring Predatory Behavior in Dogs and Implications for Training and Policy," *Frontiers in Veterinary Science*, 26 April 2021, accessed 5 October 2022, https://www.frontiersin.org/articles/10.3389/fvets.2021.675005/full.

5. *Ibid.*; Jonathan J. Cooper, Nina Cracknell, et al., "The Welfare Consequences and Efficacy of Training Pet Dogs with Remote Electronic Training Collars in Comparison to Reward Based Training. DEFRA study AW1402a," PLOS One, 3 September 2014, accessed 5 October 2022, https://journals.plos.org/plosone/article?id=10.1371/journal.pone.0102722; Lucy China, Daniel S. Mills, and Jonathan J. Cooper, "Efficacy of Dog Training With and Without Remote Electronic Collars vs. a Focus on Positive Reinforcement," *Frontiers in Veterinary Science*, 22 July 2020, accessed 5 October 2022, https://www.frontiersin.org/articles/10.3389/fvets.2020.00508/full.

6. Arnja Dale, Shivaun Statham, et al., "The acquisition and maintenance of dogs' aversion responses to kiwi (*Apteryx* spp.) training stimuli across time and locations," *Applied Animal Behaviour Science*, 8 April 2013, accessed 2 October 2023, https://researchbank.ac.nz/bitstream/handle/10652/2630/Dale%20et%20al%202013.pdf?sequence=1&isAllowed=y.

7. "Amazing facts about the kiwi bird," Legendary Nature YouTube channel, 15 April 2022, accessed 10 October 2022, https://www.youtube.com/watch?v=Vgf5JOsol34.

8. Cooper, Mills, and China, "Response: Commentary: Remote Electronic Training Aids"; Cooper, Cracknell, et al., "The Welfare Consequences and Efficacy of Training Pet Dogs with Remote Electronic Training Collars…"

9. Cooper, Cracknell, et al., "The Welfare Consequences and Efficacy of Training Pet Dogs with Remote Electronic Training Collars…"; David Bailey, "A review of AW1402A proposal, raw data and methodology into the use of electronic collars on domestic dogs in the U.K. [DEFRA study AW1402a]," ARDO, accessed 5 October 2022, https://joinardo.com/wp-content/uploads/2020/11/D-201111-Lincoln-Review-David-Bailey.pdf; Research Project Final Report" [Jonathan Cooper, Nina Cracknell, Jessica Hardiman, and Daniel Mills, "Studies to assess the effect of pet training aids, specifically remote static pulse systems, on the welfare of domestic dogs; field study of dogs in training—AW1402a", DEFRA, accessed 5 October 2022, https://randd.defra.gov.uk/ProjectDetails?ProjectID=17568 (click on link under "Project Documents").

10. Cooper, Cracknell, et al., "The Welfare Consequences and Efficacy of Training Pet Dogs with Remote Electronic Training Collars…"; China, Mills, and Cooper, "Efficacy of Dog Training With and Without Remote Electronic Collars…"

11. "A Real Case of Spontaneous Human Combustion," The Infogaphics Show, 23 December 2019, accessed 10 October 2022, https://www.youtube.com/watch?v=8DJ_2qWrqs4.

12. Patrick J. Walsh, "Behavioural approaches and conservation messages with New Zealand's threatened kiwi," *Global Ecology and Conservation* 28 (August 2021), DirectScience, accessed 10 October 2022, https://www.sciencedirect.com/science/article/pii/S2351989421002444#bbib4.

13. Ian Banatoski et al., "The role of public perceptions in reducing risks to coastal wildlife from interactions with dogs," interactive qualifying project report, Worcester Polytechnic Institute, 2 March 2017, Govt.NZ, accessed 10 October 2022, https://www.doc.govt.nz/

globalassets/documents/conservation/marine-and-coastal/dogs-and-coastal-wildlife-wpi-project-report.pdf.

14. "An Offer to ALL Force Free Dog Trainers ($55,000)," Jamie Penrith Dog Training, 12 September 2021, accessed 18 August 2022, https://www.youtube.com/watch?v=TeMeeaEqzXY.

15. "Why Do We Favor Our Existing Beliefs?" The Decision Lab, accessed 5 October 2022, https://thedecisionlab.com/biases/confirmation-bias?&adw=true&utm_campaign=21+Biases+-+Confirmation+Bias&utm_medium=ppc&utm_source=adwords&utm_term=confirmation%20bias%20examples&hsa_mt=b&hsa_net=adwords&hsa_ad=500704987803&hsa_src=g&hsa_cam=12416110011&hsa_kw=confirmation%20bias%20examples&hsa_grp=121194112474&hsa_tgt=kwd-298280949350&hsa_ver=3&hsa_acc=8441935193&gclid=Cj0KCQjw1vSZBhDuARIsAKZlijRvHOxrfjKAWtp8QQpuC3ZhTlo3HpfxidM_bcyJI6Bd__d_sL6KOgIaAl7nEALw_wcB.

16. Cooper, Cracknell, et al., "The Welfare Consequences and Efficacy of Training Pet Dogs with Remote Electronic Training Collars..."; "Research Project Final Report."

17. "Introduction to research," SOAS (School of Oriental and African Studies) University of London, accessed 2 October 2023, https://www.soas.ac.uk/courseunits/introduction-research.

18. Matthijs B.H. Schilder and Joanne A. M. van der Borg, "Training dogs with help of the shock collar: short and long term behavioural effects," *Applied Animal Behaviour Science* 85 (2004), accessed 5 October 2022, https://positively.com/files/Applied_Animal_Behaviour_Science-85-2004-319%E2%80%93334-Training_dogs_with_shock_collar.pdf.

19. Katherine Brown, "What's the future of peer review?" The Company of Biologists, 3 January 2013, accessed 5 October 2022, https://thenode.biologists.com/whats-the-future-of-peer-review/discussion/?gclid=Cj0KCQjw1vSZBhDuARIsAKZlijRxAVQ7m7XItwSo9Qyj2QoWFsDt82xwaoxBvdlJv62D63qN9Ep28RwaAvqYEALw_wcB.

20. Cooper, Mills, and China, "Response: Commentary: Remote Electronic Training Aids"; China, Mills, and Cooper, "Efficacy of Dog Training With and Without Remote Electronic Collars..."; Rebecca J. Sargisson and Ian G. McLean, "Commentary: Efficacy of Dog Training With and Without Remote Electronic Collars vs. a Focus on Positive Reinforcement," *Frontiers in Veterinary Science*, 29 April 2021, accessed 5 October 2022, https://www.frontiersin.org/articles/10.3389/fvets.2021.629746/full; "University of Lincoln Research," ARDO, accessed 5 October 2022, https://joinardo.com/lincoln-research/.

21. Cooper, Mills, and China, "Response: Commentary: Remote Electronic Training Aids."

22. Bailey, "A review of AW1402A proposal, ..."

23. Cooper, Mills, and China, "Response: Commentary: Remote Electronic Training Aids"; Cooper, Cracknell, et al., "The Welfare Consequences and Efficacy of Training Pet Dogs with Remote Electronic Training Collars..."; China, Mills, and Cooper, "Efficacy of Dog Training With and Without Remote Electronic Collars..."; "Research Project Final Report."

24. Dale et al., "Evaluation of an aversion-based program designed to reduce predation of native birds by dogs."

25. Bailey, "A review of AW1402A proposal, ..."

26. Cooper, Cracknell, et al., "The Welfare Consequences and Efficacy of Training Pet Dogs with Remote Electronic Training Collars..."; China, Mills, and Cooper, "Efficacy of Dog Training With and Without Remote Electronic Collars..."

27. China, Mills, and Cooper, "Efficacy of Dog Training With and Without Remote Electronic Collars..."

28. Sargisson and McLean, "Commentary: Efficacy of Dog Training With and Without Remote Electronic Collars..."

29. Bailey, "A review of AW1402A proposal, ..."

30. Sargisson and McLean, "Commentary: Efficacy of Dog Training With and Without Remote Electronic Collars..."

31. Cooper, Mills, and China, "Response: Commentary: Remote Electronic Training Aids."

32. China, Mills, and Cooper, "Efficacy of Dog Training With and Without Remote Electronic Collars..."

33. Cooper, Mills, and China,

"Response: Commentary: Remote Electronic Training Aids."

34. "Animal welfare: banning the use of electronic training collars for cats and dogs," DEFRA, 12 March 2018, Gov.UK, accessed 5 October 2022, https://www.gov.uk/government/consultations/animal-welfare-banning-the-use-of-electronic-training-collars-for-cats-and-dogs.

35. Dale et al., "Evaluation of an aversion-based program designed to reduce predation of native birds by dogs"; Bailey, "A review of AW1402A proposal, ..."; Sargisson and McLean, "Commentary: Efficacy of Dog Training With and Without Remote Electronic Collars..."; "University of Lincoln Research."

36. Bailey, "A review of AW1402A proposal, ..."

37. "Research Project Final Report."

38. Ibid.

39. Ian Webster, "The British pound has lost 39% its value since 2010," CPI Inflation Calculator, accessed 5 October 2022, https://www.in2013dollars.com/uk/inflation/2010

40. Xe Currency Converter, accessed 5 October 2022, https://www.xe.com/currencyconverter/.

41. Webster, "The British pound has lost 39% its value since 2010."

42. Xe Currency Converter.

43. "UK Government supports COVID-19 detection dogs trial," London School of Hygiene and Tropical Medicine, 15 May 2020, accessed 5 October 2022, https://www.lshtm.ac.uk/newsevents/news/2020/uk-government-supports-covid-19-detection-dogs-trial

44. Xe Currency Converter.

45. Claire Guest et al., "Using trained dogs and organic semi-conducting sensors to identify asymptomatic and mild SARS-CoV-2 infections: an observational study," *Journal of Travel Medicine* 29:3 (April 2022), accessed 5 October 2022, https://academic.oup.com/jtm/article/29/3/taac043/6553800?login=false.

46. Xe Currency Converter.

47. Natalie Crookham, "Fox hunting 'has no place' as Britons slam 'barbaric' practice," *The Express*, 14 July 2022, accessed 5 October 2022, https://www.express.co.uk/news/uk/1640520/fox-hunting-ban-reversed-jeremy-hunt-poll-results-spt

48. "University of Lincoln Research."

49. Rasa Žiema, "Crate training. Why is it illegal in Sweden and Finland?" Dogo, 3 November 2020, accessed 4 July 2022, https://dogo.app/crate-training-why-is-it-illegal-in-sweden-and-finland/.

50. Crookham, "Fox hunting 'has no place'..."

51. Bailey, "A review of AW1402A proposal, ..."

52. "Schilder and van der Borg, "Training dogs with help of the shock collar."

53. Ibid.

54. Ibid.

55. Ibid.

56. Ibid.

57. Ibid.

58. Ibid.

59. "The Use of Electric Pulse Training Aids (EPTAs) in Companion Animals," Companion Animal Welfare Council, June 2012, Epints.com, accessed 5 October 2022, https://eprints.lincoln.ac.uk/id/eprint/14640/1/CAWC%20ecollar%20report.pdf.

60. Cooper, Cracknell, et al., "The Welfare Consequences and Efficacy of Training Pet Dogs with Remote Electronic Training Collars..."; "Research Project Final Report."

61. Cooper, Cracknell, et al., "The Welfare Consequences and Efficacy of Training Pet Dogs with Remote Electronic Training Collars..."

62. China, Mills, and Cooper, "Efficacy of Dog Training With and Without Remote Electronic Collars..."

63. "University of Lincoln Research."

64. Bailey, "A review of AW1402A proposal, ..."

65. "Research Project Final Report."

66. "University of Lincoln Research."

67. China, Mills, and Cooper, "Efficacy of Dog Training With and Without Remote Electronic Collars..."

68. Bailey, "A review of AW1402A proposal, ..."; "University of Lincoln Research."

69. Bailey, "A review of AW1402A proposal, ..."

70. Ibid.

71. Ibid.; Sargisson and McLean, "Commentary: Efficacy of Dog Training With and Without Remote Electronic Collars..."; "University of Lincoln Research."

72. "Animal welfare: banning the use of electronic training collars for cats and dogs."

73. Cooper, Mills, and China, "Response: Commentary: Remote Electronic Training Aids"; Bailey, "A review of AW1402A proposal, ..."; Sargisson and McLean, "Commentary: Efficacy of Dog Training With and Without Remote Electronic Collars..."; "University of Lincoln Research."

74. Cooper, Mills, and China, "Response: Commentary: Remote Electronic Training Aids."

75. Ibid.

76. Ibid.

77. "University of Lincoln Research."

78. Ibid.

79. Cooper, Cracknell, et al., "The Welfare Consequences and Efficacy of Training Pet Dogs with Remote Electronic Training Collars..."; Bailey, "A review of AW1402A proposal, ..."; "Research Project Final Report."

80. Ibid.

81. Ibid.

82. Bailey, "A review of AW1402A proposal, ..."

83. Ibid.

84. Daniel F. Tortora, "Safety Training: The Elimination of Avoidance-Motivated Aggression in Dogs," *Journal of Experimental Psychology* 12:2 (1983), accessed 5 October 2022, https://cpb-us-w2.wpmucdn.com/about.illinoisstate.edu/dist/6/45/files/2019/10/tortora-1983-safety-signal-training-elimination-of-avoidance-motivated-aggression-in-dogs.pdf.

85. Ibid.

86. Ibid.

87. Firdaus S. Dhabhar, "The Short-Term Stress Response—Mother Nature's Mechanism for Enhancing Protection and Performance Under Conditions of Threat, Challenge, and Opportunity," *Frontiers in Neuroendocrinology* 49 (April 2018), National Library of Medicine, accessed 5 October 2022, https://www.ncbi.nlm.nih.gov/pmc/articles/PMC5964013/.

88. Ibid.

89. Ibid.

90. Ibid.

91. "*Clash of the Titans* (2010)— Release the Kraken! Scene (8/10)," Movieclips, 22 December 2016, accessed 5 October 2022, https://www.youtube.com/watch?v=38AYeNGjqg0.

92. "U.S. Prohibition (1920–33)," Simple History, 26 August 2017, accessed 5 October 2022, https://www.youtube.com/watch?v=_uU9GMJ8a5w.

93. Elise Kjørstad, "Wolf packs don't actually have alpha males and alpha females, the idea is based on a misunderstanding." Sciencenorway.no, 26 April 2021, accessed 18 July 2022, https://sciencenorway.no/ulv/wolf-packs-dont-actually-have-alpha-males-and-alpha-females-the-idea-is-based-on-a-misunderstanding/1850514.

94. L. David Mech, "'Alpha' Wolf?" eduweb, 15 February 2008, accessed 10 October 2022, https://www.youtube.com/watch?v=tNtFgdwTsbU; Hikari Koyasu et al., "The Gaze Communications Between Dogs/Cats and Humans: Recent Research Review and Future Directions," *Frontiers in Psychology* 11 (2020), accessed 28 July 2022, https://www.frontiersin.org/articles/10.3389/fpsyg.2020.613512/full#:~:text=Dogs%20detect%20a%20human's%20attentional,and%20change%20their%20behavior%20accordingly.

95. Mech, "'Alpha' Wolf?"

96. Koyasu et al., "The Gaze Communications Between Dogs/Cats and Humans."

Chapter Seven

1. Deb Jones, "Errorless Learning: How Could That be a Bad Thing?" K9 in Focus, 24 April 2018, accessed 23 July 2022, https://k9infocus.com/errorless-learning-how-could-that-be-a-bad-thing/.

2. "Pekingese," American Kennel Club, accessed 6 September 2022, https://www.akc.org/dog-breeds/pekingese/.

3. "Saluki," American Kennel Club, accessed 6 September 2022, https://www.akc.org/dog-breeds/saluki/.

4. "Pekingese," American Kennel Club.

5. "The Pekingese of the Chinese royal court," Christian Lilly YouTube channel, 10 March 2015, accessed 6 September 2022, https://www.youtube.com/watch?v=FIjFRKnpdyk.

6. "Saluki," American Kennel Club.

7. "Saluki—Dog Breed Information About World's Oldest Dog Breed," petmoo YouTube channel, 18 March 2020, accessed 6 September 2022, https://youtube.com/watch?v=dmZTgSLdO6Y.

8. "Saluki History: How the 5,000-Year-Old Hound Met the New

World," *American Kennel Club*, 7 July 2021, accessed 6 September 2022, https://www.akc.org/expert-advice/dog-breeds/saluki-history-5000-year-old-hound-met-new-world/.

9. *"All Creatures Great and Small*, Season 2: 'Tricki Woo Chooses Who?'" Masterpiece PBS YouTube channel, 24 January 22, accessed 6 September 2022, https://www.youtube.com/watch?v=RhDfGq-GyTo.

10. "Belgian Malinois," American Kennel Club, accessed 18 August 2022, https://www.akc.org/dog-breeds/belgian-malinois/.

11. "Beagle," American Kennel Club, accessed 6 September 2022, https://www.akc.org/dog-breeds/beagle/.

12. "Dog Drive Types—An Outdated Theory?" Chasing Dog Tales, 12 October 2016, accessed 6 September 2022, https://chasingdogtales.com/dog-drive-types-an-outdated-theory/.

13. "Dorothy's Most Savage Moments—*Golden Girls*," TV Land YouTube channel, accessed on 6 September 2022 at: https://www.youtube.com/watch?v=Ms1uYc28pD4.

14. "Dog Drive Types—An Outdated Theory?"

15. Caroline Haldeman, "What drives your dog?" Sirius K9 Academy, accessed 6 September 2022, http://www.siriusk9training.com/Tips-What-Drives-Your-Dog.htm.

16. "FAQ: Why are beagles the breed of choice for laboratory experiments?" Beagle Freedom Project, accessed 6 September 2022, https://bfp.org/faq/; Jeremy Beckham, "Why Are Beagles Used for Lab Experiments? A Look Back at the Nuclear History of This Dog Breed," One Green Planet, 2021, accessed 6 September 2022, https://www.onegreenplanet.org/animalsandnature/nuclear-history-of-lab-beagles/.

17. Jon Brady, "Scots teen has leg and arm ripped open in alleged XL Bully dog attack," *Daily Record*, 20 August 2022, accessed 6 September 2022, https://www.dailyrecord.co.uk/news/scottish-news/scots-teen-leg-arm-ripped-27772082.

18. Haldeman, "What drives your dog?"

19. Milo Boyd, "Calls for deadly dog ban after breed that killed baby chews up man's hound," *Daily Record*, 9 April 2022, accessed 6 September 2022, https://www.dailyrecord.co.uk/news/uk-world-news/calls-deadly-dog-ban-after-26673177.

20. Twitter feed of Spaniel Aid UK, 1 July 2022.

21. "10 Animals That Play Dead to Survive," 4 Ever Green YouTube channel, 18 October 2020, accessed 6 September 2022, https://www.youtube.com/watch?v=NogU_6vnPNk.

22. Katie Palmer, "A Map of the Dolphin Mind," *Discover* magazine, 1 August 2011, accessed 18 September 2022, https://www.discovermagazine.com/planet-earth/a-map-of-the-dolphin-mind; Gregory Berns, M.D., "Decoding the Canine Mind," *Cerebrum: The Dana Forum on Brain Science*, March-April 2020, on PubMed Central, 1 April 2020, accessed 18 September 2022, https://www.ncbi.nlm.nih.gov/pmc/articles/PMC7192336/.

23. Palmer, "A Map of the Dolphin Mind."

24. Ibid.

25. Ibid.

26. Berns, "Decoding the Canine Mind."

27. "Cerebral Cortex," Cleveland Clinic, accessed 18 September 2022, https://my.clevelandclinic.org/health/articles/23073-cerebral-cortex#:~:text=Your%20cortex%20is%20involved%20in,functions%20related%20to%20your%20senses.

28. Ibid.

29. J. Rubes et al., "Comparative molecular cytogenetics in Cetartiodactyla," *Cytogenetic and Genome Research* 137:2-4 (2012), on PubMed Central, 24 May 2012, accessed 18 September 2022, https://pubmed.ncbi.nlm.nih.gov/22627059/#:~:text=Cetartiodactyla%20comprises%20Artiodactyla%20(even%2Dtoed,families%20with%20almost%2080%20species.

30. Ibid.

31. Débora Jardim-Messeder et al.,"Dogs Have the Most Neurons, Though Not the Largest Brain: Trade-Off between Body Mass and Number of Neurons in the Cerebral Cortex of Large Carnivoran Species," *Frontiers in Neuroanatomy* 11:118 (12 December 2017), on PubMed Central, accessed 18 September 2022, https://pubmed.ncbi.nlm.nih.gov/29311850/.

32. Ibid.

33. Berns, "Decoding the Canine Mind."

34. "Is This Self Aware Dog Talking with Buttons?" KPassionate YouTube channel, 30 April 2022, accessed 18 September 2022, https://www.youtube.com/watch?v=jBwT94a2DXU.
35. "Cute Pet! Clever Pooch Talks to Owner Using Buttons," Caters Clips, 16 April 2022, accessed 18 September 2022, https://www.youtube.com/watch?v=l_vrMv3eYWA.

Chapter Eight

1. "Don't Ever Feed Him After Midnight"—*Gremlins* Movie Trailer, Warner Bros. UK Horror YouTube channel, 11 December 2020, accessed 21 September 2022, https://www.youtube.com/watch?v=ZDpO_rZvDg0.
2. "Dread: The Unsolved—The Dybbuk Box—S4 E7," Dread Central YouTube channel, accessed 21 September 2022, https://www.youtube.com/watch?v=uIS8HUWmHyA.
3. Wayback Machine Internet Archive, accessed 21 September 2022, https://archive.org/web/.
4. "Randall" (Christopher Gordon), "The Crazy Nastyass Honey Badger," CZG123 channel, YouTube, 18 January 2011. accessed 21 September 2022, https://www.youtube.com/watch?v=4r7wHMg5Yjg.
5. Malcolm Weir, DVM, and Ernest Ward, DVM, "Breeding for Dog Owners—Caring from Birth to Weaning," VCA Animal Hospitals, accessed 21 September 2022, https://vcahospitals.com/know-your-pet/breeding-for-dog-owners-caring-from-birth-to-weaning#:~:text=At%20the%20time%20of%20weaning,about%20four%20meals%20a%20day.
6. "5 week old puppies learning boundaries through discipline," Jamie Penrith Dog Training YouTube channel, 17 October 2017, accessed 21 September 2022, https://www.youtube.com/watch?v=Y_ESq0VO8_c.
7. Michael Dimock, "Defining generations: Where Millennials end and Generation Z begins," Pew Research Center, 17 January 2019, accessed 21 September 2022, https://www.pewresearch.org/fact-tank/2019/01/17/where-millennials-end-and-generation-z-begins/.
8. "Celebs Speak Out on How They Were Treated by Ellen," This Happened YouTube channel, 31 August 2020, accessed 21 September 2022, https://www.youtube.com/watch?v=g6kYKi0o-As.
9. "U.S. Cities Factsheet," Center for Sustainable Systems, University of Michigan. September 2022, accessed 21 September 2022, https://css.umich.edu/publications/factsheets/built-environment/us-cities-factsheet#:~:text=It%20is%20estimated%20that%2083,to%20live%20in%20urban%20areas.
10. Jan Reisen, "Most Popular Dog Breeds 2021," American Kennel Club, 15 March 2022, accessed 21 September 2022, https://www.akc.org/expert-advice/dog-breeds/most-popular-dog-breeds-of-2021/.

Chapter Nine

1. Oliver Bennett, "Dangerous Dogs," Briefing Paper Number 4348, House of Commons Library, 10 August 2016, accessed 26 September 2022, https://researchbriefings.files.parliament.uk/documents/SN04348/SN04348.pdf.
2. "Animal Fighting," RSPCA (Royal Society for the Prevention of Cruelty to Animals), accessed 26 September 2022, https://www.rspca.org.uk/whatwedo/endcruelty/investigatingcruelty/organised/animalfighting#:~:text=Animal%20fighting%20%2D%20such%20as%20dog,day%20across%20England%20and%20Wales.
3. Save Our Seized Dogs—Put BSL to Sleep UK Facebook page, accessed 26 September 2022, https://www.facebook.com/SaveOurSeizedDogs/.
4. Bennett, "Dangerous Dogs."
5. "UK Favourite Dog Breeds Which Are Banned in Other Countries," PBS Pet Travel, 9 March 2020, accessed 26 September 2022, https://www.pbspettravel.co.uk/blog/uk-favourite-dog-breeds-which-are-banned-in-other-countries/.
6. "Which Dog Breeds Are Banned in China?" PBS Specialist Pet Travel, 10 December 2019, accessed 26 September 2022, https://www.pbspettravel.co.uk/blog/which-dog-breeds-are-banned-in-china/.
7. "Weight & More Dog Size Guide," TARIGS, accessed 26 September 2022, https://tarigs.com/size-table-dog/.

8. "Which Dog Breeds Are Banned in China?"
9. Deborah L. Duffy, Yuying Hsu, and James A. Serpell, "Breed differences in canine aggression," *Applied Animal Behaviour Science* 114:3–4 (December 2008), on Science Direct, accessed 26 September 2022, https://www.sciencedirect.com/science/article/abs/pii/S0168159108001147.
10. "A List of the Dogs Banned in Beijing," *New York Times*, 22 June 2013, accessed 26 September 2022, https://www.nytimes.com/2013/06/23/world/asia/a-list-of-the-dogs-banned-in-beijing.html.
11. "French Bulldog," American Kennel Club, accessed 26 September 2022, https://www.akc.org/dog-breeds/french-bulldog/.
12. "A List of the Dogs Banned in Beijing."
13. "Dachshund—Top 10 Facts," Dogs Wiz YouTube channel, 9 December 2019, accessed on 26 September 2022, https://www.youtube.com/watch?v=ftrCm0S3lQA.
14. Duffy, Hsu, and Serpell, "Breed differences in canine aggression."
15. "Tibetan Terrier," American Kennel Club, accessed 26 September 2022, https://www.akc.org/dog-breeds/tibetan-terrier/.
16. "Tibetan Terrier—Top 10 Facts," Dogs Wiz YouTube channel, 24 April 2020, accessed 26 September 2022, https://www.youtube.com/watch?v=IZ0m6niPDtY.
17. Jan Reisen, "Most popular dog breeds of 2021," American Kennel Club, 15 March 2022, accessed 26 September 2022, https://www.akc.org/expert-advice/dog-breeds/most-popular-dog-breeds-of-2021/.
18. "The Bully Kutta—Dangerous Beast from the East?"Animal Watch YouTube channel, 25 March 2022, accessed 26 September 2022, https://www.youtube.com/watch?v=oqcMvVfZpOE (**CONTAINS SCENES OF DOG FIGHTING— VIEWER DISCRETION ADVISED.**)
19. AKC Government Relations, "ND [North Dakota] Update: Minot Repeals Breed Ban," American Kennel Club, 9 September 2022, accessed 26 September 2022, https://www.akc.org/legislative-alerts/akc-supports-minot-north-dakotas-efforts-repeal-breed-specific-law/#:~:text=Monday%2C%20by%20a%204%2D3,old%20ban%20of%20multiple%20breeds.
20. "Position Statements," American College of Veterinary Behaviorists, accessed 26 September 2022, https://www.dacvb.org/page/PositionStatement.
21. "Tustin Man Recovering after E-Cig Explodes in His Mouth," KCAL News YouTube channel, 10 June 2016, accessed 26 September 2022, https://www.youtube.com/watch?v=Jeig1a_diSg.
22. Home page, Vets Against Brachycephalism, accessed 26 September 2022, https://vetsagainstbrachycephalism.com/related-professionals/.
23. "Brachycephalic CT scans," British Veterinary Association, 16 February 2018, accessed 26 September 2022, https://www.youtube.com/watch?v=zlRO5CZSC0Y.
24. "Cute Bulldog with Obstructive Sleep Apnea," Jorge Faber YouTube channel, 5 June 2020, accessed 26 September 2022, https://www.youtube.com/watch?v=rhqf-Wm0tk8.
25. "What do I need to know about Brachycephalic dogs?" RSPCA knowledgebase, accessed 26 September 2022, https://kb.rspca.org.au/knowledge-base/what-do-i-need-to-know-about-brachycephalic-dogs/#:~:text=Some%20brachycephalic%20dogs%20are%20unable,'re%20sleeping%20%5B9%5D.
26. "Advertising guidelines—Pets in advertising: A social concern," British Veterinary Association, accessed 26 September 2022, https://www.bva.co.uk/resources-support/ethical-guidance/advertising-guidelines-pets-in-advertising-a-social-concern/.
27. Simon R. Platt, "Is Banning Breeds the Answer?" Today's Veterinary Practice, 11 April 2022, accessed 26 September 2022, https://todaysveterinarypractice.com/ethics-welfare/is-banning-breeds-the-answer/#:~:text=Norway%20and%20the%20Netherlands%20have,CKCS)%2C%20and%20Boston%20terriers; "Breeding ban for bulldogs and cavaliers in Norway," France 24, 22 February 2022, accessed 26 September 2022, https://www.france24.com/en/live-news/20220222-breeding-ban-for-bulldogs-and-cavaliers-in-norway.
28. "Breeding ban for bulldogs and cavaliers in Norway."
29. Reisen, "Most popular dog breeds of 2021."
30. "Pedigree Dogs Exposed—The Blog," 29 May 2020, accessed 26 September 2022, http://pedigreedogsexposed.blogspot.

com/2020/05/dutch-ban-short-nosed-dogs-prompts.html.
31. Platt, "Is Banning Breeds the Answer?"
32. Reisen, "Most popular dog breeds of 2021."
33. "Pedigree Dogs Exposed—The Blog."
34. "All about dogs," Blue Cross, accessed 26 September 2022, https://www.bluecross.org.uk/all-about-dogs?utm_medium=paidsocial&utm_source=facebook.com&utm_campaign=tkf-petcensus2&utm_term=competitoranimalcharity&utm_content=fb_competitoranimalcharity_resultsmulti_copy1_animalwelfare.
35. "National Dog Survey," Dogs Trust, accessed 26 September 2022, https://www.dogstrust.org.uk/how-we-help/the-future/national-dog-survey.
36. "Quarterly registration statistics for the toy group," Kennel Club, accessed 26 September 2022, https://www.thekennelclub.org.uk/media/2406/quarterly-breed-stats-toys.pdf.
37. "Quarterly registration statistics for the utility group," Kennel Club, accessed 26 September 2022, https://www.thekennelclub.org.uk/media/2407/quarterly-breed-stats-utility.pdf.
38. Ibid.
39. "Quarterly registration statistics for the gundog group," Kennel Club, accessed 26 September 2022, https://www.thekennelclub.org.uk/media/2402/quarterly-breed-stats-gundogs.pdf.
40. Ibid.
41. Duffy, Hsu, and Serpell, "Breed differences in canine aggression."
42. "81 Supporting organisations and practices," Vets Against Brachycephalism, accessed 26 September 2022, https://vetsagainstbrachycephalism.com/supporting-organisations-and-practices/; home page, Vets Against Brachycephalism.
43. "About," Association of Pet Dog Trainers, accessed 26 September 2022, https://apdt.co.uk/about/.
44. "Choosing a Puppy," Association of Pet Dog Trainers, accessed 26 September 2022, https://apdt.co.uk/choosing-a-puppy/.
45. "Merle & Health," Australian Shepherd Health & Genetics Institute, August 2013, accessed 26 September 2022, https://www.ashgi.org/home-page/genetics-info/color/merle-health#:~:text=Dogs%20that%20have%20two%20copies,pigment%20in%20the%20inner%20ear.
46. "Research of Intervertebral Disk Disease in Dachshunds Focuses on Improving Recovery," Purina Pro Club," accessed 26 September 2022, https://www.purinaproclub.com/resources/dog-articles/health/research-of-intervertebral-disk-disease-in-dachshunds-focuses-on-improving-recovery; "Dachshund—Top 10 Facts."
47. Cristina Criddle, "YouTube electric-shock dog collar videos spark anger," BBC News, 11 March 2021, accessed 26 September 2022, https://www.bbc.co.uk/news/technology-56351693?fbclid=IwAR09g-jEaIZn-49OzbeSskrITfB67huSMQVjU2iCh8qW56IoDH_2jGpuBtM.
48. "Our People—President and Patrons," ABTC (Animal Behaviour & Training Council), accessed 28 September 2022, https://abtc.org.uk/about/our-people-patrons/.
49. "Merle & Health."
50. "White fright," Australian Shepherd Health and Genetics Institute, accessed 26 September 2022, https://www.ashgi.org/home-page/genetics-info/coat-color/white-fright.
51. Criddle, "YouTube electric-shock dog collar videos spark anger."
52. Ibid.
53. Ibid.
54. "What is a Board Certified Veterinary Behaviorist?" American College of Veterinary Behaviorists, accessed 28 September 2022, https://www.dacvb.org/page/AnimalOwners.
55. Ibid.
56. "Liar, Liar—The Castaways (1965)," clotho98 YouTube channel, 18 November 2008, accessed 26 September 2022, https://www.youtube.com/watch?v=S8rCy173y7Y.
57. Amy Pike, "'Positive' Dog Training Is Not Always What It Seems," Psychology Today, 1 September 2018, accessed 26 September 2022, https://www.psychologytoday.com/us/blog/decoding-your-pet/201809/positive-dog-training-is-not-always-what-it-seems.
58. Debra Horwitz and Gary Landsberg, "Introduction to Desensitization and Counterconditioning," VCA Animal Hospitals, accessed 26 September 2022, https://vcahospitals.

com/know-your-pet/introduction-to-desensitization-and-counterconditioning.

59. "Grape, raisin, currant and sultana poisoning in dogs," PDSA (People's Dispensary for Sick Animals), accessed 26 September 2022, https://www.pdsa.org.uk/pet-help-and-advice/pet-health-hub/conditions/grape-raisin-currant-and-sultana-poisoning-in-dogs#:~:text=Print%20this%20page-,Overview,the%20fruit%20to%20become%20poorly).

60. "Man struck by lightning while walking in storm," ABC7 YouTube channel, 19 August 2019, accessed 26 September 2022, https://www.youtube.com/watch?v=ZxazDRh4frM.

Chapter Ten

1. "How Do Cults Trap People?" WMX Presents YouTube channel, 27 March 2018, accessed 29 September 2022, https://www.youtube.com/watch?v=dRO8RAkZYr4&ab_channel=WMXPresents; Stefan, Samuel, and Nick Oakley, dirs., *Cult Witness*, Arthio Films, 2010, on FilmsIsNow Movies YouTube channel, 26 December 2020, accessed 25 October 2022, https://www.youtube.com/watch?v=_cFtZRGCzYY.

2. Stefan and Oakley, *Cult Witness*; "How the Brain Is Hijacked into Compliance," Chase Hughes YouTube channel, 29 September 2022, accessed 29 September 2022, https://www.youtube.com/watch?v=n5poKK4lR5c.

3. Ibid.
4. Ibid.
5. Ibid.
6. Hughes, "How the Brain Is Hijacked into Compliance."

7. "You Will Wish You Watched This Before You Started Using Social Media," Absolute Motivation YouTube channel, 20 April 2018, accessed 29 September 2022, https://www.youtube.com/watch?v=PmEDAzqswh8.

8. Stefan and Oakley, *Cult Witness*.
9. Ibid.
10. Ibid.; Hughes, "How the Brain Is Hijacked into Compliance."
11. "Audience ad targeting," Meta, accessed 25 October 2022, https://www.facebook.com/business/ads/ad-targeting.
12. "How Do Cults Trap People?";

Hughes, "How the Brain Is Hijacked into Compliance."

13. Stefan and Oakley, *Cult Witness*.
14. "How Do Cults Trap People?"; Hughes, "How the Brain Is Hijacked into Compliance."
15. Judith Evans and Kaye Wiggins, "Going to the vet: what happens when private equity invests in a cottage industry," *Financial Times*, 20 April 2021, accessed 25 October 2022, https://www.ft.com/content/9a825fe8-8ea5-4ef3-84b7-2529bfe5ffed.
16. Ibid.
17. "Code of Ethics," Canine and Feline Behaviour Association, accessed 25 October 2022, https://cfba.uk/code-of-ethics/.
18. "Code of Ethics," Canine and Feline Behaviour Association, accessed 25 October 2022, https://cfba.uk/code-of-ethics/.
19. "Tina: Extreme OCD Case," Ivan Balabanov YouTube channel, 7 August 2022, accessed 25 October 2022, https://www.youtube.com/watch?v=9B-gt0aEtYw.
20. "The Untold Truth of the Dog Whisperer," Looper YouTube channel, 6 March 2018, accessed 24 October 2022, https://www.youtube.com/watch?v=ZO-gmaDwcZc.
21. "The A-Team TV Theme Tune," A-Team YouTube channel, 25 November 2020, accessed 24 October 2022, https://www.youtube.com/watch?v=UAO2JBjRRBk.
22. "Dog Whisperer with Cesar Millan," Wikipedia, accessed 24 October 2022, https://en.wikipedia.org/wiki/Dog_Whisperer_with_Cesar_Millan.
23. "Cesar Milan [sic]? A professional Trainer[']s opinion," Shield K9 Dog Training YouTube channel, 29 October 2021, accessed 24 October 2022 https://www.youtube.com/watch?v=wkHXqIXfUnI.
24. Ibid.
25. "Dog Whisperer with Cesar Millan."
26. "Our Mission," Victoria Stilwell Academy, accessed 24 October 2022, https://www.vsdogtrainingacademy.com/about/mission/.
27. "Introducing the newly-redesigned positively no-pull harness," Positively, accessed 24 October 2022, https://positively.com/news/introducing-the-newly-redesigned-positively-no-pull-harness/.

28. "Lives Are at Risk Around This 'Weapon on a Leash,'" It's Me or the Dog YouTube channel, 9 May 2020, accessed 24 October 2022, https://www.youtube.com/watch?v=THmtv3IP1pQ.
29. Ibid.
30. "Force-free Dog Training: How to Protect Yourself Against Frauds," Dog Training by K9-1.com YouTube channel, 18 September 2021, accessed 24 October 2022, https://www.youtube.com/watch?v=3629UOD22I8.
31. "Lives Are at Risk Around This 'Weapon on a Leash.'"
32. Ibid.
33. "Force-free Dog Training: How to Protect Yourself Against Frauds."
34. Ibid.
35. "Lives Are at Risk Around This 'Weapon on a Leash.'"
36. "Victoria Stilwell Net Worth, Income, Salary, Earnings, Biography, How much money make?" Ncert Point, 20 November 2021, accessed 24 October 2022, https://www.ncertpoint.com/2021/11/victoria-stilwell-net-worth-income-salary-earnings-biography-how-much-money-make.html.
37. "Cesar Millan Net Worth," Celebrity Net Worth, accessed 24 October 2022, https://www.celebritynetworth.com/richest-celebrities/authors/cesar-millan-net-worth/.
38. Tom Ford, "Ian Dunbar Net Worth," Net Worth Post, accessed 24 October 2022, https://networthpost.org/net-worth/ian-dunbar-net-worth/.
39. "Karen Pryor," Popular Bio, accessed 24 October 2022, https://popularbio.com/karen-pryor/.
40. Tom Ford, "Jean Donaldson Net Worth," Net Worth Post, accessed 24 October 2022, https://networthpost.org/net-worth/jean-donaldson-net-worth/.
41. "American Humane Salaries—How Much Does American Humane Pay?" Salary.com, accessed 24 October 2022, https://www.salary.com/research/company/american-humane-salary.
42. Ibid.
43. "Celebrity Supporters," American Humane, accessed 24 October 2022, https://www.americanhumane.org/initiative/celebrity-supporters/.
44. "American Humane Association," ProPublica, accessed 24 October 2022, https://projects.propublica.org/nonprofits/organizations/840432950.
45. Ibid.
46. "Choosing a Dog Collar," American Humane, accessed 24 October 2022, https://www.americanhumane.org/fact-sheet/choosing-a-dog-collar-2/.
47. XE global currency converter, XE.com, accessed 24 October 2022.
48. Kirsty Weakley, "Dogs Trust income hits £111m after rise in legacy income," Civil Society, 9 October 2019, accessed 24 October 2022, https://www.civilsociety.co.uk/news/dogs-trust-income-hits-111m-after-rise-in-legacy-income.html#:~:text=Dogs%20Trust%20saw%20its%20income,%C2%A395.8m%20in%202017.
49. XE global currency converter.
50. Ibid.
51. Ibid.
52. Weakley, "Dogs Trust income hits £111m ..."
53. Ibid.
54. XE global currency converter.
55. Ibid.
56. "Training Techniques," Dogs Trust, accessed 24 October 2022, https://www.dogstrust.org.uk/dog-advice/training/techniques.
57. XE global currency converter.
58. Weakley, "Dogs Trust income hits £111m ..."
59. XE global currency converter.
60. Weakley, "Dogs Trust income hits £111m ..."
61. "Training Techniques."
62. "Bad Newz Kennels dog fighting investigation," Wikipedia, accessed 24 October 2022, https://en.wikipedia.org/wiki/Bad_Newz_Kennels_dog_fighting_investigation.
63. Emily Giambalvo, "Frodo, the last surviving dog rescued from Michael Vick, dies surrounded by loved ones," *Washington Post*, 21 December 2021, accessed 24 October 2022, https://www.washingtonpost.com/sports/2021/12/21/michael-vick-dog-survivor-frodo-dies/.
64. "A Complete Tragedy—Violent Dogs Go Too Far," Robert Cabral YouTube channel, 16 October 2022, accessed 24 October 2022, https://www.youtube.com/watch?v=FHz3pMipJlc.
65. "Best Friends Animal Society," ProPublica, accessed 24 October 2022, https://

projects.propublica.org/nonprofits/organizations/237147797/.
66. Ibid.
67. "RVC Research study reveals consequences of extreme demand for puppies during COVID-19 Pandemic," Royal Veterinary College, 25 August 2021, accessed 24 October 2022, https://www.rvc.ac.uk/vetcompass/news/rvc-research-study-reveals-consequences-of-extreme-demand-for-puppies-during-covid-19-pandemic.
68. Ibid.
69. "A Complete Tragedy."
70. "Teaching the Guard (bark and hold)," Premier Protection Dogs YouTube channel, 17 March 2022, accessed 25 October 2022, https://www.youtube.com/watch?v=ctE-3zz19sE.
71. "Using Pinch Collar and Multiple Corrections," Gary GAZ Jackson YouTube channel, 31 October 2022, accessed 3 November 2022, https://www.youtube.com/watch?v=8DJYDlgFoBs&t=111s.
72. "Pinch Collars: are they kind or cruel?," Gary GAZ Jackson YouTube channel, accessed 25 October 2022, https://www.youtube.com/watch?v=kdFMn7WBHfo.
73. "Using Pinch Collar and Multiple Corrections."
74. "Force-free Dog Training: How to Protect Yourself Against Frauds."
75. Earthling Ed (Ed Winters), "Have You Ever Thought About This? The Ethics of Pet Ownership," Earthling Ed YouTube channel, 25 May 2019, accessed 25 October 2022, https://www.youtube.com/watch?v=hrwG1BHdHIk; "The Ethics Of Keeping Pets," Chris Hines YouTube channel, 10 July 2016, accessed 25 October 2022, https://www.youtube.com/watch?v=L42lFtzN5i4.
76. Earthling Ed (Ed Winters), "Have You Ever Thought About This?"
77. Hines, "The Ethics of Keeping Pets."
78. Earthling Ed (Ed Winters), "Have You Ever Thought About This?"; Hines, "The Ethics of Keeping Pets."

Conclusion

1. Sir Mix-a-Lot, "I Like Big Butts ["Baby's Got Back"] Lyrics," Lyrics On Demand, accessed 12 November 2022, https://www.lyricsondemand.com/s/sirmixalotlyrics/ilikebigbuttslyrics.html.
2. "An Offer to ALL Force Free Dog Trainers ($55,000)," Jamie Penrith Dog Training, 12 September 2021, accessed 18 August 2022, https://www.youtube.com/watch?v=TeMeeaEqzXY.
3. Ibid.
4. Bart Bellon website, accessed 1 September 2022, https://www.bartbellon.com/.
5. Malvika Padin, "Will pugs and French bulldogs be banned in UK? Breeds face urgent health crackdown," Mirror, 14 April 2022, accessed 29 July 2022, https://www.mirror.co.uk/news/uk-news/pugs-french-bulldogs-banned-uk-26711608.
6. "Research of Intervertebral Disk Disease in Dachshunds Focuses on Improving Recovery," Purina Pro Club, accessed 26 September 2022, https://www.purinaproclub.com/resources/dog-articles/health/research-of-intervertebral-disk-disease-in-dachshunds-focuses-on-improving-recovery.
7. "Merle & Health," Australian Shepherd Health & Genetics Institute, August 2013, accessed 26 September 2022, https://www.ashgi.org/home-page/genetics-info/color/merle-health#:~:text=Dogs%20that%20have%20two%20copies,pigment%20in%20the%20inner%20ear.
8. Darwin Awards, accessed 12 November 2022, https://darwinawards.com/.
9. Hayley Dixon, "Electric dog collar ban will lead to 'animal welfare disaster,' warn farmers," Telegraph, 3 September 2022, https://www.telegraph.co.uk/news/2022/09/03/electric-dog-collar-ban-will-lead-animal-welfare-disaster-warns/?fbclid=IwAR3I48plKVAYFEDoIsTOIifpvflENbuK_EsgAEUiasygTxj0b7MR5hoDjuE.
10. "The Most Disturbing Cult of All Time: The Ant Hill Kids," Wendigoon YouTube channel, 30 March 2021, accessed 2 November 2022, https://www.youtube.com/watch?v=jzdC1zxXgpE.
11. "A History of the Borg," Trekspertise YouTube channel, 14 May 2015, accessed 2 November 2022, https://www.youtube.com/watch?v=hNxPTk9gR54.
12. Aja Romano, "Karen: The anti-vaxxer soccer mom with speak-to-the-manager hair, explained," Vox, 5 February 2020, accessed 2 November 2022, https://www.vox.com/2020/2/5/21079162/karen-name-insult-meme-manager.
13. "Ted Bundy—He Terrorised America for 30 Years," Emma Kenny YouTube

channel, 2 March 2022, accessed 2 November 2022, https://www.youtube.com/watch?v=Ln9qrOdDzcw&t=5721s.

14. "Slavic mythology: Meet Perun, the thunder god," Kafkadesk, 12 October 2020, accessed 2 November 2022, https://kafkadesk.org/2020/10/12/what-about-slavic-mythology-meet-perun-the-thunder-god/.

Bibliography

I include a list of books which you may find of interest. A few of these books may surprise you, as some of the information they contain is really quite opposite to my own beliefs. However, it's important to concede that not everyone is right all of the time (except for my dog Mazey, naturally) and we all have a great deal which we can learn from each other.

American Kennel Club. *The New Complete Dog Book*. Fox Chapel. 2022.
Arden, J. *Mission Control: How to Train the High Drive Dog*. First Stone. 2020.
Bailey, G. *The Perfect Puppy*. Generic. 2008.
Balabanov, I., and K. Duet. *Advanced Schutzhund*. Howell. 1999.
Barnes, S. *The Way of the Dog: Training by Instinct*. CreateSpace. 2015.
Burch, M., and J. Bailey. *How Dogs Learn*. Howell. 1999.
Case, L. *Dog Smart: Evidence-Based Training with the Science Dog*. CreateSpace. 2018.
Charles River Editors. *The Domestication of Dogs: The History of Dogs' Genetic Divergence from Wolves and the Origins of Their Relationship with Human*. Self-published. 2020.
Cusack, C. *Laws, Policies, Attitudes & Processes That Shape the Lives of Puppies in America: Assessing Society's Needs, Desires, Values & Morals*. Sussex Academic Press. 2000.
Eschenweber, S. *Mental Exercise for Dogs: The 101 Best Dog Games for More Agility, Intelligence & Fun*. Self-published. 2020.
Farricelli, A. *Brain Training for Dogs*. Self-published. 2020.
Fogle, B. *The Dog's Mind*. Michael Joseph. 1992.
Gay, B. *Balanced Training: Obedience for Dogs and Their Owners*. FriesenPress. 2017.
Goody, P. *Dog Anatomy: A Pictorial Approach to Canine Structure*. J.A. Allen & Co. 1999.
Gutteridge, S. *Enrichment through Scentwork for Highly Aroused Dogs*. Self-published. 2018.
Käufer, M. *Canine Play Behaviour: The Science of Dogs at Play*. Self-published. 2011.
Kay, D. *Super Sniffer Handbook: A Guide to Scent Training for Medical Alert Dogs*. Self-published. 2013.
Krohn, L. *Everything You Need to Know about E-Collar Training*. Self-published. 2017.
Mackinnon, P. *Detector Dog: A Talking Dogs Scentwork® Manual*. Self-published. 2017.
Mann, S. *Easy Peasy Doggy Squeezy: Even More of Your Dog Training Dilemmas Solved*. Blink. 2020.
_____. *Easy Peasy Puppy Squeezy*. Blink. 2019.
Millis, D., and D. Levine. *Canine Rehabilitation and Physical Therapy*. Saunders. 2013.
Scott, J. *Genetics and the Social Behavior of the Dog*. University of Chicago Press. 2012.
Walkowicz, C., and B. Wilcox. *Successful Dog Breeding: The Complete Handbook of Canine Midwifery*. Howell. 2008.

Wycherley, J. *Losing My Best Friend: Thoughtful Support for Those Affected by Dog Bereavement or Pet Loss*. Bark at the Moon Books. 2018.

Zinc, C., and J. Van Dyke. *Canine Sports Medicine and Rehabilitation*. Wiley-Blackwell. 2018.

Index

A Team 151, 201
active submission 44–45
Adolf 2
adversive 4–21
Affenpinscher 99, 180
AK-47 207
Akita 66
All Creatures Great and Small 142
alpha roll 166, 200
America's Top Dog 49, 87
Anarchist Cookbook 227
Animal Behaviour and Training Council 181, 184
Animals (Scientific Procedures) Act 1986 122
Ant Hill Kids 222
American College of Veterinary Behaviorists 179
American Humane 203–205
American Kennel Club 173
American Pit Bull Terrier *see* Pit Bull
American Veterinary Society of Animal Behavior 199–200
Applied Animal Behaviour Science 128
ARDO (Association of Responsible Dog Owners) 129
Ark 127
Association of Pet Dog Trainers 181–182, 184
Attila the Hun 91
Australian Shepherd 182
autism 85–87

Babalanov, Ivan 31, 199
back yard breeders 63, 65, 99, 151, 205
Badger 177
balanced dog trainer 1–9, 21–22, 157–173
Barbie 85
barn hunt 142
barrier frustration 18, 78–79, 82
Beagle 143–145, 148, 176

Bedlington Terrier 177
Beelzebub 214
behavioral modification 196
behaviorists 183–186, 198–200
Beijing 176
Belgian Malinois 52–58, 143–145
Belgium 55
Bellon, B&M 31
Berlin 56, 189
Bernese Mountain Dog 177
Best Friends Animal Society 205
Blackfish 89
Blue Cross 180
BOAS 181
Boomers 166
Border Collie 48–58, 96–97, 182
Borg 222
Boston Terrier 99, 180
Botox 189
brachycephalic 8, 99–102, 114, 152, 179, 180–181
brain 153–156
Brancheau, Dawn 89–92
breed bans 174–192
breed specific legislation 98–99, 174–183
British Bulldog 177, 180
Buffett, Warren 156
Bulldog 180
Bully Kutta 178
Bundy, Ted 223
Burrhus, Frederic 23
Byrne, Keltie 89

California 89, 208
Cambridge Dictionary 18–19
Canadian National Institute for the Blind 89
Cane Corso 4, 9, 33
Canine and Feline Behaviour Association 198–199
canine compulsive disorder 97

257

Index

carnivores 154
castration 71–72, 97
cat 156
Caucasian Shepherd Dog 51
Cavalier King Charles Spaniels 180
cerebral cortex 154–155
cetaceans 154–156
charging clicker/marker word 35
China 153, 176, 177
Chihuahua 176
Chow Chow 9
Christians 153
Christmas 58
classical conditioning 35, 45–46
clicker 35–36, 42
clicker trainers 22–23, 39, 90–92
Cockapoo 181
Cocker Spaniel 99–100
coffee shop dog 6
Colvin, Margaret 65
Communists 153
competing reinforcer 22, 37, 90, 95, 192, 195–196, 224
compulsion trainers 1–9 127–28
conditioned response 46
conditioned stimulus 46
confirmation bias 121
consent *see* permission
continuous reinforcement schedule 38–39
corrections 88–101, 188–189
cortisol 133–134–136
Corvid 154
counter conditioning *see* thresholds
counter surfing 97
Court of Appeal 123
COVID-19 124, 205
cow 154
crate 135–136
Crocodile Dundee 78
cults 193–198

Dachshund 177, 181–182
Dahmer, Jeffrey 158, 206
Dalmatians 162
Dangerous Dogs Act 1991 116, 174–176
Danse Macabre 16
Darwin Award 219
defensive drive 148–151
DEFRA 114, 123–124, 133
direct reward 33–35
ditch the bowl 13, 38
Dobermann Pinscher 51
Dodo 173
dog aggression 150, 169
dog park 142–143
Dog Whisperer 200–201
Dogo Argentino 175

Dogs Trust 181, 204–205
Dogue de Bordeaux 104
dolphin 153–156
dominance 137–139
Donaldson, Jean 89, 203
donkey 149
Doodle 75, 98, 180
dopamine 41, 44–45, 155
Dremel 171
drugs *see* medications
Dukes, Daniel P. 89
Dunbar, Ian 203
Dutch Herder 97, 109
Dutch Kennel Club 180

e-collar 47, 73–75, 96, 107–116, 134–137, 141–146
Egyptian pharaohs 142
Electronic Collar Manufacturers Association 123, 132
England 54, 58, 155
English Bulldog 99, 180
English Springer Spaniels 100
emotional dog trainer 6
errorless learning 88, 140
ethics 210–211, 216
euthanasia 64–67, 99–100

Facebook 195
faint 152
fawn 152
Fenton 113–114
fight 148–151
Fila Brasileiro 175
Find Fenton 113
Finland 184
fixed interval reinforcement schedule 42–43
fixed ratio reinforcement schedule 41–42
flat collar 56–57, 102–104, 107–108, 162–163
Flexi-lead 73, 96, 173
flight 151–152, 163
flooding 186
flying monkeys 196, 222
focused heel-work 46
food deprivation 12–13, 36–38, 90–94, 224–225
food drive 148-
force free dog trainer 1–9, 157–173
fraud 1–9, 209–210
free shaping 33–34
French Bulldog 32–33, 93, 99, 173, 176, 180–181
Frisbee 13, 36
front pull harness 12, 94, 96, 103, 106–107, 201

Index

Full Metal Jacket 62
fur saver 103

games *see* play
Gen X 166
generalization 46
genetics 63–69
German Shepherd Dog 20–21, 51–54
German Shorthaired Pointer 173
Germany 189, 191
Giggy 203
Gizmo 158, 185
Goldberg, Whoopi 203
Golden Retriever 51–52, 71, 154, 173, 181
Goldendoodle 8
Google 51
Grand Theft Auto 202
Great Dane 19, 177
Griffon Belge 99, 180
Griffon Bruxellois 99, 180
Guide Dogs for the Blind 113
gut villi 95

harness 102
head collar 95–96, 102–107
Home Office 122
honey badger 162
horse 149, 153, 156, 191
house line 60
Hungarian Vizsla 97
Hungary 155
hunger 12–13

Iceland 176
IGP 49–50, 55–56, 134, 137, 209
impulse control 79
indirect reward 33–35
Instagram 21, 151, 189
IQ 50
Israel 176
It's Me or the Dog 201–202

Jack Russell Terrier 74, 98–99, 176, 181
Jackman, Hugh 203
jackpotting 38, 44
Japan 108
Japanese Chin 99, 180
Japanese Tosa 175
Jay 174
John Wick 50
Judge Dredd 109
Jurassic Park 9, 178

K9-1 202
Kennel Club 143
Kerry Blue Terrier 177
KGB 129

kill shelters 100
King Charles Spaniel 99, 180
King Charles III 156
King of the Living Room 6
Koehler Method 6
Kohn, Larry 58
Kool Aid 166, 222, 224, 226
Kraken 135
Kruger, Freddie 77

Labrador Retriever 17 51–52, 181
Lagotto Romagnolo 206
Landrace dog 8–9
leadership 17, 137–139
learned helplessness 59, 140
LIMA 19, 22
London 113
long line 73, 96
Lorenz, Konrad 24
love bombing 194
Lucifer 173, 179, 200, 227
luring 33–35
Lycra 164

Macarena 132
Magpie 154
Malaysia 176
Malines 55
management 88–101, 95–98, 120–136, 194
Mandarin 155
marker word 35–36, 42
marketing 1–9, 157–173, 202
Markle, Meghan 128
martingale collar 96, 102–108, 162–163–164
Mastiff 20
Mech, David 23, 137
medical care 5
Medical Detection Dogs 124
medications 97, 161, 171, 194
merle gene 182–183
Milgram, Stanley 194
Millan, César 200–203
Millennial 166
Minot, North Dakota 179
model-rival training 22, 91
Monopoly 15
MRI 153
Musk, Elon 156

Nazis 11
Neapolitan Mastiff 183
negative correction 25–33
negative reinforcement 25–33
NePoPo 31, 110
Netflix 60, 99, 202
Netherlands 99, 127, 180

Index

neutral stimulus 45–46
New York 89, 208
New Zealand 119, 123
no pull harness *see* front pull harness
Noah 69
Norway 180
Notweiler 173
nuns 11

off switch 136
offensive drive 149–151
olfactory apparatus (dog) 154
online training 159–161
operant conditioning 23, 25-
orca 154–156
Oslo District Court 180
osteosarcoma 71

Pac-Man 202
pack drive 148
pain 39; thresholds 19–21
Pakistan 178
partial reinforcement schedule 35–40
Patterdale Terrier 149
Pavlov, Ivan 23, 45–46
peer review 122–123
Pekingese 99, 141, 180
Penrith, Jamie 58, 121
permission 5, 72
Perun 227
Petit Brabancons 99, 180
Petsafe Ltd. 123
pig 154, 156
pinch collar 19, 47, 96, 104–109, 114–137, 162–164
Pit Bull 9, 19–20, 174–175
play 13–17, 36–38
play based dog trainer 7, 22
play drive 147
Poland 72
police dog 49–51, 55–57, 186–189
Pomeranian 20
Poo 75, 98, 180
Poodle 32
porridge 12
Portugal 176
positive correction 25–33
positive reinforcement 25–33
possum 149, 152
predation 119–121, 129–133
Premack, David 23
Presa Canario 202
prey drive 46–47, 146–147
primates 154
Prince Charming 149
Prince Harry 128
prong collar *see* pinch collar

Prohibition 137
Pryor, Karen 23, 203
Psychology Today 185
PTSD 169
PubMed 51
Pug 72–73, 99, 176, 180–181
Puggle 180
Pugweiler 102
punishment 14, 19, 75
puppies 18, 58–61, 69, 165–166, 171–183
purely positive dog trainer *see* force free dog trainer
Puss in Boots 20

quadrants 22–33
Queen Consort 124

raccoon 154, 156
random reward 40
Rapunzel 192
raven 154, 156
Red Square 153
reinforcement schedules 38–43
relationship training 22
Republic of Ireland 176
resource guarding 67
Retrievers 177
reward based dog trainer 6, 22
Rhodesian Ridgeback 32
Richmond Park 113
Romania 176
Rosenthal, Linda 89
Rottweiler 51–54, 219–220
Russia 45, 153

Saint Bernard 20, 177
salivation (dogs) 45–46
Saluki 141–145
San Francisco 89
Satanists 160
Save Our Seized Dogs—Put BSL to Sleep UK 176
scent-work 188–189
Schenkel, Rudolf 137
Schwarzenegger, Arnold 57
science 117–139
science based dog trainers 22
Scooby-Doo 49
Scotland 12, 54, 186–187
Sean Bean Appreciation Society 154
SeaWorld 89
service dog 45, 49, 51–52, 57, 164, 173, 179, 213–214
Setters 177
Shaggy 49
Shakespeare, William 129
shaping 33–35

Index

Shar Pei 177
Shih Tzus 99, 180–181
Shikashio, Michael 89
shouting 115
Shrek 20
Siberian Husky 20, 215
Sinbad the Sailor 199
Singapore 176
Skinner, B.F 19, 23, 25-
sleeve muzzle 104
slip lead 55–56, 102–108
social drive *see* pack drive
The Sound of Music 11
Spain 176
Spaniel 52, 99
Spaniel Aid UK 99
spaying 71–72, 97
Springer Spaniel 93, 100, 220
Sprocker 100
Staffordshire Bull Terrier 175, 220
Stalin 120
Stilwell, Victoria 201–203
stress 88, 134–137
suppression 78
Sweden 125, 148, 184, 190

Terminator 206
Terriers 177
testosterone 71–72
Thorndike, Edward 23
thresholds 17–18, 80, 167–172, 185–186
Tiananmen Square 153
Tibetan Mastiff 93, 177
Tibetan Terrier 177
Tik Tok 13, 159, 195, 219
Tilikum 89–92
Tinbergen, Nikolaas 24
tool bans 3–6, 46, 113–116, 190–192
tools 3–6, 20, 102–116, 18–137, 172–192
Top Gun 169
Toronto 89
Tortora, Daniel 134
Training Without Conflict 31
Tricki Woo 142

Trump University 208
Tyson, Mike 77

UAE 176
Uber 20
UK 99–100, 122–125, 174–178, 190
Ukraine 98, 176
unconditioned response 45–46
unconditioned stimulus 45
United States of America 99–100, 110, 174–176
University of Lincoln 114–115, 123–124, 129–134

Vanderpump, Lisa 203
variable interval reinforcement schedule 42
variable ratio reinforcement schedule 40–41
Velociraptor 178
veterinarians 19, 63, 71–72, 75, 137, 151–152
Vets Against Brachycephalism 179–181
Vick, Michael 205

Wagyu 108
Walmart 58, 108
Watson & Rayner 23
Watts, Adam 64
Wayback Machine 162
White, Betty 203
Wicked Witch of the West 197
Williams, Jane 181
Witchfinder General 197
wolf 137–139
wolfdog 9
Woodhouse, Barbara 62

XL Bully 99, 116, 149

Yorkshire Terrier 20, 92, 215
YouTube 155, 159, 162, 195, 202

Zoom 86, 159, 204

www.ingramcontent.com/pod-product-compliance
Lightning Source LLC
Chambersburg PA
CBHW032035300426
44117CB00009B/1066